# FROM INDEPENDENCE TO THE U.S. CONSTITUTION

*Early American Histories*

DOUGLAS BRADBURN, JOHN C. COOMBS, AND S. MAX EDELSON, EDITORS

# From Independence to the U.S. Constitution

RECONSIDERING THE CRITICAL PERIOD
OF AMERICAN HISTORY

Edited by Douglas Bradburn
and Christopher R. Pearl

UNIVERSITY OF VIRGINIA PRESS
Charlottesville and London

University of Virginia Press
© 2022 by the Rector and Visitors of the University of Virginia
All rights reserved
Printed in the United States of America on acid-free paper

*First published 2022*

1 3 5 7 9 8 6 4 2

Library of Congress Cataloging-in-Publication Data

Names: Bradburn, Douglas, editor. | Pearl, Christopher R., editor.
Title: From independence to the U.S. Constitution : reconsidering the critical period
of American history / edited by Douglas Bradburn and Christopher R. Pearl.
Other titles: Reconsidering the critical period of American history
Description: Charlottesville : University of Virginia Press, 2022. | Series: Early American
histories | Includes bibliographical references and index.
Identifiers: LCCN 2021047917 (print) | LCCN 2021047918 (ebook) | ISBN 9780813947419
(hardcover) | ISBN 9780813947426 (paperback) | ISBN 9780813947433 (ebook)
Subjects: LCSH: United States—History—Confederation, 1783–1789. | United States—Politics
and government—1775–1783. | United States—Politics and government—1783–1809. |
Elite (Social sciences)—United States—History—18th century.
Classification: LCC E303 .F766 2022 (print) | LCC E303 (ebook) | DDC 973.3/1—dc23/eng/20211012
LC record available at https://lccn.loc.gov/2021047917
LC ebook record available at https://lccn.loc.gov/2021047918

*Cover art: The Looking Glass for 1787*, Amos Doolittle.
(Library of Congress, Prints and Photographs Division, LC-DIG-ppmsca-17522)

# CONTENTS

ACKNOWLEDGMENTS    vii

Introduction    1

The Constitutional Consequences of Commercial Crisis:
The Role of Trade Reconsidered in the Critical Period    23
DAEL A. NORWOOD

America's Court: George Washington's
Mount Vernon in the Critical Period    60
DOUGLAS BRADBURN

Abolitionists, Congress, and the Atlantic Slave
Trade: Before and after Ratification    93
NICHOLAS P. WOOD

Federalism on the Frontier: Secession and Loyalty
in the Trans-Appalachian West    126
SUSAN GAUNT STEARNS

"Such a Spirit of Innovation": The American
Revolution and the Creation of States    152
CHRISTOPHER R. PEARL

Something from Nothing? Currency and Finance in the Critical Period    193
HANNAH FARBER

An Excess of Aristocracy: Democracy and the Fear
of Aristocratic Power in the 1780s   216
KEVIN BUTTERFIELD

Epilogue: Turn Down the Volume!   239
JOHANN N. NEEM

NOTES ON CONTRIBUTORS   261
INDEX   265

# ACKNOWLEDGMENTS

ALL BOOKS ARE THE work of many hands, and edited collections probably more than most. We are very grateful for all of the contributors who collaborated on this effort. We want to particularly thank the Mount Vernon Ladies' Association (MVLA), who funded a two-day workshop at the historic estate that included using the facilities of what was then the brand-new Fred W. Smith National Library for the Study of George Washington, allowing all the contributors and commentators on the papers to stay on-site and supporting the event with generous hospitality. The vision of the MVLA, to build a new research center at one of the most significant historic sites in the United States, represents an important contribution to our ability collectively to make sense of our complicated past. This volume represents just one of many contributions to the scholarship of our founding, which have directly resulted from the leadership of the MVLA.

The symposium that launched this volume included essential contributions from many people, including Jim Broussard, Denver Brunsman, Kristen Burton, Kevin Butterfield, William diGiacomantonio, Hannah Farber, Randi Lewis Flaherty, Amy Henderson, James Henretta, Warren Hofstra, T. Cole Jones, Mary Ritchie McGuire, Brian Murphy, Johann N. Neem, Dael Norwood, Brett Palfreyman, Bruce Ragsdale, Susan Gaunt Stearns, Dana Stefanelli, Mary Thompson, Nicholas P. Wood. Criticism is a compliment, and the enjoyable conversations around these essays in progress made them better.

We would also like to thank Stephen McLeod and Michael Kane. They helped make the symposium a success by taking on the herculean task of managing its logistics, communications, catering, housing, travel, and all the challenges of putting on a first-rate symposium.

This volume would not be possible without the enthusiastic support of Dick Holway, who encouraged the work through thick and thin. We also have been delighted by the guidance and support of Nadine Zimmerli, who succeeded Dick at University of Virgina Press and is already making a great mark on the field.

Finally, we would like to extend our deep gratitude to Mary Jongema, who helped in the preparation of this volume at all stages, from the organization of the events in 2014 to the final submissions to the University of Virginia Press. She has taken on the least enjoyable aspects of this process and delivered them with refreshing enthusiasm and competence.

FROM INDEPENDENCE TO THE U.S. CONSTITUTION

# Introduction

To make sense of a lost past, filled with countless avenues of human experience, historians can use a powerful shorthand to define their period of study. These are inevitably artificial, as the people living through those moments do not have the perspective to see the whole. In the historiography of the United States, there is perhaps no more popular contrivance than the idea of the "Critical Period," a moment in time starting after American independence and always looking forward to the creation of the United States Constitution. The definition itself—as a critical period—imposes a certain inevitability on the character of the 1780s. How, then, can we see the decade on its own terms? How can we define that curious interregnum starting after independence but ending before the formation of our current federal system? Is it even a national story at all? Perhaps we can take a cue from our current moment of crisis and what it can and cannot tell us about our future, revealing the power of hindsight in crafting narratives and the importance of seeing a particular time and place on its own terms while still acknowledging its deeper roots.

In winter 2019, the coronavirus pandemic began spreading throughout the world. As of this writing (May 2021), the virus has killed nearly six hundred thousand people in the United States (and counting) and efforts to contain the virus have led to massive economic disruptions, including record unemployment, bankruptcies, and unprecedented fiscal challenges at all levels of government. In the midst of the distress caused by the virus and related economic fallout, social protests have emerged worldwide, triggered by the murder of George Floyd by members of the Minneapolis Police Department—on the heels of the murders of Breonna Taylor and Ahmaud Arbery—which have resulted in an important reckoning with the nature of race relations in all aspects of American society.

In some ways, America's inability to address these crises results from a failure to tackle forcefully problems that some have argued for years require new institutions, policies, and laws. Grassroots reform movements and the American public's exasperation with patchwork efforts to handle the pandemic have been amplified by the knowledge that none of this upheaval was completely unforeseen.[1] So the United States in the second decade of the twenty-first century finds itself experiencing the worst health crisis in a hundred years, an economic and financial challenge not seen since the Great Depression, and a social reform movement reminiscent of the late 1960s.

All of this is happening as failures of governance are manifest at all levels. At the national level, the inability to find consensus and create coherent national strategies to respond to the spread of the virus and achieve social justice, or to even recognize the severity of those problems, find states and localities working alone. According to Maryland Governor Larry Hogan, "[Donald] Trump said it was the states' job" to handle coronavirus. So, "every governor went their own way." While President Trump sometimes walked back this sentiment, such a scenario, for executives throughout the United States, was, to use Hogan's words, "chilling." While some state executives sought contracts for PPE, worked with foreign states to acquire tests, mandated masks, issued stay-at-home orders, and regulated social distancing, governors elsewhere continued to act cavalierly.[2] That diffuse response failed to stem a national tide, furthering the social and economic impact of the virus. A similar divergence between national intent and state authority shaped the early rollout of the vaccine, which sometimes led to confusion and frustration. Different rules at local, state, and national levels continue to characterize the American experience of the pandemic as it lingers on into its second year.

In this lived experience we can see a real crisis of governance as the federal government, state governors, and local leaders argue over proper responses. Something as simple enforcing the use of face coverings in public has led to numerous localities and states bickering over not just the efficacy of such a measure, but who has the responsibility or the power to enforce rules. In some cases, counties refuse to enforce state mandates. Making matters worse, mayors, governors, and the national government argue over the proper way to open public schools. More seriously still, as some protests have turned violent—or have been exaggeratedly reported as such—state governors, local municipalities, and the federal government have been at odds over the ways to solve glaring inequities as well as the proper tactics and resources to deploy. After a long series of nightly clashes in Portland, Oregon, in July 2020, the governor of the state and the vice president of the United States actually needed to broker a deal to remove federal officials to try to create an environment for peace.[3] In a culmination of a year fraught with difficulties, on January 6, 2021, thousands of angry citizens assaulted the Capitol in an effort to stop the constitutional process of confirming the election of the president of the United States, threatening the peaceful transition of power and democratic governance. As Americans collectively struggle to deal with these problems, the story of America's past and the history of the founding of the country has become ground zero in a divisive culture war. We are living through something that *could be* immensely consequential to America's future.

The confluence of these challenges has led many commentators and thinkers to see the United States as a failed state or a nation in rapid decline.[4] From international influence to local control, evidence of disillusionment and disaffection abounds. A late summer 2020 Associated Press-NORC poll found only two in ten Americans said the United States was headed in the right direction.[5] Is America in another critical period? Is it a contest between villains and heroes for the fate of the country? The rhetoric of the times and the polarization of the media seem to demand such a narrative. However, the fact remains—no one knows . . . yet. This moment will be defined by what comes after, as much as what is happening now—and, really, by those who gain control over the guidance of the country to address these crises when no one can predict the future. We all have ideas and hopes about what we want to see as the outcome, but the reality of our future is further from our grasp than we can sometimes recognize.

Looking back to the revolutionary era, we can clearly see it was the federalists who initially defined what they saw as America's first critical period by declaring the 1780s an existential crisis that required a new form of government. Their vision still dominates the way we understand the 1780s today. However, we also know they only represented a segment of voices and arguments about the period and the possibilities of the future. If anything, then, our current moment clearly shows that any understanding of the Critical Period requires us to wade through such biases in an effort to forget what came after and strip the inevitability away from the experience of people living through the 1780s.

The essays in this volume attempt to do just that. When they were commissioned to coincide with the 125th anniversary of the publication of John Fiske's *The Critical Period,* we asked the authors to pose questions of the 1780s that sought to find continuities both to the period before independence and the ways it may or may not have shaped America well into the antebellum period. Before we look at how the essays of this volume should make us rethink the early history of the United States, and what it might mean for us today, we need to understand John Fiske, who defined the Critical Period for over a century.

Almost 150 years ago, the philosopher-cum-historian John Fiske wrote one of his most famous and significant works, *The Critical Period of American History, 1783–1789.* While rarely cited in scholarly works today, the book had a powerful impact on the popular understanding of the early United States during an important time in the country's reimagining and has left a lasting impression on the way we understand and ultimately debate the period today.

If Fiske were alive now, he would likely be shocked that historians would gather to reconsider the concept of a Critical Period that he did so much to popularize. After all, for most of his life he did not identify himself as an historian. He was a philosopher interested in human behavior. He came to the study of history through circumstance and financial need. It was only much later in life that Fiske would even accept the appellation "historian," and then only begrudgingly. Our reconsideration would be, perhaps, more shocking to Fiske because *The Critical Period* was not a work of original scholarship. In fact, Fiske did not even coin the term "Critical Period."

That laurel wreath belongs to William Henry Trescot, who wrote the *Diplomatic History of the Administrations of Washington and Adams* in 1857. As Andrew C. McLaughlin noted in 1905, Fiske's work was "altogether without scientific standing, because it is little more than a remarkably skillful adaptation of a very few secondary authorities, showing almost no evidence of first-hand acquaintance with the sources."[6] Despite McLaughlin's critique, Fiske did not just regurgitate past scholarship.

*The Critical Period* was a product of Fiske's intellectual progression. Throughout his many travels as a lecturer of philosophy, religion, music, and history at Harvard University; University College, London; and Washington University, he read deeply, and he enthusiastically supported the work of Charles Darwin and Herbert Spencer. His effort to grapple with their ideas and his own experiences led to the publication of his favorite work, *Outlines of Cosmic Philosophy,* the ideas of which made their way into most of his subsequent publications in one way or another. In *Cosmic Philosophy,* Fiske explained his belief in the natural progression of man, one that was providential yet still predicated on the environment—ideas that he would build upon in the coming years and that would lead him to applaud such historical interpretations as those of Frederick Jackson Turner.[7]

*The Critical Period* was the outgrowth of those formative ideas. By the early 1870s, Fiske came to believe that America, not Europe, was the seat of progress and that the natural unfettered progression of man took place there. *The Critical Period* hammered home that central point. In the 1780s, Fiske argued, Americans went through stages of progress—oppression, anarchy, and modern stability. Thus, the Americans of the 1880s were the inheritors of a stable, healthy, and prosperous nation thanks to the heroic labors of "the founders" who harnessed the revolutionary spirit, pushing through the quagmire of a disjointed and uninspired confederacy that threatened to tear asunder what little unity and commonality existed. According to Fiske, the America of the 1780s stood on the brink of collapse and could have wandered down the labyrinths of anarchy, perplexity, and ruin if not for the heroic efforts of the founders. It should be no surprise that he titled his most famous chapter "Drifting Toward Anarchy."

On the publication of Fiske's book, reviewers raved about its "sterling historical value." Fiske, they thought, "proved his assertions."[8] Soon, the

*Journal of Education,* a standard and important publication for teachers even today, deemed *The Critical Period* the third most important book for teachers to read behind only William Shakespeare's *Hamlet* and a collection of works by Joseph Addison.[9] Nor did Fiske's work lose its importance with time; a new and cheaper version was published in 1902, making it widely available. Like before, the *Journal of Education* ran review articles deeming it "a masterpiece, a book every teacher should read."[10] As late as 1941, people still claimed that "no American historian was ever more successful in unraveling the tangled skein of history and reweaving it into a pattern bright and clear."[11]

While Fiske had his detractors to be sure, it was not until Charles Beard's *An Economic Interpretation of the Constitution of the United States* that historians had to grapple with the idea of the Critical Period and its meaning for the U.S. Constitution and, through it, modern American history. Where Fiske argued that the constitution created a nation and saved a society in chaos, Beard argued that the Constitution was a coup against the states in the interests of a creditor class.

Beard's 1913 *Economic Interpretation* gave vent to ideas in circulation for decades that were often overshadowed by the likes of Fiske. During the first half of the nineteenth century, abolitionist writers who echoed the thoughts of William Lloyd Garrison, who deemed the Constitution a corrupt bargain with slaveholders. Such a view made the mere idea of the Critical Period a "skillfully directed" fiction. In a similar vein, late nineteenth- and early twentieth-century historians, including Henry B. Dawson, J. Allen Smith, Arthur F. Bentley, and A. M. Simons, argued, without much fanfare, that there was no such thing as a chaotic Critical Period. It was, they asserted, the "creation" of both historians' and elite contemporaries' "own imagination," and therefore the Constitution of the United States was a counterrevolution designed by seedy interest groups.[12]

Beard's work furthered those approaches. Highlighting social and economic interests during the battle over the Constitution, Beard found that elite moneyed men bent on protecting their way of life supported the document, while "the opposition came from the non-slaveholding farmers and debtors."[13] Beard's arguments had a huge impact, striking a nerve in a society roiled by Progressive and populist critiques of the economic and political order of the early twentieth century. Strengthened by a generation of supporters and acolytes and given support through his later synthetic work cowritten with Mary Beard (including his massive *Rise of American Civilization*), the Beardian thesis on the character of the 1780s and the Constitutional settlement seemed beyond reproach. By the early 1960s, some historians complained, Beard's work was "gospel."[14]

While "gospel" might be an overstatement, Beard did inspire an entire generation of historians and an enduring logic that still exists today and that serves as a counterweight to Fiske's framing of the 1780s. Building on Beard, Merrill Jensen and Jackson Turner Main refuted the existence of the Critical Period as Fiske imagined it. Jensen in particular emphasized the achievements of the "sovereign states" and the Articles of Confederation government, which revolutionized American political practice; instituted social, legal, and economic reforms on a scale never seen in North America; and won the war. In their telling, the Constitution was foisted on America by a conservative interest who at worst represented powerful counterrevolutionary forces.[15]

Yet, like Fiske, Beard was not without his detractors. Robert E. Thomas, Robert E. Brown, and Forrest McDonald investigated the economic landscape of the era, asserting that supporters and opponents of the constitution came from the "*same* class," and concluded Beard's interpretation did "great violence" to history. Their critiques were aided by a careful analysis of the actual votes of the federalists and antifederalists at the state level— which documented property holdings of men on either side—showing errors in some of Beard's original data, confusion in the record, and the lack of a clearly defined economic interest group in favor of ratification.[16]

The scholarship against Beard was so overwhelming that by 1969, Gordon Wood declared his perspective was "undeniably dead," but at the same time Wood recognized that "the [the idea that] Constitution was in some sense an aristocratic document designed to curb the democratic excesses of the Revolution . . . still seems to me to be the most helpful framework for understanding the politics and ideology surrounding the Constitution." In his massive *Creation of the American Republic, 1776–1787*, Wood argued against the usefulness of economic determinism to explain historical actors and concluded that ideas, as well as the social order, mattered.

According to Wood, the constitutional moment owed itself to the development and transformation of Whig political thought in revolutionary America. Recognizing the social context of ideas, Wood resurrected the notion of the Critical Period and posited that the chaos of those years, in which the states "perverted Republicanism," was an experiential incubator necessary for the intellectual progression of "the founders" to create a federal constitution predicated on an expansive notion of popular sovereignty. That new federal government, Wood maintained, was "the ultimate act of the entire Revolutionary era," with which the founders attempted "to salvage the Revolution in the face of its imminent failure."[17]

Main, who disliked much of this argument, deemed it little more than "John Fiske's interpretation in its most extreme form." Much like Wood declared about Beard, Main prophesized that "Wood's book is an excellent example of a species which has a distinguished ancestry, but which may be nearing at once a culmination and a dead end."[18] Main, in some ways, was wrong about Wood's contribution. Wood paid much more attention to social change and class politics than Main asserted. Nevertheless, Main's association of Wood with Fiske is to the point. Wood's 1780s were an anarchic period that needed to be solved by a new politics enshrined in the new Constitution.[19]

Main's belief that Wood's approach represented a "dead end" was rooted in his belief in the importance of what were then exciting trends in the development of social history. Just a year before the publication of *Creation of the American Republic*, Jesse Lemisch urged historians to work "from the bottom up," demanding they recognize that the oft-misunderstood "inarticulate," "ignorant multitude" were actually articulate and not that ignorant. They had thoughts and aspirations of their own, and it is only through an investigation of their beliefs, ideas, and experiences that historians could hope to come to grips with the revolutionary period.[20] Likewise, Gary Nash furthered our understanding of the era by criticizing the very definition of "founding fathers," preferring a far more expansive interpretation of that group to include more voices than an elite white minority.[21]

Such a focus seemed more and more possible as American historians embraced the work of early modern European scholars and a "new social history." Their eagerness to define communities' stresses and strains (using nonliterary sources) by a close attention to and analysis of quantifiable demographic trends over the *longue durée* promised a reconceptualization of the ordinary experiences of men and women that downplayed the impact of ideas and politics and highlighted broad, long-term social evolution.[22] Wood's work at first seemed to be against the tide of history, or at least history writing.

The next few decades saw an explosion of scholarship that reinvestigated the revolutionary era in new and imaginative directions, pushing the definition of the Critical Period far beyond anything Fiske or even Beard could have imagined. The phrase at one level had simply come to signify the years from 1783 to 1789. However, many continued to reject the term as too biased to represent the reality of the times. With a strong intellectual connection to Beard, Jensen, and Main, and heeding the advice of Lemisch, some historians unearthed new documents, harnessed the power of a new social history, and criticized the very idea of the Critical Period as a ruse carefully concocted by elite interests to scale back the liberating tendencies of the American Revolution. For these historians, the years 1783–1789 were when wealthy men betrayed debtors, made a bargain with slavery, and claimed the government for themselves.[23]

Nevertheless, the idea of the Critical Period did not simply go away. Some scholars saw and continue to understand the period as *critical* because of the popular forces unleashed by localized interests—a movement that promised or presaged democratic attitudes and energy—as well as the vexing and unresolved problems that frustrated an easy unity for the country after the war for independence.[24] Scholars such as David Hendrickson bluntly stated that any vision of unity under the Articles of Confederation was "a pleasing illusion," and therefore those Americans, particularly federalists, fearing disunion and dissolution of the United States "said what they meant, and meant what they said."[25]

Similarly, other historians deemed the period critical because of economic instability and its implications for both the everyday lives of people and the rapidly deteriorating status of America abroad.[26] After all, some argue, the Confederation government's acceptance of Spain's closing of the Mississippi River, which created so much sectional animosity precisely because of its broad economic impact on already suffering middling farmers, was a product of the limited diplomatic choices after the United States defaulted on its loans to the French, the Spanish, and, finally, the Dutch.[27] For historians looking at the frontier, the West made the period critical, especially the battle between "landed" and "landless" states over power and property. According to Peter Onuf, the Critical Period was defined by "deepening inter-sectional tension."[28]

Despite all the disagreement, this extensive body of work makes it clear that the idea of the Critical Period still has cachet, and it remains a battleground because it has great explanatory potential for the foundations of America and the trajectory of American history—an important if daunting realization. To a certain extent, though, it is because of that very diversity—historians' disagreement about what made the period so "critical" or if it was really "critical" at all—that the term has lost some of its explanatory power. If we look back at the history of the scholarship, one could easily feel adrift in a sea of discordant voices and confused about the very nature of the term "Critical Period."

By the turn of the twenty-first century, debate over the Critical Period seems to have ebbed. Because it is such a powerful shorthand for the postindependence, pre-Constitution United States, however, it merits a collective consideration. After all, during this period, an important war was won, constitutions and new ideas proliferated, territories and states were won and lost, new governments and institutions were constructed, laws were repealed and created, and everything seemed to be up for grabs. Those constitutions, institutions, laws, and ideas were debated, decried, and appraised. The United States first came into being as an independent country in this era—a new power on the earth. People mobilized in adulation and protest; many even rebelled. Economies foundered and rebounded. Through it all, the very essence of life was fundamentally altered for the vast peoples who inhabited this new American world, whether for good or for ill.

This volume of essays answers historical questions connected to a range of topics, from the problem of imaging a national identity before a national state existed, to international commerce, the West, early antislavery, the meaning of democracy, and local governance. Together, the essays present a window into both a new context of independence and how many of the challenges that faced the British colonies in the 1760s would continue to shape the world Americans were creating in the 1830s. The Constitution still looms large here. However, it's not a final end point to a crisis; rather, it is positioned within a series of compromises and successes that clearly served certain ends and that did not stop the tendency for unintended consequences to emerge over time. Some of the problems faced in the 1780s were still familiar to people who lived in North America in the 1840s.

Such a focus could be a useful intervention as Americans find themselves debating their history today, trying to find heroes and villains or easy clarity about the past in an effort to make moral arguments about our times and all times. The past is usable—it can be a weapon. It can shape something as large as how we see ourselves in the world, or something as small as winning a political debate to pass or deter new policies. That is why we need to grapple with that history, understand it for what it was, and think about what it was not.

An understanding of the 1780s is central to any conception of American history. Renewed exploration can help us come to terms with a recent vast scholarship, provide new avenues for inquiry, and help us gain perspective on the continuing lessons of the past—a past that can be heartening, even inspiring, and lamentable, even deplorable, at the same time. A reconsideration of the Critical Period, then, has tremendous implications, as historians have consistently shown, for our understanding of historical moments and themes that loom large over the country and that we all concede shaped the world we live in today.

In the first essay in this volume, Dael Norwood explores ground barely considered in Fiske's analysis of the crises of the 1780s, namely the challenges of international commerce felt by merchant elites in the new nation. In Norwood's telling, we clearly see that roadblocks to commercial success were often understood as failures of the Articles of Confederation government. Strengthening American commerce, which would make the United States "treaty worthy" in an increasingly globalized world, guided the actions of Americans who pursued a reformation of the articles in

Philadelphia, rather than greedy self-interest and a quest for power by the few. Norwood considerably expands our understanding of the many attitudes that shaped contemporary opinion about the viability of the new American system.

While the development of commercial ties and relations with other nations could set American identity on an international stage, the problem of imaging a community of Americans after independence would remain a challenge as long as the new states continued to pursue their own paths. As Douglas Bradburn points out, after the war ended and the army was disbanded, there were very few trappings of a national people, no unified economy, no national histories or biographies, no real capital city, and few monuments. However, there were new myths, one of which would help some Americans imagine their distinctive story—namely, the epic tale of the hero George Washington, who led the army in war and retired to his farm in peace, just like the virtuous Cincinnatus of old. As Bradburn argues, in a country with no national politics, Mount Vernon functioned as a surrogate "court" in the 1780s, both a symbolic, mythic place, but also a real center of patronage in arts, sciences, and politics where hopes for the future and contemporary statecraft converged. The confluence of people who visited and and the ideas that were patronized at Mount Vernon brought with it a national perspective that ultimately became the center of resistance to the status quo under the Articles of Confederation.

Yet, as Bradburn points out, Mount Vernon also represented the tangled fabric of slavery in the tapestry of American republican virtue—even when many sympathetic commentators ignored or dismissed the existence of slavery on the estate. The gardens of Mount Vernon, created to display republican simplicity, were tended by an enslaved population. Slavery as both a theoretical and lived experience haunted the fledgling country, resulting in divergent efforts to either enshrine the practice or abolish the system. Grappling with the important debate over slavery, the Critical Period, and the U.S. Constitution, Nicholas Wood reminds us that eighteenth-century antislavery activists saw the period as critical and problematic, though not because the U.S. Constitution made a terrible bargain. Instead, Wood argues that the Confederation government proved a significant roadblock to reform, and that is why many activists saw in the U.S. Constitution a potential to stake out real change, particularly through the prohibition on the slave trade.

Although antislavery voices and their impact would be limited, the weakness of the articles, particularly in regard to slavery in the existing states, made any concerted effort a fragmentary, disjointed, and difficult endeavor. According to Wood, the U.S. Constitution had the possibility to open doors previously closed. Nevertheless, as became increasingly clear, antislavery activism remained limited by interests and powers that reformers derided yet could not convince or control. Wood's contribution is a healthy reminder that many people in the late 1780s could not predict how the politics of slavery in the territories would challenge the union in the near future. Instead, the period immediately after independence was a moment when a variety of futures could still be imagined and, as some thought, achievable—though narrowly. However, it is that narrow opening that can make such potentialities real, a frustrating fact repeated throughout American history.

Expansive imaginations and possibilities existed across America. The "American" West, for instance, was first invented in the 1780s. From the end of the war to the official boundaries claimed by the new United States in the 1780s, the trends of British colonialism in the trans-Appalachian region would continue under a new flag in the postindependence years. In her new approach, Susan Gaunt Stearns tries to understand how these new "American" westerners in what became known as Tennessee and Kentucky related to a nascent national project. The few truly national powers of the Confederation government were intimately tied to the West, making western settlers "nationalists long before the same sentiment was widespread in the east." Yet, western experience fundamentally altered settler perceptions of the benefits of a national power. Although historians often see the West as the Confederation's greatest triumph, Stearns argues its handling of the West was one of its utmost failures. Instead of harnessing the national allegiance of westerners, living up to its charge to be a "protecting arm," government actions proved hemmed in by powerful eastern interests that ultimately alienated westerners and remained an enduring proof that they could expect no positive good from any national government or compact. In that sense, the period was critical to the national experiment, with dire consequences for its cohesiveness in the future. As Stearns shows, the crises of the West, and the resolution of the problems of American imperial development of the continent, would define and redefine the nation from the very beginning.

While the first four essays in this volume highlight challenges that the U.S. Constitution would clarify, exacerbate, or transform, Christopher Pearl's essay recognizes that many of the concerns of the revolutionary period were local and played out in revolutionary settlements in the individual states. In his recasting, the critical period is the 1760s, when a growing awareness of the illegitimacy and inadequacy of the colonial establishments gave way, in the revolutionary era, to the reconceptualization of the relationship between the "people" and the institutions of government and the way they governed. Through crucial political mobilizations that informed constitution making, institution building, and legal reform, these new states in the 1780s and 1790s worked to solve problems that had bedeviled the British colonial world for a generation or more. Unlike James Madison, and in some ways Fiske, who interpreted the states in the 1780s as indicative of the "vices of the political system," Pearl sees an effort to achieve an important *first* settlement in new states with strong and stable governments, which consolidated and centralized power in the hands of new state courts, officers, and judges that harnessed a semblance of popular sovereignty. For many Americans, the criticality of the 1780s paled in comparison to that of the 1760s. Pearl interprets the supposed chaos of the 1780s, clearly stated by revolutionaries everywhere, as the natural outgrowth of the radical transformation of the states during a destructive civil war, which would necessarily require time and patience to stabilize. Pearl's contribution reminds us again that the pro-Constitution federalists were most effective in defining a problem—to be solved by a new Constitution—that many people at the time did not believe existed.

All of these essays reflect, in one way or another, that a central aspect of the Critical Period was a debate over what kind of republican society and governments the revolution created. Central to those debates in past scholarship has been domestic economic policy and the looming threat of an American aristocracy. According to Fiske, the economy of the states faltered under the stress of debt and, for him, a ludicrous emission of paper money that tried to create "fictitious wealth." Meanwhile, Fiske imagined Robert Morris, that "one great man" or the nation's "noblest and most disinterested champion" as attempting "gigantic efforts" to usher in a new prosperity by "creating wealth out of nothing." Where Fiske saw "an epidemic" in the states and the "heroic" valor of Morris, historians such as Beard, Jensen, Woody Holton, and Terry Bouton, see the exact opposite. Paper money, land banks, and the push for readily accessible and stable credit, they argue, reflected the prodebtor democratic tendencies of the states, while Morris represented an aristocratic creditor-class bent on its destruction and therefore the overthrow of the "spirit of '76."

Hannah Farber's essay in this volume historicizes economic developments, demonstrating that paper money was neither "something out of nothing" nor revolutionary (nor even particularly innovative). Morris's economic initiatives, for example, were rooted in extensive trans-Atlantic business contacts and his own personal credit, collateral, and capital, all of which was nothing new to the Anglo-American mercantile world. Similarly, paper money had its roots in colonial history, and moreover, was backed by the land, taxes, and produce of actual people. The relative success or failure of both projects relied on establishing relationships and receiving the backing of law and the public, twin pillars of the new American states, to shore up economic legitimacy. While these initiatives are almost foreign to our modern understanding of fiscal policy, Farber reminds us that they would have been understood as normal and potentially stable economic maintenance projects. The pragmatic solutions to real- world problems of the moment guided American efforts in the 1780s and beyond.

But what of the supposed "aristocratic" character of men like Morris? As Kevin Butterfield's essay shows, there were limited possibilities of an American aristocracy rearing its ugly head during the Critical Period. Examining the debate over the Society of the Cincinnati, a fraternal and hereditary organization of Revolutionary War officers, Butterfield argues that initially the organization sparked significant opposition from an American people who feared the creation of a hereditary aristocracy with significant power to direct public policy. However, through that debate, it became more and more clear that such fears were unfounded—the impulses and institutions created in the revolution destroyed the structural possibilities of a real aristocracy, and cultural attitudes seemed to be trending towards democracy. By 1787, the debate ebbed and the threat diminished, so much so that antifederalist castigations of the U.S. Constitution as unleashing a "hideous daemon of Aristocracy" did not marshal enough people to oppose ratification. The reason, Butterfield argues, was that "by the time the Constitution was proposed, a youthful American people had grown increasingly confident that any apparent threats of a rising aristocratic power could be and would be quashed." The era may have been critical, but not because of a potential Thermidorean aristocracy.

On the surface, these essays may reflect that historians still disagree about the very nature of the "Critical Period," but together these essays bring some clarity, or at least circumspection, about who considered the period "critical" and why. The essays try to counterbalance an enduring logic about the era that characterizes much historical analysis and possesses a certain Manichaean flavor that demands that the Critical Period is an all-or-nothing scenario, in which the character of American democracy, or slavery, or Constitutional freedom were locked in for future generations. It was a crucial time, to be sure, but stark polarities are too analytically simple for our understanding of a messy history.

Wrestling with that complexity requires a collective effort to unearth the histories of the period with an eye toward their moment rather than just the power of hindsight. Practical efforts, sometimes rooted in current ideologies of problem-solving, often guide historical actors, and those efforts can and do reverberate through history, influencing but not commanding the futures of different times and places. That reality should make us assess individual moments for what they were, what people tried to address, and what actors could not foresee. Unintended consequences also always shape the ultimate meaning of decisions in the moment. These essays call for the start of a conversation that should make us reexamine the 1780s and the myriad of people who inhabited and negotiated that world on their own terms. As we live through the confusion of our own times, maybe we can take solace in the ways previous Americans grappled to find common ground and better governance in their attempt to form a more perfect union, not knowing, like us, what would come after.

## Notes

1. John Lange, "Pandemic Preparedness and Response under a Different President," *The Hill,* August 10, 2020, https://thehill.com/opinion/white-house/511320-pandemic -preparedness-and-response-under-a-different-president; Betsy McKay and Phred Dvorak, "A Deadly Coronavirus Was Inevitable. Why Was No One Ready?," *Wall Street Journal,* August 10, 2020, https://www.wsj.com/articles/a-deadly-coronavirus -was-inevitable-why-was-no-one-ready-for-covid-11597325213; Abigail Tracy, "How Trump Gutted Obama's Pandemic Preparedness Systems," *Vanity Fair,* May 1, 2020, https://www.vanityfair.com/news/2020/05/trump-obama-coronavirus -pandemic-response; Deb Reichmann, "Trump Disbanded NSC Pandemic Unit that Experts Had Praised," *Associated Press News,* March 14, 2020, https://apnews.com /ce014d94b64e98b7203b873e56f80e9a; Centers for Disease Control and Prevention, "2009 H1N1 Pandemic Timeline," last reviewed May 8, 2019, https://www.cdc.gov/flu /pandemic-resources/2009-pandemic-timeline.html; Rachel Martin, "H1N1 Swine Flu Emergency: What Does It Mean?," *ABC News,* October 25, 2009, https://abcnews.go .com/Health/SwineFluNews/h1n1-swine-flu-emergency/story?id=8913231; Uri Fried-man, "We Were Warned," *Atlantic,* March 18, 2020; Larry Buchanan, Quotrung Bui, and Jugal K. Patel, "Black Lives Matter May Be the Largest Movement in U.S. History," *New York Times,* July 3, 2020, https://www.nytimes.com/interactive/2020/07/03/us /george-floyd-protests-crowd-size.html; Ryan W. Miller, "Black Lives Matter: A Primer on What It Is and What It Stands For," *USA Today,* July 11, 2016, https://www.usatoday .com/story/news/nation/2016/07/11/black-lives-matter-what-what-stands/86963292/; Elizabeth Day, "#Black Lives Matter: How the Events in Ferguson Sparked a Movement in America, *CBS News,* August 7, 2015, https://www.cbsnews.com/news/how-the-black -lives-matter-movement-changed-america-one-year-later/; Grace Ji-Sum Kim and Jesse Jackson, "'I Can't Breathe': Eric Garner's Last Words Symbolize Our Predicament," *Huffington Post,* February 17, 2015, https://www.huffpost.com/entry/i-cant-breathe -eric-garne_b_6341634; Darnell L. Moore and Patrisse Cullors, "5 Ways to Never Forget Ferguson—and Deliver Real Justice for Michael Brown," *Guardian,* September 4, 2014, https://www.theguardian.com/commentisfree/2014/sep/04/never-forget-ferguson -justice-for-michael-brown.
2. Larry Hogan, "Fighting Alone," *Washington Post,* July 16, 2020, https://www .washingtonpost.com/outlook/2020/07/16/larry-hogan-trump-coronavirus/.https:// www.washingtonpost.com/outlook/2020/07/16/larry-hogan-trump-coronavirus/.
3. Ryan J. Foley, "Defying Governor, Iowa City Mayor Mandates Masks in Public," *Associated Press News,* July 21, 2020, https://apnews.com/146dbfdb47167b0b824f5b44ec8f0697; Jeff Amy and Ben Nadler, "Atlanta Mayor Defies Governor, Require Masks in City,"

*ABC News,* July 9, 2020, https://abcnews.go.com/Health/wireStory/atlanta-mayor-defy-governor-require-masks-city-71677421; Valeria Olivares, "Nearly 80 Texas Counties Have Opted Out of Gov. Greg Abbott's Mask Order. Others Refuse to Enforce It," *Texas Tribune,* July 9, 2020, https://www.texastribune.org/2020/07/09/texas-mask-order-enforcement/; Dirk Vanderhart and Conrad Wilson, "Oregon Gov. Kate Brown Announces 'Phased' Removal of Federal Officers from Portland," *Oregon Public Broadcasting,* July 29, 2020.

4.  George Packer, "We are Living in a Failed State," *Atlantic,* June 2020, https://www.theatlantic.com/magazine/archive/2020/06/underlying-conditions/610261/.

5.  Fadel Allassan, "Poll: 100 Days from Election, 80% Say Country Is Heading in Wrong Direction, *Axios,* July 26, 2020, https://www.axios.com/100-days-election-trump-approval-1a51a7be-9afd-4ad2-8424-72950d20644f.html.

6.  Andrew C. McLaughlin, *The Confederation and the Constitution, 1783–1789* (New York: Harper, 1905), 319–20.

7.  J. B. Sanders, "John Fiske," *Mississippi Valley Historical Review* 17, no. 2 (1930): 264–77; Lewis O. Saum, "John Fiske and the West," *Huntington Library Quarterly* 48, no. 1 (1985), 47–68.

8.  Arthur Hassall, "Review of *The Critical Period of American History, 1783–1789* by John Fiske," *English Historical Review* 5, no. 8 (1890): 388–90.

9.  "Thirty Good Books," *Journal of Education* 50, no. 18 (1899): 302.

10.  "Review," *Journal of Education* 58, no. 15 (1903): 262.

11.  Henry Steele Commager, "John Fiske: An Interpretation," *Proceedings of the Massachusetts Historical Society* 66 (1941): 338.

12.  Henry B. Dawson, "The Motley Letter," *Historical Magazine* 9, no. 2 (1871): 175; J. Allen Smith, *The Spirit of the American Government* (New York: Macmillan, 1907); Arthur F. Bently, *The Process of Government: A Study of Social Pressures* (Chicago: University of Chicago Press, 1908); A. M. Simons, *Social Forces in American History* (New York: Macmillan, 1911). For their impact on Beard, see Richard B. Morris, "The Confederation Period and the American Historian," *William and Mary Quarterly* 13, no. 2 (1956): 146–47.

13.  Charles A. Beard, *An Economic Interpretation of the Constitution of the United States* (New York: Macmillan, 1913), 17. Garrison's approach has been echoed in recent interpretations of the Constitution and the politics of slavery by Paul Finkelman, David Waldstreicher, and George Van Cleave.

14.  Charles A. Beard and Mary R. Beard, *The Rise of American Civilization,* 2 vols. (New York: Macmillan, 1927), Robert E. Brown, *Reinterpretation of the Formation of the American Constitution* (Boston: Boston University Press, 1963), 40.

15.  Merrill Jensen, *The New Nation: A History of the United States During the Confederation, 1781–1789* (New York: Knopf, 1950); Jensen, *The Making of the American Constitution* (Princeton, NJ: Princeton University Press, 1964); Jackson Tuner Main, *The Antifederalists: Critics of the Constitution, 1781–1788* (Chapel Hill: University of North Carolina Press, 1961); Main, *Political Parties Before the Constitution* (Chapel Hill: University of North Carolina Press, 1973); Main, "The Beard Thesis Defended," in *Essays on the Making of the Constitution,* ed. Leonard W. Levy (New York: Oxford University Press, 1987), 144–64.

16. Robert Thomas, "The Virginia Convention of 1788: A Criticism of Beard's *An Economic Interpretation of the Constitution," Journal of Southern History* 19, no. 1 (1953): 64; Robert E. Brown, *Charles Beard and the Constitution: A Critical Analysis of "An Economic Interpretation of the Constitution"* (Princeton, NJ: Princeton University Press, 1956), 194; Forrest McDonald, *We the People: The Economic Origins of the Constitution* (Chicago: University of Chicago Press, 1958).

17. Gordon Wood, *The Creation of the American Republic, 1776–1787* (Chapel Hill: University of North Carolina Press, 1969), 626. Even Beard's intellectual compatriots distanced themselves, claiming his work was "inconsistent, ambiguous, and incomplete." See Lee Benson, *Turner and Beard: American Historical Writing Reconsidered* (Glencoe, IL: Free Press, 1960), 127.

18. Jackson Turner Main, "Review of *The Creation of the American Republic, 1776–1787," William and Mary Quarterly* 26, no. 4 (1969): 605.

19. As Johann Neem points out in the epilogue to this volume, "Wood masterfully wove together the competing accounts of consensus and conflict, Whiggish and Progressive/neo-Progressive narratives, and ideas and interests to produce one of the classics of American historiography."

20. Jesse Lemisch, "The American Revolution Seen from the Bottom Up," in *Towards a New Past: Dissenting Essays in American History,* ed. Barton J. Bernstein (New York: Pantheon Books, 1968), 3–45.

21. Although the fullest expression of this idea came later in Nash's work as he moved his research further into the revolutionary period, his push for a more expansive definition of the "founding fathers" is certainly visible in some of his earlier works, such as *Red, White, and Black* and *Urban Crucible*. See Gary B. Nash, "Also There at the Creation: Going Beyond Gordon S. Wood," *William and Mary Quarterly* 44, no. 3 (1987): 602–11; Nash, *The Unknown American Revolution: The Unruly Birth of Democracy and the Struggle to Create America* (New York: Penguin Books, 2005). See also, Nash, *Red, White, and Black: The Peoples of Early America* (Englewood Cliffs, NJ: Prentice-Hall, 1974); Nash, *The Urban Crucible: Social Change, Political Consciousness, and the Origins of the American Revolution* (Cambridge, MA: Harvard University Press, 1979). Nash and other scholars' refusal to accept the notion that "great men do great things" had immediate implications for any understanding of the revolutionary era, resulting in studies exposing the seemingly infinite ways that race, class, gender, and politics coincided and sometimes collided in the shaping of American history. It also led to a popular backlash with an equally important impact on interpretations of the 1780s as a critical period, culminating in massive paeans to a narrowly defined list of "founders," most of whom were dedicated federalists like John Adams and Alexander Hamilton (who clearly viewed the Confederation period as "critical," in the Fiskian sense of the word). As Jeffrey L. Pasley noted in 2002, the then-emerging "founders chic" of the late 1990s and early 2000s should really be called "Federalist chic." For further information on these themes, see Pasley, "Federalist Chic," *Commonplace,* January 2002, http://commonplace.online/article/federalist-chic/, and David Waldstreicher, "Founders Chic as Culture War," *Radical History Review* 84 (2002): 185–94.

22. The four famous New England monographic town studies that all came out at nearly the same moment as Wood's *Creation* are Philip J. Greven Jr., *Four Generations: Population, Land and Family in Colonial Andover, Massachusetts* (Ithaca, NY: Cornell University Press, 1970); Kenneth A. Lockridge, *A New England Town: The First Hundred Years, Dedham, Massachusetts, 1636–1736* (New York: Norton, 1970); John Demos, *A Little Commonwealth: Family Life in Plymouth Colony* (New York: Oxford University Press, 1970); and Michael Zuckerman, *Peaceable Kingdoms: New England Towns in the Eighteenth Century* (New York: Knopf, 1970). A wonderful review essay that captures the excitement of that work and nicely contextualizes trends of the previous decade is Richard S. Dunn, "The Social History of Early New England." *American Quarterly* 24, no. 5 (1972): 661–79.

23. To name just a few of the leading and most acclaimed scholars furthering a path trod by Beard, Jensen, and Main, see Alfred Young, "How Radical Was the American Revolution?" in *Beyond the American Revolution: Explorations in the History of American Radicalism,* ed. Young (DeKalb: Northern Illinois University Press, 1993), 317–64; Woody Holton, *Unruly Americans and the Origins of the Constitution* (New York: Hill and Wang, 2007); Michael A. McDonnell, *The Politics of War: Race, Class, and Conflict in Revolutionary Virginia* (Chapel Hill: University of North Carolina Press, 2007); McDonnell, "War and Nationhood: Founding Myths and Historical Realities," in *Remembering the Revolution: Memory, History, and Nation Making from Independence to the Civil War,* ed. Michel A. McDonnell, Clare Corbould, Frances M. Clarke, and W. Fitzhugh Brundage (Amherst: University of Massachusetts Press, 2013), 19–40; Terry Bouton, *Taming Democracy: "The People," the Founders, and the Troubled Ending of the American Revolution* (New York: Oxford University Press, 2007); David Waldstreicher, *Slavery's Constitution: From Revolution to Ratification* (New York: Hill and Wang, 2009); Michael J. Karman, *The Framers' Coup: The Making of the United States Constitution* (New York: Oxford University Press, 2016).

24. Jack N. Rakove, *The Beginnings of National Politics: An Interpretive History of the Continental Congress* (New York: Knopf, 1979); Douglas Bradburn, *The Citizenship Revolution: Politics and the Creation of the American Union, 1774–1804* (Charlottesville: University of Virginia Press, 2009). See also essays by Jackson Turner Main and Merrill Jensen in *Sovereign States in an Age of Uncertainty,* ed. Ronald Hoffman and Peter J. Albert (Charlottesville: University of Virginia Press, 1982).

25. David Hendrickson, *Peace Pact: The Lost World of the American Founding* (Lawrence: University of Kansas Press, 2003), 176–77.

26. Herbert J. Storing, *The Complete Anti-Federalist* (Chicago: University of Chicago Press, 1981), 1:26. Challenging Forrest McDonald's assertion that the Critical Period was a fiction because Americans in the 1780s "had it better than they had ever had it before," Storing highlighted the economic depression of the 1780s and the inability of the Confederation government to protect and enhance international trade. For McDonald's questioning of the Critical Period, see McDonald, *The Formation of the American Republic, 1776–1790* (Baltimore: Penguin Books, 1965). In his recent book, George William Van Cleve also stresses the serious economic problems facing both the American people and the Confederation government that made the 1780s so critical. However, Van Cleve also points out that not every aspect of American society and government were

in a state of crisis and therefore has tempered the idea of an all-encompassing Critical Period. Van Cleve, *We Have Not a Government: The Articles of Confederation and the Road to the Constitution* (Chicago: University of Chicago Press, 2017).

27. Richard B. Morris, *The Forging of the Union, 1781–1789* (New York: Harper & Row, 1987). See also Mark D. Kaplanoff, "Confederation: Movement for a Stronger Union," in *A Companion to the American Revolution,* ed. Jack P. Greene and J. R. Pole (Malden, MA: Blackwell Publishing, 2004), 458–69.

28. Peter Onuf, "The West: Territory, States, and Confederation," in *A Companion to the American Revolution,* 374. See also Onuf, *The Origins of the Federal Republic: Jurisdictional Controversies in the United States, 1775–1787* (Philadelphia: University of Pennsylvania Press, 1983), 175–85.

# The Constitutional Consequences of Commercial Crisis

## THE ROLE OF TRADE RECONSIDERED
## IN THE CRITICAL PERIOD

*Dael A. Norwood*

> But if commerce forms so large a chapter in the history of the
> world, what would the history of America be if commerce and the
> men of commerce were left out?
>
> —Freeman Hunt, *Lives of American Merchants*

O N FEBRUARY 22, 1784, the ice damming New York's harbor receded, and in its wake a pair of ships escaped into the cold embrace of the wide Atlantic.[1] The *Empress of China,* a small, square-sterned ship, sailed from the East River on a trading voyage to Canton (Guang-zhou), China.[2] Managed by respected veterans of the Revolutionary War and backed by a group of prominent Philadelphia and New York merchants, the *Empress* bore hopes for a new era of prosperity along with its cargo of ginseng and Spanish silver dollars.[3] Praising the venture in verse, republican poet and editor Philip Freneau hailed it as an exercise and a proof of liberty's blessings. Americans, he wrote, could now explore "Those golden regions . . . / Where George forbade to sail before"—and reap the benefits.[4] Like the twelve-gun salute the *Empress* received on passing New York's harbor fort, and the resolution of "peculiar satisfaction" from Congress that greeted its successful return, Freneau's poem was an expression of confidence and pride in the venture, a defiant pose struck against the clouded future of American independence.[5]

The unheralded ship *Edward,* sailing the same day, demonstrated that optimism was not the only option. Bound for London, the *Edward* did not explore any new trade routes, but instead followed a familiar Atlantic track on a mission of endings. Lt. Col. David S. Franks, one of its passengers, carried a ratified copy of the "Definitive Treaty of Peace" with Britain. His mission was to complete the final procedure needed to confirm the new republic's separation from its former mother country, but this affair was far less happy than might have been expected.[6] The ratified treaty that Franks hurried to the peace commissioners in Europe differed little from the preliminary articles drafted nearly a year earlier. Crucially, the commercial relationship between the two countries remained unsettled, leaving Americans' access to their most important markets—in the British Isles and the West Indies—indeterminate and insecure. In a letter to Congress, peace commissioner John Adams marked this failure bitterly, lamenting that with "no Regulation of Commerce . . . we have thus lost Seven or eight months of our time."[7] Despite a great deal of careful diplomatic effort, the final treaty undercut what many U.S. leaders thought was a crucial support of their new nation, new China voyages notwithstanding. So Franks's departure on the *Edward* received no volleys, no poems, and no special thanks to mark the occasion.

Saluted and silently ignored, freighted with hope as well as frustration, the vessels sailing from New York on George Washington's birthday in 1784 suggest some of the ways that commerce stood at the center of American political culture in the years between the Peace of Paris and the ratification of the Philadelphia Constitution. Over the course of the 1780s, commerce became the subject of great expectations that—when disappointed—produced not only practical hardships, but also major complications in the political functioning of the American confederation, undermining its unity at home and its viability abroad. By its nature, trade inevitably involved questions of how the United States would integrate into the world of nations, and these in turn engaged debates over institutions within the new union. Commerce was not just one of the activities Americans pursued independently in the wake of their separation from Britain, but the crucial means through which they sought to perform republican politics on the global stage, to know the world, and to establish themselves as a new people in the process.

Among an influential group of nationalist revolutionaries, these layered concerns about commerce helped define the confederation period as one of crisis, a "critical period" in John Fiske's formulation.[8] When these elites saw their countrymen's trading connections repeatedly frustrated or denied in ways they had not expected, they felt their entire national project being threatened. Commercial difficulties provided Americans with a context for reexamining the inefficiencies of their own government and its unexpectedly low status among foreign powers and motivated efforts to revise and reform their confederation—a process that culminated in the creation of the Constitution and the framing of a new commercial system in the first federal Congress. From the perspective of nationalist reformers, commercial issues were not one plot among many, but the through line connecting the myriad challenges their new state faced. Highlighting the importance of trade to the political theory and national politics of the new United States reveals how the "private" world of commerce intertwined closely with the "public" work of nation building, contributing more to the dynamics of U.S. political development than historians have at times acknowledged. In the 1780s, reflecting American leaders' theoretical, moral, and practical investment in maritime trade, the consequences of commercial crisis became constitutional.

In contrast to the space it occupied in the minds of American revolutionaries, commerce has a curiously small presence in the historiography of the revolutionary era. Though it directly touches on the core concerns of many historians of the period—including the problem of U.S. sovereignty, the formation of national identity, and the path of early economic development—it has remained mostly in the background. More often, historians have focused on the struggles of the propertied against the propertyless, or the developments in ideology or political theory that shaped and resulted from these conflicts. Even scholars reinterpreting the U.S. founding within an international context have presented security dilemmas, rather than commercial frictions, as the core political issue of the 1780s.[9] Commercial affairs sometimes find voice in the literature through merchants' expressions of their own narrow interests, but more often they appear only to set the stage for more familiar domestic contests or foreign policy conflicts.[10]

More recent work, however, offers grounds for giving commerce a more central place. In their 2011 article, Staughton Lynd and David Waldstreicher argue the American Revolution was "basically a colonial independence movement and the reasons for it were fundamentally economic."[11] Noting that, again and again in the imperial crisis, disputes over commercial matters preceded constitutional debates—and connecting this pattern to how the Continental Congress consistently prioritized economic sovereignty in its policies once the revolt was underway—Lynd and Waldstreicher conclude the American transition "from colonies to neo-colony" was first and foremost a struggle for colonial independence from economic restrictions and only thereafter a movement concerned with renegotiating the polity's constitution.[12]

Lynd and Waldstreicher tie these political priorities to assumptions about government. The revolutionaries, they argue, regarded the "substance of independence" as inhering to the power to regulate the economy and thus the focus of their organizational efforts.[13] Yet although Lynd and Waldstreicher repeatedly use "economic" to describe this causal factor, their target is more specific. Rather than acting as Beardians concerned with personalty (movable property like cash, securities, or stock-in-trade), Lynd and Waldstreicher argue that revolutionaries focused on control of a specific kind of economic practice: maritime commerce. This observation makes sense: seaborne trade was the colonies' and states' primary connection to the mother country, to the rest of the world, and to each other—and readily susceptible to late eighteenth-century technologies of taxation and government control.[14]

Another long-standing object of historians' concern, sovereignty, also connects to commerce, although more indirectly. The story of how Americans forged national sovereignty out of the near anarchy of the 1780s was the principal focus of Fiske's 1888 analysis, but Fiske, like subsequent historians, downplayed the ways that commerce informed contemporaries' diagnosis of crisis and shaped their response to it.[15] More recently,

Peter Onuf and David Hendrickson, among others, have exposed the revolutionaries' preoccupation with the application of the law of nations to their independence and to the internal relations of their country. U.S. sovereignty, at least as understood by key national leaders, was premised on recognition from other powers and observed in Americans' ability to request and enforce treaty obligations, both within the bounds of the new republic and between the United States and foreign governments.[16] Eliga Gould's investigations similarly suggest that the pressure to gain European recognition as a legitimate, sovereign independent nation—to make the nation "treaty worthy"—motivated efforts to define and consolidate national power domestically for decades after the War of Independence.[17]

While these arguments concern the legitimacy of the state, broadly construed, the treaties Americans sought to secure as the means and proofs of their sovereign power were, with few exceptions, neither military alliances nor peace conventions, but commercial agreements.[18] U.S. leaders wanted commerce, and commerce alone, to be the substance of their interactions with the rest of the world—at least beyond what they intended to conquer in North America. Sentiments favoring commerce over "politics" echoed through their statements decrying "entanglement" with European powers during the confederation period and for a century thereafter.[19]

While psychological and cultural insecurities motivated Americans' desire for respect from European powers, U.S. nationalists in the 1780s had more prosaic reasons for wanting acceptance "as treaty-worthy equals."[20] Treaties would permit safe passage for American ships in international waters and provide the access to overseas markets that many revolutionaries considered necessary to the fiscal well-being of their new state. Trade would also quiet domestic political conflict. As Robin Einhorn and Max Edling have shown, U.S. leaders concluded early that a national revenue could only be secured by an impost or a tariff—taxes on commerce collectable without running afoul of sensibilities about internal taxation or the sanctity of slave property.[21] Healthy trade quickly became a sine qua non for the republican nation-state because it promised to solve many problems.

Commerce was a significant cause of the revolution. It defined the goals of the union's internal and foreign policies and shaped the process of American state formation from independence onward. Of course, problems with commerce alone did not trigger change in the confederation period; multifarious social, economic, and political tensions drove the reforms of the late 1780s. Still, what Americans thought commerce would do for both the revolution and their new nation's prospects mattered, because it propelled interest in reform. Revolutionaries' ideas about commerce's role in their new polity developed syllogistically: as the new republic's primary connection to the outside world and the lifeblood of its political economy, commerce would allow the polity to remain simple, virtuous, and civilized. Because other states and peoples needed U.S. products and markets for their own prosperity, a union of interests and free and reciprocal trade agreements would materialize, establishing U.S. sovereignty and guaranteeing its stability.[22] When this commercial logic failed in practice, some Americans, particularly those who came to define themselves as federalists, began to see the varied difficulties of the confederation period as one integrated crisis—one that could only be resolved by restructuring their union's fundamental constitution.

The revolutionaries and their supporters had grand ambitions for what their commerce needed and what it could do—and from the beginning, they linked commerce closely to sovereignty. In preparation for introducing resolutions declaring independence, Richard Henry Lee argued for a complete separation from the British empire because without it, "no State in Europe will either Treat or Trade with us."[23] The Model Treaty drafted and endorsed by the Continental Congress soon after attempted to put Lee's thinking into a contract's shape. Though the document took the form of an agreement for a political or military alliance, the text instead established "only a [reciprocal] commercial connection" between the United States and another nation.[24] Writing to Congress from Paris in 1780, the treaty's primary author, Adams, maintained that the main objective of American diplomacy should be to avoid any "entangling" with European powers and instead pursue only "Commerce, not Politicks, much less War"—a position maintained as a "guiding assumption of American foreign relations until the 1940s."[25] These ideas were not formed in a vacuum. Rather, as Felix Gilbert has observed, they were "facets of the larger complex of enlightened eighteenth-century thought." Just as the ideas of European philosophes informed American constitutional thought and republican discourse, so too did decades of Enlightenment writing about commerce as "a great instrument for bringing about a new age of peace" influence Americans' hopes for what their trade could accomplish.[26]

The confidence the revolutionaries placed in the plausibility of the Model Treaty, and the vision of commerce encoded within it, was not only based on utopian philosophy. They also thought that their independence wrought a major shift in the political economy of the Atlantic world, a significant shock to the "balance" maintained by European empires and nations. Thomas Pownall, a former governor of Massachusetts, elaborated the case for anticipating changes in a pamphlet about the revolution's effects. Following logic endorsed by Adams, Benjamin Franklin, Thomas Jefferson, and other key figures, Pownall argued American independence would hasten the end of shortsighted "monopolizing systems" that governed commerce in the Atlantic and beyond.[27] The lure of "free" trade with United States markets—that is, trade unhindered by prohibitively high taxes or outright bans—would suffice, even in peacetime, to enable Americans to establish reciprocal access to others' markets and even dictate new pacific norms to an expanded European system. The United States could become, in Pownall's formulation, "the Mediatrix of Peace, and of the polite business of the world."[28]

For some revolutionary thinkers, the promise of independent American commerce went beyond reshaping international relations to defining the future of humanity. Yale College president Ezra Stiles's well-known 1783 election day sermon dwelt on the epochal possibilities. The war's completion, Stiles averred, would see the "NAVIGATION OF THE ATLANTIC OCEAN" set free alongside "that of all the oceans of the terraqueous globe."[29] Stiles anticipated some rough patches (other nations "will not at first know how far they may safely trade with us"), but American commerce would "find out its own system, and regulate itself in time."[30] Once established, Americans would spread enlightened principles through trade: "This knowledge will be brought home and treasured up in america: and being here digested and carried to the highest perfection, may reblaze back from america to europe, asia and africa, and illumine the world with truth and liberty."[31]


What is notable about these prognostications, apart from their grandiosity, is how much they depended on commerce working independent of state power. Like many of his compatriots, Stiles did not expect the United States *government* to assure the free passage of American traders—that would flow from Europeans' recognition of their own interests. In this model, commercial regulations were counterproductive, indicating only that Americans were "still involved" in what the French political economist Anne-Robert-Jacques Turgot called "the mist of European illusions."[32] Broadly speaking, U.S. leaders shared a conviction that if *all* commerce was unhindered by prohibitions or prohibitively high tariffs—and was thus "free"—then all would benefit. Or, as Robert Morris explained to John Jay, "if all Governments were to agree that Commerce should be as free as Air I believe they would then place it on the most advantageous footing for every Country and for all mankind."[33]

Of course, revolutionaries and their liberal Enlightenment friends had diverse opinions about what good commerce might do for the republic. Richard Price, a warm supporter of the revolution and Turgot's translator, saw only the dangers of luxury and "connexions with Europe" in foreign trade and claimed that "there is no part of mankind" to which its benefits "are of less consequence than the American States."[34] A world of completely free trade would be ideal, he agreed—but saw no way to achieve it in the short run. Like later antifederalist writers, Price advised autarky to ensure republican simplicity—or as close a condition as high tariffs could create. But voices like Price's did not predominate; to the contrary, in the war's aftermath, U.S. leaders (and U.S. merchants) had high hopes that independence would lead commerce to flourish, perhaps even replacing the need for state action, whose costs weighed so heavily on the republican mind.[35]

Americans soon learned this was not to be. In the absence of reliable national data for the confederation period (one consequence of the lack of a powerful national government), it is difficult to draw definitive con-clusions—but a poor economic situation in the United States after the Revolutionary War appears to have only gotten worse through the rest of the 1780s.[36] Oddly, scholarly agreement on the postwar economy has taken decades to form. For much of the twentieth century, historians attributed the sense of commercial crisis in the 1780s to contemporaries' frustrated expectations—more an imagined depression than any "real deprivation" (though even the most dismissive scholars have given some credit to the effective power of these expressions).[37] This historiography's reliance on ambiguous literary sources, however, has been superseded by a consensus among economic historians that "something 'truly disas-trous' happened to the American economy between the Revolution and 1790."[38] By the mid-1780s, national economic growth appears to have slowed or stopped, despite an increasing population. Worse still, levels of overall trade appear to have diminished to nearly what they were before the boom of the Seven Years' War and failed to recover until well into the 1790s. Americans had good reason to lament the death of the "the high spirits and the golden dreams" they had held to immediately after the War of Independence.[39]

But bad business was not the only problem. The parlous state of U.S. sovereignty and federal union that commercial difficulties revealed were just as serious. Relations with Britain help illustrate why. Congress had removed restrictions on British shipping to American ports after the Shelburne ministry had made some promising noises during peace nego-tiations that suggested the final treaty would restore privileged access to British markets. However, as Congress's action took force, the possibility of commercial reconciliation with the mother country abruptly ended. The proximate cause was the fall of Shelburne's government in February 1783 and its replacement with a Fox-North coalition more sensitive to the political costs of commercial concessions to an independent United States.[40] The ultimate cause lay in the widespread resumption of prewar mercantilist attitudes within the British ruling class. If for a flickering moment the desire for reconciliation and peace had given some of Brit-ain's leaders cause to consider exceptions to the Navigation Acts, that candle was extinguished by the summer of 1783.[41]

Partisans of this return to form argued that British shipping, manufacturing, and credit resources made it unlikely American trade would flow in any other channel. Further, as John Holroyd, Lord Sheffield, explained in a pamphlet infamous among U.S. nationalists, "No treaty can be made with the American States that can be binding on the whole of them." The newly independent colonies, unable to "act as a nation," were not treaty-worthy partners in commerce; Americans would lack other options, so British merchants need not fear any competitors.[42] The orders-in-council proclaimed on July 2, 1783, made this shift in thinking into policy, banning American ships from trade with British West Indian ports. By December, additional regulations barred American shipping between other British ports as well and required most U.S. goods to be either transshipped through metropolitan hubs or carried in British bottoms.[43]

Britain's rejection of free, reciprocal trade did not stand alone. In another sign that European empires were reconstituting their mercantilist spheres even as they drafted final peace treaties, France, too, withdrew favorable access to West Indian ports. Though Franco-American trade increased in the postwar period, buoyed by greater tobacco exports under a special agreement negotiated in 1784, further steps toward commercial reciprocity faltered. While France and Britain still left some narrow lanes for what they regarded as beneficial American trade, by early 1784, Spanish authorities had closed many of their ports in the Americas to United States ships and cargoes entirely. As with Britain and France, calculations of power and political economy motivated these moves. Spain's representatives put "little credence" in U.S. promises that new treaties would reduce smuggling, given the national government's limited ability to control its citizens, and reported to Madrid that U.S. proposals for reciprocal free trade endangered Spanish trading interests in the Americas. Whatever their justifications, these policies significantly worsened the United States' economic outlook.[44]

Independence from Britain also exposed U.S. traders to new dangers as they ventured abroad. This threat was most acute in the Mediterranean, where in 1785, corsairs from Algiers captured two American ships. While this action was not unexpected—American diplomats had already been negotiating with Barbary powers when the capture occurred—the demonstration of weakness was a significant blow to national pride.[45] Even more serious threats lay to the west, where white settlers' invasion of the disputed lands in the Ohio and Mississippi watersheds increased tensions with native peoples—sparking bloody raiding warfare—and put stress on the national government's legitimacy. Since the Peace of Paris, Spain had blocked American navigation of the Mississippi, choking off western commerce. This policy pitted eastern farmers and merchants, who wanted to negotiate access to Spain's West Indian and South American ports, against western frontier-dwellers, who threatened secession if their rights to Mississippian navigation were not fully supported.[46]

According to some observers and a few subsequent historians, only entirely new ventures in postindependence commerce presented more opportunities than obstacles.[47] The *Empress of China's* voyage to Canton was the perhaps the most celebrated, but many similar proposals for exploring new branches of trade emerged after the war, as merchants gambled their ships and capital on new markets in the Mediterranean and the Baltic, South America as well as Asia. However, despite individual successes, "Trade with other areas of the world was not sufficient to offset the losses in traditional American exports or in the valuable benefits that Americans had enjoyed as members of the British empire."[48]

By the late 1780s, even merchants in promising new trade ventures began seeking direct government intervention. Reporting from a later China voyage in 1787, former *Empress of China* supercargo Samuel Shaw explained that monopoly companies like the British East India Company used their political and military resources to push smaller private traders like himself out of business.[49] Recalling the balance-of-power politics of the late war, Shaw wondered if a "commercial confederation" of the nations who stood to lose if Britain consolidated its grip on the East Indies trade might serve "as the best means of checking and defeating such exorbitant pretensions."[50] Reversing an earlier understanding of trade as an alternative to political power, Shaw began to think that the state's ability to form treaties was needed to secure overseas commerce even in ports thought to be beyond the reach of European politics.

Americans' hopes for a free, reciprocal, and apolitical commerce with the world faded quickly. Rather than reform the world, United States commerce exposed the weakness of the American confederation: its inability to protect its citizens, secure access to new markets, or encourage economic growth. Though some revolutionaries were quick to connect frustrations in their commerce and diplomacy, most took some time to see them as linked problems. Even then, Congress's limited powers and a suspicion of centralized authority made a national solution impractical, even unthinkable. But once bound together, the triumvirate of commerce, sovereignty, and stable union became a key motive—or pretext, depending on the perspective—driving reformers toward taking extramural and extralegal actions to restructure the national state.

Though the process of confronting the nation's commercial and structural problems culminated outside of Congress, the movement's origins lay in the national council's chambers. Revenue first made the regulation of commerce an issue in the Continental Congress. The national impost tentatively proposed in the summer of 1780 and passed in early 1781 (during the war) had limited aims. In keeping with Morris's larger program as superintendent of finance, the impost was not intended to consolidate the power of Congress over the states, but rather simply to create a reliably financed and centrally managed national debt and thereby restore public credit.[51] Recommending that the states "vest a power in Congress" to levy a 5 percent ad valorem ("according to value") duty on foreign imports and captured prizes (ships and cargoes), Congress explained to state legislatures that the money would be used to extinguish the foreign war loan debts; once those were paid, the impost would end.[52]

At first the measure seemed to meet with success, but Rhode Island's unexpectedly vehement opposition forced Congress to revisit the request.[53] A revised act, passed on April 18, 1783, still asked states to accede to an impost of 5 percent ad valorem, but also devised a tariff of duties on selected consumables (the standard "luxury" comestibles: spices, sugars, alcohols, teas, coffees, and cocoa). This new revenue measure came with safeguards for state power: states would appoint collectors, and the measure would expire after twenty-five years.[54] Led by James Madison, Congress leaned on patriotic rhetoric in its letter promoting the measure, justifying the repeated request for revenue *from trade* in part because the "debts of a revolution" had allowed "an unbounded freedom" to accrue "to commerce."[55] As before, the goal was to fund debts and secure credit—not to augment federal power over the states or improve the bargaining position of American diplomats and merchants abroad.

That focus began to expand once Congress began to review the summer dispatches from its ministers in Europe in 1783. The news was mixed: though efforts to finalize the peace through treaties had progressed, European powers had clearly "discovered great Jealousy upon the subject of American commerce" postwar. Especially worrying were Britain's orders-in-council, which curtailed Americans' participation in the carrying trade, even in their own produce, and effectively banned American shipping to Britain's West Indian holdings. Britain was not alone. While "the Court of France hath not yet explicitly disclosed her intentions," American ministers in Europe—Adams, Franklin, and Jay—suspected, correctly, that France would soon "restrain" trade, recreating their mercantilist system to parallel Britain's.[56]

Adams's reports shaped Congress's interpretation of these events significantly. Deep in negotiations with Dutch bankers to restructure wartime loans, Adams knew well the value of respectability in international affairs. At the best of times the least sanguine among U.S. diplomats, Adams was profoundly upset by the new British ministry's moves to reconstruct its closed economic system. Without access to the West Indies, he thought, the United States would be "straitened and schackeled," unable to complete "the Plan of the Happiness and Prosperity" the country needed.[57] In part, he considered Britain's actions a failure of the revolution's most advanced ideas about the humane virtues of free trade—but he also considered it a vote of no confidence in the United States' ability to act "as one Nation."[58]

His primary recommendation to Congress was, unsurprisingly, to demonstrate unity among the states by collectively striking back against British trade rules through a five percent duty on "West India Articles" imported in British ships or American produce exported in them.[59] But even Adams did not counsel government action alone. He still put stock in the power of private ventures, and advocated growing more West Indian products in the United States, to make the country more self-sufficient, or sending "ships immediately to China" to outcompete and embarrass the British.[60] Whatever means might be found, he urged Congress to find them soon: without a demonstration of strength and collective will, he feared, Americans would become "the sport of trans-atlantic Politicians" and "so far despised" that a new war—this one of conquest—would be at their door in just a "few months."[61]

Adams's gloomy letters, supported in their facts by his colleagues' correspondence, led Congress to take a new approach to commerce. It was a slow process; first the disconnect between theory and practice needed to be digested. A committee appointed to consider recommendations noted that, unfortunately, "political interests sometimes really differ from those of Commerce" and indeed, "some of those powers with whom we must necessarily maintain a Political and commercial intercourse, appear to be jealous of our power and desirous of cramping our growth." Wary of imposing policy on the "sovereign and independant" states, and aware that the consequences of European trade restrictions "will not be equally sensible to every state," Congress decided in the fall of 1783 to merely inform the legislatures of the worsening situation.[62]

The new year brought firmer resolutions. The Pennsylvania legislature recommended that Congress be vested with powers for "regulating and controlling trade" for the entire country, solving the revenue and foreign policy issues together.[63] A congressional committee made up of Elbridge Gerry, Jacob Read, Hugh Williamson, Jeremiah Chase, and Jefferson came to similar conclusions. Noting that "the fortune of every Citizen is interested in the fate of commerce: for it is the constant source of industry and wealth; and the value of our produce and our land must ever rise or fall in proportion to the prosperous or adverse state of trade," the members of the committee advised that Congress "be vested with powers competent the protection of commerce" so the United States could secure "terms of equality in their commerce with foreign nations." In particular, they recommended that Congress ask the states to grant the national assembly the temporary power to issue embargoes against nonreciprocating nations and their citizens. Unless the United States had retaliatory power to compel reciprocal trade terms from foreign powers, the committee argued, its commerce would not just decline, but "eventually be annihilated."[64] Seeking to prevent Britain's "destructive" and "unequal" measures from "growing into system"—and over the objections of Rhode Island's delegates—Congress passed resolutions on April 30, 1784, requesting new powers from the states.[65]

Once in the hands of the states, the momentum toward reforming Congress's powers over commerce slowed, but not for a lack of attention from Congress itself. Like the effort to pass an impost (to which the proposal for new regulatory powers was now linked), delegates returned again and again to the issue. As new problems developed, they added them to the list of difficulties that new commercial powers would solve—most notably the hurdles the United States faced in implementing already-signed commercial treaties in the face of diverse and often mutually incompatible state regulations on trade. In early 1785, the request for commercial powers was rolled into a larger reform effort within Congress, resulting in a detailed report specifying revisions to the Articles of Confederation themselves.[66] This plan aimed to address confusing state regulations, revenue, and the need to put a unified force behind treaty negotiations.[67]

As ever, the problem remained states' jealous protection of their own prerogatives and their unwillingness to act collectively. Even as Congress requested powers to negotiate new treaties, conflicting state regulations put existing agreements at risk.[68] Among other incidents, shipping regulations and duties passed by Massachusetts and New Hampshire led French merchants in 1785 to formally protest the measures as contraventions of the Treaty of Amity and Commerce. Secretary of Foreign Affairs Jay excused the state acts as simple mistakes, while warning Congress that without unified power over trade, "the Commerce of the United States must suffer from partial and discordant Regulations" and therefore fail to "produce the Benefits and Respectability that might be expected from it."[69]

Jay expressed a feeling common in Congress and the American diplomatic corps that state legislatures did not share. By early 1786, only four states had passed legislation fully complying with Congress's request for new powers, with little prospect of further progress.[70] Congressional delegates, suspecting that European powers refused to enter negotiations because "the States never will grant Congress such powers as are necessary," reissued their request, emphasizing how a "want of due regulation" left the United States open to these "evils of vast importance" threatening American commerce, and by extension, the nation, with "annihilation."[71] Later efforts fared similarly.[72] By late 1786, any hope of expanding Congress's control over commerce—to make new treaties, uphold existing agreements, or generate revenue—seemed dead.[73]

Part of the reason for the impasse lay in the state legislatures' growing distrust of each other and the country's low opinion of Congress. The complications created by New York provide a good example of how commercial affairs had helped sow discord and give the national assembly a poor reputation. New York's state tariffs upset neighboring states, whose trade, both domestic and foreign, was at a considerable disadvantage when it passed through New York City. In particular, New Jersey, lacking a major port of its own, suffered—and in retaliation, refused to supply Congress with requisitions until New York approved the congressional impost. Congress tried to intervene to resolve the conflict, but its delegations accomplished little. Unwilling to sacrifice its own revenues to the national treasury, the New York legislature dragged its feet, passing a "defective" act that did not meet the terms of Congress's request, only to reject an amended version in February 1787—killing through procedural means any possibility of an impost.[74]

At the same time, the most important New Yorker in the national government, Secretary of Foreign Affairs Jay, seemed to be protecting eastern states' commercial interests by selling out frontiersmen in the South and West. In August 1786, Jay brought a draft treaty with Spain to Congress and recommended that the United States accept Spain's closure of the Mississippi in exchange for access to Spanish ports in Europe and the West Indies.[75] Delegates from the South met this suggestion with outraged disbelief, unable to understand how Jay could so callously disregard their constituents' interests. South Carolina's Charles Pinckney, in wide-ranging attack on the proposal, argued against the treaty on these merits but also condemned Jay's negotiation itself, alleging that the appearance of sectional favoritism in the draft treaty would be sufficient to destroy any chance the states would grant Congress further powers over commerce.[76]

Even before affairs reached this low point, the problems of commerce and the failures to make commercial treaties or coordinate a protective commercial policy had been leading even the most ardent nationalists to wish that Americans would embrace autarky instead of engaging in so much troublesome trade. Writing to a Dutch correspondent, Jefferson hoped his compatriots would "practice neither commerce nor navigation, but to stand with respect to Europe precisely on the footing of China. We should thus avoid wars, and all our citizens would be husbandmen."[77] A few months later, Adams expressed a similar idea, albeit in a characteristically dour inversion of Jefferson's wish, arguing that the United States "might still be the happiest People upon earth and in fifty years the most powerful" even if "all Intercourse between Europe and America could be cutt off, forever, if every ship We have were burnt, and the Keel of another never to be laid."[78] Price, doling out philosophical physick to an audience of American statesmen, went even further, arguing foreign trade was only a vector for "INFECTION" for the deadly quarrels and ill mores of Europe. Dr. Price advocated a cordon sanitaire of "heavy duties on importations" as the wisest course of treatment for the new republic's sovereign body.[79]

As refreshing as such a dramatic policy might be, Jefferson and his colleagues knew it was "theory only, and a theory which the servants of America are not at liberty to follow."[80] As Adams explained, his constituents were "as Aquatic, as the Sea Fowl, and the Love of Commerce with its Conveniences and Pleasures are habits, in them as unalterable as their Natures."[81] If "the spirit of Trade which pervades these States is not to be restrained"—which all agreed it could not, even if the theoretical justifications had yet to be worked out in republican ideology—then American statesmen must reform the federal government to meet the challenges posed by Americans' interests in commerce and its expansion.[82] By late 1785, many thought, as Washington did, that strong action "cannot be done by thirteen heads, differently constructed. . . . The necessity therefore of a controuling power" was therefore "obvious."[83]

Recognizing the problem was one thing; finding a solution was another. Would-be reformers had to contend with the deep-seated and widespread suspicion of centrally organized power that they themselves had helped to instill. Even those eager to embrace reform felt no need to act because change would come on its own. As one of Jefferson's correspondents explained, "Every step Britain takes to prevent our increase of Commerce . . . will be eventually for our advantage," because it would improve the state of domestic manufacturing while heightening the contradictions sufficiently to change the public mood.[84] In time, new powers could be easily given to Congress, provided conditions got bad enough—at least, that was the hope.

In the face of suspicion and apathy, reformers decided to work outside of Congress to engineer a revision of the Articles of Confederation and increase the national government's powers over commerce. This path to the Philadelphia Constitution is well known, leading from the Mount Vernon conference to the Annapolis convention and finally to the secret debates in the Pennsylvania state house in the summer of 1787. Organized in large part by Madison, who was out of Congress but had been serving as "the leading tactician and theoretician of reform" since the fall of 1785, these extramural meetings tested ad hoc reform plans and built consensus outside the established and legitimate, if broken, political process.[85]

Securing control over commerce was the crucial motivating factor for these meetings, as they built momentum for larger reforms. The negotiations at Alexandria and Mount Vernon in March 1785 began as circumscribed efforts to regulate Potomac commerce, but ended up with a free trade and navigation compact between two states, Virginia and Maryland, with others invited to join. This agreement violated the articles, but Madison and his allies used it to push for wider reform by convening another meeting at Annapolis and subsequently submitted it to Congress for review.[86] Congress voted down the proposal, fearing that "partial regulations of commerce" would "procrastinate and impede the adoption of a general system" and might "ultimately produce divisions of the Union," making real the fear that had long haunted the revolutionaries of multiple leagues of states.[87]

These considerations came later, however, and did not slow down reformers, whose ambitions, if anything, only increased. The commissioners from five states at Annapolis in September 1786 reported they had originally met "to take into consideration the trade and commerce of the United States" and consider designing a "uniform system in their commercial intercourse and regulations," but soon realized that in order to do so they would need delegates empowered to discuss "other objects than those of Commerce."[88] Prompted by the Annapolis commissioners, Congress in February 1787 called for a new convention at Philadelphia, whose declared agenda was revising the articles to "render the federal Constitution adequate to the exigencies of Government and the preservation of the Union."[89] The wording was intentionally broad, but no one watching Congress for the prior few years—and witnessing repeated pleas for more control over commercial revenue and regulations go unanswered—could be under any illusions about what new powers would be "revised" into being at the first opportunity.

The commercially informed route that reform of the articles took institutionally challenges the argument proposed by Fiske and many subsequent historians that the focus on commercial regulations was a cover for deeper issues, and the "weightiest part of the business" aimed at by reformers was "relegated to a subordinate clause."[90] This argument misconstrues the importance of commerce to nationalist reformers. For them, commercial problems raised serious questions about the viability of the new republic's fundamental institutions. If Congress, under the articles, could not arbitrate disputes between states, fund a revenue, or negotiate treaties with other powers, then how could the nation survive, much less prosper? Americans returned to these questions constantly during the 1780s, at closed-door meetings as well as in public debates.[91] Commerce was a core constitutional issue because it was a constitutive activity for the American revolutionary project and a defining feature of the new nation's life as a polity.

But even if commerce had been a mere pretext for more extensive plans, that would in itself be telling. Appealing to a national audience steeped in a revolutionary political culture deeply suspicious of any concentrations of power, and in some cases unconvinced that the current union was dysfunctional enough to merit an overhaul, reformers thought the political problems of commerce—aggregating questions of sovereignty, revenue, and federal structure together as one challenge—could cajole their compatriots onto the road for change.

Some historians have perhaps been led astray by the records of the Philadelphia Convention itself, where the federal government's power over commerce was not much debated. This relative silence, however, should not be read as an index of unimportance, but rather of consensus. The convention had been called to revise the "exigencies" of the union under the articles, chief among them being the confederation's inability to protect U.S. commerce through treaties or to raise a revenue from it. So while the delegates in Philadelphia went well beyond their brief in many areas, providing the federal government with an explicit power to regulate and tax commerce was not one of them. Article I, Section 8 (and the clauses of Section 9 not dealing directly with slavery), were the uncontroversial results.[92] Similarly, the impost that the framers at Philadelphia imagined would be the result of their efforts was not an issue in the ratification debates; like the treaty-making power, its adoption was uncontentious.[93]

The lines of battle in the ratification debate do suggest, however, that the politically engaged public did not share the framers' consensus about the crucial importance of American commerce to the health of the body politic. The relative priority assigned to commerce—and to the nation-state's revenues and its foreign affairs—divided proponents and opponents of the new proposed constitutional order. The nationalist reformers, now federalists, considered commerce and its protection central to the maintenance of the union and the nation in a hostile world. Their opponents worried much less about the trials and travails of merchants, at least when not condemning international commerce for leading to corruption, luxury, and a loss of republican virtue.

However, this was not a divide with equal passion on each side. For the most part, antifederalists ignored the problems of commerce that federalist reformers obsessed about, instead training their attention on the dangers posed by the Constitution itself. When they did take up the issue, they suspected commerce's value as much as the importance of its regulation by the national government, reflecting the localist (or at least noncosmopolitan) perspective that formed one of the common threads among the diverse opponents of ratification. The Federal Farmer, answering Publius and others, cautioned against hasty decisions. Provided everyone remained "cool and temperate," the country was "in no immediate danger of any commotions" and in "state of perfect peace" (the activism of people like Daniel Shays aside, apparently). While Farmer admitted the difficulties state governments faced in regulating trade and securing credit and even allowed that the "uneasiness among creditors and mercantile men" was "well founded," he saw no reason to go through with any major reformations of the federal union; to do so, in fact, would be giving in to the panics of Shaysites and monied aristocrats alike.[94] For others, the old republican argument against luxury held more appeal. Arguing against ratification at the Pennsylvania constitutional convention, one antifederalist argued that Americans' "preposterous commerce"—their overreach and luxury—"has been the source of our distress, together with our extravagance," and he was unwilling "to sacrifice the rights of men" to obtain alterations in the confederation and reward such behavior.[95]

Reformers presented a mirror image to this apathy. Preparing for the Constitutional Convention, Tench Coxe wrote to remind the delegates that the disordered state of American commercial governance had provoked multiple threats to the sovereignty and unity of the country. Foreign powers lacked confidence the United States could enforce international agreements, and as a result, Americans could "hope to secure no privileges from them." Worse, the "desultory commercial acts of the [state] legislatures" had created so much "uncertainty, opposition, and errors" that in aggregate they threatened a greater distraction and evil than even European restrictions.[96] In similar anticipation, Madison worried about a "want of concert in matters where a common interest requires it," a defect he thought produced by the "perverseness of particular States, "and "most strongly illustrated in the state of our commercial affairs."[97] Oliver Ellsworth, a strong voice in favor of the new constitution in his widely read "Landholder" essays, explained the need for a stronger federal government in blunt terms: "When we call ourselves an independant nation it is false, we are neither a nation, nor are we independant. Like thirteen contentious neighbours we devour and take every advantage of each other, and are without that system of policy which gives safety and strength, and constitutes a national structure. Once we were dependant only on Great-Britain, now we are dependant on every petty state in the world and on every custom house officer of foreign ports."[98] Without greater power over commerce, Ellsworth argued, American independence was a lie.

In the influential *Federalist* essays, Publius (the joint pseudonym of Alexander Hamilton, Madison, and Jay) seemed to leave no aspect of the relation of commerce to the problems of union and government unmentioned. In essay no. 4, Jay argued that "the enterprise and address of our merchants and navigators" was leading Americans to capture a significant share of world trade. But this laudable success, Jay feared, could "*invite* hostility or insult" from European powers and thus provide cause for war—a danger Jay thought could only be sensibly countered by a more centralized union and a strong navy, institutions that would be best organized by a more powerful federal government.[99] In no. 6, Hamilton challenged Enlightenment theories about trade—commerce, history showed, did not soften the manners of men but rather provided another arena for bloody-minded competition between neighboring states. American states would meet this fate, he predicted, unless they harnessed their energies together within a strong centralized confederacy.[100] As it was, Hamilton lamented in no. 15, Americans' commerce stood at the "lowest point of declension," another prominent sign the confederation had "reached almost the last stage of national humiliation."[101] He also argued that all the powers related to "commerce, finance, [treaty] negotiation, and war" should be "lodged in the national depository" of the new federal government—although, of course, by Publius's own lights, as well as in historiographical hindsight, it is clear that contemporaries regarded the latter three powers as linked to the healthy exercise of the first.[102]

The intertwining of constitutional reform, national government, and commercial power went beyond political essays to polemical popular culture. The choruses of "The Grand CONSTITUTION," that appeared in the *Massachusetts Centinel* in October 1787 celebrated "FRANKLIN the sage" and "brave WASHINGTON" for saving the country not just from "scenes of affliction—Columbia opprest" but also "of credit expiring—and commerce distrest." Hailing the restructuring of sovereign power, the lyricist hit on the international implications of the new union, predicting the commercial victories that the reforms would guarantee: "Our trade and our commerce shall reach far and wide, / And riches and honour flow in with each tide, / Kamschatka and China with wonder shall stare, / That the Federal Stripes should wave gracefully there."[103] The "Federal Procession" that New York City's federalists organized on July 23, 1788, to honor the ratification of the "CONSTITUTION of the *United States*" marched to the same tune. The ship joiners, one of the dozens of artisan and professional groups who paraded down Broadway, carried a flag whose motto repeated a theme common to those in the procession, linking the new constitution to the return of prosperity: "This federal ship will our commerce revive, / And merchants and shipwrights and joiners shall thrive / On the ocean of time she's about to set sail, / Fair freedom her compass and concord the gale."[104]

As the New York celebrations suggest, by summer 1788, federalists and their concerns about commerce and its difficulties had carried the day. The new government their Constitution created did not wait to act. Just two days after the House of Representatives in the first federal Congress achieved a quorum in April 1789, it began debating a tariff. A few months later, the tariff, tonnage, and collection acts had passed and together created a comprehensive American commercial system.[105] This was, of course, no accident. By common consent among the new members of Congress, framing a national commercial policy became one of the most pressing agenda items for the federal legislature, since it would provide the national government with a stable revenue, American traders with protection against European systems of mercantilist regulation, and the United States with the recognized tools of sovereign authority. Reserving coastal trade to American ships and guiding trade flows through an incentive structure of duties and taxes (in particular, protecting American trade with Asia from foreign competition), the new laws provided the legible material and legal framework for U.S. political economy that aggressive nationalists had wanted since the peace.

Though some observers declared the new organization an immediate improvement, bigger changes would take longer, and the results were not always clearly attributable to the new government.[106] The federal government was certainly healthier, with dedicated revenues and the power to protect them. Treaties with Britain and Spain in 1794 and 1795 testified to those empires' new willingness to deal with the United States as a coherent body and helped stabilize some areas of trade—but this European recognition of "treaty worthiness" came at a high cost in terms of domestic unity, individual liberty, and state autonomy, as unhappy western Pennsylvanians could attest.[107] It is also unclear whether the new government was a decisive factor in these new settlements; the onset of the wars of the French Revolution likely played as large a role in convincing the courts in Madrid and London of the need for treaties as any federal restructuring. Meanwhile, the exigencies of a new global war boosted the volume of American trade to new heights in the 1790s and perhaps even shifted the nation's economy onto a trajectory of significant continuous growth.[108]

Parsing the immediate effects of 1789's constitutional settlement may be difficult, but ratification of the new order did settle the core questions about commerce and union that had pervaded national politics in the 1780s. Though in an important sense a "peace pact," the Constitution might equally be described as a customs union creating a defined domestic market. These two concepts of union were linked: for American revolutionaries, peace and prosperity, and the virtuous citizenry they would together create, depended on free-flowing commerce and the creation of a "union of interests" among the new states—a convergence that they discovered over the course of the 1780s could not occur without the oversight and management of a stronger, centralized authority.[109] As Madison explained to Jefferson in early 1786, "In fact most of our political evils may be traced up to our commercial ones, as most of our moral may to our political."[110] The Philadelphian Constitution and the economic and fiscal system Madison and his fellow federalist reformers built on its foundation were carefully targeted remedies for the nations' ills designed to address them at their commercial roots.


On the eve of a vote for Scottish independence in 2014, American political pundit Matt Yglesias took to Twitter to wonder publicly at the referendum's economic effects. Tongue firmly in cheek, he posed a question to his followers on social media: "How will independent Scotland cope with the loss of access to English colonial markets overseas?"[111] Yglesias's mocking query neatly underlines the rhetorical and substantive similarities between the debate over a failed Scottish referendum and the controversy surrounding the success of American independence. Opponents of Scotland's separation from England raised warnings about the effects of commercial exclusion similar to those Americans learned to fear over the course of the 1780s. Echoing Lord Sheffield's logic, if not (always) his gleeful scorn, supporters of continued union argued that England's interests would give it no reason to meet a former imperial partner halfway with favorable trade terms or a common defense. Instead, the new country on the Atlantic periphery would have had to make its own way in the cold world, disadvantaged by a small population, shorn of significant resources, and hobbled by untested institutions.[112] (It is perhaps an irony, but not a surprise, that the same arguments applied to the United States in 1776 and Scotland in 2014 reappeared, in 2016, as a counter to the push for a UK "Brexit" from the European Union).

Indeed, such circumstances prevail beyond the North Atlantic. For new nations, the status and durability of commercial connections to the rest of the world carry an outsized importance for the strength and stability of the state. Seen from this transnational, transhistorical perspective, it is unsurprising that trade was a key component of the struggle for political order in the United States during the 1780s, creating fiscal and interstate union problems as well as feeding a perception of a looming crisis among elites. Similarly, the resurgence of commerce as a major partisan issue in American politics during the 1790s and early 1800s appears less unusual considering its long-standing connections to sovereignty, legitimacy, and constitutional structure. In the early United States, commerce was central to debates over political economy and the nature and purpose of the polity.

Whether considered over the ruled lines of a ledger book in a countinghouse near New York's ice-packed harbor; regarded through the shadow-streaked, wooded back acres of a frontier farm in Kentucky; or contemplated from the stuffy confines of a stifling meeting hall in Philadelphia, commerce and the production of commercial opportunity were core components of the still-diffuse concept known as the "United States of America" in the 1780s. Commerce was a key part of the practical political economy of the early American nation-state, but also an important part of the *theory* of that state. In an integrated Atlantic world, and within an intermittently globalized economy, how could it be otherwise? During the 1780s, nationalist reformers saw commerce as a thread running through disparate political disputes—the friction between states, persistent fiscal instability, practical sovereignty in foreign affairs, even the frustration of the epochal promise of republican politics. From their perspective, the failure to secure a firm purchase in international politics and a prosperous union at home were twinned disasters, rooted in commercial vexations. This concern for commerce created an impetus for reform in the late 1780s and explains why commerce was so constitutionally consequential for the early American republic in the years after its founding. Anxious for their trade, Americans remade their state.

## Notes

I wish to thank the anonymous reviewers at University of Virginia Press for their insightful comments, as well as Chris Pearl and Doug Bradburn for their expert guidance. This essay was first presented as a paper at the Founding Debates: Leadership, Conflict, and Crisis in the Critical Period, 1784–1789 conference, hosted at the Fred W. Smith National Library for the Study of George Washington at Mount Vernon. I am indebted to Doug Bradburn and Brian Phillips Murphy, the coorganizers of that fantastic event, for the invitation to consider the Critical Period anew, as well as the opportunity to discuss this material with them and the other scholars gathered for the conference. Hannah Farber read revisions and gave me the benefit of her trenchant, actionable suggestions, a service for which I am deeply, deeply grateful. This essay is reprinted with the permission of the University of Pennsylvania Press.

It appeared first in print as Dael A. Norwood, "The Constitutional Consequences of Commercial Crisis: The Role of Trade Reconsidered in the 'Critical Period,'" *Early American Studies* 18, no. 4 (Fall 2020): 490–524. My sincere thanks to University of Pennsylvania Press for their permission to republish it and to the journal's staff—especially editor Roderick McDonald—for shepherding it through with their keen eyes, deep knowledge, and kind instruction. Financial support for the research for this essay was provided by the Mount Vernon Ladies' Association and the Cassius Marcellus Clay Postdoctoral Fellowship at Yale University.

Epigraph from Freeman Hunt, *Lives of American Merchants* (New York: Office of Hunt's Merchants' Magazine, 1856), 1:iv.

1. *Independent Gazette (New York)*, February 26, 1784, 3.

2. Samuel Shaw, *The Journals of Major Samuel Shaw: The First American Consul at Canton; With a Life of the Author*, ed. Josiah Quincy (Boston: Crosby and Nichols, 1847), 133–34; Philip Chadwick Foster Smith, *The Empress of China* (Philadelphia: Philadelphia Maritime Museum, 1984), 3.

3. The venture's most prominent backer was Robert Morris, who had served as superintendent of finance for the Continental Congress. The business and sailing of the *Empress of China*'s voyage is most fully described in Smith, *The Empress of China*. See also Morris, "Appendix I: Early Records of Robert Morris's Involvement in American Trade with China," in *The Papers of Robert Morris, 1781–1784*, ed. E. James Ferguson (Pittsburgh: University of Pittsburgh Press, 1995), 8:857–82; Clarence L. Ver Steeg, "Financing and Outfitting the First United States Ship to China," *Pacific Historical Review* 22, no. 1 (1953): 1–12; Dane A. Morrison, *True Yankees: The South Seas and the Discovery of American Identity* (Baltimore: Johns Hopkins University Press, 2014), 3–30. On the ship's design and characteristics, see Smith, *The Empress of China*, 25–26, 67–69, 129–133, 306n15; Shaw, *The Journals of Major Samuel Shaw*, 337. Morris found himself bankrupted a few years later, partially as a result of his overextension of optimism, and credit, in voyages like the *Empress*'s. Jonathan M. Chu, *Stumbling Towards the Constitution: The Economic Consequences of Freedom in the Atlantic World* (New York: Palgrave Macmillan, 2012), 3.

4. Philip Freneau, "On the First American Ship (*Empress of China, Capt. Greene*) That Explored the Rout to *China*, and the East Indies, After the Revolution, 1784," in *Poems Written and Published during the American Revolutionary War*, 3rd ed. (Philadelphia, 1809), 2:181–82.

5. Shaw, *The Journals of Major Samuel Shaw*, 134, 113.

6. Both Franks and the other messenger carrying the ratified treaty, Colonel Josiah Harmar, were delayed by bad weather. Franks reached London on April 7, 1784, and proceeded from there to Paris. See "Philadelphia, May 22," *Pennsylvania Packet*, May 22, 1784, 3; "New-York, Thursday, May 27," *New-York Journal*, May 27, 1784, 3. On the ratification exchange process, see Worthington C. Ford et al., eds., *Journals of the Continental Congress, 1774–1789* (Washington, DC: Government Printing Office, 1928), 26:34–36, http://memory.loc.gov/ammem/amlaw/lwjc.html (henceforth *JCC*); Charles Thomson to Jay, Annapolis, January 15, 1784, in *The Emerging Nation: A Documentary History of the Foreign Relations of the United States Under the Articles of Confederation, 1780–1789*, ed. Mary A. Giunta, J. Dane Hartgrove, and Mary-Jane M.

Dowd (Washington, DC: National Historical Publications and Records Commission, 1996), 2:277–78; and *The Papers of Thomas Jefferson,* ed. Julian P. Boyd, Main Series (Princeton, NJ: Princeton University Press, 1959), 6:461–62 (henceforth, *Jefferson Papers*). For Congress's proclamation declaring the treaty ratification and the formal end of the War of Independence, see Francis Wharton, ed., *The Revolutionary Diplomatic Correspondence of the United States* (Washington, DC: Government Printing Office, 1889), 6:754–57.

7. Adams to the president of Congress, Paris, September 1, 1783, in *The Adams Papers: Papers of John Adams, June 1783–January 1784,* ed. Gregg L. Lint (Cambridge, MA: Harvard University Press, 2010), 15:241 (henceforth, *Adams Papers*).

8. John Fiske, *The Critical Period of American History, 1783–1789* (Boston: Houghton Mifflin, 1888). For a reconsideration of Fiske's analysis, see Max M. Edling, "Consolidating a Revolutionary Republic," in *The World of the Revolutionary American Republic: Land, Labor, and the Conflict for a Continent,* ed. Andrew Shankman, Routledge Worlds (New York: Routledge, 2014), 165–94.

9. E.g., David C. Hendrickson, *Peace Pact: The Lost World of the American Founding* (Lawrence: University Press of Kansas, 2003); David C. Hendrickson, *Union, Nation, or Empire: The American Debate Over International Relations, 1789–1941* (Lawrence: University Press of Kansas, 2009); Robbie J. Totten, "Security, Two Diplomacies, and the Formation of the U.S. Constitution: Review, Interpretation, and New Directions for the Study of the Early American Period," *Diplomatic History* 36, no. 1 (2012): 77–117; David M. Golove and Daniel J. Hulsebosch, "Civilized Nation: The Early American Constitution, the Law of Nations, and the Pursuit of International Recognition," *New York University Law Review* 85, no. 4 (2010): 932–1066; William Earl Weeks, *Dimensions of the Early American Empire, 1754–1865,* vol. 1, New Cambridge History of American Foreign Relations (New York: Cambridge University Press, 2013).

10. For a thorough review of the literature touching on the 1780s and efforts to reform the confederation, see Totten, "Security, Two Diplomacies, and the Formation of the U.S. Constitution," 80–89. Douglas Irwin's magisterial survey of American trade policy puts commerce at the center of American politics but understands these debates—and the regimes they produced—primarily as political expressions of economic interests. Douglas A. Irwin, *Clashing over Commerce: A History of US Trade Policy* (Chicago: University of Chicago Press, 2017).

11. Staughton Lynd and David Waldstreicher, "Free Trade, Sovereignty, and Slavery: Toward an Economic Interpretation of American Independence," *William and Mary Quarterly* 68, no. 4 (2011): 599.

12. Ibid., 630.

13. Ibid., 629.

14. On the role of the coasting and carrying trades in creating bonds of union that shaped the new constitutional order, see Maeve Herbert Glass, "These United States: A History of the Fracturing of America" (PhD diss., Princeton University, 2016), http://arks .princeton.edu/ark:/88435/dsp016d5700036. For an excellent and extended consideration of how U.S. authorities exercised control over maritime trade, see Gautham Rao, *National Duties: Custom Houses and the Making of the American State* (Chicago: University of Chicago Press, 2016).

15. Fiske, *The Critical Period of American History*.

16. Peter S. Onuf, *The Origins of the Federal Republic: Jurisdictional Controversies in the United States, 1775–1787* (Philadelphia: University of Pennsylvania Press, 1983); Peter S. Onuf and Nicholas G. Onuf, *Federal Union, Modern World: The Law of Nations in an Age of Revolutions, 1776–1814* (Madison, WI: Madison House, 1993); Hendrickson, *Peace Pact*. For recent work considering and extending this model, see David Armitage, *The Declaration of Independence: A Global History* (Cambridge, MA: Harvard University Press, 2007); Golove and Hulsebosch, "Civilized Nation"; Eliga H. Gould, *Among the Powers of the Earth: The American Revolution and the Making of a New World Empire* (Cambridge, MA: Harvard University Press, 2012); Totten, "Security, Two Diplomacies, and the Formation of the U.S. Constitution"; Tom Cutterham, "The International Dimension of the Federal Constitution," *Journal of American Studies* 48, no. 2 (May 2014): 501–15.

17. Gould defines "treaty worthiness" less as being tied to specific treaties and "more on the broader process by which Americans sought to make themselves appear worthy of peaceful relations with other nations." A key part of his analysis—though not one attended to here—concerns how Americans constructed their own hierarchies of race, creed, and class to define other peoples (Africans, Indians, Muslims) as less than treaty worthy. Gould, *Among the Powers of the Earth*, 12–13. In broad agreement with Gould's analysis, Golove and Hulsebosch also identify European recognition as critical, but they implicitly periodize the development of Americans' approach to winning recognition by arguing that before the Treaty of Peace, Americans regarded "taxation and commercial regulation" as "essential markers of sovereignty," but coordinating foreign policy did not necessarily violate individual states' independence. Golove and Hulsebosch, "Civilized Nation," 954. Mining a parallel vein, Max Edling's study of the fiscal history of the early United States argues that efficient fiscal institutions and a good reputation among international lenders were key to the nation's imperial successes and rise to great power status. Because Americans' establishment of a good public credit preceded the nation's accordance of diplomatic heft, we might perhaps say "creditworthiness" was necessary for treaty worthiness. See Max M. Edling, *A Hercules in the Cradle: War, Money, and the American State, 1783–1867* (Chicago: University of Chicago Press, 2014).

18. The exceptions were the Franco-American military alliance, the Peace of Paris, and the Treaty of Ghent. Edling argues that the Jay Treaty should also be seen primarily as a peace treaty; however, seeing it as such does not preclude understanding its commercial aspects as fundamental to nation building—a perspective buttressed by Lawrence Hatter's work on the treaty's long-term effects on Laurentide trade, citizenship standards, and the state's role in western settlement. Max M. Edling, *A Revolution in Favor of Government: Origins of the U.S. Constitution and the Making of the American State* (New York: Oxford University Press, 2003), 133–34; Lawrence B. A. Hatter, "The Jay Charter: Rethinking the American National State in the West, 1796–1819," *Diplomatic History* 37, no. 4 (2013): 693–726.

19. Washington's Farewell Address is perhaps the best-known statement of this type, but his comments were echoed by virtually every American diplomat and executive official from the beginning of the revolution through to the late nineteenth-century overseas

interventions in Spain's colonies. This is not to say the United States did not have an ongoing imperialism of its own in North America and surrounding territories—it certainly did—but not one motivated by alliances with or direct ties to European powers, specifically.

20. Gould, *Among the Powers of the Earth*, 119. For analyses of Americans' cultural and psychological insecurities, see Brendan McConville, *The King's Three Faces: The Rise and Fall of Royal America, 1688–1776* (Chapel Hill: University of North Carolina Press, 2007); Kariann Akemi Yokota, *Unbecoming British: How Revolutionary America Became a Postcolonial Nation* (New York: Oxford University Press, 2011).

21. Robin L. Einhorn, *American Taxation, American Slavery* (Chicago: University of Chicago Press, 2006), 117–56; Edling, *A Revolution in Favor of Government*, 74. For an examination of just how light, and just how efficient, that state became after the constitution, see Edling, *A Hercules in the Cradle*, 50–80.

22. Thomas Ruston's reply to Sheffield articulates this understanding of the connection between commerce and foreign relations: "Trade is to the body politic what the blood is to the human body; it diffuses itself by the minutest channels into every part of the nation, and gives life and vigour to the whole. Without it no country can either be happy in herself or be able to withstand the attacks of powerful adversaries from without." *Remarks on Lord Sheffield's Observations on the Commerce of the American States: By an American* (London, 1784), 1.

23. Lee to Patrick Henry, Philadelphia, April 20, 1776, in *The Letters of Richard Henry Lee*, ed. James Curtis Ballagh (New York: Macmillan, 1911), 1:178.

24. "Plan of Treaties: 12 June—17 September 1776," in *Adams Papers*, 4:260–301. As Gould notes, the treaty also made grand claims for the extent and coherence of the United States' national empire. Gould, *Among the Powers of the Earth*, 1–13, 222n1.

25. Adams to the president of Congress, Paris, April 18, 1780, in *Adams Papers*, 9:151; Weeks, *Dimensions of the Early American Empire*, 23.

26. Felix Gilbert, *To the Farewell Address: Ideas of Early American Foreign Policy* (Princeton, NJ: Princeton University Press, 1970), 69, 68. For a periodization of how Americans' ideas about their position in world trade and particular trade policies evolved, see Robert Bruce Bittner, "The Definition of Economic Independence and the New Nation," (PhD, University of Wisconsin–Madison, 1970).

27. Thomas Pownall, *A Translation of the Memorial to the Sovereigns of Europe Upon the Present State of Affairs, Between the Old and the New World, into Common Sense and Intelligible English*, ed. Edmund Jenings and John Adams (London, 1781), 41. On general American support for logic similar to Pownall's, see Hendrickson, *Peace Pact*, 168–70.

28. Pownall, *A Translation of the Memorial to the Sovereigns of Europe*, 26.

29. Ezra Stiles, *The United States Elevated to Glory and Honor: A Sermon, Preached Before His Excellency Jonathan Trumbull, Esq L.L.D, Governor and Commander in Chief, and the Honorable the General Assembly of the State of Connecticut, Convened at Hartford, at the Anniversary Election, May 8th, 1783* (New Haven, CT, 1783), 50.

30. Ibid., 30.

31. "This great american revolution, this recent political phaenomenon of a new sovereignty arising from among the sovereign powers of the earth, will be attended to and contemplated by all nations. Navigation will carry the american flag around the globe

itself; and display the thirteen stripes and new constellation at *bengal* and *canton,* on the *indus* and *ganges,* on the *whang-ho* and the *yang-tse-kiang;* and with commerce will import the wisdom and literature of the east. That prophecy of Daniel is now literally fulfilling . . . that there shall be an universal travelling *too and fro, and knowledge shall be increased.* This knowledge will be brought home and treasured up in america: and being here digested and carried to the highest perfection, may reblaze back from america to europe, asia and africa, and illumine the world with truth and liberty." Ibid., 52, emphasis in original. Also quoted, and commented upon, in Drew R. McCoy, *The Elusive Republic: Political Economy in Jeffersonian America* (Chapel Hill: University of North Carolina Press, 1980), 88–89.

32. Anne-Robert-Jacques Turgot, "Letter from M. Turgot to Dr. Price, Paris, March 22, 1778," in *Observations on the Importance of the American Revolution, and the Means of Making It a Benefit to the World: To Which Is Added, a Letter from M. Turgot, Late Comptroller-General of the Finances of France; With an Appendix, Containing a Translation of the Will of M. Fortuné Ricard, Lately Published in France,* ed. Richard Price (London, 1785), 116.

33. Morris to Jay, Philadelphia, November 27, 1783, in Giunta, Hartgrove, and Dowd, *The Emerging Nation,* 1:955.

34. Richard Price, *Observations on the Importance of the American Revolution* (London, 1785), 76, 75.

35. For a survey of the debate over commerce and "luxury" in the 1780s, see McCoy, *The Elusive Republic,* 95–104.

36. For a discussion of the data's difficulties, see James F. Shepherd and Gary M. Walton, "Economic Change after the American Revolution: Pre- and Post-War Comparisons of Maritime Shipping and Trade," *Explorations in Economic History* 13, no. 4 (1976): 397–422.

37. A good example is Gordon S. Wood, *The Creation of the American Republic, 1776–1787* (Chapel Hill: University of North Carolina Press, 1969), 395. Wood's conflicted admission of hard times is sometimes contrasted with Merrill Jensen's famous positivity (Jensen argued "the period was one of extraordinary economic growth"). But Jensen was not alone; Beard's interpretation was also based on a deep skepticism of merchants' and manufacturers' claims to poverty. Merrill Jensen, *The New Nation: A History of the United States during the Confederation, 1781–1789* (New York: Knopf, 1950), 423; Charles A. Beard, *An Economic Interpretation of the Constitution of the United States* (New York: Macmillan, 1921), 41–49.

38. Quote from John J. McCusker and Russell R. Menard, *The Economy of British America, 1607–1789,* Needs and Opportunities for Study Series (Chapel Hill: University of North Carolina Press, 1985), 373. For a classic (and much imitated) example of pairing literary sources, see Gordon C. Bjork, "The Weaning of the American Economy: Independence, Market Changes, and Economic Development," *Journal of Economic History* 24, no. 4 (1964): 541. Benjamin Franklin's much-cited but suspiciously Panglossian comments were responses to European claims that the United States was in dire straits. "Consolation for America, or remarks on her real situation, interests, and policy—by his excellency Benjamin Franklin, esq. president of the commonwealth of Pennsylvania," *American Museum* 1, no. 1 (January 1787): 5–8, and Franklin to Louis-Guillaume Le Veillard, Philadelphia, March 6, 1786, Unpublished Papers, in Franklin,

*The Papers of Benjamin Franklin Digital Edition,* ed. Ellen R. Cohn (New Haven: Yale University Press, 1959), http://franklinpapers.org.

For a summary of the new(er) consensus on the 1780s as a period of economic depression, see Jacob Price, "Reflections on the Economy of Revolutionary America," in *The Economy of Early America: The Revolutionary Period, 1763–1790,* ed. Ronald Hoffman et al. (Charlottesville: University of Virginia Press, 1988), 303–22; Cathy Matson, "The Revolution, the Constitution, and the New Nation," in *The Cambridge Economic History of the United States,* ed. Stanley L. Engerman and Robert E. Gallman, vol. 1, The Colonial Era (New York: Cambridge University Press, 1996), 363–401. The data we do have allow for comparisons of the pre- and post-Revolutionary economy and bears out the interpretation of a 1780s depression—or at best, stagnation—as a general, national trend. For an econometric analysis, see Bjork, "The Weaning of the American Economy" and Shepherd and Walton, "Economic Change after the American Revolution." Note, however, that whether the new constitutional arrangements were what spurred growth after 1789 is a separate question. A few recent studies of the grain and coffee trades suggest there were areas of growth before the reformation of the federal government under the Constitution, but it is not clear that these specific cases explain more than what the structural conditions might suggest for the national stage. See Brooke Hunter, "The Prospect of Independent Americans: The Grain Trade and Economic Development during the 1780s," *Explorations in Early American Culture* 5 (2001): 260–87; Michelle Craig McDonald, "The Chance of the Moment: Coffee and the New West Indies Commodities Trade," *William and Mary Quarterly* 62, no. 3 (2005): 441–72. Frank W. Garmon Jr.'s recent work analyzing insolvency rates in Virginia suggests that even in individual states, regional patterns of development diverged sufficiently to provide a basis for both economic pessimism and optimism. Frank W. Garmon Jr., "Mapping Distress: Taxation and Insolvency in Virginia, 1782–1790," *Journal of the Early Republic* 40, no. 2 (Summer 2020): 231–65.

39. Tench Coxe, "23. An Enquiry into the Principles of a Commercial System Philadelphia, 19 May [1787] (Excerpt)," in *The Documentary History of the Ratification of the Constitution,* ed. John P. Kaminski et al. (Charlottesville: University of Virginia Press, 2009), 13:102.

40. Giunta, Hartgrove, and Dowd, *The Emerging Nation,* 2:vii–viii; Weeks, *Dimensions of the Early American Empire,* 28–30, 36–37. The key piece of legislation was the "American Intercourse bill," drafted by John Pownall and supported by Shelburne. For a perceptive analysis of Shelburne's thoughts on political economy and political aptitudes, see Charles R. Ritcheson, "The Earl of Shelbourne [*sic*] and Peace with America, 1782–1783: Vision and Reality," *International History Review* 5, no. 3 (1983): 322–45.

41. The reversion to prewar trade policy and its applicability to postwar circumstances are most famously articulated in John Holroyd, Earl of Sheffield, *Observations on the Commerce of the America States with Europe and the West Indies Including the Several Articles of Import and Export: And on the Tendency of a Bill Now Depending in Parliament* (London, 1783). For a detailed time line of the shift in British orientation toward American commerce, see the original documents collected in Giunta, Hartgrove, and Dowd, *The Emerging Nation,* 2:115–17, et seq.

42. Sheffield, *Observations on the Commerce of the America States,* 69, 68.

43. Chu, *Stumbling Towards the Constitution*, 15.

44. Francisco Rendón to José de Gálvez, Philadelphia, April 20, 1784, in Giunta, Hart-grove, and Dowd, *The Emerging Nation*, 2:342; Matson, "The Revolution, the Constitution, and the New Nation," 373–78; Chu, *Stumbling Towards the Constitution*, 8–13.

45. The Barbary captures had a significant effect, not only underscoring the republic's impotence, but also providing fodder for partisan competition and heightening American debates around slavery. See Robert J. Allison, *The Crescent Obscured: The United States and the Muslim World, 1776–1815* (New York: Oxford University Press, 1995); Lawrence A. Peskin, *Captives and Countrymen: Barbary Slavery and the American Public, 1785–1816* (Baltimore: Johns Hopkins University Press, 2009); Christine E. Sears, *American Slaves and African Masters: Algiers and the Western Sahara, 1776–1820* (New York: Palgrave Macmillan, 2012).

46. Weeks, *Dimensions of the Early American Empire*, 37–39.

47. For example, "The only really bright spot on America's trade horizon was its incipient China trade, which would yield handsome profits while stimulating America's shipbuilding industry and providing experience for future American naval officers." Giunta, Hartgrove, and Dowd, *The Emerging Nation*, 1:ix.

48. Matson, "The Revolution, the Constitution, and the New Nation," 374.

49. Shaw, *The Journals of Major Samuel Shaw*, 352–56.

50. Ibid., 353, 354. Shaw was effectively calling for an Asian-waters version of the Atlantic world League of Armed Neutrality that Russia had organized among neutral powers to oppose British search and seizure during the American Revolution.

51. Jack N. Rakove, *The Beginnings of National Politics: An Interpretive History of the Continental Congress* (New York: Knopf, 1979), 282–84, 302–4.

52. *JCC*, 17:758–59; 19:105–6, 110–13, 124–25.

53. Ibid., 23:771, 783–84.

54. Ibid., 24:144, 170–74, 188–92, 257–62. Congress also requested a revision to the eighth Article of Confederation, shifting the way Congress assessed state responsibility for revenue from land values to population totals (counting each enslaved individual as three-fifths of a person).

55. Ibid., 24:278.

56. Ibid., 25:617.

57. Adams saw conspiracy in the proclamations, calling them a piece of "Refugee Politicks"—the result of pressure from exiled loyalists. Adams to Robert Livingston, Paris, July 16, 1783, in *Adams Papers*, 15:123–24.

58. Adams to Livingston, Paris, July 14, 1783, in ibid., 15:112. "The United States of America have propagated far & wide in Europe the Ideas of the Liberty of Navigation and Commerce. The Powers of Europe, however, cannot agree as yet, in adopting them to their full extent." Ibid., 15:109.

59. Adams to Livingston, Paris, July 16, 1783, in ibid., 15:124.

60. Ibid. Adams does not specify the means for sending "ships to China," but it is unlikely he meant direct government financing; in keeping with the tenor of the rest of his letter, it seems more probable that he favored merely official exhortation, or, at best, encouragement through favorable duties.

61. Adams to Livingston, Paris, July 18, 1783, in ibid., 15:138–39.

62. *JCC*, 25:661–63.

63. Ibid., 26:71.

64. Ibid., 26:269–71.

65. Ibid., 26:318–22.

66. Ibid., 28:201–5. A little over a year later, another, even more sweeping, attempt at reforming the articles included a significant expansion of congressional powers over commerce. This latter proposal was never accepted by Congress, but, unusually, it was published in the newspapers. See ibid., 31:494–98; Rakove, *The Beginnings of National Politics*, 371.

67. The need for reform was also expressed by Congress's policy managers—Jay, considering a treaty proposal, offered that he thought it unwise (or impossible) to negotiate new treaties of commerce without first adopting "a System for regulating the Trade of the United States." *JCC*, 28:367.

68. On state experiments in commercial regulation—including Virginia's efforts to establish "free" ports and other states attempts at commercial retaliation—see Bittner, "The Definition of Economic Independence and the New Nation," 152–231.

69. "John Jay's Report on Complaints from French Merchants, October 7, 1785," in Giunta, Hartgrove, and Dowd, *The Emerging Nation*, 2:846.

70. *JCC*, 30:93–94.

71. Ibid., 30:87–88.

72. Ibid., 31: 613–19.

73. On the especially long and tortured failure of the impost, see Fiske, *The Critical Period of American History*, 218–20; Rakove, *The Beginnings of National Politics*, 338–42.

74. Rakove, *The Beginnings of National Politics*, 341–42; Fiske, *The Critical Period of American History*, 219–20.

75. *JCC*, 31:467–84, 566–70, 935–48, 951–53.

76. "Is it to be supposed, that if it is discovered a treaty is formed upon principles calculated to promote the interests of one part of the union at the expence of the other, that the part conceiving itself injured will ever consent to invest additional powers? Will they not urge, and with great reason, the impropriety of vesting that body with farther powers, which has so recently abused those they already possess? I have no doubt they will." Ibid., 31:945–46.

77. Jefferson to G. K. van Hogendorp, Paris, October 13, 1785, in *Jefferson Papers*, 8:633.

78. Adams to Jay, Grosvenor Square, December 6, 1785, in Giunta, Hartgrove, and Dowd, *The Emerging Nation*, 2:943.

79. Price, *Observations on the Importance of the American Revolution*, 76, 77.

80. Jefferson to van Hogendorp, Paris, October 13, 1785, in *Jefferson Papers*, 8:633.

81. Adams to Jay, London, December 6, 1785, in Giunta, Hartgrove, and Dowd, *The Emerging Nation*, 2:943.

82. Washington to James Warren, Mt. Vernon, October 7, 1785, in *The Papers of George Washington*, ed. W. W. Abbot, Confederation Series (Charlottesville: University Press of Virginia Press, 1994), 3:299–300.

83. Ibid.

84. John Langdon to Jefferson, Portsmouth, NH, December 7, 1785, in *Jefferson Papers*, 9:84.

85. Rakove, *The Beginnings of National Politics*, 368; Bruce Ackerman and Neal Katyal, "Our Unconventional Founding," *University of Chicago Law Review* 62, no. 2 (1995): 475–573.

86. Ackerman and Katyal, "Our Unconventional Founding," 492–94.

87. Henry Lee to Edmund Randolph, New York, May 15, 1787, in *Letters of Delegates to Congress, 1774–1789*, ed. Paul Hubert Smith (Washington DC: Library of Congress, 1976), 24:280. See also *JCC*, 32:76–77, 114, 271–72 and Edward Carrington to Edmund Randolph, New York, April 2, 1787, in Smith, *Letters of Delegates to Congress*, 24:193.

88. *JCC*, 31:678–79.

89. Ibid., 32:74.

90. Fiske here refers specifically to the clause in New Jersey's instructions to its commissioners suggesting that the Annapolis meeting consider "other important matters" besides creating a uniform system of commercial regulations. Fiske, *The Critical Period of American History*, 217. Jonathan Elliot, compiling a documentary history of the formation of the Constitution at a generation's remove from the events themselves, was less circumspect about assigning questions around commerce key importance, even as he lauded the wisdom and genius of the framers. The section of his multivolume *Debates* covering the confederation period is titled "Proceedings which led to the Adoption of the Constitution"; it is a legislative history containing only the Continental Congress's acts, reports, and debates about drawing revenue from commerce and regulating commerce to protect American trade against a European "system" and leaves no doubt as to what Elliot, like many Americans, considered to be the heart of the matter. Jonathan Elliot, ed., *The Debates in the Several State Conventions on the Adoption of the Federal Constitution*, 2nd ed. (Washington, DC, 1836), 1:92–120.

91. "The issue of Congress' control over commerce had occupied the public attention since the end of the Revolution and it continued to do so after Congress called the Constitutional Convention on 21 February 1787. After that date, newspapers, pamphlets, and letters were filled with statements recommending that the Convention propose that Congress be given the power to regulate commerce." Kaminski et al., *The Documentary History of the Ratification of the Constitution Digital Edition*, 13:50.

92. Einhorn, *American Taxation, American Slavery*, 149–50.

93. The opposite of controversial, in fact: "The impost was the only tax Congress could adopt without talking about slavery." Ibid., 120.

94. *Observations Leading to a Fair Examination of the System of Government: Proposed by the Late Convention; And to Several Essential and Necessary Alterations in It, In a Number of Letters from the Federal Farmer to the Republican* (New York, 1787), 4, 36, 37. The series is alternately attributed to Richard Henry Lee or Melancton Smith.

95. John Smilie, December 3, 1787, in Kaminski et al., *The Documentary History of the Ratification of the Constitution Digital Edition*, 2:459.

96. Coxe, "23. An Enquiry into the Principles of a Commercial System Philadelphia" in ibid., 13:103–4.

97. Madison, "Vices of the Political System of the United States," in *The Papers of James Madison*, ed. Robert A. Rutland and William M. E. Rachal, Congressional Series (Chicago: University of Chicago Press, 1975), 9:350 (henceforth, *Madison Papers*).

98. "254. A Landholder II, Connecticut Courant, 12 November [1787]," in Kaminski et al., *The Documentary History of the Ratification of the Constitution Digital Edition*, 14:92.

99. No. 4 (John Jay), in Hamilton, Madison, and Jay, *The Federalist*, ed. George W. Carey and James McClellan, Gideon edition (Indianapolis: Liberty Fund, 2001), 14, 13.

100. No. 6 (Hamilton), in ibid., 20–26.

101. No. 15 (Hamilton), in ibid., 69.

102. No. 17 (Hamilton), in ibid., 80. Arguments in favor of granting commercial powers to the federal government are also developed in *Federalist* nos. 22, 45, and 46 and mentioned inter alia throughout the series.

103. An image, and perhaps a sentiment, that Francis Scott Key might have appreciated. "135. The Grand Constitution Massachusetts Centinel, 6 October [1787]," in Kaminski et al., *The Documentary History of the Ratification of the Constitution Digital Edition*, 13:344–45.

104. "Federal Procession, in Honor of the CONSTITUTION of the *United States*," *New-York Packet,* August 5, 1788. The parade's organizers had postponed the event in the hope that New York's constitutional convention would "accede to the union," but after a month waiting for the delegates in Poughkeepsie to finish their debates, they decided that nine states' ratification votes, being enough to make a new national union, would suffice for a citywide celebration. The "federal ship" the ship joiners referenced was both a figurative allusion to the new government and a literal reference to a model frigate, the *Hamilton,* that served as the procession's centerpiece float. Twenty-seven feet long and ten feet wide at the beam, fully crewed and featuring working guns, a full set of sail, and even its own canvas waves, the ship "made a fine appearance" sailing down the city's thoroughfares, according to the *New-York Journal.* See *New-York Journal,* July 24, 1788, 3; *New-York Packet,* June 27, 1788, 3; "FEDERAL PROCESSION," *New-York Packet,* July 22, 1788, 3.

105. These were the second, third, and fifth laws passed, respectively. The first act passed was to regulate oaths: Act of June 1, 1789, ch. 1, 1 Stat. 23 ("An Act: To regulate the time and manner of administering certain oaths"). The specific pieces of legislation are as follows—the Tariff: Act of July 4, 1789, ch. 2., 1 Stat. 24 ("An Act: For laying a duty on goods, wares, and merchandises imported into the United States"); the Tonnage Act: Act of July 20, 1789, ch. 3., 1 Stat. 27 ("An Act: Imposing duties on tonnage"); the Collection Act: Act of July 31, 1789, ch. 5, 1 Stat. 29 ("An Act: To regulate the collection of the duties imposed by law on the tonnage of ships or vessels, and on goods, wares, and merchandise"). Like Robin Einhorn, I have followed contemporaries' language in terming the revenue act of July 4, 1789, a "tariff" rather than an "impost"; the latter refers to any trade tax, while the former more specifically designates a trade tax that enumerates specific rates of duty on some goods. Other historians have not made this distinction. Einhorn, *American Taxation, American Slavery*, 293n4. Cf. Edling, *A Hercules in the Cradle,* 50–51.

106. Phineas Bond, the British consul resident at Philadelphia and no friend to American commerce, told his superiors that as early as November 1789, he saw an improvement in the state of the economy, at least in the mid-Atlantic states: "These inconveniences are gradually wearing away—the eyes of the people seem now to be opened to their true interests—the prospect of an efficient government has greatly encouraged them

industry has succeeded to idleness and husbandry appears to be in a progressive state. "59. To the Duke of Leeds. Philadelphia, Nov. 10, 1789," in Bond, "Letters of Phineas Bond, British Consul at Philadelphia, to the Foreign Office of Great Britain, 1787, 1788, 1789," in *Annual Report of the American Historical Association for the Year 1896*, ed. J. Franklin Jameson (Washington, DC: Government Printing Office, 1897), 1:628.

107. Gould, *Among the Powers of the Earth*, 134–39.

108. Douglass C. North, *The Economic Growth of the United States, 1790–1860* (New York: Norton, 1966).

109. Though they do not focus specifically on the links between sovereign power, as recognized from without, and the problems of union, as organized from within, the development of the idea of a "union of interests" in the American context is best explored in Cathy D. Matson and Peter S. Onuf, *A Union of Interests: Political and Economic Thought in Revolutionary America* (Lawrence: University Press of Kansas, 1990).

110. Madison to Jefferson, March 18, 1786, in *Madison Papers*, 8:502.

111. Matthew Yglesias (@mattyglesias), "How Will Independent Scotland Cope with the Loss of Access to English Colonial Markets Overseas?," Twitter, September 8, 2014, https://twitter.com/mattyglesias/status/508952104170688512.

112. "The Facts—the Economy," *Better Together*, Wayback Machine, accessed September 8, 2014, https://web.archive.org/web/20140914194307/http:/bettertogether.net/the-facts/entry/economy.

# America's Court

## GEORGE WASHINGTON'S MOUNT VERNON
### IN THE CRITICAL PERIOD

*Douglas Bradburn*

Nassau or Marlbro' should not brighter shine,
In bolder figures or a smoother line:
Ensigns and trophies should adorn his bowers,
And Vernon's Mount rise high
as Blenheim's towers.

—Thomas Thornton

After achieving independence, the new United States of America was a strange nation. The country lacked a center of power, lacked political traditions and a distinctive national character, lacked an integrated financial system, lacked large and impressive public buildings and monuments, lacked biographies or histories of its founding and founding heroes, and perhaps most jarring for the many former Britons who made up the American citizenry, lacked even a true head of state.[1] By September 1784, James Madison was calling the Continental Congress an "impotent remnant."[2] The "Glorious Cause" complete, it was not at all clear that the United States would remain a union, let alone a perpetual union. What kept the country together after independence?

The new nation did have a hero, General George Washington—and he lived, the world would learn, at a place called Mount Vernon. At Mount Vernon, in the aftermath of the American War of Independence, the

Early published image of Mount Vernon. *Mount Vernon*, George Isham Parkyns, c. 1797. Aquatint, from G. I. Parkyns, *Sketches of select American Scenery*, No. 1 (Philadelphia, Pa 1799). "This celebrated Domain, unites in picturesque beauty, all that can be attractive to an admirer of elegant nature. Wood, water, gently swelling hills and cultivated fields, form the most exquisite scenes. . . ." (Mount Vernon Ladies' Association; gift of Honorable and Mrs. Robert Woods Bliss, 1951 [M-1657])

legend of the "illustrious Washington" and the best wishes for the future of the country converged. Washington's plantation—which was not the site of a battle or a parliamentary debate, or a meeting of a revolutionary committee, or even of a "Liberty Tree"—became a hallowed place for the remembrance of sacrifice and virtue, a spot to learn the proper style of republican simplicity or to imagine the future of the republic under a stronger union. Mount Vernon, universally known as "the seat of General Washington," became the first truly national symbolic place in America. In a trend fueled by the nascent public sphere of print consumption, the home of the Washingtons helped a nation with no identity other than the memory of a long and brutal war begin the process of imagining a shared country after independence as the property became celebrated in poems, travel journals, and countless letters.

More than a symbol, George Washington's estate on the Potomac served as a surrogate court for the nation.[3] Visited by diplomats, curious travelers, artists, and improvers, with resident historians and memoirists, Mount Vernon became an important center of conversation on the problems and possibilities of the young American republic. In agricultural reform, commercial development, diplomacy, and the support and patronage of literature and the arts, Mount Vernon played a leading role. Ultimately, Mount Vernon became the ideological and political center for the movement to reform the Articles of Confederation, a movement at once despairing and optimistic that would define the crisis of the "Critical Period," as well as prescribe the solution. After the Constitution was ratified, Mount Vernon would never again be as significant in the political, cultural, social, and economic life of the United States, and it did not need to be. While historians have recognized the significance of taverns, parades, sermons, the republic of letters, and the "public sphere" in the creation of the American nation, they have missed the importance of this alternative and definitive creative space in the years following independence—America's court on the Potomac.[4]

## Imagining Mount Vernon: Otium cum Dignitate

Mount Vernon's status as America's favorite home began with a highly anticipated, highly scripted national drama: the resignation of George Washington. From the beginning of the revolution, Washington had been promising to quit when the job was done, and by the fall of 1783, newspapers were reporting the impending event.[5] Washington's movements were closely followed, and his plans circulated widely. In New York in early December 1783, newspapers noted that Washington "proposes to make a short stay at Philadelphia, will thence proceed to Annapolis where he will resign his Commission." "Immediately after which," reports emphasized, "his Excellency will set out for his Seat, named Mount Vernon, in Virginia." In resigning in such a way, he was "emulating the example" of the "virtuous

Roman General, who, victorious, left the tented field, covered with honor, and withdrew from public life, *otium cum dignitate*"—leisure with dignity.[6]

Over the final month of 1783, Washington played out his role of a lifetime, and upon returning his commission to Congress on December 23, as every newspaper in the country would note, "he immediately set off for Mount Vernon, in Virginia." As one author wrote, "like the heroes of old."[7] By resigning, Washington immediately became, in the words of George III, "the greatest man in the world."[8] To the true believers, he became a living example of ancient dignity and virtue—a modern version of something timeless, authentic, rare and heroic. Mount Vernon was where "the Great Man" lived.[9] An early description of the house, one of the most widely circulated in the 1780s, called the place "ancient, but magnificent."[10] It possessed spiritual power to some Americans. As one enthusiastic visitor noted in early 1785, "I had feasted my imagination for several days in the near prospect of a visit to Mount Vernon, the seat of Washington. No pilgrim ever approached Mecca with deeper enthusiasm."[11]

Before the American Revolution, the main house and the estate at Mount Vernon were a significant property for a gentry planter, but they were by no means a transcendent statement. Up to the mid-1770s, Washington's near neighbors—the Fairfaxes at Belvoir and the Masons at Gunston Hall—possessed better claims to the finest estates in the county, let alone the entire colony. Washington's mansion house, which had been expanded piecemeal since the 1740s, and which possessed some unfashionable, ungainly elements, was not even built in brick, the standard of elite Chesapeake housing since at least the late seventeenth century. It was not the largest, or the most well appointed, or even the best-known estate in colonial Virginia. Some of the great houses built in the early eighteenth century, like Mann Page's Rosewell in Gloucester, dwarfed the mansion house at Mount Vernon.

However, Washington's fame, and the cultural significance of his retirement, immediately transformed Mount Vernon into America's most well-known seat. It was the essential place for the completion of the great first American myth—the virtuous retirement of Washington, "like the heroes of old." To have an "ancient" and monumental figure for such a new country added a sense of permanence and destiny to what was still an uncertain future. Washington could not be *Cincinnatus* without Mount Vernon. The estate took on the luster of the first great founding myth of the United States, and visitors by the thousands, and print references by the hundreds in the 1780s, publicized the "seat of the illustrious Washington" as the indispensable estate for America's indispensable hero. In the 1780s, Mount Vernon mattered in the story and significance of America's revolution as much as Bunker Hill, Trenton, and Yorktown.

The announcement of Washington's retirement and "immediate" return to Mount Vernon circulated well into 1784 and began a regular flow of "news" and reminders of Washington's presence or absence from Mount Vernon. In every week of every year from 1784 until Washington assumed the presidency in New York, some reader of some newspaper or pamphlet or almanac, or geography, or book of poems, could read a reference to George Washington's Mount Vernon. From the mundane (advertisements of the stud opportunities available at Mount Vernon) to the sublime (poetry extolling the inspirational haunts of "grass-green Vernon,"), American readers could regularly imagine and be reminded of the estate of the first citizen of the country. When Washington's voice appeared in the paper between 1784 and his ascension to the presidency in 1789, it usually appeared with the dateline "Mount Vernon." He appeared often, thanking various official guests and municipalities for their well wishes, endorsing various publications, subscribing to many others, and later in the 1780s, as we shall see, approving of support for the Constitution.[12]

The first poetic description of Mount Vernon appeared in the newspapers years before independence had been secured, and Washington was already being compared with Cincinnatus of Rome and Timoleon of Greece (who kept the Greek colony of Syracuse free against the Carthaginians and retired to private life)—two exemplars of ancient virtue. Mount Vernon was depicted as "at once the hero's and the sage's seat" where "bounteous Nature spreads her choicest gifts / Of woods and lawns along thy ancient cliff." Wedded love, the Graces, and Wisdom "roam" while "sweet Simplicity had fix'd her home." Leaving for such "tranquil scenes of domestic life," Washington "shall be . . . what Timoleon was." The poem imagined a future after independence had been secured, when sailors plying the commerce-swelled Potomac would point to Mount Vernon and announce, "There once liv'd Washington, the good the great / Whose arms preserv'd, whose wisdom guides the state." The sailors describe "yon temple, rising 'midst the encircling grove" built by "a grateful people's love" to "Fame and him." Where "Nature's God receives Religion's pray'r" at the spot where Washington, before he died, would "muse away the noon-tide hour" on "Columbia's future bliss and pow'r." That this anonymous poet assumed that grateful Americans would build a monument to Washington and "Freedom" at Mount Vernon was not only fairly good prophecy, it dramatically illustrates that Mount Vernon would hold a powerful place in the American imagination immediately after the end of the war—once independence had actually been achieved.[13]

In the postwar years, poetic references to Mount Vernon abounded. The "Extempore Verses" of a gentleman on a visit to the estate first appeared on January 1, 1784, within days of Washington's return from the war. Written in the fashionable pseudoclassical tone, the poem argued that all feeling people would be overcome with patriotic sensations and visions of "rescu'd human kind" upon seeing the "enchanting seat."

Most poetry in which the estate was mentioned reinforced the link between Washington's greatness, his retirement, and the destiny of America. As a poem of February 1784 implored, "behold, Columbia's Chief retire" to "MOUNT VERNON too, thrice happy spot." Enjoining Washington "with peace and plenty blest" to watch over "Your INDEPENDENT country," for "Long may you live to see your empire grow / The world's great terror and the tyrant's foe."[14] In a small poem written in 1785 "at Chester Country," Pennsylvania, Washington's retirement to "Vernon's groves" followed the common narrative:

> Now hurrying from the busy scene,
> Where thy Patomak waters flow,
> May thee enjoy thy rural reign,
> And every earthly blessing know.
> Thus he comes, proud legions sway'd
> Return'd and sought his sylvan shade.[15]

Another effort, by Reverend Thomas Thornton, which appeared first in newspapers and later became attached to an early biography of Washington, explicitly linked the greatness of the estate to the greatness of the man. Comparing Washington favorably with the heroes of antiquity and modern Europe, including Maurice of Nassau and the Duke of Marlborough, Thornton wished that "Ensigns and trophies should adorn" Washington's "bowers," and "Vernon's Mount rise high as Blenheim's towers."[16]

Other, more significant, productions would follow. The Connecticut Wits—Timothy Dwight, Joel Barlow, Lemuel Hopkins, John Trumball Jr., and especially David Humphreys—would make Mount Vernon into an active player in the great destiny of America, in which they interwove a series of providential and millennial themes, which would come to take on a potent political symbolism by the end of the decade. Each of these men believed the American Revolution represented a transformational epoch in the history of the world—the end of history—fulfilling the great prophecy that empire and civilization followed the sun, from east to west. Timothy Dwight's effort "The Prospect for America" took the familiar line, congratulating Washington for his bold and unprecedented retirement:

> Once more to thy fair seats we view thee come
> While each pleas'd neighbor gratulates thee home
> On grass-green Vernon lovelier beams the morn
> And glad Potowmack murmurs thy return.[17]

Collectively, they called Washington "Vernon's sage," elevating the retired general to an oracle of America's challenges and promise.[18]

Humphreys, George Washington's friend and former aide-de-camp, who lived at Mount Vernon for extended periods in the 1780s, published a steady stream of verse and prose celebrating, describing, and enhancing Mount Vernon with powerful significance. His long poem, "On the happiness of America," originally published in London, lamented leaving "Vernon's shades," and the "sage" of the Potomac, now engaged in "the works of peace."[19] For Humphreys, Mount Vernon serves the story of Washington's generous service and retirement—and the greatness of the estate enhanced the original sacrifice. However, he also gave Washington an active political role at Mount Vernon: speaking to the people of

America about the crisis of the 1780s. In "On the Happiness of America," Humphreys has Washington speaking at length to the American people, offering advice, emphasizing harmony, the rule of law, and payment of "honest debt." He declares, "Be just! Be wise!" and "Beware the feuds whence civil war proceeds / Fly mean suspicions / Shun inglorious deeds." Washington implores his fellow citizens to "increase the fed'ral ties, support the laws, Guard public faith, revere religion's cause."[20] Humphreys's most widely circulated work in the 1780s was his "Ode to Mount Vernon," an extremely popular poem/song that appeared in newspapers and pamphlets throughout the late 1780s. Humphreys wrote the poem while he was living at Mount Vernon in the fall of 1786. He frames the estate by the retirement.

> By broad Potowmack's azure tide,
> Where Vernon's mount, in sylvan pride,
> Displays its beauties far,
> Great Washington to peaceful shades,
> Where no unhallow'd wish invades,
> Retir'd from fields of war.

The estate is a mystical place, and "inspires" Humphreys's song. With "gay perennial blooms," "bow'r wilderness of sweets," perfumed air, pleasing walks, ample farms, and "cool retreats," Mount Vernon was a world of "philosophic ease" where no "vulgar converse" intruded. Rather, visitors would enjoy enlightened conversation on "nature's charms," on exploits of the past, or "future scenes unfold."[21]

While the most imaginative descriptions of Mount Vernon appeared in the poetry of the 1780s and placed the estate firmly into the providential destiny of the United States, the most descriptive accounts appeared, serving an ideological end, in early attempts to explore the life of George Washington. The earliest biography came from an anonymous Marylander writing from London who was familiar with the estate, and the two most widely circulated descriptions were written by Noah Webster and Humphreys. The ubiquitous Humphreys intended to write the first official biography of Washington and succeeded, but on a much smaller scale than originally intended. His life of Washington would circulate anonymously—most widely as a section of Jedidiah Morse's popular *American Geography* books.[22] Both Morse and Webster believed the nation and a true national character could be cultivated with stories of America's past and present, and they used their schoolbooks, dictionaries, geographies, and biographical squibs to introduce the American citizenry to their own nation. The only private home described in their works in the 1780s was Washington's Mount Vernon. As such, the description served important patriotic ends.[23]

The popular visitation to the estate stands out among all other private homes or even public buildings in the 1780s. There simply was nothing approaching the popularity of Washington's Mount Vernon, which, unlike a market building or state house, did not exist to serve official public ends. One list of visitors to Mount Vernon from 1784 to 1789 contains 579 individuals: men and women; friends, neighbors, and strangers; citizens and foreigners.[24] Although some of these people are anonymous, and a few are local farmers, tenants, or tradesmen, most were people of gentry rank, or "polite society," the sort of people who would be listed in Washington's diary, or as he explained to his mother, "people of the first distinction."[25]

While it is impossible to capture the exact number of people who traveled to the estate, anecdotal evidence suggests that Mount Vernon saw unprecedented visitation in the 1780s—certainly more than any other home in North America. Many travelers remarked on the numbers and diversity of guests. As Londoner Robert Hunter Jr. wrote, "People come to see him here from all parts of the world; hardly a day passes without."[26] Italian botanist Count Luigi Castiglioni, who spent four days in 1785, wrote that he received "the greatest hospitality," as did all "who come in great numbers to admire such a famous personage."[27] His countryman Philip Mazzei insisted that "there is not one single officer on the whole continent" who did not attempt to spend a "few days with his General" and "no European traveller who does not eagerly wish to visit General Washington." The result, Mazzei noted, "is that his house is continuously filled with strangers who bring with them an even larger number of servants and horses; as there is no village in the vicinity and no inn within reach, the General has to take charge of everything."[28] Agricultural reformer and author Charles Varlo, who stayed at Mount Vernon in 1784 while researching an American version of his "New System of Husbandry," similarly noted Washington's hospitality and wrote that the "General's house is open to poor travelers as well as rich; he gives diet and lodging to all." Lost in the woods, Varlo was led to the estate by a "woman with a child on her back" who told him that Washington "gave orders to his servants to entertain all that came; that she had lain there two or three times before, though she lived above two hundred miles distance."[29] In 1787, Washington himself compared his house to "a well resorted tavern, as scarcely any strangers who are going from north to south, or from south to north do not spend a day or two at it."[30]

Also remarkable was the extent to which American newspapers marked the journeys of celebrities to and from Mount Vernon. The visits of the Marquis de Lafayette filled the newspapers, and Lafayette's letters from Mount Vernon documented his movements and eventual departure from America.[31] Visits of two French ambassadors, the Spanish ambassador, governors, congressmen, and artists found a place in the public papers. Even the unfortunate Georgian James MacKay was noted to have died "en route to Mount Vernon."[32] The great Whig historian Catherine Macaulay Graham, with her young husband, spent more than a week at Mount Vernon and became fast friends of George and Martha Washington. Eager newspapers gossiped of her visit and noted that she intended to write a great history of American Revolution. Newspapers not only reported her movements but also the occasion of the meeting between the great historian and the great man.[33]

In the 1780s, people flocked to Mount Vernon, and wrote poetry about it, and told tales of life at Mount Vernon—and in doing so, created the truth in the first legend of the founding. Mount Vernon served a fundamental role in the effervescence of American national identity in independence. As the seat of the "illustrious" Washington, the estate was the home of the most famous man in the Eurocentric world, whose act of retirement was the first and most fundamental legend in the American founding. Located along the main route south from Philadelphia and north from Fredericksburg, visitors of all types descended upon the place for curiosity, for counsel, and for inspiration. In a country without monuments or even monumental architecture, Mount Vernon evoked a sense of permanence in a time of great uncertainty. Washington, though a private citizen, represented the nearest thing to a symbolic head of state that could be imagined in the Confederation years. Although the country was "in its infancy," Mount Vernon was "ancient" and "magnificent." Unlike the capital of the new United States, which moved from Philadelphia, to Annapolis, to Trenton, and to New York, the seat of George Washington stayed in the same place—and would always exist, as one poet hoped, "while no dark tyrant o'er Columbia frowns."[34]

## Washington's Court

If George Washington had actually retired to a life of quiet contemplation—of "philosophic ease" as the poets would have it—the importance of Mount Vernon in the course of events in the 1780s might have remained largely symbolic. Immediately after his return to the estate, Washington liked to claim that he was happily retired, living "under my own Vine & my own fig tree" where the "bustle of camp & the intrigues of a Court" would never again disturb his "serenity of mind." To Lafayette, he noted that he would be able to "gently move down the stream of life, until I sleep with my Fathers."[35] If he ever believed the rhetoric, it was clear by the fall of 1784 that his retirement would not be free from public action or political intrigue and would allow little time for quiet contemplation.

At Mount Vernon, his initial interest in securing his financial future became his route back into public life. On a trip west in 1784 to collect rents and investigate the status of his western properties, which included land both east and west of the Allegheny Mountains, including 30,000 acres bordering the east bank of the Ohio River, Washington found his next great cause.

Marred by poor weather, intractable squatters, and hostile Native Americans, Washington's trip to his western lands made two facts clear. First, the people who lived on the other side of the mountains were only tenuously connected to the United States. Second, his own lands would never be worth much unless those lands could be connected with the East. In the last entry in his western journal, he wrote an elaborate explanation of the problem and outlined the solution. He turned the entry into a series of letters calling for a public effort to improve the navigation of the Potomac River into the Ohio. As he wrote to Benjamin Harrison, governor of Virginia:

> I need not remark to you Sir, . . . how necessary it is to apply the cement of interest, to bind all parts of the Union together by indissoluble bonds—especially that part of it, which lies immediately west of us, with the middle States. For, what ties, let me ask, shou'd we have upon those people? . . . What, when they get strength, which will be sooner than most people conceive (from the emigration of foreigners who will have no particular predilection towards us, as well as from the removal of our own Citizens) will be the consequence of their having formed close connexions with both, or either of those powers in a commercial way? It needs not, in my opinion, the gift of prophecy to foretell.

The "Western Settlers," he noted, "stand as it were upon a pivot—the touch of a feather, would turn them anyway," and he intended to give them a push—he would improve the Potomac River. [36]

Washington's solution required politics. Though tackling the problem would be too expensive for any private individual, he successfully lobbied both the Virginia and the Maryland legislatures to incorporate a public company that could raise the capital to cover investment; labor; and the creation of roads, sluices, dams, locks, and some bypass canals. With the passage of identical bills, Virginia and Maryland ultimately created the first multistate corporation in the United States in 1785, the Potomac Navigation Company. George Washington with his office in the mansion house at Mount Vernon, was the first president. In the service of the project, Mount Vernon would become a visiting point for mechanics of all types—engineers and inventors of "useful" improvements. He particularly encouraged James Rumsey, a "man of genius" whom he employed as his chief engineer and who would exhibit the first working steamboat on the Potomac twenty years before Robert Fulton. [37]

When Maryland and Virginia agreed to incorporate the company, the states needed to agree on the legal uses and commercial regulations of the Potomac. To negotiate a settlement, both states appointed commissioners, who met at Mount Vernon. The ultimate success of the "Mount

Vernon Compact," a diplomatic agreement between sovereign states, led directly to the movement for larger conventions at Annapolis and eventually Philadelphia. The road to a new Constitution began at Mount Vernon.

As Washington worked to improve commercial relations between states and managed the largest infrastructure project in the nation, he also redesigned the landscape of his estate, destroying the colonial order he had imposed and instituting a vision intended to reflect his new republican sensibilities. He leaned upon various tendencies of English and continental gardening and relied on pattern books and common practices, but he lived in an American environment, and his landscape, although evocative of some British trends, was wholly his own. Especially important were his extensive use of native plants and his desire to perfect an American landscape. He used very little ornamentation. There were no follies or flights of fancy at Mount Vernon.

Inside the mansion house, during the same years in which he transformed his landscape and entertained hundreds of visitors, Washington begin to finish his "New Room." Begun before the war as part of Washington's extension of the footprint of the house, the addition on the north side of the mansion was intended to be a grand showpiece. Washington demanded that it be precise in its proportions and masterfully executed. Born out of a long tradition of grand rooms, salons, and galleries, the room came to be the stateroom of the mansion house, the ultimate expression of Washington's sense of taste. In the 1780s, it was a work in progress. The finished, faux-painted doors were installed in 1785. The impressive ceiling plaster was completed in 1786. While the room would eventually become a gallery of portraits, prints, and landscapes, with its walls papered and tastefully painted and the room beautifully appointed, in the 1780s it would have been sparse. However, the partially finished and still largely unadorned character of the New Room in the 1780s served the emphasis on "simplicity" that the Washingtons cultivated to create their "republican style." [38]

Visitors to the estate as a whole often remarked on the simplicity, plainness, and neatness of the estate. Francis Adrian van der Kemp, a Dutch minister, was delighted to reach "Mount Vernon, where simplicity, order, unadorned grandeur, and dignity, had taken up their abode."[39] For Jean-Pierre Brissot de Warville, "Every thing has an air of simplicity in

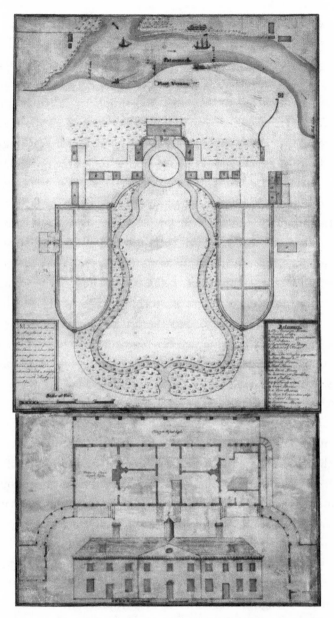

Samuel Vaughn captured the newly redesigned landscape in his presentation print, based upon his sketches from his visit in 1786. *Drawing of Mount Vernon,* Samuel Vaughan, 1787. Ink, watercolor, laid paper. (Mount Vernon Ladies' Association; purchase, 1975 [W-1434])

his house."[40] When he received the multiple boxes containing the marble mantelpiece sent from Samuel Vaughn, Washington worried that it was "too elegant & costly by far I fear for my own room, & republican stile of living."[41] For Lafayette, Washington at his estate was an extraordinary specimen; as he wrote to his wife, "His simplicity is truly sublime." [42] When Washington later corresponded with Gouverneur Morris about the furniture for the president's table, Morris agreed with Washington that it should not be extravagant, but should be "majestically plain, made to endure." Washington himself was often declared to be "majestic," but of course also "simple" and plain. Like "unadorned grandeur," the notion of "majestic simplicity" was a term often used in Europe to speak to timeless taste or, more particularly, to describe the taste of the ancients. Humphreys emphasized the importance of the Washingtons in setting the example of taste in architecture, fashion, and lifestyle, appropriate to a republican rather than a monarchical country. As he wrote, "The virtuous simplicity which distinguishes the private life of Gen. Washington, though less known than the dazzling splendor of his military achievements; is not less edifying in example, or worthy the attentions of his countrymen."

Martha Washington served a critical role in the creation of the Washington style in the 1780s. The house was a site of importance for men and women, and the rotating society of Mount Vernon created spaces in which men and women interacted, discussing the topics of the day. Agriculture, the Potomac canal, and the fragile state of the union, as well as reminiscences of the war, might engage both women and men, but Martha's convivial presence and mastery of polite sociability served a crucial role in opening the mansion house to wide influence. While the general would spend much of the day among his farms, on horseback, or secluded with his correspondence, Martha and the women of the house maintained the high standards of hospitality and conversation. As Lafayette noted after relaxing in his room, he would reenter the social life of the house to find "Mrs. Washington with visitors from the neighborhood." She had a "simple dignity," Brissot pronounced; she "possesses that amenity and manifests that attention to strangers, which render hospitality so charming."[43]

While much has been made of Martha's role in the socio-political world of the "republican court" after Washington would become president, her role at the center of fashionable and polite society began not in Philadelphia but at Mount Vernon. Her manners, fashion, and behavior reinforced the emphasis on "simplicity" that the Washingtons projected for the emulation of the country, and although the rituals at Mount Vernon were less formal, they were nonetheless regular and impactful. It was a cast of characters who served with her at Mount Vernon, enslaved and free, including Tobias Lear and Humphreys, who would help create the procedures of the formal levees at the president's house in Philadelphia.[44]

Washington's most enthusiastic reforms occurred in agriculture. Scientific agriculture was all the rage among the enlightened of the eighteenth century, and Washington embraced improvement for practical, financial, and moral purposes. As he would complain to George William Fairfax, "Our course of Husbandry in this Country, & more especially in this State, is not only exceedingly unprofitable, but so destructive to our Lands, that it is my earnest wish to adopt a better."[45] He wanted to transform Mount Vernon into a model for the future of the country. He hired an English farmer. In the 1780s, he expanded his experiments with various grains and grasses, implemented systematic crop rotation, widespread use of manure, close attention to breeding of stock, and the use of barns and pens for animals. He used the best implements and assistants, new barns and fences, even gifts of giant Spanish and Maltese donkeys to put his estate at the forefront of American farming techniques. Washington's reputation as a farmer was supreme. As one of many observers noted in the 1780s, Washington was "indisputably the best if not the only good farmer in the State."[46] His efforts in agricultural reform were well known across the country, and people came to his estate to see his techniques. A letter written by Washington celebrating the importance of the improvers of agriculture circulated widely in the 1780s. In the letter, he declared that agriculture was "the only source from which we can at present draw any real or permanent advantage."[47]

Washington became a regular correspondent with the most renowned English agricultural reformer, Arthur Young. It was Young who initiated the relationship. Like a transatlantic courtier, Young threw himself into

Washington's orbit. As he wrote to the general, "you must allow me to consider myself as your agent for everything that concerns agriculture."[48] Washington took him up on his offer, immediately ordering plows, seeds, and advice. Young complied and became one of a series of agricultural writers and reformers whose friendship Washington cultivated. His relationship with Young was celebrated by visitors and writers. Ultimately, Washington's agricultural significance enhanced the legend of his retirement. The conclusion of Metcalf Bowler's treatise on practical agriculture and husbandry, published in 1786, celebrated Washington's leadership in scientific agriculture: "Like the heroes of old[,] [Washington] resigned all military employments, and retired to his rural seat of Mount Vernon, on the Potowmack, with the blessings of his fellow-citizens; where he still continues to shed his beneficial influence by the promotion of agriculture, and the patronage of arts and sciences."[49] Washington's "patronage of arts and sciences" and his promotion of agriculture enhanced his legend and raised Mount Vernon to new heights.

For the promotion of history and biography, Washington's Mount Vernon served a fundamental purpose in the 1780s—it was the largest archive of revolutionary material available for scholars. In August 1783, twenty-eight volumes of Washington's papers, including letters to Congress, orders and letters to various officers and foreigners, and private letters, were shipped to Mount Vernon in anticipation of Washington's retirement.[50] The collection represented an essential body of sources for the operations of the American army over the long conflict, and Washington, after receiving permission from the Congress, readily made his archive available to writers at his estate.

William Gordon, author of one of the first complete histories of the American Revolution, spent over two weeks examining, copying, and researching in Washington's papers. As he wrote enthusiastically to Horatio Gates, Washington gave him access to "thirty and three folio volumes of copied letters of the General's, besides three volumes of private, seven volumes of general orders, and bundles upon bundles of letters to the General." Washington would eventually purchase two sets of Gordon's history.[51] Brissot likely had a "peep" at Washington's papers to aid in his own plans to "write the History of America."[52] Humphreys used Washington's papers not only for his incomplete biography of Washington but also for his lengthy biography of General Israel Putnam. He finished the work at Mount Vernon in June of 1788 and mailed it to the Connecticut Society of Cincinnati, calling it "the first effort in Biography that has been made on this continent." Humphreys hoped that his effort would "prompt some more skillful hand to portray the illustrious group of patriots, sages, and heroes, who have guided our councils, fought our battles, and adorned the memorable epocha of independence."[53]

Washington hoped to spur and encourage work on the history of the revolution. Richard Bland Lee—the brother of "Light Horse Harry" Lee—visited Mount Vernon in 1787 and informed Washington of his eagerness to "write a memoir of the events of the late revolution," a task he thought would be "so great an undertaking, so full of glory, so flattering to my ambition," that he worried he did not have the skill, time, or leisure to complete the task. Ultimately, he decided to "yield however reluctantly this rich harvest of glory to some one, to whom fortune has been more indulgent, and on whom Nature has bestowed the qualities requisite for the undertaking." Washington replied that if ever Lee changed his mind, "any aid" that he could offer "from my papers, or information," would be granted "with pleasure."[54]

Mount Vernon also became a center of ambition in the fine arts. Painters and sculptors worked regularly at the estate in the 1780s, including Jean Antoine Houdon, considered one of the greatest sculptors of Europe. Robert Edge Pine spent at least three weeks at Mount Vernon in the spring of 1785 with ambitions to paint a series of grand history paintings of the American Revolution. Washington hoped he would succeed, as "his present design, if well executed, will do equal credit to his imagination and Pencil; and be interesting to America."[55] In 1787, painter Anne Flore Millet, the marquise de Bréhan, in company with her husband and the ambassador of France, visited the estate to great fanfare. Washington, now familiar sitting for likenesses and portraits of all kinds, noted that although he was once impatient with the experience, "no dray moves more readily to the Thrill, than I do to the Painters Chair." These men and women would exploit the popularity of their subject and helped spread Washington's image far and wide.

Washington was not a passive subject of artistic ambition, but a patron and enthusiast for nascent American productions. Perhaps the greatest poem published by an American in the 1780s was Joel Barlow's "The Vision of Columbus," considered by critics at the time to be a work of genius. Washington obtained twenty copies, more copies than any other subscriber except the king of France, to whom the work was dedicated. Washington distributed these poems widely, sending them to France and giving them away to influential women in Philadelphia's social and political world, including Elizabeth Willing Powell, Ann Allen Penn, Sarah Franklin Bache, and Elizabeth Meredith Clymer. [56]

In recommending Barlow to Lafayette, who also subscribed to ten copies of the poem, Washington ruminated on the importance of the fine arts in the establishment of American greatness. Poets were the "priests and doorkeepers to the temples of Fame," and these, he noted, "are no vulgar functions." All great ages and great men have had their poets. Alexander, Washington noted, "lamented that" he had "no Homer,"[57] while Julius Caesar was "well known to have been a man of highly cultivated understanding and taste." Louis XIV and Queen Anne's era were known for the greatness of the arts, he continued, and Washington himself wished to help launch a similar outbreak of American greatness. "Although we are yet in our cradle, as a nation," he wrote, it is clear that we can "refute (by incontestable facts) the doctrines of those who have asserted that every thing degenerates in America." So it can be shown in "the performances of our poets and painters," despite the lack of the many advantages "which operate powerfully among older nations." He meant the lack of leisure, luxury, wealth, and government, "for it is generally understood, that excellence in those sister arts has been the result of easy circumstances, public encouragements and an advanced stage of society." He was delighted to see that "the Critics in England . . . speak highly of the American poetical geniuses." [58]

In the representations of Mount Vernon circulating in newspapers, pamphlets, geographies, and published travel accounts in the 1780s, the enslaved men, women and children who made up the majority of the population of Mount Vernon and performed the hard work of keeping up the estate and farms, were almost never mentioned. The great estate stood as a symbol of freedom, contemplation, virtue, and reform, never as a typical plantation dependent on enslaved labor. Neither the poems nor the biographies and geographies mention the existence of slavery at Mount Vernon. This remarkable fact becomes even more surprising given that many authors were highly critical of the institution, both philosophically and morally. One example can be seen in the descriptions of Brissot, who contrasted the surrounding countryside, filled with worn-out lands, poor peasants, crime, and "miserable huts, and miserable negroes," with the reforming intelligence of Washington. For Brissot, the problem with Maryland and Virginia was the existence of slavery. "In countries cultivated by slaves" Brissot wrote, "there is no industry and no domestic economy." Slavery destroyed all incentive for labor, and so poverty, ignorance, and lack of ingenuity marked the countryside. Washington alone, "constantly occupied in the care of his farm and improvement of cultivation," understood the science of agriculture. "You have often heard him compared to Cincinnatus," Brissot wrote, and "the comparison is doubtless just." [59] Yet, Brissot failed to emphasize the widespread use of enslaved labor on Washington's estate, where he spent "three days in the house of that celebrated man."[60]

However, while the representations of Mount Vernon circulating in print in the 1780s excised slavery from the picture, Washington participated in several conversations at his home relating to the problem of slavery in America in the 1780s. Shortly after his long-awaited visit in 1784, Lafayette proposed a radical experiment of emancipation in the West Indies. Gordon clearly overheard and likely participated in their conversations on the matter, writing, "you wished to get rid of all your Negroes, & the Marquis wisht that an end might be put to the slavery of all of them." Gordon hoped such an event would occur, and "give the finishing stroke & the last polish to your political characters."[61] Other visitors noted that Washington expressed his opinions on slavery openly. Philip Morgan argues that the mid-1780s proved an important turning point in Washington's thinking, and by mid-decade Washington wrote openly that he hoped the institution could be ended in some manner "by legislation." [62] By the end of the decade, Humphreys was reporting Washington's private regret over "the unfortunate condition of the persons, whose labour in part I employed" and his desire to prepare his young slaves "for a destiny different from that in which they were born," hinting at a plan to free his slaves in his will.[63]

The most tantalizing context for the role Mount Vernon played in America's halting conversations on the possible reform of slavery is Washington's relationship to Ferdinando Fairfax, who published one of the earliest known complete plans for the emancipation of slaves in America.[64] Ferdinando was George Washington's godson and the nephew and heir of his great friend George William Fairfax. After he inherited Belvoir, Ferdinando visited Mount Vernon in the late 1780s, and Washington wrote a letter of introduction for Fairfax to Samuel Powell, mayor of Philadelphia. The short tract, which appeared in Mathew Carey's *American Museum* magazine in 1790, emphasized the ongoing debates in Virginia about slavery. Would Washington have encouraged Fairfax to come up with a plan? Did Fairfax even tell Washington of his inclinations? Had they spoken of the institution at Mount Vernon?

Whatever enthusiasm Washington expressed for the ending of slavery in the 1780s, it was not a cause that would be associated with Mount Vernon until after his death and the publication of his last will and testament. In the years after independence, the great reform Washington would successfully champion was the reform of the union. In representing the nation, Mount Vernon would become the seat of opposition to the independence of the states.

## Mount Vernon and the Origins of Federalism

In the 1780s, Washington held positions unlike any in the new country. As the president of the Society of Cincinnati, Washington was at the pinnacle of the only truly national private organization in the United States in the 1780s, which required him to correspond regularly with many influential Americans, as well as Europeans. His official correspondence with members of the Cincinnati, calling for national meetings, were emblazoned as "circulars" in the newspapers.[65] As the head of the Potomac Navigation Company, Washington was president of the only multistate corporation in North America, and his office for both of these unique roles was on the first floor of his mansion house at Mount Vernon.

His status as the great hero of the revolution and the informal roles he (and Martha Washington) played in diplomacy, agricultural reform, society, and the patronage of the arts and sciences, ensured that Washington wielded tremendous influence. In describing his place in the universe of politicians in America, Humphreys emphasized the number and quality of visitors to Mount Vernon. In addition to "every foreigner, of distinction who visits America," all the "members of Congress & other dignified Personages" did not "pass his house without calling to pay their respects." The information these guests brought to Mount Vernon, combined with the unrelenting correspondence and "numerous periodical Publications & News Papers" which Washington regularly read, made Mount Vernon "the focus of political Intelligence for the New World."[66]

Washington used his influence regularly to promote his own belief that a crisis existed in the affairs of the nation. He also cultivated a powerful network of like-minded leaders, men who would become the core of the movement to reform the Articles of Confederation. They were the original federalists.

The political message emanating from Washington's Mount Vernon in the years following the end of the war emphasized the critical need to save the union and strengthen the government. Action to save the nascent country was required on multiple fronts. As he would write forcefully to Henry Knox in December 1786, "Vigilance in the watching, & vigour in acting" has "become indispensably necessary." As he continued, "If the powers are inadequate" in the articles as constituted, "amend or alter them" but no matter what, "do not let us sink into the lowest state of humiliation & contempt, & become a byword in all the earth."[67] There was never a moment in Washington's so-called retirement in which he was not calling for the strengthening of the union to avert inevitable ruin.

In his private correspondence, in every month of every year between 1784 and the ratification of the Constitution, Washington emphasized to someone, foreign or domestic, the urgent need to strengthen the union and to encourage states to honor their obligations, as well as the great possibilities that would come if Americans would look to their "federal" ties, rather than their local prejudices. Within days of his return to Mount Vernon, Washington deplored the "jealous and contracted temper which seems to prevail in some of the States" and the "present unsettled and deranged state of public Affairs."[68] A few weeks later Washington complained to Harrison of the behavior of "the individual States," which seemed intent on being "all-wise & all-powerful" within themselves, which would lead inevitably to "our downfall as a Nation," if there was not "a change in the system." "If we cannot conquer our prejudices" he argued, the hard won "peace & independency" served "very little purpose." Such a scenario, he noted, was "as plain to me as A.B.C." The network of correspondents he would cultivate would more and more come to share and reflect Washington's point of view. The sense of crisis and the need for action, the sense that America was engulfed in a critical period, was created by the conversation and correspondence emanating to and from Mount Vernon. From 1784 to 1787, Mount Vernon served as a center of opposition to the status quo under the Articles of Confederation. However, the seeds of such an attitude were planted even earlier.

The origins of the federalist persuasion—the need to strengthen the Articles of Confederation to save the union from impending disaster, secure respect abroad, and save the country from inevitable dissolution—received its first widely read formulation in Washington's "Circular to the States," which he issued in early June 1783.[69] Called by Washington "his last official communication," the circular came to be known also as Washington's "Legacy" or his "Last Legacy." Before the ratification of the United States Constitution, Washington's Legacy was considered one of the crucial founding documents of the United States. All but forgotten now—supplanted by his later final thoughts, the "Farewell Address"—the Legacy is a powerful critique of the Articles of Confederation and should perhaps be considered the first of the *Federalist* papers.

Washington began the essay by celebrating the great "opportunity for political happiness" in the new country. The "citizens of America" created their nation in "an Epocha when the rights of mankind" were better understood than ever before. Commerce, literature, the arts, the "refinement of Manners," and the growing "liberality of sentiment" made the present a most "auspicious period." However, American future happiness was not assured. People still had a "choice" to be "respectable and prosperous, or contemptible or miserable as a Nation." This was the time, Washington wrote, "of their political probation, this is the moment when the eyes of the World are upon them," and it would be "the moment to establish or ruin their national Character forever." The stakes were high. Success would depend on whether the citizens of America gave "such a tone to our Federal Government" and therefore enabled "it to answer the ends of its institution" or relaxed the powers of the union and annihilated "the cement of Confederation." Calling for a strengthening the powers of Congress, Washington noted that it was still to be decided "whether the Revolution must ultimately be considered a blessing or a curse, not to the present age alone, for with our fate will the destiny of unborn Millions be involved." So Washington helped to create a notion of crisis, or of a critical period, even before he had resigned.[70]

Themes of the danger of anarchy and disunion would fill his letters in the 1780s. The "sales pitch" that Washington used to encourage investment in the Potomac Navigation Company always emphasized the significance, importance, and potential of improving the navigation of the Potomac into the interior of America to the ultimate creation of a strong, united, and prosperous country. There was money to be made, to be sure, but as he wrote to Robert Morris, the venture "is pregnant with great public utility."[71] Letters coordinating the business of the Potomac Navigation Company regularly noted a crisis of the union. In forwarding a petition of the directors of the Potomac Navigation Company to Thomas Johnson in the fall of 1786, Washington called for action on the strengthening of the union: "The want of energy in the fœderal government; the pulling of one State, & parts of States against another; and the commotions among the Eastern People, have sunk our national character much below par; & have brought our politics and credit to the brink of a precipice. A step or two more must plunge us into inextricable ruin. Liberality, justice & unanimity in these States, wch do not appear to have drank so deep of the cup of folly, may yet retrieve our affairs; but no time is to be lost in essaying the reparation of them."[72]

Other correspondence regularly commented on the state of the union. In a note describing his opinions on the relationship between constituents and representation and the general usefulness of local "patriotic" societies, Washington chastised his nephew Bushrod for his group's lack of attention to "the inefficiency of the Fœderal government." Everyone "who considers the present Constitution" and "sees to what it is verging" knew that it "now totters to the foundation, and without support must soon fall."[73] In fall 1785, Washington would lay out the case to James McHenry, urging him to support the strengthening of the powers of Congress to tax commerce. Without these new powers, he wrote, "we stand. . . . in a ridiculous point of view in the eyes of the Nations of the Earth," as the United States lacked the power to enforce treaties, raise funds, or engage in a "war of Imposts." As he argued, "We are either a United people under one head, & for Fœderal purposes, or, we are thirteen independent Sovereignties, eternally counteracting each other."

It is common for historians of the ratification of the Constitution—and most textbooks that look into the matter in detail—to note that the "the federalists" achieved a rhetorical coup by seizing the name for their political movement—which somehow implied that their vision was not as threatening as the name "nationalists" or "centralizers." In fact, the title of their movement reflects the approach of this circle around George Washington and the perspective clearly established in the Legacy." "Federal" was the term used by Washington to emphasize those who thought of the national interest, rather than local and provincial concerns. As he wrote to Bushrod, who would become Supreme Court justice, "In speaking of National matters I look to the Fœderal government which in my opinion it is the interest of every state to support." Federalists supported the national interest above state prejudices. He continued, "as there are a variety of interests in the Union," there has to be "a yielding of the parts to coalesce the whole."[74]

The term "antifederalist," used to describe a political faction, was first used by Humphreys, who commonly talked with Washington about the need for more federal thinking. Informing Washington of the collaborative satirical poem "The Archianaid"—written jointly by Humphreys, Barlow, and J Trumball—Humphreys used the term that would become the stock description for opponents to the ratification of the Constitution. Noting that "the force of ridicule has been found of more efficacy than the force of argument" in opposition to "the Antifederalists & Advocates for Mobs & Conventions," Humphreys branded opponents to "federal" causes with an epithet that would be deployed two years later in the campaign to ratify the Constitution.[75] Written only a few months after his "Ode to Mount Vernon," it is possible that Washington and Humphreys used the term often in their long talks about the state of the union.

In the autobiographical poem, Humphreys placed himself at the estate as the constant companion and confidant of Washington, a status born out in Washington's diaries and correspondence.[76] "'Twas mine," Humphreys wrote, "returned from Europe's courts, to share his thoughts partake his sports, and sooth his partial ear."[77] The Washington he depicts is filled with doubt. "O God, the source of light supreme," Washington prays, "shed on our dusky morn a gleam / To guide our doubtful way." Who would want to live in "so querulous an age," the hero cries? How could Americans have lost their way, Washington sighed, "To find the country still despise the Legacy he gave," and "half he fear'd his toils were in vain."[78] The reference to the Legacy would have been well understood as Washington's call for a stronger union. But after this momentary lapse into pessimism, Humphrey's Washington immediately changes tune. Providence would continue to watch over the country, for "that pow'r benign too much had done" to "leave an empire's task begun / Imperfectly achieve'd." So the poem ends on a high note—Washington's "Skies assumes a lovelier blue" and "fairer blooms his flow'rs." The poem fixed the heart of Federalism at Mount Vernon.[79]

When Washington returned to Mount Vernon after the Constitutional Convention in Philadelphia, his estate would play a significant role as the center of political intelligence for the federalist movement. Humphreys spent the time "engaged in literary pursuits" living with Washington as news flowed in from across the country, and together they would collect and share news and propaganda. Washington collected pamphlets and sent them on to be published in other parts of the country. He also appeared in print, supporting ratification in letters that were as widely circulated in the newspapers as any of the *Federalist* papers. His letter congratulating the Marylanders on their approval of the Constitution, in which he encouraged Virginians to do the same and also hoped for an easy reconciliation between those who disagreed, was printed in thirty newspapers.

Mount Vernon in the 1780s helped shape American identity as well as the future course of the country. As a symbol of America, the estate served the great legend of Washington's retirement, which immediately made the story of America's founding something extraordinary. In a sense, Mount Vernon belonged to America, as Washington served as a surrogate head of state. He was the "hero and sage" of American independence. As a center for reforms, a destination for travelers, a site of experimentation, a place of patronage of arts and letters, a theatre of performance of American republican taste, and the fountainhead for conversation among the leading figures in the United States, Mount Vernon played a powerful and influential role in a county without a stable center or capital. The court at Mount Vernon ultimately became a powerful political counterweight to the continuation of the union under the weak Articles of Confederation. When the Constitution was ratified, the celebrations on the Potomac, with cannonades at Alexandria and Georgetown, were memorialized in a poem:

> Mount Vernon hears, with patriotic pride,
> The glorious news adorn the thund'ring tide.
> Belss'd tide! On whose fair form-reflecting breasts,
> Our HERO's seat, and scenes Elysian rest.
> Here, may thy surface, lucid, smooth and slow,
> As conscious of his fame, for ever flow.
> But now, in one swift ebb's effusive space,
> Thy course out o'er the vast Atlantic traces.
> And, widely spread, as its circumfluous wave,
> To all the Eastern World our glory lave.[80]

# Notes

1. I have written extensively about the problem of national identity and consensus in the founding era in *The Citizenship Revolution: Politics and the Creation of the American Union, 1774–1804* (Charlottesville: University of Virginia Press, 2009), 1–25, passim, but many other authors have emphasized this problem as well. Some important essays include John Murrin, "A Roof without Walls: The Dilemma of American National Identity," in *Beyond Confederation: Origins of the Constitution and American National Identity* (Chapel Hill: University of North Carolina Press, 1987), 333–47; T. H. Breen, "Ideology

and Nationalism on the Eve of the American Revolution: Revisions Once More in Need of Revising," *Journal of American History* 84, no. 1 (1997): 13–39; and David Waldstreicher, "Rites of Rebellion, Rites of Assent: Celebrations, Print Culture, and the Origins of American Nationalism," *Journal of American History* 82, no. 1 (1995): 37–61.

2. James Madison to Thomas Jefferson, September 7, 1784, *The Papers of Thomas Jefferson*, ed. Julian P. Boyd (Princeton, NJ: Princeton University Press, 1953), 7:416–18.

3. "Courts" in early modern Europe were institutions of power, patronage, and cultural significance in the life of a state or society. Most often associated with the official legal power of a prince, king, or noble figure (but not always), courts were important centers of thought, art, or patronage and, when not the court of the head of state, were often centers of a particular political faction or ideology. Mount Vernon served all of these purposes in the 1780s. Courts are often contrasted with more public spaces, such as coffeehouses, taverns, or even print culture, but are often conflated or compared with salons or other high settings of intrigue and cultural effervescence. In American historiography, the "republican court" literature explores some similar concerns to this essay but is mostly interested in the history of social, cultural, and political life in Philadelphia in the 1790s, and the men and women who—through their sociability, their taste, and their display, as well as their ability to bring politicians and their wives together in informal settings—created and reinforced their role at the top of American society and culture. The term was first used by Rufus Griswold, *The Republican Court or American Society in the Days of Washington with Twenty-One Portraits of Distinguished Women* (New York, 1855), which is a work of antiquarianism, but the notion of a "republican court" has taken on new life to highlight the significance of the elite families who circulated around George and Martha Washington in New York and Philadelphia during the late 1780s and 1790s. See, in particular, David Shields's and Frederika Teute's essays on republican courts; Susan Branson, *These Fiery Frenchified Dames* (Philadelphia: University of Pennsylvania Press, 2001); Catherine Allgor, *Parlor Politics: In Which the Ladies of Washington Help Build a City and a Government* (Charlottesville: University Press of Virginia, 2000); Amy Hudson Henderson, "Furnishing the Republican Court: Building and Decorating Philadelphia Homes, 1790–1800" (PhD diss., University of Delaware, 2008); and, most recently, François Furstenburg, *When the United States Spoke French: Five Refugees Who Shaped a Nation* (New York: Penguin, 2014).

4. The following list is not exhaustive but speaks to the range of methods and ways historians have tried to describe the process by which Americans created, performed, or displayed their new national identity in the founding era: David Waldstreicher, *In the Midst of Perpetual Fetes: The Making of American Nationalism, 1776–1820* (Chapel Hill: University of North Carolina Press, 1997); Simon Paul Newman, *Parades and the Politics of the Street: Festive Culture and the Early American Republic* (Philadelphia: University of Pennsylvania Press, 1997); Len Travers, *Celebrating the Fourth: Independence Day and the Rites of Nationalism in the Early Republic* (Amherst: University of Massachusetts Press, 1997); Joseph Fichtelberg, *Critical Fictions: Sentiment and the American Market, 1780–1870* (Athens: University of Georgia Press, 2003); Michael Warner, *The Letters of the Republic: Publication and the Public Sphere in Eighteenth-Century America* (Cambridge, MA: Harvard University Press, 1990); Larzer Ziff, *Writing in the New*

*Nation: Prose, Print, and Politics in the Early United States* (New Haven, CT: Yale University Press, 1991); Sarah J. Purcell, *Sealed with Blood: War, Sacrifice, and Memory in Revolutionary America* (Philadelphia: University of Pennsylvania Press, 2002); Andrew W. Robertson, "'Look on This Picture . . . And on This!': Nationalism, Localism, and Partisan Images of Otherness in the United States, 1787–1820," *American Historical Review* 106 (2001): 1263–80.

5. In his "Circular to the States" of June 1783, Washington publicized his intention to "pass the remainder of his life in a state of undisturbed repose." George Washington, "Circular to the States," *The Writings of George Washington from the Original Manuscript Sources, 1745–1799*, ed. John C. Fitzpatrick (Washington, DC: Government Printing Office, 1938), 26:483–96.

6. For an introduction to the eighteenth-century enthusiasm for certain figures from ancient history who sacrificed their own comforts for the public good and who refused to seize unlawful authority (in particular, Cincinnatus), see Garry Wills, *Cincinnatus: George Washington and the Enlightenment; Images of Power in Early America* (New York: Doubleday, 1984).

7. "The Following Conclusion of Mr. Bowler's Ingenious Treatise upon Practical Husbandry, Lately Published in Rhode Island," *New Hampshire (Portsmouth) Gazette*, November 2, 1786, 1.

8. Joseph Farington, *The Farington Diary*, ed. James Greig, 3rd ed. (New York: George H. Doran, 1922), 1:278.

9. Washington was often called "the great man" by visitors to Mount Vernon without irony. For three examples out of many, see Francis T. Brooke, "Some Contemporary Accounts of Eminent Characters: From 'A Narrative of My Life For My Family,' by Judge Francis T. Brooke," *William and Mary Quarterly*, ser. 1, 17 (July 1908): 2n, 1n; and Gijsbert Karel van Hogendorp, as quoted in Douglas Southall Freeman, *George Washington: A Biography* (New York: Scribner's, 1954), 6:34–35; Philip Mazzei, 1788, in *George Washington as the French Knew Him: A Collection of Texts*, ed. Gilbert Chinard (Princeton, NJ: Princeton University Press, 1940), 82–85.

10. John Maxwell, *The American patriot and hero: A brief memoir of the ilustrious conduct and character of His Excellency General Washington [. . .]* (Philadelphia, 1795), 8.

11. Elkanah Watson, memoirs, January 23–25, 1785, in *The Founders on the Founders: Word Portraits from the American Revolutionary Era*, ed. John P. Kaminski (Charlottesville: University of Virginia Press, 2008), 491–93.

12. For examples of "official" visits and resolutions of groups to Mount Vernon, see *Virginia Journal and Alexandria Advertiser*, August 26, 1784, 2; *Independent Gazetteer (Philadelphia)*, August 28, 1784, 2; *New Jersey (Trenton) Gazette*, August 30, 1784, 2; *New-York Journal, and State Gazette*, September 2, 1784, 2; *Thomas's Massachusetts Spy: Or, Worcester Gazette*, September 2, 1784, 3. For Washington's endorsements, see *Pennsylvania (Philadelphia) Mercury and Universal Advertiser*, August 21, 1788, 4; *Independent Gazetteer (Philadelphia)*, August 29, 1788, 4; *City Gazette and Daily Advertiser (Charleston, SC)*, September 26, 1788, 4. For advertisements, see *Maryland Journal and Baltimore Advertiser*, March 16, 1787, 3; *Connecticut (Hartford) Courant, and Weekly Intelligencer*, May 21, 1787, 3. For three of many almanacs that list "directions" to Mount Vernon on the road south from Philadelphia, see Daniel George, *An almanack,*

*for the year of our Lord, 1786 [. . .]* (Boston, 1785); *The universal calendar, and the North-American's almanack [. . .]* (Boston, 1787); Edmund Freebetter, *The New-England almanack, and gentlemen & ladies diary, for the year of our Lord Christ, 1789 [. . .]* (Boston, 1788).

13. *Providence (RI) Gazette and Country Journal,* March 24, 1781, 2.

14. Juvenis, *Political Intelligencer (New Brunswick, NY),* February 5, 1784, 4.

15. John Maxwell, *The American patriot and hero: A brief memoir of the illustrious conduct and character of His Excellency General Washington [. . .]* (Philadelphia, 1795), 43–44.

16. *Pennsylvania (Philadelphia) Packet, and Daily Advertiser,* February 29, 1788, 3; [Thomas Thornton,] *A true and authentic history of His Excellency George Washington [. . .]* (Philadelphia, 1789), n.p.

17. [Timothy Dwight], "The Prospect of America," *The Poems of Arouet* (Charleston, SC, 1786), 15.

18. David Humphreys, Joel Barlow, John Trumbull, Lemuel Hopkins, *Anarchiad: a New England poem, 1786–1787* (New Haven, CT: Thomas H. Pease, 1861), 50.

19. David Humphreys, "A poem, on the happiness of America: Addressed to the citizens of the United States" (Hartford, CT, 1786), 24.

20. Ibid., 7.

21. For the popularity of "Ode to Mount Vernon," see *Connecticut (Hartford) Courant, and Weekly Intelligencer,* October 9, 1786, 3; *The Massachusetts (Boston) Centinel,* September 18, 1786, 4, October 18, 1786, 36, and February 21, 1787, 179; *Daily Advertiser: Political, Historical, and Commercial (New York),* October, 16, 1786, 2; *Pennsylvania (Philadelphia) Packet, and Daily Advertiser,* October 17, 1786, 3; *Maryland Journal and Baltimore Advertiser,* October 24, 1786, 4; *Fowle's New-Hampshire (Portsmouth) Gazette, and the General Advertiser,* October 26, 1786, 4; *Worcester Magazine Massachusetts Spy* November 2, 1786, 376; *United States Chronicle (Providence, RI): Political, Commercial and Historical,* November 2, 1786, 4; *Carlisle (PA) Gazette, and the Western Repository of Knowledge,* November 8, 1786, 4; *New-York Journal, or the Weekly Register,* November 16, 1786, 4; *New-Haven Gazette, and the Connecticut Magazine,* November 16, 1786, 314; *Vermont (Windsor) Journal, and the Universal Advertiser,* November 20, 1786, 4; *State Gazette of Charleston, South Carolina,* December 25, 1786, 3. The poem would continue to be circulated in the late 1780s and in collections of Humphreys's work into the early nineteenth century. See *The Miscellaneous Works of David Humphreys Late Minister Plenipotentiary from the United States of America to the Court of Madrid* (New York, 1804), 223–25.

22. David Humphreys, *David Humphreys' "Life of General Washington," with George Washington's "Remarks,"* ed. Rosemarie Zagarri (Athens: University of Georgia Press, 1991). Often thought to have never been published outside of Jedidiah Morse's version, the biography was indeed printed anonymously in 1789. [Humphreys,] *A true and authentic history of His Excellency George Washington [. . .],* n.p.

23. Douglas Bradburn, "A Nation Made Easy: Geography, Pedagogy, and American Identity," *Mapline* 91 (Summer/Fall 2000); Jill Lepore, *A Is for American: Letters and Other Characters in the Newly United States* (New York: Vintage, 2003); Martin Brückner, "Lessons in Geography: Maps, Spellers, and Other Grammars of Nationalism in the Early Republic," *American Quarterly* 51, no. 2 (June 1999): 311–43.

24. Compiled by Mount Vernon research historian Mary Thompson, in possession of author, available at Fred W. Smith National Library for the Study of George Washington, Mount Vernon, VA.

25. Geroge Washington to Mary Ball Washington, February 15, 1787, *Papers of George Washington, Confederation Series,* ed. W.W. Abbot (Charlottesville: University of Virginia Press, 1997), 5:35 (hereafter *PGW*).

26. Robert Hunter Jr., travel diary, November 16, 1785, in Kaminski, *The Founders on the Founders,* 493–96, 493n.

27. Luigi Castiglioni, *Luigi Castiglioni's Viaggio: Travels in the United States of North America, 1785–1787,* ed. and trans. Antonio Pace (Syracuse, NY: Syracuse University Press, 1983), 112–13.

28. Philip Mazzei, 1788, in *George Washington as the French Knew Him,* 82–85.

29. Charles Varlo, *The Floating Ideas of Nature* (London, 1796), 1:90–94. Washington subscribed to Charles Varlo's *A New System of Husbandry* (Philadelphia, 1785).

30. George Washington to Mary Ball Washington, February 15, 1787, in *PGW,* 5:35.

31. *New-York Journal, and State Gazette,* August 12, 1784, 2; *American Mercury (New York),* August 16, 1784, 2; *American Herald (Boston),* September 6, 1784, 1; and many others.

32. *Virginia Journal and Alexandria Advertiser,* December 1, 1785, 3.

33. *Pennsylvania (Philadelphia) Mercury and Universal Advertiser,* June 24, 1785, 3; *Freeman's Journal: or, The North-American Intelligencer,* June 22, 1785; *Independent Gazetteer (Philadelphia),* June 18, 1785, 2; *Independent Ledger and the American Advertiser (Boston),* May 30, 1785, 4; and many others.

34. [Timothy Dwight,] "The Prospect of America," 15.

35. Washington to François-Jean de Beauvoir, Chevalier de Chastellux, February 1, 1784, in *PGW,* 1:85; see also Washington to Charles Thomson, January 22, 1784, ibid., 74; Washington to Gilbert du Motier, Marquis de Lafayette, February 1, 1784, ibid., 87–90.

36. Washington to Benjamin Harrison, October 10, 1784, in *PGW,* 2:91.

37. Robert J. Kapsch, *The Potomac Canal: George Washington and the Way West* (Morgantown: West Virginia University Press, 2007).

38. See Thomas A. Reinhart and Susan Schoelwer, "'Distinguished by the Name of the New Room': Reinvestigation and Reinterpretation of George Washington's Grandest Space," in *Stewards of Memory: The Past, Present, and Future of Historic Preservation at George Washington's Mount Vernon,* ed. Carol Borchert Cadou (Charlottesville: University of Virginia Press, 2018), 41–69; Joseph Manca, *George Washington's Eye: Landscape, Architecture, and Design at Mount Vernon* (Baltimore: Johns Hopkins University Press, 2012), 5–8, 100–134; and the excellent chapter on decorative arts in the 1780s at Mount Vernon by Carol Borchert Cadou, "Cincinnatus Returns Home: George Washington the War Hero 1788–1789," in *The George Washington Collection: Fine and Decorative Arts at Mount Vernon,* ed. Cadou (New York: Hudson Hill Press, 2006), 99–107.

39. Helen Lincklaen Fairchild, ed., *Francis Adrian Van der Kemp, 1752–1829: An Autobiography, Together with Extracts from His Correspondence* (New York: Knickerbocker Press, 1903), 114–16.

40. J. P. Brissot de Warville, *New Travels in the United States of America* (New York: T&J Swords, 1792), 235.

41. Washington to Samuel Vaughn, February 5, 1787, in *PGW,* 2:326.

42. Lafayette to Adrienne de Noailles de Lafayette, August 10, 1784, in *Lafayette in the Age of the American Revolution: Selected Letters and Papers, 1776–1790*, ed. Stanley J. Idzerda and Robert Rhodes Crout (Ithaca, NY: Cornell University Press, 1983), 5:237–38.

43. Brissot, *New Travels*, 235.

44. See, for instance, Abagail Adams to her sister, Mary Cranch, August 9, 1789, in Kaminski, *The Founders on the Founders*, 524–25.

45. Washington to George William Fairfax, June 30, 1785, in *PGW*, 3:87.

46. Samuel Vaughn, *Samuel Vaughan's Journal: Or "Minutes Made by S.V., from Stage to Stage, on a Tour to Fort Pitt,"* ed. Edward Williams (Mount Vernon: Mount Vernon Ladies' Association, 1961), 273.

47. Washington to Bolwer Metcalf, August 19, 1786, in *PGW*, 4:220–21.

48. Arthur Young to Washington, February 1, 1787, in *PGW*, 5:5–6.

49. Bowler, *A Treatise on Agriculture and Practical Husbandry [. . .]* (Providence, RI, 1786), n.p.

50. Washington to Richard Varick, January 1, 1784, in *PGW*, 1:2.

51. William Gordon, *The History of the Rise, Progress, and Establishment, of the Independence of the United States of America: Including an Account of the Late War; and of the Thirteen Colonies, from Their Origin to That Period* (London, 1788). William Gordon to Horatio Gates, August 31, 1784, in "Letters of the Reverend William Gordon, Historian of the American Revolution, 1770–1799," *Proceedings of the Massachusetts Historical Society* 63 (1929–30): 506; William Gordon to Washington, September 24, 1788, in *PGW*, 1:1.

52. Lafayette to Washington, May 25, 1788, in *PGW*, 6:294.

53. David Humphreys, *An Essay on the Life of the Honorable Major-General Israel Putnam* (Hartford, CT, 1788), 8, 14.

54. George Washington to Richard Bland Lee, March 25, 1788, in *PGW*, 6:177.

55. Washington to Francis Hopkinson, May 16, 1785, in *PGW*, 2:562n1.

56. Washington to Ann Allen Penn, September 18, 1787, in *PGW*, 5:334; Washington to Elizabeth Powel, June 6, 1787, in *PGW*, 5:223.

57. This sentiment was widespread in the 1780s and even appeared in a poem written "on the Resignation of his Excellency General Washington." *Litchfield (CT) Monitor*, November 22, 1785, 4.

58. Washington to Lafayette, May 28, 1788, in *PGW*, 6:298–99. He concluded this uncharacteristic letter by remarking on how uncharacteristic it was: "I hardly know how it is that I am drawn thus far in observations on a subject so foreign from those in which we are mostly engaged, farming and politics, unless because I had little news to tell you."

59. Brissot, *New Travels in the United States Performed in 1788* (Dublin: P. Byrne et al., 1792), 426, 428–30.

60. Ibid., 431.

61. William Gordon to Washington, August 30, 1784, in *PGW*, 1:64.

62. The definitive study on slavery at Mount Vernon and Washington's attitude toward his enslaved workers, as well as slavery in the abstract, can be found in Mary V. Thompson, *"The Only Unavoidable Subject of Regret": George Washington, Slavery, and the Enslaved Community at Mount Vernon* (Charlottesville: University of Virginia Press, 2020); also see Philip D. Morgan, "'To Get Quit of Negroes'": George Washington and Slavery," *Journal of American Studies* 39 (December 2005): 403–39.

63. Humphreys, *David Humphreys' "Life of General Washington,"* 78.

64. Ferdinando Fairfax, "Plan for Liberating the Negroes within the United States," *American Museum* 7 (December 1790), 285–87.

65. Three examples of many: "Mount Vernon, October 31st 1786. Circular," *Independent Gazetteer (Philadelphia)*, April 26, 1787, 2; *Carlisle (PA) Gazette, and the Western Repository of Knowledge,* May 23, 1787, 2; *Columbian Herald or the Patriotic Courier of North-America (Charleston, SC),* May 24, 1787, 3.

66. *David Humphreys' "Life of General Washington,"* 35–36.

67. Washington to Henry Knox, December 26, 1786, in *PGW,* 4:481.

68. Washington to Jonathan Trumball Jr., January 5, 1784, in *PGW,* 1:12.

69. Washington, "Circular to the States," *The Writings of George Washington from the Original Manuscript Sources, 1745–1799,* ed. John C. Fitzpatrick (Washington, DC: Government Printing Office, 1931–44), 26:483–96. See *A Collection of Papers* (New York: Samuel Loudon, 1784) for a popular reference to the Legacy. See also *Carlisle (PA) Gazette,* May 1787, 3: "The following extracts from that much admired Letter of General Washington, commonly styled his 'Last Legacy,' to the governors of the several states, we flatter ourselves, in the present stage of our political degeneracy, be deemed uninteresting to readers."

70. Washington, "Circular to the States," 483–86.

71. Washington to Robert Morris, in *PGW,* 2:315.

72. Washington to Thomas Johnson, November 12, 1786, in *PGW,* 4:359–60.

73. Washington to Bushrod, November 15, 1786, in *PGW,* 4:368.

74. Washington to Bushrod, November 15, 1786, in *PGW,* 4:369.

75. David Humphreys to Washington, November 16, 1786, in *PGW,* 4:373.

76. For David Humphreys's regular attendance with Washington on hunts and appearances in the diaries, see Donald Jackson and Dorothy Twohig, eds., *The Diaries of George Washington* (Charlottesville: University of Virginia Press, 1979), 5:221, 222, 224, 230, 234, 235.

77. David Humphreys, *The Miscellaneous Works of David Humphreys,* 223–25.

78. See note 69.

79. See note 21.

80. *Pennsylvania (Philadelphia) Packet, and Daily Advertiser,* July 12, 1788, 3.

# Abolitionists, Congress, and the Atlantic Slave Trade

### BEFORE AND AFTER RATIFICATION

*Nicholas P. Wood*

A T THE FEDERAL CONVENTION of 1787, southern delegates negotiated several advantageous compromises that benefited slaveholders. These compromises included protecting the Atlantic
slave trade for twenty-one years, guaranteeing their right to recapture runaway slaves across state bounds, calculating three-fifths of their enslaved
populations when enumerating political representation, and enlisting
the federal government in putting down "domestic insurrections." When
the Constitution was presented to the public, abolitionists immediately
recognized and denounced its concessions to slaveholders. Massachusetts Quaker William Rotch proclaimed the Constitution's "cornerstone"
was "founded on *Slavery* and that is on *Blood*."[1] His denunciation anticipated the fiery rhetoric of the yet-unborn William Lloyd Garrison, the
more famous Massachusetts abolitionist who later described the Constitution as a "covenant with death" and an "agreement with Hell."[2] During
the antebellum era, Garrison and many of his supporters refused to vote
or participate directly in politics, which they viewed as irredeemably corrupt and proslavery.[3]

In contrast to the later Garrisonians who repudiated the Constitution
and electoral politics, many abolitionists in the early republic overcame
their initial qualms and supported ratification. Their support may seem
surprising, especially as a growing number of scholars endorse Garrison's
interpretation of a "proslavery" Constitution. In one sense, such reconciliation could suggest that abolitionists—many of whom were merchants

in port cities—prioritized the economic stability they hoped the new government would bring above their concern for enslaved Black people. However, early abolitionists also evaluated the "proslavery" character of the Constitution in its broader context. The Constitution's compromises were obviously "proslavery" in comparison to the types of provisions that abolitionists and African Americans would have liked. However, it was not clear whether the Constitution was worse than the Articles of Confederation in regard to slavery. Abolitionists who supported ratification hoped that their political influence would increase under the new Constitution.

Examining the views and experiences of abolitionists in the years immediately before and after ratification can help refine scholarly arguments over the Constitution's relationship to slavery. A growing number of scholars highlight what they see as southerners' proslavery victories at the Federal Convention. From the 1960s through the 1990s, historians in this camp generally portrayed the framers as betraying the American Revolution's egalitarian promise. In this view, the natural rights rhetoric of the revolution created an ideological imperative and a political opportunity to eradicate racial bondage fully, but a failure of moral leadership and the growth of racism allowed a proslavery counterrevolution at the Federal Convention (which the 1793 invention of the cotton gin subsequently entrenched further).[4] More recently, scholars such as David Waldstreicher and George Van Cleve tend to see continuity rather than betrayal, emphasizing the extent to which slaveholders had shaped the American Revolution from its outset.[5] A few scholars go so far as to argue that the patriots declared independence in part to protect slavery from imperial meddling.[6] Many historians have dissented from the proslavery interpretation, arguing that the Federal Convention was characterized by compromises rather than proslavery victories. The compromises, they claim, were not intended to perpetuate slavery and did not foreclose antislavery politics.[7] Although conceding that some compromises ultimately facilitated slavery's growth, these scholars often defend the framers by insisting that they sincerely believed slavery would wither away once slave importations ceased.[8] Some historians, such as Sean Wilentz, further stress that the Constitution did not explicitly sanction the concept of "property in man," which many slaveholders had wanted.[9]

The abolitionists of the early republic often held views about the revolution and Constitution that do not conform to current historiographical divisions. On one hand, most leading abolitionists were Quaker pacifists who had been deeply ambivalent about the War of Independence and skeptical of patriots' professed commitment to natural rights principles. They recognized slaveholders' political power and held no naive expectation that slavery was on track to wither away on its own. On the other hand, they were frustrated with Congress's inability to curtail the Atlantic slave trade under the Articles of Confederation, and they hoped that the Constitution would prove more conducive to antislavery reform.

Comparing the effects of abolitionists' national efforts during the 1780s and 1790s underscores the obstacles they faced throughout the era while also revealing the growth, rather than diminution, of their influence after ratification. Although Congress never considered a national program of emancipation, the Constitution established a political structure that proved more receptive to antislavery politics than had the Articles of Confederation. After ratification, Quaker abolitionists quickly built a political coalition against the Atlantic slave trade that would have been previously impossible. In 1790, this coalition undermined some of the protections the Constitution had seemingly given to slave traders and importers. Four years later, Congress passed the Foreign Slave Trade Act of 1794 based on an enlarged understanding of its antislavery powers. These victories by abolitionists may have been incomplete, but they would have been impossible under the Articles of Confederation.

## Quaker Antislavery and the American Revolution

Most of the antislavery reforms passed during and after the American Revolution resulted from the efforts of enslaved Black people and white Quakers. Africans had resisted their enslavement from the beginning, and the disruption of war provided new opportunities to escape (often joining the British against their former masters) or negotiate concessions from slaveholders and legislatures, such as earning freedom through military service.[10] Antislavery had become a central component of Quakers' collective identity during the French and Indian War (1754–1763), which many Friends interpreted as divine chastisement for slaveholding and other sins. Anthony Benezet, for example, warned that God would continue punishing the colonists until they conformed the Lord's commands as recounted in Isaiah 58:6: "to loose the Bands of Wickedness, to undo the heavy Burden, to let the Oppressed go free, and . . . break every Yoke."[11] In 1758, the Philadelphia Yearly Meeting of Friends (PYM, which established policies for the mid-Atlantic colonies) instructed members to begin freeing their slaves; during the 1770s, Quakers began disowning recalcitrant slaveholders.[12] The Philadelphia Meeting for Sufferings (PMS), the activist committee of PYM, promoted antislavery reform throughout the nation.[13]

Although the American Revolution strengthened Quakers' commitment to antislavery, it gave them little hope that independence would naturally lead to emancipation. Based on their pacifism and deference to government authority, most Quakers opposed the revolution and suffered persecution as a result.[14] They expected little from patriot leaders, whom one abolitionist described as "talking much & making a shew of promoting the cause of Liberty & Virtue, while they have nothing less in view, than merely prostitute those terms to serve their base & wicked purposes."[15] Nonetheless, after American independence, Quakers in the United States sought to rebrand their prerevolutionary antislavery efforts as a nonsectarian and national cause. In doing so, they strategically overstated popular support for emancipation as a goal of the revolution.[16]

The experience of Quakers during the War of Independence makes their retroactive celebration of the antislavery character of the revolution all the more striking. PMS activist John Drinker, who was imprisoned by patriots in Virginia, observed: "Surely these are not the Men to let the Oppressed go free & loose the Bonds of Wickedness, have they not for many years been wantoning in Blood, & holding in a severe, merciless captivity, thousands of their fellow Men. . . . Can Righteousness be expected from men so depraved & corrupt? verily nay."[17] At times during the war, southern state governments even sought to reverse the effects of Quakers' antislavery exertions. When Virginia Quakers refused to pay wartime taxes (on account of their pacifism), officials seized free people of color whom the Quakers had manumitted and "sold them as Slaves" to help fund a war fought in the name of liberty.[18] North Carolina officials similarly reenslaved over one hundred Black men, women, and children whom Quakers had freed.[19] Northern legislatures such as New Jersey's also used slavery to fund the war, confiscating and selling Loyalists' human property.[20] Some Friends had hoped that wartime destruction—the "Dispensation of divine Chastisement"—would produce a spirit of repentance among the populace; instead, they reported that "a contrary Disposition of Mind & Conduct is sorrowfully prevalent."[21] Quakers were therefore disgusted but not surprised when American citizens, "deluded by the Gain of Oppression," revived the "detestable Trade carried on to the Coast of Africa" once the war ended.[22]

*A Serious Address to the Rulers of America, on the Inconsistency of Their Conduct Respecting Slavery,* published by New Jersey Quaker David Cooper in 1783, typified Quakers' cynicism and pessimism. Although happy that Pennsylvania had initiated a program of gradual abolition during the war, Cooper feared that "after the sunshine of peace takes place, we have little more to expect." Hoping to shame patriots into action, the Quaker juxtaposed references to natural rights from the Declaration of Independence and other political documents with examples of white Americans' continued exploitation of enslaved Black people.[23] PMS leader James Pemberton praised Cooper's pamphlet for taking the "arguments which have been published by the professing advocates for liberty" and turning their rhetoric "upon themselves."[24] Even as Quakers dismissed the patriots' sincerity, they hoped to shape the revolution's legacy on behalf of antislavery.[25]

In October 1783, Cooper, Pemberton, and 533 other Quakers signed a petition from the PYM calling on the Confederation Congress to abolish the slave trade and promote emancipation. Slavery was not only "contrary to every righteous consideration," but "in opposition to the solemn declarations often repeated in favour of universal liberty." Whereas the newly independent Americans should be expressing their "thankfulness to the all wise controller of human events," the revival of the slave trade instead threatened to provoke "future calamities."[26] The aging Anthony Benezet led a Quaker delegation delivering the petition to Princeton, New Jersey, where Congress was meeting at the time.[27]

Congress's response to the Quaker petition demonstrated both the disorganized state of national affairs and the obstructionist power of sectional minorities under the Articles of Confederation. The Quakers read their petition to Congress on October 8, 1783, but the "unsettled State of Congress in respect to fixing on a place for their residence" prevented the legislators from addressing the petition before they moved from New Jersey to Annapolis, Maryland.[28] The issue surely would have been lost in the shuffle without the intervention of David Howell, a delegate from Rhode Island whose father-in-law, Moses Brown, had signed the petition.[29] Congress finally took action on December 18, referring the petition to a committee led by Howell, who issued a report on January 7, 1784.

Howell's report praised the Quakers' commitment to the "rights of mankind" and "the essential good of their Country" (although Congress subsequently struck out the latter phrase). The report then proposed that Congress "recommend" that the state legislatures revive the slave trade ban that had been part of the Continental Congress's 1774 boycott of British trade. Under the Articles of Confederation, such a recommendation would have had no binding power. Nonetheless, slaveholding delegates from the Lower South still blocked Congress from adopting the Howell report, killing the toothless recommendation.[30] Across the Atlantic, a similar petition presented by British Quakers to Parliament failed to overcome the power of the West India lobby.[31]

Rebuffed by Congress, American Quakers published 5,000 copies of the British Friends' petition, hoping to attract public support as well as a sense of national competition.[32] They sent copies to every congressman, as well as legislators in Pennsylvania and New Jersey.[33] Yet for much of fall 1784, the peripatetic Congress remained in an "unsettled state," often lacking a quorum of members.[34] Eventually, the abolitionists, aided again by Howell, brought their concerns before Congress in January 1785.[35] Manuscript notations on the back of the Quakers' letter to Richard Henry Lee, the president of Congress, indicate that their address was read in Congress, but the body made no official record of the episode.[36]

The Atlantic slave trade was far from universally popular among southern slaveholders. Only South Carolina and Georgia were importing slaves at this time, while Virginia and Maryland were selling their surplus enslaved laborers via a growing interstate slave trade; thus economic self-interest encouraged slaveholders in the Upper South to oppose the slave trade from Africa.[37] However, the Confederation Congress had no power to regulate commerce; banning the slave trade would have required unanimous support for an amendment to the articles. Thus, even if a coalition of northern and Upper South delegates supported slave trade abolition, Lower South delegates could block such a measure. The Quaker abolitionists later learned that their address had prompted opposition from "some of the Southern States" on the grounds that "Congress had not the Power of Legislation" regarding the slave trade.[38] Moreover, the Confederation Congress would have had no power to enforce such a ban.

In 1786, Quaker activists drafted another petition. Although conceding that the Confederation Congress lacked authority to prohibit the slave trade, they hoped that a declaration of Congress's "sincere disapprobation of this public Wickedness . . . might not be void of Effect." They again argued that ending the "national inequity" was the best means of ensuring "divine Blessing."[39] In December, a delegation from the PMS traveled to New York, where Congress was then meeting. However, Congress again lacked a quorum and had not yet chosen a new president. As Pemberton explained to his brother: "[The Congress] being then without a head, we could not fully accomplish the business."[40] The Pennsylvania Quakers left the petition with their coreligionists in the New York Meeting for Sufferings, hoping they would have an opportunity to present it; however, no "seasonable Opening" occurred.[41] (The best news the New York Quakers could report was the death of Abner Nash, a North Carolina delegate who had "expressed sentiments very unfavourable in respect to the poor Blacks."[42])

When the PMS had first proposed the petition campaign in 1783, their London brethren had presciently cautioned that they "must expect to meet with the greatest Opposition from the Combination of interested parties."[43] Pemberton subsequently reported that Congress's refusal to act indicated its members' "sense of Liberty to be more founded on partial political views than real Justice & Equity."[44] Moreover, the Congress itself was in an "unsettled state," often unable to maintain a quorum of members, and "much declined in the estimation of the people."[45] Three years of annual lobbying stalled in the face of slaveholder opposition as well as from the general weakness of Congress. Fortunately, the abolitionists' state-level lobbying had been more fruitful, and they could report to British Quakers that "several of the Legislatures of these (dis)united States have made some further advances."[46] Nonetheless, much remained to be done. The state governments in Pennsylvania and New England had begun dismantling slavery, but New York, New Jersey, and every state south of Pennsylvania resisted calls for emancipation. South Carolina and Georgia continued importing enslaved Africans, and many New England merchants participated in this trade, as well as slave trade to foreign markets, often in violation of state laws.[47]

## The Constitution and the Atlantic Slave Trade

By 1787, antislavery activists had made significant strides but also hit many walls. In March, Edmund Prior of the New York Meeting for Sufferings complained that Congress yet again lacked a quorum. Still, he suggested that abolitionists shift their attention to the upcoming convention in Philadelphia, which Congress had called to amend the Articles of Confederation. Prior reported that Massachusetts politician Rufus King had mentioned that the slave trade fell under the convention's proposed focus on commerce and suggested that "some hints thrown before that body on that business might . . . be useful."[48] In response, the Pennsylvania Abolition Society (PAS) drafted a petition to the Federal Convention. The PAS had been established in 1775, revived after the war in 1784, and reorganized in April 1787.[49] It shared many prominent members with the PMS, such as James Pemberton, and the decision to have the nominally nondenominational PAS submit the petition was almost certainly a calculated strategy intended to demonstrate that antislavery sentiment was not limited to Quakers.

In their petition, the PAS members "implore[d] the present Convention to make the Suppression of the African trade in the United States, a part of their important deliberations."[50] They were "deeply distress[ed] . . . to observe that peace was scarcely concluded before the African trade was revived." Warning that "this inhuman traffic" threatened to bring down "the righteous vengeance of God in national judgments," they suggested the recent capture and enslavement of American sailors by Algerian corsairs was "intended by Divine Providence" to remind them of their moral duty to end the slave trade.[51] The abolitionists had hoped that Benjamin Franklin—newly appointed as the president of the PAS—would present the petition to the Federal Convention, but the elderly statesmen declined to submit a petition he knew would have exacerbated existing sectional tensions among the delegates.[52] The New York Manumission Society, founded in 1785 with a disproportionate involvement of Quakers, also prepared an antislavery petition to the convention.[53] John Jay drafted the petition, but it appears that Alexander Hamilton, another of the group's non-Quaker members, dissuaded the society from presenting it.[54]

Even without the antislavery petitions, the Atlantic slave trade proved a contentious subject at the Federal Convention. Many delegates from the North and Upper South called for its abolition, while those from South Carolina and Georgia portrayed continued slave importations as a precondition for a stronger central government. Eventually, a compromise— apparently facilitated by some New Englanders in return for Lower South support on other commercial policies they prioritized—forbade Congress from banning slave importations until 1808, while allowing the imposition of a tax in the meantime. The euphemism-laden first clause of Article I, Section 9, read: "The Migration or Importation of such Persons as any of the States now existing shall think proper to admit, shall not be prohibited by the Congress prior to the Year one thousand eight hundred and eight, but a Tax or duty may be imposed on such Importation, not exceeding ten dollars for each Person." Scholars who emphasize the proslavery elements of the Constitution argue that this clause was a significant victory for the Lower South.[55]

Critics of the proslavery interpretation counter that the slave trade clause was carefully worded to avoid giving national sanction to the concept of "property in man."[56] They also argue that the framers sincerely—if naively—believed the clause was a minor concession that merely delayed slavery's inevitable death. "By all accounts," Wilentz asserts, "Americans in 1787 believed that slavery would still require additional importations of Africans to flourish; and it followed that permanently closing the trade would hasten slavery's doom."[57] Gordon Wood argues that the "Founders' self-deception and mistaken optimism were understandable," and they "concluded that if the slave trade could be cut off, slavery would wither and die."[58] As evidence for this position, both scholars quote Oliver Ellsworth's claim at the convention that "as population increases; poor laborers will be so plenty as to render slaves useless. Slavery in time will not be a speck in our Country."[59]

Yet it is important to note that the framers who claimed to be most optimistic about slavery's inevitable death were generally motivated by their desire to *discourage* antislavery action.[60] Ellsworth, a delegate from Connecticut, was defending the slave trade clause, apparently because of a quid pro quo in which Lower South supported a provision that allowed New England more control over commercial legislation (by requiring a simple rather than two-thirds majority to pass such laws). In the same speech, Ellsworth also recognized that "slaves multiply so fast in Virginia and Maryland that it is cheaper to raise than import them." Other delegates also pointed out that Virginia "will gain by stopping the importations. Her slaves will rise in value, and she has more than she wants."[61] It seems the framers recognized not only that the Upper South had financial reasons for opposing the Atlantic slave trade, but also that the interstate slave trade would continue even after Congress ended importations from abroad, allowing slavery's indefinite growth. Abolitionists were not privy to secret debates at the Federal Convention, but when the Constitution was made public, they initially directed most of their criticism at the slave trade clause.[62]

Despite their misgivings, many American abolitionists ultimately supported ratification. Benjamin Rush happily informed a correspondent that the "the quakers in Pennsylvania" were almost unanimous in support of ratification and viewed the Constitution's slave trade clause as "a great point obtained from the Southern States."[63] Abolitionists' praise of the slave trade clause did not reflect naivete; they held no illusions that ending slave imports would cause slavery itself to die out. (It is true that Noah Webster did predict that slavery would wither away "without any extraordinary efforts to end it"—but he estimated the process might take "two centuries."[64]) Abolitionists in the Upper South, such as the Quaker Warner

Mifflin in Delaware, had already recognized that the growing interstate slave trade would enable slavery's expansion in the Lower South.[65] They realized ending slave importations would not lead to emancipation on its own, but they still identified it as an essential first step. In sum, no abolitionist would have interpreted the Constitution's slave trade clause as merely delaying slavery's inevitable demise. However, when abolitionists evaluated the Constitution in comparison to the Articles of Confederation—under which there was no expectation that Congress would *ever* have the power to abolish the slave trade, the delay of twenty-one years was more tolerable.[66]

Abolitionists who supported ratification described the slave trade clause not as a great triumph but as the best that could be expected given political realities. Writing on behalf of the PAS, Pemberton reminded British abolitionists that the Constitution was designed "to remedy the defects in our *federal* System, & to strengthen the ties by which we as several independent States were *united to each other,* & not to regulate the peculiar arrangements of the separate States." It would have been naive to expect radical changes in favor of antislavery. In regard to the slave trade, he observed: "It is not doubted that the States will *separately* abolish the African trade in much less time, which they may do at any period, & . . . should Interest unhappily shut the ears to the voice of the wretched African the [1808] clause alluded to will come into their relief."[67] A Virginian made similar arguments in response to an antifederalist who had called on antislavery Quakers to oppose ratification.[68] Although abolitionists would have written a different constitution for the nation, they believed that the Constitution had more antislavery potential than the Articles of Confederation.

## Antislavery Politics After Ratification

Abolitionists continued pushing state-level antislavery reforms while the Constitution was being ratified, achieving some important gains, such as northern state laws forbidding participation in any form of the Atlantic slave trade.[69] By the end of 1787, even South Carolina banned slave importations, albeit temporarily and based on financial considerations.[70] Abolitionists celebrated "the Progress made in this Work of Righteousness & Benevolence," but also reported the "difficulties & Disappointments [that] continue to impede the work."[71] Proceeding with religious zeal but limited optimism, abolitionists organized a campaign that culminated with three antislavery petitions submitted to the new Federal Congress in February 1790. The ensuing debates have attracted considerable scholarly attention, but remain poorly understood. Historians often characterize the episode as a major defeat for abolitionist analogous to the congressional gag rules that silenced antislavery debate in the 1830s and 1840s.[72] Placed in proper context, the 1790 debates are better understood as an important victory for abolitionists compared to their experiences under the Articles of Confederation.

Before abolitionists petitioned the new Congress about slavery, congressmen introduced the subject themselves in May 1789. During the debates over a revenue bill, Josiah Parker of Virginia proposed including a $10 tax on imported slaves.[73] Although many congressmen from the Upper South and mid-Atlantic favored the measure, the proposal ultimately came to naught. Nonetheless, the debates and the resulting revenue bill demonstrated that a new era of national politics had arrived. Under the Constitution, small minorities had lost their ability to easily obstruct the will of the majority. The Lower South representatives only prevented the slave trade tax by allying with New Englanders, apparently as part of another quid pro quo that lowered duties on the molasses that New England distillers imported from the West Indies.[74]

During the summer and fall of 1789, abolitionists geared up for another lobbying campaign. The PAS printed 1,500 copies of a slave ship diagram produced by British abolitionists showing how hundreds of Africans were crammed together during the Middle Passage. They distributed the image publicly and sent copies to members of Congress.[75] In late September, the PYM appointed a committee to petition Congress.[76] Congress was on recess until January, and the Quakers appointed a committee from the Meeting for Sufferings, including John Parrish and Mifflin, to deliver their petition in February 1790. A few days before the Quaker committee set off for New York (then the capital), Pemberton called a special meeting of the PAS and convinced them to send a delegation with their own petition as well.[77] Upon arriving in New York, several of the Philadelphia Quakers attended a gathering of the New York Meeting for Sufferings. The New Yorkers had recently petitioned their state legislature for a law preventing slave traders from using New York ports and reiterating their desire for the "Emancipation of *Slaves* in general." The legislature had ignored the call for emancipation and told the Quakers that under the new federal Constitution, they should direct petitions about the slave trade to Congress. The New York Quakers therefore joined the two delegations from Philadelphia with a petition of their own.[78] The Quakers presented the first two petitions to Congress on February 11, 1790.[79]

The PYM petition observed that when they had petitioned the Confederation Congress in 1783, the delegates had "generally acknowledged" the "gross national iniquity of trafficking in the persons of fellow-men," but had "lacked the power to apply a remedy." Now that the Constitution had been ratified, the petitioners asked Congress to use "the full extent of your power" to encourage "the Abolition of the slave trade."[80] The petition from the New York Yearly Meeting focused more narrowly on the foreign slave trade. The Quakers complained that although New York had banned slave importations, some slave traders were still using the port as a base of operations to transport slaves from Africa for sale elsewhere. They hoped Congress would use the federal government's new powers over commerce in order "to restrain vessells from fitting out and clearing out in any of the ports in this State for the purpose of a trade to Africa for slaves."[81]

The Senate quickly voted to lay both petitions on the table without taking any further action, but the House of Representatives began a lively debate over whether they should create a committee to consider the requests. James Jackson of Georgia and William L. Smith of South Carolina raised the most vocal opposition against discussing the slave trade. By contrast, some Upper South representatives, such as Josiah Parker and James Madison, used the debate as an opportunity to revive their call for a $10 duty on imported slaves. After several hours of debate, the House members determined to resume the discussion the following day.[82]

The next day, February 12, 1790, Congress received the third petition, signed by PAS president Benjamin Franklin. This petition focused more broadly on the evils of slavery, which the PAS described as incompatible with "the Christian Religion" and the "Political Creed of America." The petitioners felt "themselves *bound to use all justifiable endeavours to loosen the bands of slavery*" and looked to Congress for aid. Believing that the Constitution's reference to the "*blessings of liberty*" vested Congress with "many important & salutary Powers," they hoped that Congress would "be pleased to countenance the *Restoration of liberty*" to slaves. This request most likely referred to the reenslavement of the Black North Carolinians whom Quakers had manumitted, though some contemporaries and scholars interpreted it as a call for universal emancipation. The petition concluded by asking Congress to "step to the very verge of the Powers vested in you for discouraging every Species of Traffick in the Persons of our fellow Men."[83] Again, some scholars have interpreted this as calling for emancipation, but the PAS and Franklin more likely hoped that Congress would work within the boundaries of the Constitution to discourage slave trading.

Congressmen then debated what to do with the petitions even more heatedly than the previous day.[84] South Carolinians and Georgians demanded "tabling" the petitions (thus ending debate without taking action), thereby discouraging abolitionists from submitting more in the future. They defended slavery while castigating the Quakers for failing to support the War of Independence.[85] However, the House of Representatives eventually voted 43 to 11 to create a committee on the subject, leaving Smith to complain that his opposition was "ineffectual."[86] During the House debates, Quakers and abolitionists filled the galleries, lobbied individual congressmen (including those from the Lower South), and subsequently met with the special committee appointed to consider the petitions.[87] The Quakers were not always welcome, and Parrish described the lobbying experience as "a kind of warfare."[88]

The abolitionists' influence was evident when the committee, headed by Abiel Foster of New Hampshire, issued its report on March 5, 1790. Although Foster's report began with three resolutions reiterating the constitutional restraints on congressional power over slavery and slave trading, these were followed by the acknowledgment that Congress could impose a $10 tax on imported slaves and—more surprisingly—two resolutions declaring broad implied powers to ban the slave trade to foreign markets and to regulate the importation of enslaved Africans prior to 1808. A seventh resolution stated "that in all cases to which the authority of Congress extends, they will exercise it for the humane objects of the memorialists, so far as they can be promoted on the principles of justice, humanity, and good policy."[89] In sum, Foster's report encouraged Congress to address the abolitionists' grievances as far as possible.

The Foster report provoked fierce opposition from Lower South representatives (and a minority of those from the Upper South), with some of them warning of disunion. Beginning on March 17, the House of Representatives debated the report at length, ultimately issuing an amended report by the "committee of the whole House" on March 23. This second report preserved all the essential elements of the Foster report, except for the seventh resolution. Lower South representatives therefore found it almost equally obnoxious. Congressmen eventually voted 29 to 25 to print both reports, representing a rebuke to the Lower South and an important victory for the abolitionists.[90]

Abolitionists were pleased with Congress in 1790, especially in comparison to the fate of their petitions during the 1780s. They were happy that their "persevering Solicitations" had finally paid off.[91] Pemberton informed his British correspondents that although their petitions had been "violently opposed by a train of invective speeches" from Lower South slaveholders, "it is however agreed that the momenteous cause we are engaged to promote has been greatly advanced by this measure."[92] To French abolitionists, Pemberton wrote: "Our application to Congress in behalf of these unhappy Men, did not meet with that Success which their most zealous friends expected, yet we have great reason to be satisfied with the measure."[93] The abolitionists were confident that their first petitioning effort after ratification had strengthened their cause, and they were optimistic that the two committee reports would lead to congressional legislation.

With few exceptions, historians have understood the result of the 1790 debates as a "clear victory for the South" and have characterized the abolitionists as self-deluding in their positive response.[94] Even scholars who disagree about the character of the Constitution agree on this point. Those who characterize the Constitution as proslavery from the beginning argue that the 1790 debates further entrenched this attribute, while those who argue that the Constitution was *not* inherently proslavery identify the 1790 debates as a watershed moment when a proslavery interpretation of the Constitution gained broader acceptance.[95] Few scholars have taken the abolitionists' perception of progress seriously.[96] The contrast between the ways abolitionists and most modern scholars have viewed the episode results from a tendency of historians to exaggerate the antislavery character of the Foster committee's report, thus making the second report by the House appear as a great setback.

The confusion revolves around the meaning of the second resolution in the Foster report. The resolution in question, along with the first resolution to which it refers, reads as follows:

> First. That the General Government is expressly restrained from prohibiting the importation of such persons "as any of the States now existing shall think proper to admit, until the year one thousand eight hundred and eight."
>
> Second. That Congress, by a fair construction of the Constitution, are equally restrained from interfering in the emancipation of slaves, who already are, or may, *within the period mentioned,* be imported into, or born within, any of the said states.[97]

It is virtually certain that the italicized clause was intended to qualify only the subsequent clause; that Congress could never free slaves in the states *except* those who might be illegally imported *after* 1808. In other words, after 1808, Congress could prohibit the importation of slaves and could free illegally imported Africans, but they could *never* liberate slaves who were either born in the United States or had been legally imported before 1808.[98] This resolution should not have been controversial; the more important resolutions, as discussed below, dealt with banning or regulating branches of the Atlantic slave trade.

However, South Carolina's William L. Smith portrayed the second resolution as a Trojan horse for emancipation. He declared: "The report of the committee appeared to hold out the idea that Congress might exercise the power of emancipation after the year 1808; for it said that Congress could not emancipate slaves prior to that period."[99] Smith needed to make such exaggerated claims because the Lower South could no longer unilaterally block legislation as they had under the Articles of Confederation. By misrepresenting the Foster report's second resolution, Smith hoped to enlist Upper South congressmen against the entire report, thereby protecting the Atlantic slave trade from any regulation before 1808. Most of Smith's contemporaries recognized that he only "affected to believe" that Congress was contemplating emancipation.[100]

Smith's rhetorical hyperbole, however, has been accepted at face value by many historians, leading them to exaggerate the stakes of the debate. Wilentz writes that the Foster report contained "the possibility that Congress possessed the power to emancipate slaves born in the United States after 1808—a staggering proposition." Van Cleve asserts that the resolution "implied that Congress also had power to emancipate slaves both in existing states and new states after 1808." Other scholars have similarly assumed that the Foster report would have opened the door to national emancipation after 1808.[101] Following from this belief, the second resolution appears as the "key provision" of the Foster report, and its absence in the second "emasculated" report by the whole House seems to have "destroyed the antislavery implications of the [Foster] report."[102] According to this narrative, Congress seriously considered an interpretation of the Constitution that would have allowed them to emancipate slaves after 1808 before instead embracing a proslavery report establishing a proslavery consensus on the Constitution. However, as Douglas Bradburn has argued, most historians have "misread this fundamental debate." Bradburn notes that the Lower South representatives failed to block either report from being printed and were the congressmen least satisfied with the final result.[103]

A careful examination of the evidence—facilitated by the publication of *Documentary History of the First Federal Congress*—indicates that nobody at the time intended or advocated the second resolution as containing the emancipatory power that Congressman Smith and modern scholars have commonly ascribed to it.[104] Responding to Lower South insinuations that

Congress was "disposed to prohibit not only the slave trade, but abolish slavery likewise," Virginia's John Page insisted: "Not one member has even hinted that he entertained an idea of that kind."[105] Northern members also disavowed the view that any of the resolutions indicated a power to interfere with slavery itself, before or after 1808. Virtually all contemporaries understood this resolution as *restraining* rather than empowering Congress.[106] The subsequent change in the second report simply condensed and combined the second and third resolutions without altering the meaning; both versions had merely reiterated constitutional restraints on federal power.[107] Abolitionists from neither Pennsylvania nor New York expressed any disappointment about the modification.[108]

By treating the debates as if they were about emancipation, historians also lose sight of the actual battle and the site of the abolitionist victory: the declaration of broad powers to regulate the Atlantic slave trade prior to 1808.[109] In a significant defeat for the Lower South, the Committee of the Whole preserved all the essential elements of the Foster committee's fifth resolution on American participation in the slave trade to foreign markets while making the language more concise: "That Congress have authority to restrain the citizens of the United States from carrying on the African trade, for the purpose of supplying foreigners with slaves, and of providing, by proper regulations, for the humane treatment, during their passage, of slaves imported by the said citizens into the States admitting such importation."[110] In other words, Congress could completely prohibit Americans from delivering slaves to foreign markets and, although they could not ban Americans from importing slaves until 1808, they could immediately regulate conditions on slave ships servicing the United States. The Committee of the Whole also voted to preserve the Foster report's sixth resolution in its entirety: "That Congress have also authority to prohibit foreigners from fitting out vessels, in any port of the United States, for transporting persons from Africa to any foreign port."[111] Because this resolution was alone preserved verbatim from the Foster report, the Committee of the Whole did not reprint it in their revisions.[112] Several historians have mistaken its apparent absence for a deletion that further "protected both the interests of slave traders and those states that wanted to import slaves."[113] In sum, the historians who characterize the debates as a setback for abolitionists—or even a missed opportunity to abolish slavery after 1808—have misinterpreted congressional procedures and fundamentally misunderstood the stakes of the controversy.

Congress never considered claiming power to abolish slavery, but both committee reports went beyond the explicit text of the Constitution to enumerate implicit powers that Congress could use to curtail and regulate slave trading before 1808. Antislavery lobbyists were therefore pleased with the result. John Parrish celebrated "the Voats of the House" determining that "Congress have it in their Power to prevent [the sale of slaves to foreigners] with out infringing on the Constitution."[114] Mifflin was similarly happy that Congress claimed the power "greatly to obstruct the purposes of avarice in the pursuit of this iniquitous traffic, if not to put an effectual stop thereto."[115] Abolitionists emerged from the 1790 debates feeling not like the defeated group that historians have portrayed, but confident that the federal Congress would prove much more receptive to their goals than the Confederation Congress ever had.[116] Moreover, the debates proved that under the Constitution, Lower South representatives could no longer block legislation by themselves.

Abolitionists were disappointed, however, that Congress did not immediately create legislation based on the reports. The petitioners had interrupted Congress's consideration of Treasury Secretary Alexander Hamilton's controversial proposal to transfer state debts to the federal government, and the House of Representatives quickly returned to this topic after issuing their reports on the antislavery petitions. Congress then moved on to other issues and showed little inclination to revisit the controversial subject of the slave trade.

Throughout the next four years, abolitionists repeatedly lobbied government officials and petitioned Congress to pass legislation based on the 1790 reports.[117] In January 1794, delegates from six states attended the first annual American Convention of Abolition Societies and drafted a new petition to Congress, requesting "that a law may be passed, prohibiting the traffic carried on by citizens of the United States for the supply of slaves to foreign nations, and preventing foreigners from fitting out vessels for the slave-trade in the ports of the United States."[118] This effort soon led to the Foreign Slave Trade Act of 1794.

The Foreign Slave Trade Law of 1794 implemented most but not all of the powers outlined in the relevant sections of the 1790 resolutions. It banned both Americans and foreigners from using American vessels or ports to engage in "any trade or traffic in slaves, to any foreign country."[119] The PMS praised the law as "nearly conformable" to their requests, and abolitionists throughout the nation celebrated it as the culmination of the petitioning campaign Quakers had begun in 1783 under the Articles of Confederation.[120] Some historians have dismissed the 1794 Foreign Slave Trade law as "ultra-cautious;" but given the restraints of the federal Constitution, the law could not have been much more ambitious.[121] Indeed, in 1787 the Constitution had given no reason to expect any limitation on slave trading before 1808; the 1794 law reflected the 1790 reports' broadened interpretation of the Constitution's anti–slave trade potential. Not only was the foreign carrying trade the only branch of the Atlantic slave trade that Congress could constitutionally restrict, it also made tactical sense to focus on it because the vast majority of voyages by American slave traders supplied foreign markets, especially Spanish colonies. After 1787, when South Carolina had (temporarily) prohibited slave imports, about 90 percent of American slave ships transported slaves from Africa to the West Indies rather than into the United States.[122] Under the 1794 law, this behavior became illegal.

Still, one should not overstate the importance and effect of the Foreign Slave Trade Act. Although the 1794 law resulted in dozens of prosecutions and an initial drop in American involvement in the foreign trade, illegal American participation in trade reached new heights by 1797. Enforcement was difficult because virtually all of the illegal activity occurred outside of the United States at a time when there was rising foreign demand for slaves and the Napoleonic Wars impeded the operations of European slavers.[123] Moreover, the young federal government remained weak in the international sphere. Its infant navy could not effectively protect American sailors from enslavement by Barbary corsairs, impressment by the

British Navy, or molestation by French privateers—all of which were much higher priorities than protecting Africans from enslavement.[124]

Despite its limitations, the Foreign Slave Trade Act of 1794, like the 1790 congressional reports, represented an antislavery victory that would have been impossible during the Confederation period. Moreover, the legislation was based on an antislavery interpretation of implied powers contained in the Constitution's slave trade clause, indicating that the compromises over slavery were still open to reinterpretation. Scholars have increasingly recognized that the American Revolution had contradictory implications for slavery, and it is essential to recognize that the Constitution did as well.

In general, the Constitution merely formalized privileges that slaveholders had enjoyed during the Confederation period; in some cases, it even reduced slaveholders' influence. Van Cleve has persuasively argued that "historians have underestimated the protection that the Articles of Confederation provided to slavery," and he has shown that the Constitution's fugitive slave clause followed existing policy.[125] Moreover, even with the three-fifths clause, slaveholders could not control the new Federal Congress and had less obstructionist power than in the Confederation Congress. With equal representation under the Articles of Confederation, Georgia and South Carolina had had as much voting power as more populous states such as Pennsylvania and New York and could essentially veto legislation regulating commerce. Under the Constitution, state equality was preserved in the Senate, but northern states gained a decisive majority in the House of Representatives (despite the three-fifths clause).[126] States' rights and federalism protected slavery from the central government, but this had been even more true under the Articles of Confederation.

In the end, the provisions of the Constitution that allowed the United States to expand territorially into a massive "empire for slavery" were less the clauses specific to slavery than the more general development of a stable government that could effectively mobilize fiscal-military resources. Over the ensuing decades, slaveholders were able to exploit contingent developments and geopolitical concerns about international trade, borders, and western loyalty to expel Native Americans and expand slavery across the southwest. By the 1850s, the "slave power"—slaveholders' political influence—dominated the federal government, employing its resources to expand and protect slavery.[127] However, that future was unwritten during the 1790s, and abolitionists found that the Constitution had increased Congress's responsiveness to antislavery activism.

## Notes

1. William Rotch Sr. to Moses Brown, Nantucket, MA, November 8, 1787, *Documentary History of the Ratification of the Constitution: Digital Edition* (hereafter *DHRC*), ed. John P. Kaminski et al. (Charlottesville: University of Virginia Press), http://rotunda.upress.virginia.edu/founders/RNCN.html.

2. Garrison as quoted in Paul Finkelman, "Slavery and the Constitutional Convention: Making a Covenant with Death," *Beyond Confederation: Origins of the Constitution and American National Identity,* ed. Richard Beeman, Stephen Botein, and Edward C. Carter II (Chapel Hill: University of North Carolina Press, 1987), 188–225.

3. Aileen S. Kraditor, *Means and Ends in American Abolitionism: Garrison and His Critics on Strategy and Tactics, 1834–1855* (New York: Pantheon Books, 1967), 185–217; W. Caleb McDaniel, *The Problem of Democracy in the Age of Slavery: Garrisonian Abolitionists and Transatlantic Reform* (Baton Rouge: Louisiana State University Press, 2013). Many of Garrison's contemporary abolitionists disagreed with his strategy, embraced politics, and argued that the Constitution was inherently antislavery. See, e.g., Corey M. Brooks, *Liberty Power: Antislavery Third Parties and the Transformation of American Politics* (Chicago: University of Chicago Press, 2016).

4. Staughton Lynd, *Class Conflict, Slavery, and the United States Constitution* (New York: Bobbs-Merril, 1967), 153–213, esp. 179–83; Finkelman, "Slavery and the Constitutional Convention"; Gary B. Nash, *Race and Revolution* (New York: Rowman & Littlefield, 1990), 25–56; Paul Finkelman, *Slavery and the Founders: Race and Liberty in the Age of Jefferson* (Armonk, NY: Sharpe, 1996).

5. David Waldstreicher, *Slavery's Constitution: From Revolution to Ratification* (New York: Hill and Wang, 2009); George William Van Cleve, *A Slaveholders' Union: Slavery, Politics, and the Constitution in the Early American Republic* (Chicago: University of Chicago Press, 2010). For historiographical essays challenging the notion that the American Revolution offered a missed opportunity to end slavery, see Christopher Leslie Brown, "The Problems of Slavery," in *Oxford Handbook of the American Revolution,* ed. Edward G. Gray and Jane Kamensky (New York: Oxford University Press, 2012), 427–46; Matthew Mason, "A Missed Opportunity? The Founding, Postcolonial Realities, and the Abolition of Slavery," *Slavery and Abolition* 35 (2014): 199–213.

6. The strongest proponents of this proslavery interpretation of the American Revolution assert that "one of the primary reasons the colonists decided to declare their independence from Britain was because they wanted to protect the institution of slavery" at a time when antislavery sentiment was growing in Britain. See Nikole Hannah-Jones's introductory essay to the *New York Times Magazine's* special 1619 Project issue: "Our Democracy's Founding Ideals Were False When They Were Written. Black Americans Have Fought to Make Them True," August 14, 2019, https://www.nytimes.com/interactive/2019/08/14/magazine/black-history-american-democracy.html. See also Gerald Horne, *The Counter-revolution of 1776: Slave Resistance and the Origins of the United States of America* (New York: New York University Press, 2014), esp. 209–33; Alfred W. Blumrosen and Ruth G. Blumrosen, *Slave Nation: How Slavery United the Colonies and Sparked the American Revolution* (Naperville, IL: Sourcebooks, 2005).

7. See, e.g., William Wiecek, *The Sources of Antislavery Constitutionalism in America, 1760–1848* (Ithaca, NY: Cornell University Press, 1977); Howard A. Ohline, "Slavery, Economics, and Congressional Politics, 1790," *Journal of Southern History* 46 (August 1980): 335–60; Earl M. Maltz, "The Idea of a Proslavery Constitution," *Journal of the Early Republic* 17 (April 1997): 37–59; Don E. Fehrenbacher, *The Slaveholding Republic: An Account of the United States Government's Relations to Slavery* (New York: Oxford University Press, 2002).

8. Gordon S. Wood, *Empire of Liberty: A History of the Early Republic* (New York: Oxford University Press, 2009), 518–23.

9. Sean Wilentz, *No Property in Man: Slavery and Antislavery at the Nation's Founding* (Cambridge, MA: Harvard University Press, 2018), 58–114.

10. Douglas Egerton, *Death or Liberty: African Americans and Revolutionary America* (New York: Oxford University, 2009).

11. The biblical quotation, misidentified as Isaiah 58:7, appears as the epigraph on the cover of [Anthony Benezet], *Observations on the Inslaving, Importing and Purchasing of Negroes, With Some Advice thereon extracted From the Epistle of the Yearly-Meeting of the People Called Quakers, held at London in the year 1748 [sic, 1758],* 2nd ed. (Germantown, PA: Christopher Sower, 1760).

12. Thomas E. Drake, *Quakers and Slavery in America* (New Haven, CT: Yale University Press, 1965), 86–99; Sydney V. James, *A People among Peoples: Quaker Benevolence in Eighteenth-Century America* (Cambridge, MA: Harvard University Press, 1963); Jack D. Marietta, *Reformation of American Quakerism, 1748–1783* (Philadelphia: University of Pennsylvania Press, 1984), 113–28, 273–88. On the Quakers' slow embrace of abolitionism, see also Jean R. Soderland, *Quakers and Slavery: A Divided Spirit* (Princeton, NJ: Princeton University Press, 1985).

13. Historiographical divisions between Quaker studies and scholarship on formal abolitionist societies has obscured the continued prominence of the Philadelphia Meeting for Sufferings (PMS) and Quaker meetings for sufferings in other states within the national antislavery movement after 1783. For the importance of PMS activism after the revolution, see Drake, *Quakers and Slavery in America,* 84–113; Nicholas P. Wood, "A 'Class of Citizens': The Earliest Black Petitioners to Congress and Their Quaker Allies," *William and Mary Quarterly* 74 (January 2017): 109–44.

14. Marietta, *Reformation of American Quakerism,* 215–48.

15. Henry Drinker to Elizabeth Drinker, Winchester, 10 mo. 12, 1777, Henry Drinker Correspondence, 1777–1778, Haverford College Library, Haverford, PA. (When citing Quaker manuscripts, I have preserved their practice of numbering rather than naming months [e.g., "1st month" or "1mo" for January]). See also PMS to the London Meeting for Sufferings (LMS), 17th: day of 7th: mo: 1783, PMS Minutes, 2:399–403, Haverford. PMS publications interpreted the imperial crisis and war as divine chastisement designed to encourage righteous reform, including the abolition of slavery. PMS, *The Antient Testimony & Principles of the People Call'd Quakers* (Philadelphia, 1776); PMS, *A Short Vindication of the Religious Society Called Quakers against the Aspersions of a Nameless Writer* (Philadelphia, 1780). See also Marietta, *Reformation of American Quakerism,* 252–56.

16. My thinking on this point has been influenced especially by Kirsten Sword, "Remembering Dinah Nevil: Strategic Deceptions in Eighteenth-Century Antislavery," *Journal of American History* 97 (September 2010): 315–43, esp. 315–18, 325–26, 334–35. See also Christopher Leslie Brown, *Moral Capital: Foundations of British Abolitionism* (Chapel Hill: University of North Carolina Press, 2006), 431–41.

17. Henry Drinker to Elizabeth Drinker, Winchester, 11 mo. 20, 1777, Henry Drinker Correspondence, 1777–1778, Haverford.

18. "The Memorial of a Committee of the People Called Quakers to the Speaker and House of Delegates in Virginia," November 29, 1780, Legislative Petitions of the General Assembly, 1776–1865, Accession Number 36121, box 290, folder 23, Library of Virginia. See also Edward Stabler to [John Pemberton], Petersburg, 11 mo: 23d 1780, Cox Parrish Wharton Collection (hereafter CPW), box 15, Historical Society of Pennsylvania (hereafter HSP).

19. Larry E. Tise, "'Taking Up' Quaker Slaves: The Origins of America's Slavery Imperative," in *Varieties of Southern Religious History: Essays in Honor of Donald G. Mathews,* ed. Regina D. Sullivan and Monte Harrell Hampton (Columbia: University of South Carolina, 2015), 35–50.

20. James J. Gigantino II, *Ragged Road to Abolition: Slavery and Freedom in New Jersey, 1775–1865* (Philadelphia: University of Pennsylvania Press, 2016), 31, 60–61.

21. PMS to LMS, Philadelphia, 15th: Day of the 6th: mon: 1780, PMS Minutes, 2:269–72, Haverford.

22. PMS to New York Meeting for Sufferings, Philad[delphi]a, 20th: day of the 11th: mo: 1783, PMS Minutes, 2:410–11, Haverford; PMS to New England Meeting for Sufferings, Philada[delphia], 20th: day of the 11th: mo: 1783, PMS Minutes, 2:409–10, Haverford.

23. [David Cooper], *A Serious Address to the Rulers of America, On the Inconsistency of Their Conduct Respecting Slavery: Forming a Contrast Between the Encroachments of England on American Liberty, and American Injustice in Tolerating Slavery* (Trenton, NJ: Isaac Collins, 1783), 17.

24. James Pemberton to John Pemberton, Philad[elphia], 7th mo. 19th: 1783, Pemberton Papers, vol. 39, HSP.

25. On the revolution's legacy as unsettled at this time, see James Alexander (Alec) Dun, "Atlantic Antislavery, American Abolition: The Problem of Slavery in the United States

in an Age of Disruption, 1770–1808," in *The World of the Revolutionary American Republic: Land, Labor, and the Conflict for a Continent,* ed. Andrew Shankman (New York: Routledge, 2014), 228–45.

26. Philadelphia Yearly Meeting (PYM), "To the United States in Congress Assembled, The Address of the People called Quakers," in *A Necessary Evil? Slavery and the Debate over the Constitution,* ed. John P. Kaminski (Madison, WI: Madison House, 1995), 26–27.

27. Drake, *Quakers and Slavery,* 90–94. On Benezet, see Maurice Jackson, *Let This Voice be Heard: Anthony Benezet, Father of Atlantic Abolitionism* (Philadelphia: University of Pennsylvania Press, 2009).

28. James Pemberton to John Pemberton, Phila[delphia], 11th mon: 28th: 1783, Pemberton Papers, vol. 39, HSP; PMS Minutes, 2:399–403 (16 10mo 1783), Haverford; *Journals of the Continental Congress,* ed. Worthington C. Ford et al. (Washington, DC: 1922), 25:654, 660.

29. Moses Brown to James Pemberton, Providence, 22d, 5th mo. 1782, Pemberton Papers, vol. 36, HSP; James Pemberton to Moses Brown, Philad[elphia], 4mo. 9th: 1784 (draft), Pemberton Papers, vol. 40, HSP.

30. *Journals of the Continental Congress,* 26:13–14. A writer in *The Friend* later claimed that the 1783 petition had inspired the 1784 proposal to ban slavery in the western territories after 1800. Whether or not this was the case, the proposal was defeated, though passed in a different form in the Northwest Ordinance of 1787. "Relics of the Past: Warner Mifflin, No. 7," *Friend* 17 (1844): 181–82.

31. Brown, *Moral Capital,* 412–26.

32. *The Case of Our Fellow-Creatures, the Oppressed Africans, Respectfully Recommended to the Serious Consideration of the Legislature of Great-Britain, By the People Called Quakers* (Philadelphia: Joseph Crukshank, 1784); PMS Minutes, 2:429–30 (19 8mo 1784), Haverford.

33. PMS Minutes, 2:437 (16 12mo 1784), Haverford. See also PMS Minutes, 2:441 (17 3mo 1785); PMS to LMS, 16th 6th mo. 1785, PMS Minutes, 2:451–54, Haverford.

34. James Pemberton to John Pemberton, Philad[elphia], 21st. 11mo: 1784, Pemberton Papers, vol. 42, HSP. James Pemberton to David Howell (in Congress at Trenton, NJ), Philadelphia, 12mo: 21st: 1784 (copy), ibid.

35. James Pemberton to David Howell (in NY), Philad[elphia] 26. 1mo., 1785 (2 drafts), Pemberton Papers, vol. 42, HSP.

36. PYM to Richard Henry Lee and Congress, Philadelphia, 26th of First mo., 1785, Papers of Continental Congress, reel 57, "Remonstrances and Addresses to Congress, 1776–88," 347, accessed June 11, 2014, ttp://www.fold3.com/image/184874/.

37. Steven Deyle, "Irony of Liberty: Origins of the Domestic Slave Trade," *Journal of the Early Republic* 12 (Spring 1992): 37–62.

38. PMS Minutes, 2:457–58 (24 9mo 1784), Haverford.

39. PMS to Congress, 20th: of the 10mo: 1786, PMS Minutes, 3:38–39, Haverford.

40. James Pemberton to John Pemberton, Philad[elphia]: 29th: 11thth mo. 1786, Pemberton Papers, vol. 47, HSP.

41. PMS Minutes, 3:41–42 (21 12mo 1786), Haverford. Edmund Prior to James Pemberton, New York, 3 M 15, 1787, Pemberton Papers, vol. 47, HSP.

42. John Murray Jr. to James Pemberton, New York, 12 Mo. 8. 1786, Pemberton Papers, vol. 47, HSP.

43. LMS to PMS, London, 4th: of the 4th: mo 1783, PMS Minutes, 2:394–95.

44. James Pemberton to John Pemberton, 6 mo 14 1784, Pemberton Papers, vol. 41, HSP.

45. James Pemberton to John Pemberton, Philad[elphi]a, 21st. 11mo: 1784, Pemberton Papers, vol. 42, HSP.

46. James Pemberton to William Dillwyn, 6mo, 19th: 1786, Pemberton Papers, vol. 46, HSP.

47. Jay Coughtry, *Notorious Triangle: Rhode Island and the Slave Trade, 1700–1807* (Philadelphia: Temple University Press, 1981); James A. McMillin, *The Final Victims: Foreign Slave Trade to North America, 1783–1810* (Charleston: University of South Carolina Press, 2004).

48. Edmund Prior to James Pemberton, New York, 3M 18, 1787, Pemberton Papers, vol. 47, HSP.

49. On the Pennsylvania Abolition Society (PAS), see Gary B. Nash and Jean R. Soderlund, *Freedom by Degrees: Emancipation in Pennsylvania and Its Aftermath* (New York: Oxford University Press, 1991); Richard S. Newman, *The Transformation of American Abolitionism: Fighting Slavery in the Early Republic* (Chapel Hill: University of North Carolina Press, 2002); Paul J. Polgar, *Standard-Bearers of Equality: America's First Abolition Movement* (Chapel Hill: University of North Carolina Press, 2019); Sword, "Remembering Dinah Nevil."

50. PAS petition to the Honourable Convention of the United States now Assembled in the City of Philadelphia, June 2d: 1787, PAS Papers, reel 25, HSP.

51. PAS petition of June 2, 1787, in *Pennsylvania Packet (Philadelphia)*, February 14, 1788.

52. Waldstreicher, *Slavery's Constitution*, 103–4. The PAS nonetheless managed to reach a public—and international—audience for their petition by having it published in the newspapers; see *Pennsylvania Packet (Philadelphia)*, February 14, 1788; *Massachusetts Centinel (Boston)*, March 19, 1788; Appendix, *Edinburgh Magazine or Literary Miscellany* 6 (1787): 453; *Gentleman's Magazine* 2 (1787): 925; *Scots Magazine* 49 (1787): 564.

53. On the New York Manumission Society (NYSM), see Thomas Robert Mosely, "A History of the New-York Manumission Society, 1785–1849," (PhD diss., New York University, 1963); David N. Gellman, *Emancipating New York: The Politics of Slavery and Freedom, 1777–1827* (Baton Rouge: Louisiana State University Press, 2006), 56–77; Polgar, *Standard-Bearers of Equality*, 53–57, 63 and passim; Sarah Levine-Gronningsater, "Delivering Freedom: Gradual Emancipation, Black Legal Culture, and the Origins of the Sectional Crisis in New York, 1759–1870," (PhD diss., University of Chicago, 2014), 76–79 and passim.

54. Ron Chernow mistakenly assumes the NYMS petition was delivered to the convention, and he suggests—completely misrepresenting the historical record—that Hamilton deserves credit for proposing the petition; see Ron Chernow, *Alexander Hamilton* (New York: Penguin, 2005), 239. The NYMS papers indicate that John Jay, president of the NYMS, helped draft the petition to the Federal Convention on August 16, 1787. The next day Hamilton arrived, having left the Federal Convention early. The NYMS minutes recorded that "the Committee appointed last Evening to draw a Memorial to the federal Convention reported that they had prepared one which was read and

approved, but the Society being informed that it was probable the Convention would not take up the Business, resolved not to send the same." See New York Manumission Society Records, vol. 6, Meeting Minutes, 69–73, New-York Historical Society.

55. Lynd, *Class Conflict, Slavery, and the United States Constitution*, 185–213; Finkelman, *Slavery and the Founders*, 19–31; Waldstreicher, *Slavery's Constitution*, 93–98; Van Cleve, *Slaveholders' Union*, 144–53.

56. E.g., see Wilentz, *No Property in Man*, 73–101.

57. Wilentz, *No Property in Man*, 134 (see also 16, 187).

58. Wood, *Empire of Liberty*, 519, 523.

59. Ellsworth quoted in Kaminski, *A Necessary Evil?*, 59–60 and cited by Wood, *Empire of Liberty*, 525, and Wilentz, *No Property in Man*, 83.

60. Douglas R. Egerton similarly concludes that Ellsworth's "sanguinity may be regarded as a rhetorical ploy" in *Death or Liberty*, 245. Brown makes this point more generally about patriots' antislavery rhetoric in "The Problems of Slavery," 439.

61. Kaminski, *A Necessary Evil?*, 59 (Ellsworth), 60 (Charles Coatesworth Pinckney).

62. William Rotch Sr. to Moses Brown, Nantucket, MA, November 8, 1787; James Pemberton to John Pemberton, Philadelphia, September 20, 1787; Moses Brown to James Pemberton, Providence, October 17, 1787; Samuel Hopkins to Moses Brown, Newport, October 22, 1787; Moses Brown to James Thornton Sr., Providence, November 13, 1787; James Pemberton to Moses Brown, Philadelphia, November 16, 1787; Edmund Prior to Moses Brown, New York, December 1, 1787; James Thornton Sr. to Moses Brown, Byberry, Philadelphia County, December 17, 1787; Jeremy Belknap to Benjamin Rush, Boston, February 12, 1788, all available in Kaminski, *DHRC*.

63. Benjamin Rush to Jeremy Belknap, Philadelphia, February 28, 1788, in Kaminski, *DHRC*. See also William Rotch Sr. to Moses Brown, Nantucket, MA, November 8, 1787, ibid.

64. Webster's point was that antislavery activism was "highly necessary" to expedite abolition; see Noah Webster, *Effects of Slavery on Industry* (Hartford, CT: Hudson and Goodwin, 1793), 37.

65. Warner Mifflin to James Pemberton, Kent ye 3th Day of 2mo: 1787, Pemberton Papers, 47, HSP; Warner Mifflin to John Parrish, Kent ye 9th of 2 mo. 1787, CPW, box 1, HSP. On Mifflin's efforts against the interstate slave trade in the 1780s, see Gary B. Nash, *Warner Mifflin: Unflinching Quaker Abolitionist* (Philadelphia: University of Pennsylvania Press, 2017), 138–39.

66. Anthony Wayne made this comparison in marginalia on the proceedings of the Pennsylvania ratification debates, writing: "What were the Southern States to gain by the Constitution? No restraint in the *Articles* of *Confederation*. In this [Constitution] the restraint [is] 21 *years*. A duty amounting to a prohibition." See [Pennsylvania] Convention Debates, December 3, 1787, in Kaminski, *DHRC*.

67. PAS to the London Committee, 20th of the 5th. Month, copied in PAS Minutes, 35–38, HSP.

68. "One of the People Called Quakers in the State of Virginia," *Virginia Independent Chronicle*, March 12, 1788, Kaminski, *DHRC*.

69. Arthur Zilversmit, *First Emancipation: The Abolition of Slavery in the North* (Chicago: University of Chicago Press, 1967), 156–62.

70. South Carolina's 1787 ban on slave imports had little to do with abolitionists or humanitarianism. Instead, it represented efforts by legislators to encourage the payments of taxes and debts by preventing the outflow of specie to slave traders. Lacy K. Ford, *Deliver Us From Evil: The Slavery Question in the Old South* (New York: Oxford University Press, 2009), 82–96.

71. PMS to the LMS, Philad[delphi]a, 18th: 12th: mo: 1788, PMS Minutes 1785–1802, 96–98, quotations from 98, Haverford; PMS LMS, Philadelphia, 19th: day of the 11th Mo: 1789, PMS Minutes, 3:115–17, quotation from 116, Haverford.

72. See especially Richard Newman, "Prelude to the Gag Rule: Southern Reaction to Antislavery Petitions in First Federal Congress," *Journal of the Early Republic* 16 (Winter 1996): 571–99.

73. For discussion of Parker's proposal, see Kenneth Morgan, "Proscription by Degrees: The Ending of the African Slave Trade to the United States," in *Ambiguous Anniversary: The Bicentennial of the International Slave Trade Bans,* ed. David T. Gleeson and Simon Lewis (Columbia: University of South Carolina Press, 2012), 16–17; W. E. B. DuBois, *The Suppression of the African Slave-Trade to the United States of America, 1638–1870* (New York: Longmans, Green, and Co., 1896), 74; Donald L. Robinson, *Slavery in the Structure of American Politics, 1765–1820* (New York: Harcourt Brace Jovanovich, 1971), 299–301; Fehrenbacher, *Slaveholding Republic,* 137–38.

74. At various points in the April and May debates, congressmen made none-too-subtle remarks about sectional bargaining in reaching a compromise about duties on molasses and slaves. In response to the high duty proposed for molasses, George Thatcher of Massachusetts cautioned: "If the pernicious effects of New England rum have been justly lamented, what can be urged for negro slavery? Certainly there is no comparison; but I will avoid the enumeration of its evils, and conclude with a hope that, if the House will not condescend to strike it out, they will reduce it to two cents." *Annals of Congress, First Congress, First Session* (hereafter, *AC [Congress #]-[Session #]*), 224 (28 April 1789). Later, Thomas Tudor of South Carolina hinted, "I may think the duty too high on molasses, and may be disposed to make it five cents, or less, if a reduction is made in other articles" *AC 1–1,* 338 (11 May 1789). The next day the House voted to lower the duty on molasses from six to five cents per gallon, and various proposals indicated that it might be lowered further at a later date. After Parker proposed the $10 duty on slaves, James Jackson of Georgia appealed directly to congressmen "to the eastward [i.e. in New England]"; he knew they viewed the slave trade in an "odious light," but hoped they would help "those who have assisted in lightening their burdens." *AC 1–1,* 349 (14 May 1789). New Englanders then helped defeat the $10 slave duty and the final law further lowered the molasses duty to two and a half cents. "An Act for laying a Duty on Goods, Wares, and Merchandise imported into the United States" (4 July 1789), *US Statues at Large,* I:24–27.

75. PAS Minute Book 1787–1800, 86 (6 7mo 1789), 88 (20 7mo 1789), HSP.

76. PMS Minutes, 3:110 (26 9mo 1789), Haverford.

77. PAS Minute Book 1787–1800, 111 (3 2mo 1790), HSP.

78. New York Meeting for Sufferings Minutes, vol. 1, 233–35 (12 1mo 1790), quotation from 234, 237–38 (9 2mo 1790), Swarthmore College, Swarthmore, PA.

79. The petitions, a timetable, and relevant documents are collected in *Documentary History of the First Federal Congress* (hereafter, *DHFFC*), ed. Kenneth R. Bowling, William Charles diGiacomantonio, and Charlene Bangs Bickford, vol. 8 (*Petitions Histories*) of 26 (Baltimore: Johns Hopkins University Press, 1998), 314–48. Much of the relevant correspondence between abolitionists James and John Pemberton has been reprinted in Bowling, diGiacomantonio, and Bickford, *DHFFC*, vol. 19.

80. Memorial of the Philadelphia Yearly Meeting, October 3, 1789 (presented February 11, 1790), in Bowling, diGiacomantonio, and Bickford, *DHFFC*, 8:322–23.

81. Ibid., 323–24.

82. For the February 11, debates, see *AC 1–2*, 1224–33; Bowling, diGiacomantonio, and Bickford, *DHFFC*, 12:270–92.

83. Memorial of the PAS, 3 February 1790, (presented 12 February 1790), in Bowling, diGiacomantonio, and Bickford, *DHFFC*, 8:324–27. Quaker testimony given before a congressional committee suggests that the PAS's request to "countenance the Restoration of liberty" was not a call for total emancipation (which they knew would never be granted) but recognizing the freedom of Black people whom southern Quakers had manumitted (often in technical violation of state laws). The Quakers complained that manumitted Blacks in North Carolina had been enslaved under "an ex post facto law" and that slaves illegally imported into Virginia were similarly enslaved even though state law "clearly declared [them] free." See "Testimony to the Committee, 15 February 1790," in *DFFC*, 8:324–28. On the North Carolina context see Wood, "A 'Class of Citizens.'"

84. *AC 1–2*, 1239–47 (12 February 1790); Bowling, diGiacomantonio, and Bickford, *DHFFC*, 12:295–313.

85. Robert G. Parkinson, "'Manifest Signs of Passion': The First Federal Congress, Antislavery, and Legacies of the Revolutionary War," in *Contesting Slavery: The Politics of Bondage and Freedom in the New American Nation*, ed. John Craig Hammond and Matthew Mason (Charlottesville: University of Virginia Press, 2012), 49–68.

86. Smith to Edward Rutledge, 13 February 1790, in Bowling, diGiacomantonio, and Bickford, *DHFFC*, 18:511. *AC 1–2*, 1247 (13 February 1790). (In the *Annals*, the vote is mistakenly recorded as 43–14, but the recorded names represent the correct numbers.)

87. Ohline, "Slavery, Economics, and Congressional Politics"; diGiacomantonio, "'For the Gratification of a Volunteering Society': Antislavery and Pressure Group Politics in the First Federal Congress," *Journal of the Early Republic* 15 (Summer 1995): 169–97; Richard Newman, "Prelude to the Gag Rule: Southern Reaction to Antislavery Petitions in First Federal Congress," *Journal of the Early Republic* 16 (Winter 1996): 571–99.

88. John Parrish to Henry Drinker, New York, 2Mo/ 25. 1790, Vaux Family Papers, box 2, Haverford.

89. The Foster committee report is printed in *AC 1–2*, 1465–66 (8 March 1790) and again, with the committee of the whole report (discussed below), on 1523–25 (23 March 1790). Also in Bowling, diGiacomantonio, and Bickford, *DHFFC*, 8:335–36.

90. *AC 1–2*, 1523 (23 March 1790). It should be noted that the House did not vote to replace the special committee's report with that of the committee of the whole (as some

historians assume), but merely to print both. All voting representatives from South Carolina and Georgia voted against the measure, indicating that they opposed both reports. The Upper South and northern states were divided in their votes.

91. PMS to North Carolina Standing Committee, 15: 7mon. 1790 (draft), PMS Miscellaneous Records, 1790:3, Haverford.

92. J[ames] P[emberton] to London Society, Ph[il]ad[elphia]a: 2nd. 4. Mo. 1790, PAS Letter Book, 1:24–26, HSP. See also PAS to London Society, Philad[elphia]a 5 Mo: 3d: 1790, PAS Letter Book, 1:32–35, HSP.

93. PAS to Amis de Noirs, Philadelphia, August 30th, 1790, PAS Letter Book, 1:37–41, HSP.

94. Davis, *Slavery in the Age of Revolution*, 133. Van Cleve describes the PAS's optimism as "inexplicabl[e]" and writes: "While it is understandable that PAS officials were pleased that Congress had debated slavery, judging from its results they appear to have attended a different debate than the one Congress conducted." *Slaveholders' Union*, 202.

95. E.g., Ohline, "Slavery and Congressional Politics," 354; Van Cleve, *Slaveholders' Union*, 202.

96. The exceptions, noted below, are Douglas Bradburn and William diGiamantonio.

97. *AC* 1–2, 1524 (23 March 1790, my emphasis).

98. Congress acted on this commonplace understanding in various laws during the following decades. For example, a 1798 law banning the Atlantic slave trade to the Mississippi Territory freed illegally imported slaves (constitutional because Mississippi was not a state). During the debates over the 1807 law abolishing the slave trade, Congress initially considered freeing illegally imported Africans, but eventually decided to allow the individual states to determine their status. The 1819 Slave Trade Act implemented Congress's ability to free illegally imported Africans.

99. *AC* 1–2, 1504 (17 March 1790); Bowling, diGiacomantonio, and Bickford, *DHFFC*, 12:750–51 (17 March 1790). Alexander White of Virginia viewed the first three resolutions as "unnecessary," as they simply reiterated what was already in the Constitution. Bowling, diGiacomantonio, and Bickford, *DHFFC*, 12:761 (17 March 1790).

100. Ebenezer Hazard to Jeremy Belknap, 5 June 1790, in Bowling, diGiacomantonio, and Bickford, *DHFFC*, 19:711–12.

101. Van Cleve, *Slaveholders' Union*, 194; Wilentz, *No Property in Man*, 160. See also Joseph J. Ellis, *Founding Brothers: The Revolutionary Generation* (New York: Vintage, 2002), 117; Robinson, *Slavery in the Structure of American Politics*, 305. Ohline, "Slavery and Congressional Politics," 346.

102. Ellis, *Founding Brothers*, 117; Robinson, *Slavery in the Structure of American Politics*, 310; Ohline, "Slavery and Congressional Politics," 351. See also Van Cleve, *Slaveholders Union*, 199–200; Newman, "Prelude to the Gag Rule," 596; Wilentz, *No Property in Man*, 160–62; Kaminski, *A Necessary Evil?*, 203.

103. Douglas Bradburn, *The Citizenship Revolution: Politics and the Creation of the American Union, 1774–1804* (Charlottesville: University of Virginia Press, 2009), 248–53, quotation from 249. DiGiacomantonio is another noteworthy exception to the standard historiography. He suggests that the PAS petition overreached in this request, but he also demonstrates the sophistication of the abolitionists' lobbying techniques and

recognizes that the second report preserved the essential features of the first report. DiGiamantonio, "For the Gratification of a Volunteering Society."

104.   The *DHFFC* contains additional debate coverage drawn from numerous newspapers not found in the *Annals of Congress,* along with committee papers and correspondence among politicians and with their constituents.

105.   Bowling, diGiacomantonio, and Bickford, *DHFFC,* 12:779 (18 March 1790). See also 825 (Vining, 22 March 1790).

106.   E.g., the speeches of Elias Boudinot, Theodore Sedgwick, Fisher Ames, George Clymer, and Elbridge Gerry on March 18, 1790: Bowling, diGiacomantonio, and Bickford, *DHFFC,* 12:764, 766–68, 770.

107.   Meanwhile, the element of the third resolution that slaveholding opponents had found most offensive—the expectation that states would provide any regulations that "humanity" required—remained in the final version, representing a victory for the abolitionists. The new version stated "that Congress have no authority to interfere in the emancipation of slaves, or in the treatment of them within any of the States; it remaining with the several States alone to provide any regulations therein, which humanity and true policy may require." *AC 1–2,* 1524 (23 March 1790).

108.   In response to the change, John Pemberton wrote simply, "The second & third provisions of the committee were to be struck out & Madison proposes some lines which were adopted in stead of them." John Pemberton to James Pemberton, New York. 3d mo; 18th. 1790, *DHFFC,* 12:771. See also New York Meeting for Sufferings, vol. 1, 242–43 (9 3mo 1790), 243 (13 4mo 1790), Swarthmore.

109.   Given that two of the three petitions had focused solely on the foreign slave trade, it is surprising that most historians have given little attention to these gains. The main exceptions are Fehrenbacher, *Slaveholding Republic,* 139; Wilentz, *No Property in Man,* 161–62.

110.   The original version had read: "That Congress have also authority to interdict, or (so far as it is or may be carried on by citizens of the United States, for supplying foreigners) to regulate the African trade, and to make provision for the humane treatment of slaves, in all cases while on their passage to the United States, or to foreign ports, so far as it respects the citizens of the United States." The change clarified, but did not affect, the meaning. *AC 1–2,* 1524–25 (23 March 1790).

111.   *AC 1–2,* 1522 (22 March 1790), 1524 (23 March 1790).

112.   E.g., the revised report read "strike out the seventh clause," but made no reference to the sixth. *AC 1–2,* 1524 (23 March 1790).

113.   DuBois correctly shows that the sixth resolution of the special committee report was preserved as the fourth resolution of the committee of the whole House report (*Suppression of the African Slave-Trade,* 80), but Kaminski assumes it was deleted (*A Necessary Evil?,* 229), as does Van Cleve (*Slaveholders' Union,* 200, 340n57).

114.   John Parrish to James Madison, Philadelphia, 5th mo. 28. 1790, Founders Archives, National Archive, http://founders.archives.gov/documents/Madison/01-13-02-0162. See also James Pemberton to Robert Pleasants, 4. mo. 20th. 1790, Robert Pleasants Papers, box 12, Huntington Library (hereafter HL); James Pemberton and the PAS to the Washington [PA] Abolition Society, Philad[elphi]a. 25th. October 1790, PAS Letter Book, 1:49–52, HSP.

115. Warner Mifflin to Members of the House of Representatives, 2nd 6mo 1790, *American Museum* (October 1790), 156–58; Bowling, diGiacomantonio, and Bickford, *DHFFC*, 19:1638.

116. James Pemberton to Robert Pleasants, 4. mo. 20th. 1790, Robert Pleasants Papers, box 12, HL. See also James Pemberton and the PAS to the Washington [PA] Abolition Society, Philad[elphi]a, 25th. October 1790, PAS Letter Book, 1:49–52, HSP.

117. PAS, *Memorials Presented to the Congress of the United States of America [. . .]* (Philadelphia: Francis Bailey, 1792).

118. *Minutes of the Proceedings of a Convention of Delegates from the Abolition Societies Established in Different Parts of the United States, Assembled at Philadelphia* (Philadelphia: Zacharah Poulson Jr., 1794), 28.

119. "An Act to prohibit the carrying on the Slave Trade from the United States to any foreign place or country," *US Statutes at Large* I:347–49 (22 March 1794). It is important to note that this did *not* ban Americans from transporting slaves from Africa or the West Indies *into* the United States, only from transporting them for sale *outside* of the United States. Finkelman mistakenly asserts that the law banned all American participation in the trade as sailors while permitting slave importations into the United States "only on foreign ships with foreign crews." *Supreme Injustice: Slavery in the Nation's Highest Court* (Cambridge, MA: Harvard University Press, 2018), 77, see also 22, 54. Leonard Marquez correctly characterizes the law in *The United States and the Transatlantic Slave Trade to the Americas, 1776–1867* (New Haven, CT: Yale University Press, 2016), 27.

120. PMS to New England Meeting for Sufferings, Philadelphia, 17th: of the 4th: mon. 1794, PMS Minutes, 3:259–61, quotations from 261, Haverford. PAS to London Committee, Philadelphia, 5mo. 6th 1794, PAS Letter Book, 1:111–13, HSP.

121. Seymour Drescher, "Divergent Paths: The Anglo-American Abolitions of the Atlantic Slave Trade," in *Migration, Trade, and Slavery in an Expanding World: Essays in Honor of Pieter Emmer*, ed. Wim Klooster (Leiden: Brill Academic Publishers, 2009), 270.

122. Because many slave traders operated illegally, the data are incomplete, and it is difficult to determine the nationality of some vessels. Between 1787 and 1794, 69 of 76 (90.7 percent) of slaving voyages that began their voyage in mainland North America supplied foreign markets. See "Trans-Atlantic Slave Trade: Database," Slave Voyages, accessed August 11, 2019, https://slavevoyages.org/voyages/qclokuPK.

123. Fehrenbacher, *Slaveholding Republic*, 140–41; Coughtry, *Notorious Triangle*, 212–21; Leonardo Marques, "Slave Trading in a New World: The Strategies of North American Slave Traders in the Age of Abolition," *Journal of the Early Republic* 32 (Summer 2012): 233–60.

124. Lawrence Peskin, *Captives and Countrymen: Barbary Slavery and the American Public, 1785–1816* (Baltimore: Johns Hopkins University Press, 2009); David J. Dzurec, *Our Suffering Brethren: Foreign Captivity and Nationalism in the Early United States* (Amherst: University of Massachusetts Press, 2019).

125. Van Cleve, *Slaveholders' Union*, 53–56, quotation on 46.

126. Leonard Richards emphasizes the role of the three-fifths clause and doughfaces (northerners who voted with the South) in explaining southern influence in national politics, but he concedes that Senate parity was often the more decisive factor. *The*

*Slave Power: The Free North and Southern Domination, 1780–1860* (Baton Rouge: Louisiana State University Press, 2000), 47, 88.

127. Fehrenbacher, *The Slaveholding Republic;* David F. Ericson, *Slavery in the American Republic* (Lawrence: University of Kansas Press, 2011); John Craig Hammond, "Slavery, Sovereignty, and Empires: North American Borderlands and the American Civil War, 1660–1860," *Journal of the Civil War Era* 4 (June 2014): 264–98; Matthew Karp, *This Vast Southern Empire: Slaveholders at the Helm of American Foreign Policy* (Cambridge, MA: Harvard University Press, 2016).

# Federalism on the Frontier

## SECESSION AND LOYALTY IN
## THE TRANS-APPALACHIAN WEST

*Susan Gaunt Stearns*

I N HIS SEMINAL WORK *Original Meanings and the Origins of the Constitution,* Jack Rakove contended that in the 1780s, to "most Americans . . . national politics mattered little." Instead, "When Americans thought about politics at all, they directed their concerns toward local and state issues." The people gave or withheld their loyalty—along with their taxes and their militia service—to the states, and not to the federal government. In return, the states provided, as the Virginia Declaration of Rights termed it, for the "protection, and security of the people, nation, or community." By extension, the national government was of little concern to most Americans. Their experiences as colonists had taught Americans to fear the effects of centralized authority; far better to have immediate, local control over political decision-making.[1] After all, as Rakove points out, for the majority of Americans, the local, and not the national, was the "[level] of governance whose decisions affected their daily lives."[2]

This was emphatically not true in the trans-Appalachian West, where the most pressing local issues fell under the purview of the federal government. There, foreign policy was a key component of everyday affairs. The Euro-American residents of Kentucky and the Tennessee River Valley were surrounded by hostile rivals, both European and Indigenous.[3] To the north lay the powerful remnants of the British empire, which refused to evacuate its troops from the territory south of the Great Lakes that Britain had ceded following the revolution. To the south and to the west, the Spanish colonies of Louisiana and East and West Florida encircled the new settlements in Kentucky and the Tennessee Valley, contesting the United States' claims to sovereignty over the region and controlling westerners' access to markets through control of New Orleans. On all sides, powerful and embattled Indian nations fought to retain the same lands the Euro-Americans hoped to claim. The Articles of Confederation explicitly vested Congress, and not the states, with the power to treat with foreign powers, including Indians, as well as the primary responsibility for military defense. Westerners thus cultivated a unique relationship to the federal government—one that developed along dramatically different lines than did the rest of the nation's. In the words of one early Kentucky attorney, "Congress," and not the Virginia legislature, was "the immediate Sovereign" of settlers in the trans-Appalachian West.[4]

Nowhere was the vexed problem of imperium in imperio more glaring than on the trans-Appalachian frontier, where Congress's lack of executive authority, but nominal control over affairs of defense and foreign relations, consistently placed westerners in opposition to the rest of the nation. Westerners occupied a liminal space, straddling a fine line between statehood and statelessness, between subjects and citizens, dependent on the federal government, yet unable to affect it.[5] Westerners' reliance on the federal government made them nationalists long before the same sentiment was widespread in the East.

This contention is in direct opposition to most of the historical literature on the United States under the Articles of Confederation. Historians have long recognized the crucial role that the West played in the politics of the United States during the "Critical Period." John Fiske began his chapter on the "Germs of National Sovereignty" with a discussion of events in the trans-Appalachian West; almost every historian of the period at least mentions the debates surrounding the cession of western lands as a barrier to the creation of the union and the adoption of the Articles of Confederation.[6] Most historians of the United States under the Articles of Confederation also mention the role that many contemporaries, including Tom Paine, imagined for the lands of the trans-Appalachian West, which were envisioned as a "the fund by which the debt of America would in the course of years be redeemed."[7] Indeed, for many historians, if the Congress of the Confederation had a victory, it was the passage of the

Northwest Ordinance, which (in theory) provided for the future sale and orderly settlement of the territory north of the Ohio River, both offering a pathway to reduce the crushing public debt and creating a truly national domain.[8] The West was the one realm in which "all the thirteen old states had a common interest," as Fiske described it. "Without studying the creation of a national domain between the Alleghanies [sic] and the Mississippi," Fiske reminds us, "we cannot understand how our Federal Union came to be formed."[9]

However, for all the value both historians and contemporaries accorded to western lands, western people have proven far more problematic to account for in narratives of the nation's founding. Few historians today would, along with Fiske, characterize the Anglo-American settlers of the trans-Appalachian West as a "lawless population of 'white trash'" or their "troublesome neighbors" the Cherokee as "bloodthirsty Indians."[10] Yet, despite the enormous growth in studies of the Ohio River Valley, the relationship between the people who occupied those regions and the development of federal authority—particularly with regards to their relationship to the Congress of the Confederation and the creation of the Constitution—has remained understudied.[11] When Anglo-American westerners do appear in the history of the union writ large, it is often as a cautionary tale: the further one traveled from the revolutionary core of the Eastern Seaboard, the weaker the pull of union in the decade following the war. In particular, the two western secession movements, the creation of the state of Franklin in eastern Tennessee in 1784 and the Spanish Conspiracy in Kentucky in 1787–1788, often appear as examples of what historian Douglas Bradburn has called "a centrifugal tendency toward disunion [that] tugged at the boundaries of the country."[12]

This view of the two western secession movements distorts the nature of westerners' relationship to the federal government by conflating what was, in fact, a stark change over time. In 1784, nearly half of the population of Kentucky and the residents of the Washington District of what is now Tennessee supported calls to secede from the states of Virginia and North Carolina, respectively, and form their own, independent states under what one western petition termed "the protecting Arm of the foederal government."[13] In the immediate aftermath of the revolution, westerners hoped that the union would be the protector of their liberties, the defender of their rights to life, liberty, and the pursuit of happiness. By 1787, the long arm of the government no longer looked protective, but instead, threatened an ominous infringement on western liberties. "We have," one Kentucky author lamented in 1787, "no security to barr [sic] [Congress's] terronical [sic] hand or prevent her lawless thirst of domination."[14] The radically different tenor of these two sentiments necessitates rethinking our understanding of the relationship of the trans-Appalachian West with Congress and the federal government. The West was not where the federal government was at its weakest; instead, the West was where it was most necessary.[15] Thus, the West was also the site where the failures of the Congress of the Confederation were most obvious.

Rather than seeing western discontent as arising from a crisis of loyalty, I argue here that we should examine it from the perspective of a crisis of federalism—a fundamental failure of the separation of power between the states and the central government under the Articles of Confederation.[16] In the years prior to the Constitution, the white residents of Kentucky and the Tennessee River Valley found themselves dependent on congressional action to pursue their individual needs, yet the Articles of Confederation were silent on the subject of the relationship between the American people and the national government. Examining western attitudes toward the union in the 1780s presents an alternative view of the Critical Period and of the western secession movements. While westerners' desire for greater local autonomy and anger with state and federal policies toward the Indians and land speculation played a significant role in the rise of western radicalism, ultimately it was westerners' reliance on Congress to meet local needs, and Congress's failure to meet them, that led westerners to abandon their nationalist sentiments, thereby threatening to fracture the nation along the fault line of the Appalachian Mountains.[17]

Between 1775 and 1790, the Euro-American population of the trans-Appalachian West grew from almost nothing to over 100,000 souls, and by the late 1780s, the region's population was increasing rapidly as thousands of new residents arrived every year.[18] Both poor farmers and ambitious land speculators were drawn to the West by the lure of rich and cheap lands. In Kentucky, the bulk of these settlers lived in the rapidly expanding settlements of the Bluegrass region, or else at the Falls of the Ohio near what would become the city of Louisville. The various Kentucky counties fell under the governance of the Virginia legislature in Richmond, some five hundred miles away. To the south of Kentucky lay North Carolina's western settlements along the Cumberland River at what is now the city of Nashville, and the older, more established communities along the Holston and Nolichucky Rivers in eastern Tennessee. The Holston Valley settlers had proven their usefulness during the revolution at the Battle of King's Mountain in October 1780, where they had inflicted heavy casualties on Loyalist militia. They had been joined in the fight by residents of Washington County, Virginia, in the far southwestern corner of the state, near where the Cumberland Gap formed the only overland route connecting the western settlements to the parent states. In 1777, North Carolina designated its western settlements as Washington County.[19] It was in these new western communities, many of which had formed only within the previous decade, that western separatist movements arose.

Residents who judged the West by its political actions in the early 1780s would have been surprised by the animosity toward the federal government that emerged later in the decade. From 1780 to 1785, Kentuckians had dispatched a flurry of petitions to Congress. The political rhetoric adopted by the petitions of the citizens settled along what were known as the "western waters"—the rivers that flowed westward into the Mississippi River and ultimately into the Gulf of Mexico, instead of into the Atlantic Ocean—evinced a strong regard for the Continental Congress and the importance of the broader political union.[20] These petitions received new ammunition in 1784, when Congress and Virginia finally settled on the terms by which Virginia would transfer its claims to the territory north of the Ohio River to Congress. In response to the cession, Congress passed the Ordinance of 1784 to provide a plan of governance for the new public domain. Congress resolved that all those who chose to move to the "territory ceded or to be ceded" to the federal government had the right to create their own provisional elected government; when the population reached 20,000, the territory was eligible to apply to join the states "on an equal footing with the . . . original states," but as under the Articles of Confederation, the consent of nine states was necessary for a new state to join.[21]

The passage of the Ordinance of 1784 and its implied governmental approval for the creation of new states led to a renewed influx of petitions to Congress from Kentucky and Western Virginia, petitions that clearly emphasize westerners' affection for the federal union. Adopting the flowery language and hyperbole typical of petitions, westerners described themselves as protonationalists. Declaring themselves to be the "first occupants and aborigines of this Country; freemen claiming natural rights and the privileges of American Citizens," the citizens of Washington County (VA) repeatedly emphasized their loyalty to the national union, not to the state of Virginia.[22] Resolving that "it is the duty of every American citizen to entertain a sacred regard for the principles of the continental Union," the residents of Washington vowed to "ever display an ardent zeal for those generous principles of union, and be ready to resign all partial considerations of private interest or the interest of particular States when they would undermine the interests of the confederacy, and endanger the glorious priviledges [sic], which the Confederacy is designed to defend and preserve."[23] That same year, the settlers of Kentucky followed suit in a petition to the Virginia legislature, impressing on the legislature that a "connexion" between Kentucky and "any Community beyond the Apulachian [sic] Mountains, other than the Federal Union" had always been "irreconcileable" with the principles of justice and "free Government."[24] Part of their desire for a separate state was, westerners claimed, created by their high regard for Congress as the protector of the values of the revolution and of the rights and liberties of the American people. Throughout their petitions, westerners purported the highest regard for the wisdom of the United States in Congress assembled and were confident that "plans of Congress," and not those of the states of North Carolina or Virginia, were "the best, tending to benefit all alike."[25]

Westerners went so far as to contend that their faith in Congress made them better Americans than their cis-Appalachian cousins. "Instead of disregarding the authority of that august body, or treating their requisitions with contempt; the western people looks up to them with reverence, as the faithful arbiters of the rights and interests of all component parts of the empire."[26] In short, westerners were citizens not of Virginia or North Carolina, but of the "United States of America at Large."[27]

Congress's western petitioners were clearly following the long-standing tropes of the petition genre, which required petitioners to describe themselves as helpless supplicants and loyal adherents of a superior political entity. Until 1776, American colonists were used to addressing the king as the object of their allegiance and the ultimate source of their hopes for protection. The western petitioners adopted the same tone of subservience that had characterized prerevolutionary petitions, yet with a new revolutionary flair that emphasized their position as good republican citizens. Yet in choosing to appeal to Congress, as opposed to the state governments, westerners were demonstrating how they understood their relationship to the union. Unlike in the East, where the state legislature might reasonably be expected to resolve the issues confronting their citizens, westerners understood Congress as the nation's supreme ruling body long before the Constitution enshrined it as such. In the very act of addressing their petitions, westerners elevated Congress over the state legislatures as the ultimate protector of their rights.[28]

Despite this appeal to the principles of union, westerners were strongly in favor of a federal—not consolidated—government. Indeed, one of their primary concerns in seeking a separation was to obtain greater local autonomy in the face of distant state governments.[29] Part of the problem was the sheer distance and rugged geography that separated westerners from the state governments. The distance from Kentucky, or even Washington County, to the Virginia state capital at Richmond produced nearly intolerable difficulties. Kentuckians complained that "our sequestered situation, from the seat of Government, with the intervention of a mountainous desart [sic] of two hundred miles, always dangerous, and passable only at particular seasons, precludes every Idea of a conexxion [sic], on Republican principles" with the state government in the East.[30] For those settled in North Carolina's western districts, the situation was, if anything, worse: the only way to travel to the Tennessee River Valley communities from North Carolina was by venturing through Virginia. Consequently, the Washingtonians came to believe that "our local situation is such that we not only apprehend we should be separated from

North Carolina, But almost every sensible disinterested traveler has declared it incompatible with our Interest to belong in Union with the Eastern part of the State, For we are not only far removed from the Eastern parts of North Carolina, But separated from them by high & almost impasable [sic] Mountains, which Naturally divide us from them."[31]

While distance and the difficulty of travel were real problems, both Kentuckians and their southern neighbors sought a separation primarily in order to protect their own interests. Whatever state claimed the land possessed the ability to dispose of it, and for both Virginia and North Carolina, western lands constituted their only real asset in the face of their crushing revolutionary debts. Both states repeatedly passed laws that benefited some groups more than others: the North Carolina "Land Grab Act" of 1783, for instance, placed four million acres of western lands up for sale, the vast majority of which ended up in the hands of speculators, many of whom were government officials.[32] Those who had actually settled in the West, unable to capitalize on the legislatures' actions, resented the lack of local control over the distribution of land, a resentment that was especially strong among the social and political elites of western society. Creating a separate state would, they believed, allow greater local autonomy over land distribution.[33] Widespread anger over the Land Grab Act, and over Virginia's Land Law of 1779, spurred western opposition to the state governments. It was acts like these that would ultimately lead the residents of the Holston River settlements to declare that not only was their "Interest . . . in many respects distinct from the inhabitants on the other Side," but that they were "much injured by a Union with" the eastern part of the state.[34]

Isolated geographically, westerners felt disconnected from their parent states. In the case of the most famous western secession movement, the creation of the state of Franklin in 1784, this was literally true. In April 1784, North Carolina, driven by a desire to lessen the state's share of the federal debt (which would be assessed based on territory), had followed Virginia's example and agreed to cede its claims to western lands. The North Carolina Act of Cession transferred control of the district to Congress, leaving those already settled in Tennessee in a quandary. If they were no longer part of North Carolina, yet they had not yet been accepted by Congress, then what was their political status? Although North Carolina quickly and abruptly reversed its decision to cede the western district two months later, the damage to political relations between the two regions was already done. Some western residents argued that by ceding its westernmost residents, North Carolina had thrown them into a state of nature. In August 1784, representatives from North Carolina's three western counties of Washington, Sullivan, and Greene, met to create their own, independent state that would join the federal union under the terms of the Ordinance of 1784. They named their new entity "the State of Franklin."[35]

In April 1785, Governor Alexander Martin of North Carolina denounced the secession, calling the new government a "self-created power and authority unknown to the Constitution of the State," "a mock Government, without the essentials, the shadow without the substance," whose supporters had betrayed the "national pride in all Kingdoms and State that inspires every Subject and citizen," a pride that was "the grand cement and support of every Government."[36] (Martin meant the nation of North Carolina, not the broader American nation.) Franklinites, in contrast, viewed their relationship to the state in a dramatically different light. In a widely circulated defense of the creation of the new state, a Franklinite styling himself Freelander described the conflict of federalism that the ceded westerners faced. North Carolina had relinquished not only its lands but also its citizens to the federal government. The state legislature now claimed "that although the state had ceded its western territory, yet she by no means had relinquished her sovereignty and jurisdiction" over her former citizens. Such a situation struck the Freelander as preposterous. It was "a curious phenomenon," Freelander pointed out, if "in a free country, the lands to belong to one power, and the inhabitants of the same lands to another."[37] Such a system would, in the eyes of yet another western statehood petition, render every westerner "a tenant and not a landlord, a vassal and not a freeman," a subject and not a citizen.[38]

As soon as the Franklinites declared their independence, they dispatched a representative to Congress to appeal for admission to the union. This petition, like all the others Congress received from the residents of the trans-Appalachian West, placed Congress in a difficult situation. The Articles of Confederation granted Congress the ability to adjudicate "in all disputes and differences now subsisting or that hereafter may arise between two or more States concerning boundary, jurisdiction or any other causes whatever"; they did not give Congress the authority to intervene in conflicts that occurred between a state's government and its populace.[39] During the revolution, the residents of Vermont repeatedly tested this resolve, but Congress ultimately refused to admit them into the union, arguing that Congress lacked the authority to destroy the territorial integrity of one of its component states.[40] As representatives of the states, congressional delegates were wary of infringing on any state's sovereignty. Moreover, it was not clear to them that they had the right to do so.

Western secession movements also placed Congress in another quandary. Did the Articles of Confederation even give the people the right to petition for a separate state? Congress was convinced that the articles did not; only the state legislatures could give permission for westerners to create states. By appealing to Congress for separate statehood, westerners had hoped to gain greater local autonomy from the distant state legislatures, ironically by becoming subject to an even more distant federal power. However, the failure of western statehood movements, none of which were successful under the Articles of Confederation, left westerners in a particularly vulnerable condition. On the one hand, settlers had already demonstrated the inability of the states to secure their obedience and loyalty, preferring to offer it to Congress; on the other hand, Congress had done little to earn their devotion.

Westerners' position at the interstices of state and federal sovereignty placed them in a dangerous situation. Throughout the decades following the American Revolution, the single most important factor affecting daily life in the trans-Appalachian West was violence. While Cornwallis's surrender at Yorktown and the subsequent signing of the Treaty of Paris in 1783 brought about an end to fighting along the Atlantic seaboard, warfare continued in the continental interior. Tides of violence ebbed and flowed across the region regularly. Anglo-American settlers and various Indian groups (e.g., Shawnee, Delaware, Creek, Cherokee, Chickasaw, Miami, Wabash) engaged in a near-genocidal conflict for control of the Ohio Valley. One 1782 estimate, almost certainly inflated to cast Kentucky's residents as particularly distressed, claimed that, in the preceding six years,

860 settlers of a single Kentucky county had been killed. According to another contemporary estimate, from 1783 to 1787, 300 settlers on the Kentucky frontier lost their lives; another 50 were taken captive; and over 2,000 horses, valued in excess of 20,000 dollars, were stolen by Indians from north of the Ohio River.[41] Although both of these accounts were exaggerated, violence and potential violence remained central facts of everyday life.

Nor, by any means, were Native Americans the only perpetrators of frontier violence, which was overwhelmingly in response to American efforts to dispossess native peoples of their lands. Whites regularly perpetrated acts of violence without immediate provocation: in March 1781, John Sevier, the future governor of Franklin, led a party of volunteers in a surprise attack on the Cherokee village of Tuskasegee; in 1782, 160 members of the Pennsylvania militia slaughtered over a hundred Delaware and Mohican converts to Moravianism who had been engaged in peacefully gathering corn.[42] Anglo-American militia and western settlers more broadly often failed to distinguish between friendly and enemy Indian peoples; in 1786, the council of Lincoln County, Kentucky, issued the Upper Cherokee a scant "apology" for its militia, which in February of that year had attacked a party of the Upper Cherokee while in pursuit of a Chickamauga war party, arguing that the militia's actions were "purely accidental, [as] it was impossible to distinguish" between the members of the two groups. Moreover, the council went a step further, warning the Upper Cherokee that if they failed to restrain the Chickamauga (who, though Cherokee, were politically distinct from the Upper Cherokee), "the blood which may be shed in our taking an indiscriminate revenge must lie on their own Heads."[43]

Frontier violence revealed a stark problem in the nature of the divided sovereignty created by the Articles of Confederation. The articles granted Congress the "sole and exclusive right and power of determining on war." However, declaring war on the frontier was one exception to Congress's exclusive right: the articles provided that if a state "be actually invaded by enemies . . . and the danger is so imminent as not to admit of a delay till the United States in Congress assembled can be consulted," then the state could mobilize its militia to fight against the invading enemy.[44] Ironically for westerners, the uncertainty created by this dual obligation for defense left them unprotected. Both Kentucky and the settlements claimed by North Carolina maintained militia that were ultimately controlled by the state assemblies in Richmond and Hillsborough, respectively, which possessed the power of the purse. Western militia leaders needed permission from the governor before any extensive expedition could be mounted; there was no guarantee before departing on militia service that the state would decide to pay for it. Given it took well over a month to make the round trip journey from Kentucky to Richmond, or even longer to travel from the Cumberland region to Hillsborough, westerners grew continuously frustrated as their ability to respond to immediate dangers was hampered by the necessity of obtaining permission from the East. To protect themselves and their families, westerners wanted an army, not a militia, and the army fell under the purview of Congress.

In June 1784, in response to western violence, James Monroe of Virginia proposed that Congress immediately dispatch 350 men to protect the frontier, with another 700 to be raised in the next several months. His proposal was met with suspicion. The end of the revolution had diminished the necessity of maintaining an expensive and unruly army, and many in Congress were opposed to creating a new one.[45] Elbridge Gerry of Massachusetts questioned whether, now that the revolution was over, Congress even possessed the right to requisition troops from the states. The nation was, Gerry believed, in a time of peace. If Congress required the states to send troops to protect the frontier, it would be creating a standing army, which would be "inconsistent with the principles of republican Governments, dangerous to the liberties of a free people, and generally converted into detestable destructive engines for establishing despotism."[46] Effectively, Gerry argued that forcing the states to protect the frontier threatened the safety of the states themselves. Gerry suggested that, rather than requisition troops, Congress should recommend to the states that troops be provided. The measure was adopted.

Congress's decision that the threat to states' liberties posed by a standing army outweighed the ongoing threat to the lives of westerners reveals the liminal position that westerners held in the union. In evaluating whether to require the states to send troops to the frontier, Congress was essentially pondering whether attacks on North Carolina's and Virginia's westernmost citizens constituted an attack on the nation at large. To Gerry, clearly they did not. From the safety of Philadelphia, the nation was at peace. Such a vision of the nation was only true, however, if it did not include the West.

The debates surrounding expanding the army portended the troops' eventual ineffectiveness. Recommending troops instead of requiring them proved a dismal failure as a method of defense. The regiment raised in Connecticut, for instance, did not arrive at Fort Pitt—present-day Pittsburgh—still hundreds of miles upriver from the Kentucky and Ohio frontiers—until October 1785, more than a year after Congress had called for its creation; no federal troops were ever dispatched to Franklin, where the new state government launched a particularly brutal war against the Cherokee.[47] Even as federal troops trickled into the West, it became clear to western settlers that the federal government could not meet the need for protection. Three hundred and fifty men could never have protected five hundred miles of frontier. Moreover, the federal troops were charged not only with protecting the frontier, but also with preventing "unwarrantable intrusions on lands belonging to the United States."[48] The soldiers proved far better at removing squatters from federal land than they did at deterring Indian attacks. Most western settlers ultimately recognized that the federal troops were useless. As Harry Innes, Kentucky's first attorney general, saw it, congressional troops provided only the "specious appearance of protection," rather than the safety Kentuckians believed they deserved from the union.[49] Innes' assessment appears right on: in March 1786, Captain Walter Finney, commander of the federal troops at the mouth of the Miami River, wrote to General George Rogers Clark of Kentucky requesting the militia be called up to help protect the troops.[50] Clearly, the federal government was incapable of—or, more ominously, to many western settlers—unwilling to protect the western frontier.

In 1786, some westerners once more began threatening secession; but this time, it was secession not just from their parent-states but from the union entirely. The cause of the rupture was treaty negotiations between the United States and the crown of Spain.[51] At the heart of the negotiations were two concerns: trade and the status of the Mississippi River. In

1784, alarmed by the United States' rapid expansion and frustrated by the terms of the Treaty of Paris, Spain closed the Mississippi River to American trade as an opening gambit in negotiations for a commercial treaty between the two nations. The move cut to the heart of the financial prospects of the trans-Appalachian West.

The Mississippi River was the "key to the . . . western continent," as every westerner knew.[52] Between western settlers and the rest of the nation lay two hundred miles of rugged, heavily forested mountains that made it impossible for westerners to transport the bulky produce of their farms to eastern markets. The simplest outlet for goods produced in the trans-Appalachian West was to send them down the Ohio River or one of its many tributaries to its confluence with the Mississippi; from there, goods traveled downriver through Spanish territory to the port of New Orleans, where vessels involved in the "coasting" trade carried the produce to Atlantic world markets. The Mississippi was thus the chief pathway by which westerners could hope to prosper from their lands; as one writer in the *Kentucke Gazette* summarized, without "an unrestrained use of the Mississippi," Kentucky would always be "poor and oppressed."[53]

Unfortunately for westerners, New England's prosperity depended far more on relations with Spain than it did on relations with the trans-Appalachian West. At the end of the revolution, Britain refused American ships access to its colonial ports, plunging the commercial ports of New England and the mid-Atlantic into a recession. Ships and sailors sat idle, and stevedores had little to do as the United States worked to negotiate trade arrangements that would give them access to new ports. Spain, in particular, was an attractive trade partner to American shippers. Not only did Spain's colonies in the Caribbean rely on food imports, continental Spain's Catholic population ate fish on Fridays and for the forty days of lent. New England merchants hoped that any treaty would provide them with the ability to make sure that the fish that the Spanish ate were New England cod.

The negotiations between Don Diego de Gardoqui, the Spanish minister plenipotentiary, and John Jay, the U.S. secretary of foreign affairs, lasted from spring 1785 until summer 1786, when Jay reported to Congress that the two parties had reached a stalemate. Jay proposed a compromise:

rather than insist on an American right to navigate the Mississippi, the United States should offer to *forbear* using the river for a period of twenty or thirty years. Driven largely by delegates from the northern states who were eager to gain trade concessions, Congress agreed to Jay's idea.[54]

Congress's agreement to cede the Mississippi River shattered the already-frayed social contract that had loosely tied the Anglo-American settlers of the trans-Appalachian West to Congress and the eastern states, thereby severing the bonds of union and destroying westerners' loyalty to the broader concept of nationhood. Although the treaty was never ratified, Congress had acted in direct opposition to the West's interests: it had failed to protect their right—as they conceived it—to the "pursuit of happiness." Whereas in 1784 westerners had described the state governments as tyrants, they now used the same language to refer to the federal government. A convention held in Kentucky declared unanimously that the negotiations were "subversive of justice[,] good faith, and the great foundations of moral rectitude, and particularly of the principles which gave birth to the late revolution."[55] More dangerously for American federalism, they were "strongly repugnant to all confidence in the foederal [sic] government, and destructive to its peace, safety, happiness and duration."[56] Another western voice concurred: Congress had violated the obligations that tied westerners to the union, and in the process, it had abandoned America's republican principles. If Congress could cede away western prosperity, what was to stop it from going even further and stretching "her [sic] arbitrary hand to private property and upon the same principle of reasoning from one usurpation to another reduce us to a state of Vassalage."[57]

As the nation had proved in 1776, there was only one appropriate reaction to tyranny. The "Spanish Conspiracy" of the trans-Appalachian West comprised efforts on the part of western elite—and Spanish officials in New York and Louisiana—to sever the West from the nation and create a separate western state. Congress's inability to reopen the Mississippi had convinced many westerners that aligning themselves with Spain represented their best course for obtaining river trade; by becoming vassals of a distant foreign power, they hoped that they could overcome the difficulties they faced as part of a republic closer at hand. The most famous of these attempts was James Wilkinson's 1787 journey to New Orleans, but

Wilkinson was hardly alone in establishing relations with Spanish officials in the aftermath of the Jay-Gardoqui negotiations.[58] In New York,
John Brown of Kentucky, the West's first and only congressional delegate
to serve under the Articles of Confederation, and North Carolinian James
White, who himself had speculated heavily in Tennessee Valley lands,
both met repeatedly with Gardoqui, while in Kentucky, numerous members of the elite, including Harry Innes, contemplated secession. In the
final days of the state of Franklin, John Sevier, the governor, met with
White and dispatched his son, James Sevier, to speak to Gardoqui. While
each of these movements was motivated by unique circumstances, they
all occurred in the broader context of the West's gradual disillusionment
with the prospects of nationalism.[59]

Across the West, a widespread sense of betrayal came to permeate
westerners' interactions with the federal government. The same day that
the Constitutional Convention concluded its work and submitted its new
plan for a "more perfect union" to the states, a convention met in Danville, Kentucky, proposing secession from Virginia and the creation of an
independent western state. Unlike movements for statehood in 1784, by
1787, the Virginia legislature had repeatedly given westerners permission
to form their own state, provided that Congress was willing to admit the
new state to the union, but in light of Congress's failure to protect the
frontier and its willingness to sacrifice Mississippi trade, some Kentuckians were no longer sure they wanted to become one of the "united" states.
The petition that Kentucky's statehood convention sent to Congress
threatened the real possibility of westerners severing their ties not only
with Virginia, but with Congress as well. The threat was subtle but nonetheless potent: "If we be unsuccessful in this application" for independent
statehood, the convention warned, "we shall not consider ourselves in
any manner answerable for the future conduct of our constituents."[60]

Given the difficulties the West faced under the Articles of Confederation, western opposition to the Constitution and to strengthening the
union is at first glance surprising. Georgia, which was poised on the brink
of war with the Creek in 1787, ratified the Constitution immediately in
the hopes of securing military aid. In the area surrounding Fort Pitt, a
convention of western Pennsylvanians, who were nearly as dependent

on the navigation of the Mississippi as Kentuckians and Tennessee River Valley residents, determined "that of all people it becomes us of the western country more especially to desire an object of this kind, as from the weakness of Congress to take proper measures with the courts of Spain and Britain, we are on the one hand deprived of the advantages of the Missisippi trade, which is our natural right, and on the other, are liable to the incursions of the savages ."[61] Although by 1789, the state of Franklin had collapsed, western resentment lingered. Congress had proven unable to resolve the thorny problems of land distribution, endemic warfare, and Mississippi River trade. Both in Kentucky and in North Carolina's western districts, opposition to the Constitution was widespread.

In reacting to the Constitution, westerners drew a clear line between themselves and their eastern brethren. The Constitution struck "immediately at the happiness & greatness of the Western Country." While there were "many Objections thrown Out against [the Constitution] which are of a general Nature and affect the interests of the States at large," there were also "Others of a local Nature" that were threatening to westerners alone.[62] Kentuckians were convinced, one western reporter recorded, that "in case of a new govt. the Navigation of the Mississippi would infalliably [sic] be given up."[63] Virginia's antifederalists were well aware of the western fears and used them to convince Kentucky's fourteen delegates to vote against adopting the Constitution. At the ratifying Convention, Patrick Henry, Virginia's most vocal opponent of the Constitution, stressed repeatedly the dangers that the new Constitution posed for Kentuckians. Calling the Constitution "that fatal policy," Henry warned the convention that adopting the Constitution would essentially sever the bonds between the eastern half of the state and the Kentuckians. Mississippi navigation was "necessary to [the West's] very existence," Henry contended, but the Constitution would make it easier for eastern interests to cede the river. Within the new union, the West would never be more than a "contemptible minority," unable to protect its interests against the more numerous states of the East.[64] Thus, even if Kentuckians could enter the union, their problems with federalism would persist. Power would remain firmly vested in eastern hands.

Henry's words struck a powerful chord with westerners; Harry Innes informed John Brown that he was "certain . . . that if the Constitution is adopted . . . that we shall be mere vassals of Congress." "The consequences" for Kentucky of the ratification of the Constitution, he concluded, "are horrible & dreadful."[65] On such terms, separation seemed preferable to subjugation.

In 1784, the West had looked to congress as the "dernier" (last) force, the ultimate arbiter and protector of their rights, but by 1787, westerners had come to regard it as inimical to their interests and dangerous to their liberties. Throughout the 1780s, there was a growing sense in both the West and the East that western "interests and the interests of the Eastern states are so diametrically opposite to each other" that a union between the two hardly seemed tenable.[66] Rufus King of Massachusetts believed as early at 1786, and was "every day more confirmed in the opinion[,] that no paper engagements, or stipulations, can be formed which will insure a desirable connection between the Atlantic States and those which will be erected [on the other side] of the Apalachian or Alleghany Mountains. . . . The pursuits and interests of the people on the two sides," King concluded, "will be so different, and probably so opposite, that an entire separation must eventually ensue."[67] However, King believed that the inevitable separation was hardly a matter for despair. Nor was it the result of treasonous or disloyal behavior on the part of westerners. Instead, the ensuing disunion would result because there was nothing to bind the two halves of the nation together. The bonds of union could stretch just so far, but no further.

Thus, when James Madison wrote of the advantages of a large republic over a small republic in *Federalist*, no. 10, his analysis flew in the face of the experience of the nation during the previous five years. While dissent and disorder had been problems throughout the states, it was along the nation's far-flung edges that the bonds of union had come closest to dissolving. Yet this was not due, as the petitions for statehood of 1784 and 1785 demonstrate, to a lack of patriotism on the frontier. Nor was did it result from a gradual weakening of Congress's authority with distance from the capital. Instead, the conflict arose because westerners' vision of union exceeded that of even the most nationally minded of the founding fathers. They came to recognize far earlier than most that the collective survival of the union depended on concerted action; certainly, theirs did. By the time the rest of the nation came to believe the same, westerners' willingness to wait had already ended. They were determined to not need a nation that had already demonstrated that it did not need them.

The ideological basis for federalism—the division of sovereignty between states and the federal government, and the distribution of particular powers between the two—faced its greatest threat in the trans-Appalachian West, where unique problems, like frontier warfare and Spain's closure of the Mississippi, challenged the effectiveness of American claims to sovereignty over the region. In 1784, the desire to obtain greater local autonomy led the Franklinites to embrace the federal government as the source of independent statehood, but Congress's unwillingness to allow a separation left a vacuum of effective authority on the frontier. The ongoing violence of frontier warfare exacerbated the problem, demonstrating the weakness of both the state governments and Congress and leading to increasing western resentment of both. Thus, in 1786, when Congress agreed to exchange western access to the Mississippi River—and with it, westerners' best hope for future prosperity—for trade concessions with Spain, westerners' resentment grew to new bounds. The Spanish Conspiracy can thus be viewed as an attempt, on the part of some elite western settlers, to claim for themselves the local autonomy they had been clamoring for since the end of the revolution.

The ratification of the Constitution did not make the West any less dependent on the federal government than it had been during the 1780s, nor did its passage suddenly reconcile westerners to being subject to distant authorities.[68] Indian policy and foreign treaties remained constant points of contention between westerners and the newly constituted federal government. Ironically, it was in the West, far from the new capitals at New York, Philadelphia, and Washington, that the federal government continued to have the greatest influence over its citizens' day-to-day lives. Although arguments in favor of a western separation remained politically potent in the West throughout the 1790s, the crisis of the 1780s had passed. In part, the change occurred as westerners gradually gained a greater voice in national politics. The advent of Kentucky and Tennessee statehoods in 1792 and 1796 gave westerners a continuous voice within the federal government; Washington's shrewd decision to appoint many western elites who had previously opposed centralized authority to positions of authority in his new administration also helped to quiet western discontent.[69] The army's defeat of the northwest Indians at the Battle of Fallen Timbers in 1794, and the influx of cash that accompanied the army's deployment in the region, along with the 1795 ratification of Pinckney's Treaty (which reopened the Mississippi) went a long way toward reconciling westerners with the new government.[70] Moreover, the advent of the new political regime resolved the problem of sovereignty the West had faced under the Articles of Confederation. While the resultant union was by no means "perfect," it did ultimately accomplish what westerners had urged since 1784: it made all citizens into "one people in a national view"—a view that might just as easily face east as west.[71]

## Notes

1. The elevation of the local over the national was profound; Woody Holton has demonstrated that New Englanders in the 1780s believed "true sovereignty lay in the towns"; Woody Holton, "An 'Excess of Democracy'—or a Shortage? The Federalists' Earliest Adversaries," *Journal of the Early Republic* 25, no. 3 (October 2005): 346.

2. Jack N. Rakove, *Original Meanings: Politics and Ideas in the Making of the Constitution* (New York: Knopf, 1996), 28–29.

3. Historian François Furstenberg calls the period from 1754 to 1815 the "long war for the American West." Throughout the eighteenth century, there was intense competition between Britain, France, Spain, and Indian peoples for control of the Ohio River Valley. See François Furstenberg, "The Significance of the Trans-Appalachian Frontier in Atlantic History," *American Historical Review* 113, no. 3 (June 2008): 650; Eric Hinderaker, *Elusive Empires: Constructing Colonialism in the Ohio Valley, 1673–1800* (New York: Cambridge University Press, 1997). Determining what to call the various Euro-American communities that fall within what would eventually become known as Kentucky and Tennessee is challenging. Euro-American occupation of what would become Kentucky began in 1775; by 1776, Virginia created Kentucky County to include several communities forming south of the Ohio River on land claimed by Virginia. In the Tennessee Valley, Euro-American settlement began in 1769 with the formation of a settlement along the Watauga River in what is now eastern Tennessee. In 1776, these communities petitioned North Carolina for recognition as Washington County; in 1779, Euro-American occupation of the Cumberland Basin, centered around Fort

Nashborough, began. In this essay, when I refer to "Kentuckians," I mean Euro-Americans living within the boundaries created by Kentucky County; I will refer to the residents of the Tennessee River Valley as either "residents of Washington County" or as "Franklinites." On Kentucky, see Craig Thompson Friend, *Kentucke's Frontiers: A History of the Trans-Appalachian Frontier* (Bloomington: Indiana University Press, 2010), 75; on the Tennessee River Valley, see Kevin T. Barksdale, *The Lost State of Franklin: America's First Secession* (Lexington: University Press of Kentucky, 2009), 18–20; John R. Finger, *Tennessee Frontiers: Three Regions in Transition* (Bloomington: Indiana University Press, 2001), 77–80.

4. Daniel Walker to Benjamin Harrison V, January 19, 1784, in *Calendar of Virginia State Papers and Other Manuscripts . . . Preserved in the Capitol at Richmond: 1782–1784; 1782–1784,* ed. William P. Palmer (Richmond, VA, 1883), 3:555.

5. Douglas Bradburn makes the distinction between a citizen, who is part of a compact, and a subject—a "feudal status of perpetual allegiance and inferiority." *The Citizenship Revolution: Politics and the Creation of the American Union, 1774–1804* (Charlottesville: University of Virginia Press, 2009), 11.

6. Merrill Jensen, *The New Nation: A History of the United States During the Confederation, 1781–1789* (New York: Knopf, 1962), 25–27; Jack N. Rakove, "Ambiguous Achievement: The Northwest Ordinance," ed. Frederick D. Williams, *The Northwest Ordinance: Essays on Its Formulation, Provisions, and Legacy* (East Lansing: Michigan State University Press, 1989), 9; Peter S. Onuf, *The Origins of the Federal Republic: Jurisdictional Controversies in the United States, 1775–1787* (Philadelphia: University of Pennsylvania Press, 1983), 75–102; George Van Cleve, *We Have Not a Government: The Articles of Confederation and the Road to the Constitution* (Chicago: University of Chicago Press, 2017), 138–39; Alan Taylor, *American Revolutions: A Continental History, 1750–1804* (New York: Norton, 2016), 337–39.

7. Thomas Paine, "The Public Good," in *The Works of Thomas Paine* (Philadelphia, 1797), 1:232.

8. Carol Berkin, in her popular account of the drafting of the Constitution, states that "the Northwest Ordinances . . . were, without question, the government's finest peacetime accomplishment." Carol Berkin, *A Brilliant Solution: Inventing the American Constitution* (New York: Harcourt, 2002), 23.

9. John Fiske, *The Critical Period of American History, 1783–1789* (Cambridge, MA, 1888), 188.

10. Fiske, *The Critical Period of American History,* 199, 30.

11. Numerous books on the United States under the Articles of Confederation discuss westerners briefly—but rarely for more than a few pages out of several hundred. Some, like Gordon S. Wood, ignore them completely. Wood, *The Creation of the American Republic, 1776–1787* (New York: Norton, 1993); Woody Holton, *Unruly Americans and the Origins of the Constitution* (New York: Hill and Wang, 2007); David C. Hendrickson, *Peace Pact: The Lost World of the American Founding* (Lawrence: University Press of Kansas, 2003). Notable exceptions include Eli Merritt, "Sectional Conflict and Secret Compromise: The Mississippi River Question and the United States Constitution," *American Journal of Legal History* 35, no. 2 (April 1991): 117–71; Onuf, *Origins of the Federal Republic;* Patrick Griffin, *American Leviathan: Empire, Nation, and*

*Revolutionary Frontier* (New York: Hill and Wang, 2008); Gregory Ablavsky, "The Savage Constitution," *Duke Law Journal* 63 (2014): 1000–1089; William H. Bergmann, *The American National State and the Early West* (New York: Cambridge University Press, 2012); John Robert Van Atta, *Securing the West: Politics, Public Lands, and the Fate of the Old Republic, 1785–1850* (Baltimore: Johns Hopkins University Press, 2014). At the same time, there are numerous books that focus on the region yet engage rarely with the question of the concurrent national development. On Kentucky, see Stephen Aron, *How the West Was Lost: The Transformation of Kentucky from Daniel Boone to Henry Clay* (Baltimore: Johns Hopkins University Press, 1996); Patricia Watlington, *The Partisan Spirit: Kentucky Politics, 1779–1792* (New York: Atheneum, 1972); Friend, *Kentucke's Frontiers;* Ellen Eslinger, *Citizens of Zion: The Social Origins of Camp Meeting Revivalism* (Knoxville: University of Tennessee Press, 1999); Elizabeth Ann Perkins, *Border Life: Experience and Perception in the Revolutionary Ohio Valley* (Chapel Hill: University of North Carolina, 1998); Honor Sachs, *Home Rule: Households, Manhood, and National Expansion on the Eighteenth-Century Kentucky Frontier* (New Haven, CT: Yale University Press, 2015); Barksdale, *Lost State of Franklin,* 2009; Kristofer Ray, *Middle Tennessee, 1775–1825: Progress and Popular Democracy on the Southwestern Frontier* (Knoxville: University of Tennessee Press, 2007); Finger, *Tennessee Frontiers.*

12. Bradburn, *Citizenship Revolution,* 64–65; James E. Lewis, *The Burr Conspiracy: Uncovering the Story of an Early American Crisis* (Princeton, NJ: Princeton University Press, 2017).

13. On the population of Kentucky that supported a congressional claim, see Watlington, *Partisan Spirit,* 52–53, especially n65; on Tennessee, see Robert Ewing Corlew, Stanley John Folmsbee, and Enoch L. Mitchell, *Tennessee: A Short History* (Knoxville: University of Tennessee Press, 1990), 77. "Petition to Congress, Washington County, Virginia," April 7, 1785, Papers of the Continental Congress: Memorials of the Inhabitants of Illinois, Kaskaskia, and Kentucky, 1780–89, M247, reel 62:297, National Archives and Record Administration (NARA).

14. Harry Innes to John Brown, Danville, KY, December 7, 1787, Harry Innes Papers, Manuscript Division, Library of Congress (hereafter LC), Washington, DC.

15. Brian Balogh makes a similar argument for a later period with radically different consequences. Balogh argues that it was along the frontiers that the nation was able to be at its most effective; in contrast, during the Confederation period, it was along the frontiers that the federal government failed most spectacularly. Brian Balogh, *A Government Out of Sight: The Mystery of National Authority in Nineteenth-Century America* (New York: Cambridge University Press, 2009), 153–54.

16. Onuf recognized this point in his book *The Origins of the Federal Republic.* Onuf's primary focus, though, is on the creation of the American state system and the contest for authority between the states and the federal government. As a result, he uses the western secession movements as a means of examining the creation of ideas about statehood and not as a means of examining the conflicts westerners had with the federal government. Onuf, *Origins of the Federal Republic,* 37.

17. In an excellent 2017 essay, Jessica Choppin Roney argued that the Franklin statehood movement of the mid-1780s highlighted a battle over what entities—the people or the federal government—would be able to control the creation of new states. While Roney's essay looks forward to the construction of the American empire in the late

eighteenth and early nineteenth centuries, this essay looks backward at how the Articles of Confederation set up a particularly challenging logistical issue for residents of Kentucky and Tennessee, especially over the issues of warfare and international relations. Jessica Choppin Roney, "1776, Viewed from the West," *Journal of the Early Republic* 37, no. 4 (2017): 655–700.

18. The 1790 census placed the population of Kentucky at 73,677, including 12,430 enslaved people, and the population of the Southwest Territory—which included the Tennessee River Valley communities—had grown to 35,691 residents, including 3,400 enslaved people. Of these approximately 35,700 people, nearly 29,000 lived in the Washington district. For state-level census data, see Richard L. Forstall, ed., *Population of States and Counties of the United States: 1790–1990* (Washington, DC: U.S. Government Printing Office, 1996), 4. On the Southwest Territory, see Paul H. Bergeron, Stephen V. Ash, and Jeanette Keith, *Tennesseans and Their History* (Knoxville: University of Tennessee Press, 1999), 59.

19. Finger, *Tennessee Frontiers*, 67.

20. Peter J. Castor presents an interesting discussion of the secession movement in Washington County, framing these events within the perspective of a conflict between competing local elites. Kastor's chronology, however, is inaccurate. Kastor places the origins of the state of Franklin earlier and the movement for separation from Virginia in Washington County later than most other historians of the region. "'Equitable Rights and Privileges': The Divided Loyalties in Washington County, Virginia, during the Franklin Separatist Crisis," *Virginia Magazine of History and Biography* 105, no. 2 (April 1997): 193–226. For the best description of the separation movement from the perspective of Kentucky, see Watlington, *Partisan Spirit*, chap. 2; for the same events viewed from the perspective of the future state of Tennessee, see Barksdale, *Lost State of Franklin*.

21. "III. Report of the Committee, 1 March 1784," *The Papers of Thomas Jefferson*, ed. Julian P. Boyd (Princeton, NJ: Princeton University Press, 1952), 6:603–7.

22. Styling westerners involved in a colonizing mission as "aborigines" is a sentiment that can only strike the modern reader as ironic, given the petitioners' roles in the violent dispossession of the regions' native peoples.

23. "The Memorial of the Freemen Inhabiting the Country Westward of the Allegany or Apalachian [*sic*] Mountain, 1784," Papers of the Continental Congress: Memorials of the Inhabitants of Illinois, Kaskaskia, and Kentucky, 1780–89, M247, reel 62:281–82, NARA.

24. "To the Honorable the General Assembly of Virginia," September 23, 1785, in *Petitions of the Early Inhabitants of Kentucky to the General Assembly of Virginia, 1769–1792*, ed. James Rood Robertson (Louisville, KY: Filson Club Publication, 1914), 81.

25. "Copy of the Justisicative Memorial of the State of Franklin," *Freeman's Journal* (Philadelphia), November 23, 1785.

26. Ibid.

27. "Petition of the Inhabitants of Kentucky," Papers of the Continental Congress: Memorials of the Inhabitants of Illinois, Kaskaskia, and Kentucky, 1780–89, M247, reel 62:245, NARA.

28. On the language and mechanics of petitioning, see Richard L. Bushman, *King and People in Provincial Massachusetts* (Chapel Hill: University of North Carolina Press, 1985), 47–54.

29. Barksdale, *Lost State of Franklin;* Watlington, *Partisan Spirit.*

30. Robertson, *Petitions of Kentucky,* 80.

31. "Letter from the Franklin [state] General Assembly to Alexander Martin," in *The Colonial and State Records of North Carolina,* ed. Walter Clark (Goldsboro, NC: Nash Brothers, 1907), 17:604.

32. Thomas Perkins Abernethy, *From Frontier to Plantation in Tennessee: A Study in Frontier Democracy* (Chapel Hill: University of North Carolina Press, 1932), 58.

33. Watlington, *Partisan Spirit,* 47; Finger, *Tennessee Frontiers,* 109–13; Roney, "1776, Viewed from the West," 685.

34. "William Cage and Others to Gov. Alexander Martin," Jonesborough, NC, March, 22, 1785, in Clark, *The Colonial and State Records of North Carolina,* 22:639–640.

35. For specialist accounts of the creation of the state of Franklin, see Barksdale, *Lost State of Franklin* and Roney, "1776, Viewed from the West"; a more general overview can be found in Finger, *Tennessee Frontiers,* 110–24. The only example of a similarly situated Euro-American community were the French-Métis communities of Kaskaskia and Vincennes in the Illinois Country. Conquered by Virginia during the war, yet then ceded to Congress's control, the residents of these river towns lacked both a court and political authority throughout the Confederation period. They are not considered at length here, as they never implemented a secessionist movement.

36. "Manifesto by Alexander Martin concerning the secession of inhabitants of western North Carolina and the creation of the state of Franklin," April 25, 1785, *The Colonial and State Records of North Carolina,* 22:642–47.

37. "Justisicative Memorial," *Freeman's Journal (Philadelphia),* November 23, 1785.

38. Bradburn, *Citizenship Revolution,* 11. "Petition of the inhabitants of the Country westward of the Allegany Mountains [Washington County, VA]," November, 1784, Papers of the Continental Congress: Memorials of the Inhabitants of Illinois, Kaskaskia, and Kentucky, 1780–89, M247, reel 62:281–82, NARA.

39. U.S. Art. of Confed., Art. IX (March 1, 1781), https://avalon.law.yale.edu/18th_century /artconf.asp.

40. Onuf, *Origins of the Federal Republic,* 18–19.

41. Harry Innes to John Brown, Danville, KY, December 7, 1787, Papers of Harry Innes, LC. Watlington adds another detail: "In Jefferson County during the first nine months of 1781 Indians killed or took prisoner 131 people, about 13 percent of the total population." Watlington, 27.

42. Rob Harper, "Looking the Other Way: The Gnadenhutten Massacre and the Contextual Interpretation of Violence," *William and Mary Quarterly,* 3rd ser., 64, no. 3 (July 2007): 621–44; Griffin, *American Leviathan.*

43. "Lincoln County Resolution of Committee of Officers, &c., 1786," in Palmer, *Calendar of Virginia State Papers,* 4:221.

44. U.S. Art. of Confed. (March 1, 1781), http://avalon.law.yale.edu/18th_century /artconf.asp.

45. This was particularly true in the aftermath of the Newburgh Conspiracy of 1783, when officers of the Continental Army had nearly mutinied over their pay. C. Edward Skeen and Richard H. Kohn, "The Newburgh Conspiracy Reconsidered," *William and Mary Quarterly,* 3rd ser., 31, no. 2 (April 1974): 273–98.

46. *Journals of the Continental Congress,* June 2, 1784, ed. Gallard Hunt (Washington, DC: Government Printing Office, 1928), 27:518.

47. C. W. Heart, ed., *Journal of Capt. Jonathan Heart: On the March with His Company from Connecticut to Fort Pitt, in Pittsburgh, Pennsylvania [. . .]* (Albany, 1885), viii.

48. Charles Thomson to Certain States, April 12, 1785, in *Letters of Delegates to Congress, 1774–1789,* ed. Paul H. Smith (Washington, DC: Library of Congress, 1976), 22:330. On the failure to send troops to the future Southwest Territory, see Andrew R. L. Cayton, "'Separate Interests' and the Nation-State: The Washington Administration and the Origins of Regionalism in the Trans-Appalachian West," *Journal of American History* 79, no. 1 (June 1992): 39–67.

49. Harry Innes to Virginia Delegates, Danville, KY, April 4, 1788, Papers of Harry Innes, LC.

50. Temple Bodley, *Reprints of Littell's Political Transactions in and Concerning Kentucky: Letter of George Nicholas to His Friend in Virginia; General Wilkinson's Memorial* (Louisville, KY: Morton, 1926), 281. Bodley notes that George Rogers Clark, who was not a commissioned militia officer at the time, could not have come to Finney's aid. That Finney would write to Clark, rather than to Benjamin Logan, the commander of the Kentucky militia, speaks to Clark's preeminence among military men on the western frontier.

51. The two best treatments of these debates are still Samuel Flagg Bemis, *Pinckney's Treaty: A Study of America's Advantage from Europe's Distress, 1783–1800* (Baltimore: Johns Hopkins University Press, 1926) and Arthur Preston Whitaker, *The Mississippi Question, 1795–1803: A Study in Trade, Politics and Diplomacy* (Gloucester, MA: Smith, 1962).

52. John Filson, *The Discovery, Settlement and Present State of Kentucke* (Wilmington, DE, 1784), 30–31.

53. *Kentucke Gazette,* September 13, 1788.

54. Bemis, *Pinckney's Treaty,* 84.

55. *Kentucke Gazette,* January 26, 1788.

56. Ibid.

57. Harry Innes to John Brown, Danville, KY, December 7, 1787, Harry Innes Papers, LC.

58. Intimations of a Spanish conspiracy first appeared in the newspaper *The Western World (Frankfort, KY)* in 1806. The accusations were countered by William Littell's *Political Transactions in and Concerning Kentucky: From the First Settlement thereof, until it became an Independent State in June, 1792* (Frankfort, KY, 1806), before subsequently being expanded on in Humphrey Marshall's *The History of Kentucky: Including an Account of the Discovery, Settlement, Progressive Improvement, Political and Military Events, and Present State of the Country,* 2 vols. (Frankfort, KY, 1824). Other important sources on the topic include Thomas M. Green, *The Spanish Conspiracy: A Review of Early Spanish Movements in the Southwest* (Cincinnati, 1891) and John M. Brown's *The Political Beginnings of Kentucky: A narrative of public events bearing on the history of that state up to the time of its admission into the American Union* (Louisville, KY, 1889). Spanish sources only became available later, so these accounts are incomplete. Subsequent works on the Spanish Conspiracy include William R. Shepherd, "Wilkinson and the Beginnings of the Spanish Conspiracy," *American Historical Review* 9, no. 3 (April 1904): 490–506; "Papers Bearing on James Wilkinson's Relations with Spain, 1787–1816," *American Historical Review* 9, no. 4 (July 1904): 748–66; Arthur Preston Whitaker, "James Wilkinson's First Descent to New Orleans in 1787," *Hispanic*

*American History Review* 8, no. 1 (February 1928): 82–97; John Edward Weems, *Men without Countries: Three Adventurers in the Early Southwest* (Boston: Houghton Mifflin, 1969); and Andro Linklater, *An Artist in Treason: The Extraordinary Double Life of General James Wilkinson* (New York: Walker, 2009).

59. On Brown, see Patricia Watlington, "John Brown and the Spanish Conspiracy," *Virginia Magazine of History and Biography* 75, no. 1 (January 1967): 52–68; on White and Sevier, see Barksdale, *Lost State of Franklin*, 145–55.

60. "Extracts from the Journals of the Convention, begun and held at Danville . . . on Monday, the 17th day of September, 1787," in Littell, *Political Transactions in and Concerning Kentucky*, 86.

61. *Pittsburgh Gazette,* November 17, 1787.

62. Circular Letter to the Fayette County Court, Danville, KY, February 29, in *The Documentary History of the Ratification of the Constitution: Ratification by the States; Virginia,* ed. John P. Kaminski et al. (Madison: Wisconsin Historical Society, 1988), 1:433.

63. Hugh Williamson to James Madison, New York, June 2, 1788, in Elizabeth Gregory McPherson, "Unpublished Letters from North Carolinians to James Madison and James Monroe," *North Carolina Historical Review* 14, no. 2 (April 1937): 160.

64. Jonathan Elliot, ed., *The Debates in the Several State Conventions, on the Adoption of the Federal Constitution, as Recommended by the General Convention at Philadelphia, in 1787,* 2nd ed. (Philadelphia: Lippincott, 1901), 3:352.

65. Harry Innes to John Brown, Danville, KY, February 20, 1788, Harry Innes Papers, LC.

66. Ibid.

67. Rufus King to Elbridge Gerry, New York, June 4, 1786, in Smith, *Letters of Delegates to Congress, 1774–1789,* 23:331.

68. On the continued conflicts—and resulting petitions—between Congress and Kentucky, see Michelle Orihel, "'Mississippi Mad': The Democratic Society of Kentucky and the Sectional Politics of Navigation Rights," *Register of the Kentucky Historical Society* 114, nos. 3 and 4 (September 2016): 399–430.

69. Susan Gaunt Stearns, "Borderland Diplomacy: Western Elites and the 'Spanish Conspiracy,'" *Register of the Kentucky Historical Society* 114, nos. 3 and 4 (September 2016): 371–98.

70. Both Andrew Cayton and, more recently, Michael Bergmann have argued that the U.S. Army brought an infusion of cash to the Ohio frontier in the 1790s; some of this cash trickled into Kentucky and helped to revive the economy of the region. Bergmann, *American National State and the Early West;* Bergmann, "A 'Commercial View of This Unfortunate War': Economic Roots of an American National State in the Ohio Valley, 1775—1795," *Early American Studies* 6, no. 1 (April 1, 2008): 137–64; Cayton, "'Separate Interests and the Nation State.'"

71. "Petition to Congress, Washington County, Virginia," April 7, 1785, Papers of the Continental Congress: Memorials of the Inhabitants of Illinois, Kaskaskia, and Kentucky, 1780–89, M247, reel 62:245, NARA.

# "Such a Spirit of Innovation"

## THE AMERICAN REVOLUTION AND
## THE CREATION OF STATES

*Christopher R. Pearl*

I N JUNE 1776, JOHN Winthrop, a famous scientist and the head of mathematics at Harvard, wrote hysterically to his friend, John Adams, about the dangerous mood of revolutionary America. In May of that year, Congress resolved that each colony should create new governments to meet the "exigencies of their affairs," a measure that Winthrop thought unleashed "such a spirit of innovation" amongst the populace. It seemed "as if every thing was to be altered. Scarce a News paper but teems with new projects." In just one week, people in Massachusetts laid out plans for county assemblies and new governmental offices and institutions to administer and regulate their lives better. Although Winthrop favored independence, such a "spirit of innovation" frightened him. He did not believe this "a proper time to make so many alterations."[1] For many Americans such modifications were exactly what the May congressional resolve and potential independence from Britain entailed.

The "spirit of innovation" Winthrop witnessed unveils the centrality of governance to the revolutionary era. As colonists debated the merits of severing their bond with the empire, they also began to readjust the contours of their belonging and their understanding of and relationship with political power. They also reassessed other key aspects of governance, particularly where ultimate authority lay and who or what they appealed to for justice. As they weighed the possibilities, they looked to their past, comparing the governance that could be with the governance that existed. During this centrifugal assessment, colonists and eventually newly dubbed citizens harnessed an innovative spirit to alter the institutions, officers, and laws of their governments, and in the process, created states.

Such a focus on governance and state formation builds on recent scholarly trends that have moved the field and challenged long-held assumptions. One such long-standing interpretation has its roots in John Fiske's 1888 work, *The Critical Period of American History, 1783–1789*. In that work, Fiske investigated what he deemed the "Critical Period" of the 1780s, when, he argued, chaos ensued, embroiling the states and its peoples in riots, rebellions, and newly exaggerated political rivalries. For Fiske, much of this discontent stemmed from the early years of revolution, where a lack of innovation in statecraft failed to provide order in a changing world. According to Fiske, the American Revolution was "the most conservative revolution known to history." To back up that claim, he looked to the new states and found that they were not "revolutionary" in "character." The basic forms of governance "all remained substantially unchanged." The revolution, then, merely continued what Americans "had always enjoyed." For Fiske, the U.S. Constitution and the heroic labors of its framers saved a country on the brink of failure.[2]

American historiography has come a long way since Fiske, yet there remain strong currents of his interpretation in the literature. Jack P. Greene's work, for instance, often showcases the importance of continuity rather than change in the revolutionary era. For Greene, the American Revolution was a constitutional dispute that allowed Americans "with a deep aversion to change" to enjoy basic liberties enshrined in their colonial past under a largely nonexistent government in an empire with limited coercive power. According to Greene, early Americans were "wary" of "any fundamental political change," and therefore, "possibilities for change during and after the American Revolution were drastically circumscribed." After all, Greene argues, Americans lacked "interest in enlarging the public sphere."[3] Even Gordon Wood, who disagrees with Greene about social change in the revolution, has accepted the limited nature of statecraft outside the constitutional moment of 1787.[4]

In Wood's work, though, central aspects of governance remain central to any understanding of the revolution. Moreover, the flurry of work

Wood stirred, whether to support or to challenge, remains fundamental to our understanding of governance during the revolutionary era. The emergence of the "Republic Synthesis" and the excellent effort by teams of historians to unearth the stories of peoples excluded from the revolutionary narrative has trained our collective attention on the ideologies and the economic, cultural, and social aspects of governance, particularly people's understanding of and experience with power—all of which have informed how we view the limits of government in revolutionary thought. Nevertheless, what governments should do, how they should govern, and what, if any power, they should have, are still powerful questions we need to fully comprehend. In essence, how did early Americans understand and debate the limit, as well as the power, of government? The answer to such questions can be situational, as it depends on where and what circumstance we explore. Debate over the reach and remit of the federal government, for instance, was different from similar conversations over the place and power of the individual states. Grappling with such questions and such distinctions pushes us to reevaluate the importance of government and active governance to the revolutionary era.

There are trends in American historiography that help focus our attention on those other areas of governance and statecraft in the revolutionary era. The work of Peter Onuf, Daniel Hulsebosch, David Hendrickson, Douglas Bradburn, Brian Philips Murphy, Gary Gerstle, William Novak, and Steven Pincus all show the importance of state formation and statehood to the revolutionary experience.[5] In some ways resurrecting the early works of Oscar Handlin and Mary Handlin—as well as Louis Hartz, who searched in vain for a clear "liberal tradition" in the revolution, or, rather, the revolutionary origins of laissez-fair—these scholars highlight the astounding power of the states, particularly their ability to regulate the domestic economy as well as the public and at times private lives of the people within their jurisdictions.[6] In addition, works by Max Edling and Patrick Griffin have demonstrated the key importance of governance and government to the everyday lives of early Americans. Edling and Griffin show that ordinary people, too, contributed to thoughts on governance and affected the scope and nature of government in the revolutionary era.

Early Americans, they argue, were concerned with enlarging the public sphere, rather than wary of government or more concerned with their individual pursuits of happiness.[7]

Combining and building on these trends in the literature, this essay tackles how early Americans thought about and debated the proper role and nature of government and tried to execute their ideas in the creation of new states. During this generative moment of revolution, early Americans altered the design, structure, and implementation of state institutions and officers. They understood that they were creating states, not glorified colonies. When they celebrated election days and anniversaries of independence, they toasted "the rising States of America."[8]

These exalted states underwent vast transformations in the revolutionary period. Many of their laws and the institutions and the officers that enforced them were entirely new. If revolutionaries did not create new ones, they altered, reformed, and even abolished others. Such change has important ramifications for the way we view and interpret both the revolution and the Critical Period of the 1780s. While Fiske and some historians since him blamed the perceived chaos of that period on the lack of significant innovation in American statecraft, the crisis owed its existence to the sheer totality of change rather than the absence of it. In these years, people on the ground mobilized for fundamental changes to the very nature of how governments governed and who could and should control the basic levers and function of power. In the process, the judicial, legal, and police powers of the states were decisively changed.

Yet, we cannot expect that those newly crafted, enhanced, and revised systems of government would work seamlessly overnight. Nor can we expect the allegiance of all the people to the power and authority of those institutions. The states were established during a destructive civil war by the fiat of nascent polities that did not have, as one contemporary pointed out, "habits of obedience and opinion."[9] They were bound to encounter realities, exigencies, and challenges that necessitated further reflection, debate, reform—and, significantly, time. Many of those reforms took place on the ground through the energy of collective pressure and resistance, forcing executives, judges, and legislatures to alter timeworn practices, policies, and institutions to achieve some kind of revolutionary settlement. That creativity and the ongoing reform of the 1780s, while it certainly engendered a feeling of instability and produced a divisive political environment, was nonetheless the product of a revolutionary transformation in the states.

To comprehend the magnitude of change and the significance of statecraft in the revolutionary period, one must look both forward and backward, tracking how long-held grievances over laws, institutions, and officers during the colonial period continued to shape the formation of states in the revolutionary era. The colonial and revolutionary experiences of New Hampshire, Pennsylvania, and Virginia demonstrate that point. In those places, the colonial governments suffered severe challenges. Patronage, prerogative, and an exclusive rather than inclusive political system undermined the efficiency, effectiveness, and overall reach of the governments. Societal transformations—particularly demographic growth, geographic expansion, and economic change—only exacerbated those tensions and strained the paltry institutions of government on the outpost of Britain's ever-extending empire.

In response, people mobilized for change, fomenting a revolution that harnessed a semblance of popular sovereignty in order to craft states that could, some thought, govern vast jurisdictions and adjust themselves when needs and interests demanded. The American Revolution, from that vantage point, was vital to the creation of strong, centralized, and powerful states that would dominate both the late eighteenth and much of the nineteenth centuries.[10]

The colonies of New Hampshire, Pennsylvania, and Virginia, while representing different peoples, polities, and geographic locations, all shared certain legal and political characteristics that shaped early American visions of governance. We can see in each of those colonies the interplay of patronage, prerogative, place, and power—attributes central to a monarchical world— and their impact on everyday governance. Equally significant, each of those colonies experienced societal transformations that challenged the governments' closed networks of interest that was cultivated and controlled. The inability of colonial leaders to revise timeworn practices and their unwillingness to shift the locus of power away from the hands of a few to meet the challenges societal transformations resulted in significant animosity between the generality of the people and the few at the top who attempted to rule them. That hostility served as the driving force of revolution and influenced statecraft in the postindependence period.

In New Hampshire, monarchical patronage networks and the exertion of royal power through the refractory lens of the executive defined the legal system. Perhaps in no other colony did the combination of prerogative and power have such a total effect on the basic administration of justice. Since 1717, a single family, the Wentworths, had controlled the colony's executive branch. To perpetuate family control, the Wentworths directed political appointments and circumscribed the geographic limits of office holding. In 1740, for example, the majority of the twenty-five justices of the peace (JPs) in the colony lived in Portsmouth. A year later, the son of Governor John Wentworth, Benning Wentworth, came to power and furthered the dominance of the seaport by doubling the number of JPs there. Jeremy Belknap, the contemporary chronicler of New Hampshire's history, noted that "in the latter part of his time, appointments of this kind became so numerous, and were so easily procured, that the office was rendered contemptible." It is easy to imagine why. Wentworth only appointed men who demonstrated their commitment to him and his interest, and most of those were related to him by marriage, if not by blood. Wentworth even appointed his own young sons and a ten-year-old nephew to significant official positions.[11]

Not only did Wentworth and his network control places of honor and profit, but they also directed most legal proceedings in the province. Until 1771, all legal business occurred in a tiny eastern corner of the colony, Portsmouth. The inferior courts and the high court convened in that port town, allowing the governor and his councilors to control colonial legal affairs. Governor appointees—often council members, friends, and relatives—manned the inferior courts for both civil and criminal proceedings. Similarly, the governor and his councilors staffed the high court, a court with both law and chancery powers. In all, law was a family affair. In 1772, during the administration of John Wentworth (Benning Wentworth's nephew), the governor's father sat on the high court's bench, along with five uncles and two cousins.[12]

The concentration of legal power in the Wentworth family had an astounding and, some argued, contemptible impact on the administration of justice. In the courts, the governor, council, and allied judges let their own interests guide their decisions.[13] The Wentworths made their money through land and the lucrative masts trade. Moreover, that family and its extended network supported the Anglican Church, guarded that establishment's interest, and attempted to confine entrance into the "principal families" who governed the province to that religious persuasion.[14] Together, economics and religion proved a noxious mixture, especially since most of the population adhered to a congregational faith and, as small farmers, were at odds with the land and commercial interests of the colonial elite who controlled the courts. According to Belknap, because of this public dissonance, the judges in the lesser courts attempted to manipulate decisions by *"watering the jury."* If a claimant disapproved of the lower court's judgment, they could only appeal to the high court, where the governor and his councilors ruled without juries. Moreover, many of the councilors also sat on the lower court benches, thus "the final sentence was often passed by the same persons who had been concerned in the former decisions." Obviously, "frequent complaints were made of partiality."[15]

Other factors contributed to a general disgust with and complaints against the government. Like every other colony, New Hampshire had experienced considerable societal transformations. Between 1740 and 1775, the population more than doubled. [16] As the population grew, the settlements extended away from the seaport. Such changes challenged the structure, substance, and culture of the legal system. As one colonist noted in 1774, "It will be found that Laws and Regulations, which prove very effectual for small Communities, and that serve to keep them within the strictest Bounds of Decorum, &c, will by no Means answer the same good Ends, when they, either through Emigration or their own natural Population, become more extensive." When "numbers increase," he warned, "Difference in Opinion, Ways and Means for Support, opposite Interests, & c." will "grow in Proportion, which must inevitably render the Plan formed by the Few, insufficient for the Many."[17] More to the point, another colonist argued, "the province is so increased" that "it is now of great importance to dissolve a family combination which has already been productive of so much injustice."[18]

These authors, writing between 1773 and 1774, were responding to over a decade of political strife and inconclusiveness. By the late 1760s, the legal and political system had come under severe attack. Since its inception, New Hampshire had had no county governments, allowing Portsmouth to control the legal and political affairs of the colony. By the 1760s, colonists demanded that the government create counties to grant representation in the legislature to excluded settlers and provide easier access to the law through local courts. Upon his entrance as governor in 1767, John Wentworth realized the seriousness of these complaints. Societal change without the commensurate alteration of the government could have disastrous consequences, especially for his personal rule. In response, the young governor pushed for the creation of counties and courts. He also sought to extend his power through the construction of roads to connect the westernmost limits of the province to Portsmouth.[19]

On paper, the government seemed to redress many of the grievances harbored by inhabitants. Roads were to be constructed, new courts created, and new seats in the legislature would open. Reality proved a different thing, however. Prominent men in Portsmouth feared the incorporation of the areas outside the town into the governance of the province and actively worked to derail reforms. As one Portsmouth resident groaned, in a few short years, settlers who secured lands outside of the seaport "will send such a Number of Representatives" to the legislature and "out-vote" the "Town-born Children in all important Matters."[20] As a result, the four counties outside Portsmouth only received twelve legislative seats, while Portsmouth's home county held 22, giving the port's junto the ability to circumvent outside influence.[21] In addition, the roads remained underfunded, and the governor only appointed a few local men as JPs. Most of the officers in the new counties remained governor's men, outsiders in the local communities, who made sure the counties stayed dependent on their eastern leaders.[22] Although the assembly, council, and governor had different motives, they all disrupted reform. As historian Jere R. Daniell aptly put it, "It was a well-conceived plan, but it didn't work."[23]

Irritated that the new system rectified little, colonists sent petitions to the government and popularized their grievances in the press. They were perturbed that "very little if any thing was benefited by the late Division of this Province into Five Counties." Many inhabitants lived anywhere from forty to sixty miles from "the Courts of Justice." In result, justice was at a premium and many waited "sometimes Eleven, nine or six months" for the courts to process cases.[24] Similarly, others railed that judges "were selected rather for the purpose of advancing the governor's interest than with the view of administering justice." Still others claimed that judges were "biased, careless or otherwise unfitted for the work they were expected to perform."[25] To rectify these problems, petitioners requested the creation of new counties, new boundaries for existing counties, and new courts in more central geographic locations. Colonists also requested the restructuring of the high court with judges outside the governor and his council and equal political representation to assure action on these reform initiatives.[26]

As the colonial period closed, inhabitants realized that they could expect no redress of their grievances. Not only was parliament at odds with the American people, but so were the politicians at home. One irritated colonist groaned, a few "Wiseacres," "over a Bowl of Punch" in their "nocturnal Assemblies" have denied all requests for reform, refused the inclusion of the bulk of the population in decision making, perpetuated a system that guards power for the few, and, in the process, "have destroyed the very Basis of Liberty."[27] By the early 1770s, the entire imperial government, on both sides of the Atlantic, required significant reform.

Like New Hampshire, prerogative and power in Pennsylvania were deeply felt. Although a proprietary colony, Pennsylvania had an executive and judicial structure similar to any other royal colony. The governors not only held their office at the proprietor's discretion, but also the crown's, and were to guard, with a vengeance, the "royal prerogative." The governor had the power to appoint judges who held their offices during royal pleasure. Judges received their commissions from "GEORGE the Second by the Grace of God" to keep "our Peace" in "our said Province" as "our Justices."[28]

Leading men coveted these offices because they represented the highest authority in the empire, and therefore, like elsewhere, nepotism and patronage ruled the day. Elite families connected to the governor, the proprietor, and royal officials across the Atlantic controlled the political and legal spheres of the province. Take the Allen family, for instance. William Allen, whose daughter married a Penn, also held kinship ties to the longest-sitting governor of Pennsylvania, James Hamilton, and had important contacts in London. Through these connections, Allen was appointed the chief justice of the supreme court and JP for Northampton County. His son, Andrew Allen, served as the king's attorney general, and his other son was a JP for Northampton County. Edward Shippen, an in-law of William Allen and a close friend of Hamilton, simultaneously held the positions of prothonotary, clerk of the orphans' court, clerk of quarter sessions, recorder, deputy register, and JP for Lancaster County. His sons likewise held positions as prothonotaries, councilors, and judges. By the close of the colonial period, the blue bloods "at the head of affairs, have in many instances behaved as though they thought they had a sort of fee simple in them and might dispose of all places of Honour and profit as pleased them best."[29]

This politically charged system of nepotism and patronage had serious implications for the everyday reality of governance in the province. Like New Hampshire, Pennsylvania experienced demographic growth and geographic expansion, yet the institutions and officers of the law did not adapt to these major changes. A small, geographically confined elite controlled the few offices and governmental institutions that existed in the eleven large counties of Pennsylvania. In each of those counties, the courts situated in eastern county seats remained "upwards of an Hundred" miles from "the most inhabited part of" the province. Similarly, local law enforcement officials were "upwards of Fifty miles" away.[30] In Bucks County, for instance, nine out of the seventeen justices lived in the three oldest and richest townships on the eastern seaboard. This geographic distribution proved problematic, as the ten towns with the largest number of taxable inhabitants had only four JPs, and they resided in three of the ten towns. The six most populated towns, representing the central part of Bucks, had no JPs. A similar geographic concentration of JPs existed for the rest of the counties.[31]

Societal transformations tested these limited and geographically confined colonial institutions. Not only were these courts nearly inaccessible for large segments of the population, but they could barely handle the work that came before them. Administering large counties, some of which were more than 3,000 square miles with a growing population, proved impossible. Chester County magistrates stated simply, "Much business comes before us, which cannot be accomplished."[32] Similarly, mounting caseloads led to delays in the courts, hampering attempts to govern effectively. For one thing, subpoenaed jurors and witnesses had to travel nearly insurmountable distances to attend court without knowing whether their case would be heard that session, potentially wasting valuable time better spent on the farm or in the shop. Eventually, this judicial problem became more acute; jurors and witnesses refused to attend, further hindering legal processes. In Northampton County, failing to attend trials at quarter sessions contributed to a continuance docket in 1776 that included 140 cases dating back almost a decade.[33] In sum, as petitioners noted, "justice is delayed" and "totally obstructed."[34]

Like the county courts, the supreme court felt the pressure of societal transformations. That court acted as a court of appeals and had original jurisdiction for all capital cases. As the population grew and settlements expanded westward, the court's business, as Chief Justice Allen complained, was "thirty times as much as it was." By 1774, the high court faced a docket over eighty pages long listing over two hundred cases.[35] Yet, the court demanded most trials take place in the city of Philadelphia, an onerous obligation that over 1,200 petitioners called "a Burden so unreasonable and oppressive."[36] Just as the local courts had found, the supreme court could not oblige people to make the difficult journeys to attend sessions.[37]

To make matters worse, trying all capital offenses in Philadelphia required the few officers of the counties to arrest and convey violent criminals to the city with limited means of transportation. Captives and their associates often violently assaulted local officers during such journeys.[38] In one instance, a known serial outlaw almost beat a local constable to death with the handle of an axe and then terrorized inhabitants who tried to help local officials. The outlaw threatened one local tavernkeeper that he would "cut him to Pieces, and make a Breakfast of his Heart" if he supported local authorities.[39] Obviously, there were problems with the colony's ability to govern.

While inhabitants could not help "considering the Insecurity of their Lives and Estates as worth the Attention of the Legislature," their appeals resulted in no appreciable change to the government.[40] Factional disputes between the assembly and governor blocked attempts for reform of the judiciary in 1762, 1764, 1767, and 1773. Similarly, between 1710 and 1776, the crown vetoed six of eight laws that altered the structure of the courts because they impinged on the royal prerogative. Unreformed courts, large sprawling counties, and "the want of magistrates to enforce the laws of the province" resulted in "Vexation and Terror," as "Rapine, Violence and Injustice are suffered to pass unpunished, and the lives as well as the Properties of the Inhabitants are rendered insecure."[41] By the late 1760s, both inhabitants and some officials complained that the government was "toothless and precarious," or more bluntly, that Pennsylvania had "no Government" at all.[42]

Patronage and power also dominated colonial Virginia's legal system and circumscribed the reach and effectiveness of the government. The highest court in the colony refused to leave the comforts of Williamsburg while a self-perpetuating oligarchy ran the business of government in local spaces. By mid-century, societal transformations challenged this governing structure. The royal governor and powerful local oligarchies, fearing the loss of power, refused to restructure the legal system. In result, the colonial government faced the same outspoken opposition and criticism as existed in New Hampshire and Pennsylvania.

The main institutions that adjudicated the wrangling of the average subject were the county courts, but frequently, those courts did not work at all. Part of the problem had to do with societal change. In the early eighteenth century, the courts could sit for a day to handle county administration and their caseloads. By mid-century, however, the population drastically increased and economic exchanges became more complex. The number of cases before the courts swelled, and it took at least four or five days and numerous sessions to settle legal business. Feeling the strain of attendance, local judges shirked their duties, making it difficult for the courts to maintain a quorum. The first day of a court session would often start with a full bench, but by the second day, the number of judges dwindled and the courts ground to a halt.[43] Between 1746 and 1751, for example, the local court in Lunenburg County skipped almost half of its meetings.[44] In 1772, Landon Carter, criticizing the indolence of his fellow judges, noted that he had to travel around "to get Justices enough to hold court." Irritated, Carter threatened to leave the bench.[45]

Ordinary subjects complained in petitions, and the press even looked into "the Causes of Delay in the County Courts" and demanded reform. Feeling public pressure, the governor and council deemed "the Delay of Justice" the result of "the too great Number and Neglect of Justices, to remedy the said Inconvenience and Grievances, & expedite the Business of the said Courts."[46] Nevertheless, the council could not agree on proper reforms beyond interrogating and in some instances reprimanding court clerks. Virginians, however, wanted more than a piecemeal strategy to solve the issue. For example, in 1746, petitioners from Fairfax County demanded notable institutional change. They argued for the creation of quarterly courts and legally binding penalties for justices who failed to clear the dockets.[47] Although the government demurred, colonists refused to part with the plan. In 1771, the anonymous PHILO VIRGINIAE begged the "Notice of the Legislature" to initiate those same reforms "for the Good of the Society I live in."[48]

Various were the proposed solutions to fix the legal system. Some colonists demanded salaried judges who would consistently attend court. Others pushed for new counties to make judicial jurisdictions smaller and increase the number of justices. Still others demanded the removal of courts, prisons, and judges to more central geographic locations.[49] Regardless of such plans, reforms were not forthcoming. Local justices, many of whom held seats in the House of Burgesses, fought against reforms they thought threatened their positions of authority. Although the "public Gazettes" attempted to "spirit Gentlemen up to a diligent discharge of their duty," the judges demonstrated little "inclination even to incomode the least private concern for the sake of the public." An annoyed Landon Carter continued to document the "lazyness" of "each person concerned with the Court."[50]

By the early 1770s, Virginians, irritated by the inaction of their representatives and local magnates, defied the authority of the local courts and challenged the deference that those courts and their officers had demanded for over a century. William Rind, printer of the *Virginia Gazette,* noted in 1771 that Virginians filled the papers with "illiberal Reflections on the Justices."[51] On the ground, those expressions turned into intense displays of contempt. In March 1771, colonists in Richmond County, reeling from a poor economy and angered by a legal system that did not have their interest at heart, offered "an Insult of the most Extravagant Nature" by plastering the magistrates' bench "with Tar and Dung."[52] Similarly, just a few years earlier in Loudon County, inhabitants had "set up in the courthouse in the chair of the judge" a "dead and stinking hog with a most scandalous libel in his mouth greatly reflecting on the said court and the officers thereof."[53]

The county courts, however, were the least of colonial legal problems. The apex of a theoretically integrated court system was the general court, a body made up of royal councilors and the governor. In that court, which sat in Williamsburg, the "judges" dealt with all cases concerning capital offenses and heard appeals from the county courts. Like the local courts, the general court felt the pressure of societal transformations as its caseload markedly increased. The failure of the county courts also augmented the general court's dockets through appeals to overrule the decisions of local judges. By the late 1760s, the general court faced a caseload that some estimated it would take at least three years of continuous work to clear.[54]

Much like the public's reaction to the failure of the county courts, inhabitants censured the slowness, inconvenience, and, some argued, the corruption of the general court. Demanding all trials take place in Williamsburg put serious strains on the lives of ordinary Virginians. Claimants, victims, defendants, witnesses, and jurors had to make the long, arduous treks to the general court without knowing whether the judges would even hear their cases. One contemporary worried about bringing his case to the general court because "Judgment wou'd not be obtained in less than three years."[55] By the mid-1760s, these grumblings turned still more sour. One writer blasted the whole makeup of the general court, arguing that it went against all ideas and values that separated powers for the protection of "LIBERTY and PROPERTY." Not only was the court slow, but each "judge" symbolized the "union in one person of the discordant and heterogeneous dignities of Privy Councellor, Judge of the G C. and Member of the intermediate body of the Legislature."[56] These censures against official collusion, when combined with the vociferous rhetoric of the imperial crisis against royal creatures and coteries, had serious implications.

By the close of the colonial period, Virginia had a two-tiered judicial system that was out of step with colonial needs and incapable of reform. Monarchical networks, court rings with the ability to control legislative initiative, and even executive fiat deterred any reform that threatened the dominance of the local ruling elite. The conflation of local legal authority with provincial political power resulted in serious confrontations and acrimony among leading families and between the squirearchy and the general populace that darkened public opinion and lessened the public image of the judiciary.

Popular grievances regarding the legal and political systems of Virginia, Pennsylvania, and New Hampshire coalesced with the politicization and mobilization of people during the growing imperial dispute. That combination resulted in the dramatic overthrow of the colonial establishments and calls for significant revolutionary reform.

New Hampshire serves as an early and poignant example of that fact. As early as 1774, nearly all authority in that colony was at an end, as colonists let loose their vengeance on the symbols, offices, institutions, and men who had been a source of contention for so long. In December of that year, almost one-sixth of the adult white male population demonstrated their rejection of royal authority by sacking an imperial fortress and hauling "down the king's colours." In addition, on the same day, thousands descended on Portsmouth and threatened the governor with their "cry about liberty." The colony, the governor complained, had succumbed to the "rage of the ruling multitude" who "do not support the Magistrates."[57] Less than a year later, the governor and all remaining vestiges of royal authority had been forcibly removed from the colony.

While some contemporaries and even modern historians have viewed this train of events as an odd rupture, it was the product of strong currents of discontent permeating the colony.[58] Since at least 1765, the growing imperial dispute had sharpened rather than detracted from the internal problems of New Hampshire. Grievances leveled at the judicial and political systems were heightened, given new meaning amid a universal struggle in colonial North America, and, significantly, a collective purpose. Moreover, public discussion of constitutional issues transformed the way colonists envisioned imperial authority on both sides of the Atlantic. In that critical period, not only did colonists debate the right of parliamentary taxation, but they also scrutinized and condemned the very governments that had claimed to represent them. Inhabitants linked the calls of "No Taxation without Representation" to their own internal troubles. That maxim, one subject intoned, "is Part of the American's political Creed, yet not so much in Practice as in Theory," as "we annually see this very Right violated and infringed upon in almost every Province in America."[59] Similarly, inhabitants "justly complain, that the British Parliament imposes its Taxes upon us without Consent—But are our internal Grievances less, or have we ever yet tried to obtain Redress of them?"[60]

As colonists explained, fighting for "our Liberty" not only meant resisting a distant parliament, but tackling the "internal Grievances" they had at home. After all, "Our Property, when contested . . . may finally be decided by a Court, whose Constitution is destructive to the most sacred Priviledges of Englishmen, viz. Tryal by Jury." A jury's decision "may be overthrown by a Judicature, whose Jurisdiction is so indeterminate, that it is either a Court of Law, Chancery or Equity, as the Exigence of the Case may require."[61] In their petitions and addresses to the public, inhabitants interwove both domestic and imperial grievances. At a town meeting in Portsmouth in 1774, locals submitted 13 instructions to their representatives during the "present critical Situation of Public Affairs." Of the 13 points, only one addressed the dispute over parliamentary sovereignty, whereas the bulk addressed the domestic problems of governance in the colony. While colonists wanted their legislature to join in the general fight against the "novel Claim of the Parliament," they also demanded "all internal Grievances may be redressed." They wanted the government to reform the high court by separating its duties in law from chancery or equity. They requested new independent judges removed from "the Grants of this Government," new counties, new roads, and new local officers and administrative buildings to house legal records. Colonists also demanded equal political representation, annual rather than triennial elections, and the opening of the legislature's doors so they can be "no longer SHUT against their CONSTITUENTS." In all, they requested an overhaul of the government and a radical reorientation of the relationship between the people and political power.[62]

The imperial crisis served as a crucible, giving ordinary colonists the confidence to push for what those in power considered extraordinary claims and demands. Only the public and private discussions that that imbroglio instigated could produce the boldness of someone like "Americanus," who coolly asserted, "The People being now better informed of the Nature of Government, can better judge their own Importance."[63] Yet men in control refused to abide popular instructions, never mind the calls by the "weak and ignorant" for political inclusion.[64] As a result , popular calls for inclusion and reform turned into violent recriminations. Colonists castigated "a few fawning Sycophants," those "Placemen or Pensioners . . . chiefly dependent on the Province for their Sustenance," as the epitome of a broken system.[65] In the back parts of the colony, inhabitants erected liberty poles, intimidated local magistrates, and ripped JPs from their slumbers and chased them out of town.[66] In Portsmouth, hundreds gathered, taunted, threatened, and even assaulted loyal subjects of the king and the governor.[67] The warning signs were everywhere. As "The DEVIL in a Passion" counseled, "Administration is tyrannie, and if its Measures are not speedily softened, Destruction and Damnation will alight somewhere."[68]

By early 1775, the governor and his circle of favorites could only bewail that such damnation alighted on their doorsteps while they commanded an unpopular government that proved "a miserable example of its own weakness."[69] Those who had, for so long, been in power "were almost Frightened out of their wits" that they would be "killed & having their throats cutt."[70] The rage against the Wentworth clan and the government they created and controlled worsened as people privately and publicly debated the seriousness of their domestic grievances. As one writer proclaimed, the turbulence of the times owed its existence to the politicization of grievances leveled at the judiciary, at local officers, at unequal representation, and at "many other Complaints too trifling to be canvased."[71]

Many thought that the recent politicization of grievances, coupled with the collective power harnessed by extralegal committees birthed in the resistance to imperial measures, would provide enough pressure on existing political institutions to achieve substantial reform. As one Pennsylvanian put it, they needed to "seize the present opportunity of redressing our provincial grievances, and let us repair the faults which time and experience have discovered in our constitution."[72] Much to their chagrin, that was not the case. They may have felt their collective might, but such a mobilization failed to move the needle in a closed political system.

This circumstance turned a reform movement into a revolutionary scenario that undermined existing governments and ushered in a wave of change. As Wentworth lamented in May 1775, "Thus government is in a great measure unhinged, for though the form as yet remains . . . there is not much of the reality."[73] Within a month, the government did not even exist in form. In New Hampshire, a violent crowd descended on the governor's mansion and leveled a cannon at his door. They wanted to frighten the governor and punish one of his "most useful magistrates," then dining at the mansion.[74] Their tactic worked; the officer surrendered, and the governor fled to Fort William and Mary. By June 1775, the font of all sovereign power in the colony, a man who represented a family that dominated the government for almost a century, resided in a dilapidated fort "entirely cut off" from the world.[75]

Similar situations occurred in Virginia and Pennsylvania. In Virginia, the governor fled the colony and the legal institutions collapsed. In Pennsylvania, the governor and assembly faded out of all significance as extralegal groups wrested control of the basic administration of government. Like New Hampshire, colonists there distanced themselves from an established form of governance to declare new sovereign powers of their own. On the eve of independence, inhabitants asserted in loud and vocal ways that they lived "under a species of government which has always been reprobated by good men as the worst in the world."[76] They would not, colonists inferred, do so anymore.

The void created by the collapse of government opened up new possibilities. In May 1776, the Continental Congress called on the colonies to fashion new governments to meet the "exigencies of their affairs." Together, the absence of government and the congressional appeal unleashed a plethora of ideas on the proper forms, functions, and purposes of government. Not only did Americans debate the merits of unicameral versus bicameral legislatures and plural executives versus powerful governors that have been the mainstay of histories written about the revolution, but they also discussed and demanded the reform of the laws, institutions, and officers most important to the everyday function of government. Judges, justices, sheriffs, courts, prisons, and penal codes all necessitated reform, writers urged.

In Pennsylvania, inhabitants immediately published government plans that shed light on how the vagaries of the colonial past influenced the revolutionary moment. The work of the anonymous "Demophilus" is particularly revealing. For that author, the "Ancient Saxon Constitution" seemed the perfect blueprint for a government. While the author praised and explored the democratic elements of that government, he spent most of his time and energy laying out its "internal police." The author devoted so much attention to this subject because the Saxon form was "so excellent" compared to Pennsylvania's "circumstances." What made that government "so excellent" was its use of "distributive justice." Magistrates, instead of being located in a few geographically confined areas, lived and worked in each of the towns in a county. Moreover, instead of large, sprawling counties, the Saxons had smaller shires for easier access to the courts. Therefore, Demophilus concluded that Pennsylvania should break each county up into small districts from which "the Conservators, or justices of the peace" should live and serve. If Pennsylvanians followed this model, it would "give such a new face to the affairs of this colony" and "improve its internal police."[77]

Demophilus rooted his plan in the existing disputes over the inadequacy of the colonial government. For Demophilus, the colony did not live up to its proper role as an arbiter of liberty. In fact, the entire imperial system threatened liberty. According to Demophilus, the "Creator formed Man for society, and that society cannot subsist without regulations, laws, and government." The imperial and executive "negative power on acts" had denied Pennsylvanians these three pillars of liberty. The "whole business" of government "is to *restrain*, and in some cases to take off such members of the community as disturb the quiet and destroy the security of the honest and peaceable subject." Pennsylvania's government, however, did not meet those basic expectations. Demophilus's plans provided an obvious juxtaposition for his readers: the ideal government in relation-ship to liberty with the reality of their own.[78]

The thoughts of revolutionary reformers like Demophilus represent a significant moment. Newly independent Americans had the ability to revise their legal codes and apparatuses. They could and did collect their general laws together, hewing and winnowing away the archaic, reform-ing the mediocre, and creating new laws that would, some thought, be the dawn of a new age. They all, in one way or another, partook in actions that standardized law and centralized power throughout their states. Revolutionaries were creating states, in some ways modern in form, in some ways not, but nonetheless fundamentally different from the gov-ernments of the colonial past.

One way to see this change is through popular calls for the indepen-dent states to become countries of "laws and not of men." This revolu-tionary motto can seem an abstraction in its generality, but nonetheless spoke to the goals of reformers to demolish the squirearchy, court rings, and patronage networks that unbalanced the governing system by cater-ing to the needs, ideas, and aspirations of a few.

In response, the new states, over the course of the 1770s, 1780s, and 1790s, created laws and inaugurated reforms establishing institutions and officers of state that would function like, as Thomas Jefferson argued, "mere machines." Jefferson's use of the word "machines" highlights the transformation of the state in the revolution. Such an idea denotes a mechanical impersonalism that differed greatly from the colonial world. Monarchical conceit prized personal fealties and connections. Colonial offices represented persons and personalities. However, machines are not persons, and in the postindependence states, revolutionaries declared that impersonal offices and institutions should be created and should rule. At the same time, localities, with all of their distinctiveness in law and identity, with their leading families and clientele, faded away as the state rose in power through the initiatives of republican reformers.[79]

In New Hampshire, the transition from colony to state was divisive and long-drawn-out. After the government fell apart in 1775, the colony had to figure out a stopgap measure. For a time, a provincial congress and the revolutionary committees of safety filled the void, but that proved an ineffectual and potentially dangerous scenario if prolonged. In November 1775, the Continental Congress advised New Hampshire to create a government on the "full and free representation of the people," but only "during the continuance of the present dispute between Great Britain and the colonies." That last stipulation, while reasonable, inhibited the framing of a permanent, well-thought-out constitution and therefore continued acrimonious political disputes and divisions over the proper form and function of government. The new constitution had no declaration of rights, nor did it provide a structural outline of a government like the constitutions many of the states adopted in 1776. Instead, it offered a bare-bones framework that barely addressed the limits of legislative, executive, and judicial powers. Nevertheless, the constitution and the debate it inspired put in place a formidable and centralized legal system that defined state power well into the next century.

Despite the limited nature of New Hampshire's constitution, it did institute several crucial changes that the state built upon over the course of the 1780s. The constitution stipulated a significantly different way to appoint judges and JPs. Instead of being appointed by and holding their office at the pleasure of a royal governor, the legislature chose the justices. This alteration, on its own, seems rather insignificant. However, when combined with the modifications of the legislative branch, it produced profound changes. The number of towns represented in the legislature increased from 36 to nearly 100, giving inhabitants outside Portsmouth a greater say in legislative initiative and judicial appointments.[80] As a result, the number of justices and judges increased in some areas and decreased in others, highlighting a new and expansive geographic distribution of these important officers of the law. Obviously, through such a change there would be massive turnover from the colonial period. In Hillsborough County, for example, all the magistrates were wholly new to their offices.[81]

Not only were these justices new, but they had far more expansive powers. Over the course of the 1770s and 1780s, the state increased the realm of summary justice for the JPs, gave them police powers to regulate the daily activities of citizens and apprehend suspected criminals, and, just as important, granted them discretionary power over the detection and detainment of suspected state enemies. By 1786, some worried that "the Justices of the Peace" are "a growing order . . . dangerous to the real interest of the people."[82] Nevertheless, like it or not, the JPs became integral to the whole scheme of state law enforcement.

The state also centralized power by altering the structure—and, many hoped, the function—of the judiciary. In one of its first acts, the legislature abolished the high court, granting both appellate power and original jurisdiction for capital crimes to the state superior court, a structure that remained in place until 1901. Through these changes, citizens could hear their cases and try appeals in one of nine district courts, rather than traveling to the distant town of Portsmouth. Such changes tied once local, disparate, and excluded areas to the highest court in the state.[83] New Hampshire also brought local spaces more directly under the control of state institutions by moving some of the meetings of the legislature and the executive from Portsmouth to the centrally located town of Concord.

While the governmental structure was in place, in function, it still suffered from problems that had existed in the past, particularly the manipulation of the legal system by special interest groups and individuals. Since at least the 1760s, citizens had demanded the strict separation of powers between the different branches of government. It was, many thought, the only way to wrest control of the legal system away from the Wentworth clan. Although the legislature eased part of that grievance by abolishing the high court, it never stipulated distinct powers between the branches. It was not until a new state constitution in 1784 that the organization introduced such a separation.

Regardless of such a change, the legislature, which had risen to significant power, consistently encroached on the judiciary's authority. That body annulled the decisions of both the inferior and the superior courts and passed a slew of private bills returning people "to their law." Individuals with social and economic clout and political connections could and did use the legislature to influence the decisions of the judiciary and therefore undermine the whole legal system. It seemed, one angry citizen argued, that the government changed in form rather than function. "Scarcely had we the pleasure of beholding the fair frame of liberty completed," the author argued, "but our malignant servants attempt the destruction of the beauteous building." The whole scheme smacked of a time "when every department of the *Province* was filled by a relation or a dependent of a servant of the crown."[84]

This last statement epitomizes the frustration citizens felt toward their government. Nevertheless, because of the activity of the citizenry, the state took these grievances head-on and came out of the 1780s far different than it had been in the past. The transformation of the state judiciary demonstrates that fact. The institution was structurally strong on paper yet still suffered from problems of allegiance and confidence that undermined the entire system. The courts faced a difficult situation; they represented a new polity without the luxury of settled allegiance and were staffed by men who had never held positions of power.

Over the course of the 1780s, the courts worked hard to craft an image of authority and gain the respect of the rest of the population. During those trying years with "money scarce, business dull, and our feeble government unhinged," future governor William Plummer wrote, the "Courts of Law are firm, and in these degenerate days, dare to be honest."[85] As this quote implies, the judiciary attempted, for the first time, to match the structural authority granted to it through revolutionary reforms. By the late 1780s, the courts, particularly the superior court, began to garner the respect and allegiance of the citizens. That court entered the 1790s at the apex of the state government and would remain, throughout the nineteenth century, the cornerstone of state authority. It and only it served as the foremost enforcer of state policy and shaped citizens' daily lives by regulating their social and economic interactions.

We can see the rise of the superior court in two court cases. In the early 1790s, a farmer, irritated by a court ruling in a case over two stolen pigs, appealed to the legislature to have the case dismissed. The legislature immediately passed an act requiring the superior court to grant the defendant a new trial. When this piece of special legislation reached the superior court, the chief justice "promptly pronounced the act utterly void, and refused to obey it." Then, the court denied the defendant an appeal. Not to be outdone, the legislature demanded the court of common pleas retry the case. Emboldened by the refusal of the superior court and wary of acting contrary to its ruling, the local bench "determined they would do nothing with it," effectively rejecting legislative interference.[86]

In another 1791 court case, *Gilman v. M'Clary,* the superior court denied the constitutionality of legislative meddling.[87] These cases highlight the rise of the superior court. Not only did that court challenge legislative authority, but it had also earned the allegiance of the inferior courts, who acquiesced to its rulings.

These court cases also represent a general transformation of the state in the late 1780s and early 1790s. Special acts of the legislature not only allowed prominent individuals to manipulate the legal system, but such interference left law open to the vagaries of legislative pleasure, thus resulting in, as one legal historian argues, "uncertainty" that failed to "provide clear legal rules around which parties could plan."[88] Such "ludicrous" circumstances, many contemporaries thought, represented "the total abolition of justice."[89] However, the actions and decisions of the superior court "tended much to bring such special acts of the Legislature . . . into ridicule and deserved contempt" and resulted in the increasing standardization of law throughout the state.[90] After 1791, the number of special acts dramatically decreased. Between 1790 and 1795, acts restoring people to their law dropped by almost 90 percent, and legislation on other judicial matters, such as modifying court rules or granting the estate of a deceased citizen to another person without a trial, dropped by over 50 percent. Moreover, in just one year (1790–1791), general statutes to set statewide procedures, which used to be settled on a case-by-case basis with special legislation, increased from 15 to 55 acts.[91]

Just as important, the executive and legislative branches worked together on a general revision of the laws to adopt "them to our present situation" and disperse them to the public through local and state courts and officers. Such a move ensured "that the people at large may know what are the Laws that are now in force" in "this state."[92] Rev. Stephen Peabody noted in a sermon that these revisions helped bring the vast areas of the state into "a complete and harmonious whole."[93] By the mid-1790s, not only did state institutions bring state law to those most local of spaces, but that law was no longer variable and uncertain—instead, it was codified and standardized.

Like New Hampshire, structural change in Pennsylvania happened almost immediately in the wake of the toppling of the oligarchy. In the convention that framed the state constitution, delegates not only debated suffrage qualifications and the propriety of doing away with a powerful executive, but also demanded penal reform, prison reform, the establishment of laws to eradicate "Vice and Immorality," and the restructuring of the judicial system. In effect, the framers of the constitution focused on altering the internal police of their state as much as implementing democracy. One convention delegate believed plans to reform the state's police powers proved that the convention was "resolved to clear every part of the old rubbish out of the way and begin upon a clear foundation."[94]

Clearing away the "old rubbish," in part, meant heeding the advice of revolutionary reformers like Demophilus and his plans for "distributive justice." In the constitution, the framers stipulated that citizens from specific judicial districts would elect every justice of the peace in the state. Importantly, no districts existed in the colony; the mere mention of districts represented a completely new judicial structure. While historians often point out the elective portion of the constitutional section pertaining to justices, they just as often ignore the significance of the framers' conscious use of the word "district." The creation of districts in the state substantially altered the geographic distribution of JPs and therefore the reach of state law.[95] While magistrates had been unevenly distributed during the colonial period—as in Bucks County, where JPs resided in eleven of twenty-eight townships and nine of the seventeen JPs lived in and around the borough of Bristol—through the creation of districts, eighteen of twenty-eight townships had JPs, and no town held a majority of the officers. Like Bucks, Cumberland County's distribution of JPs changed dramatically. In 1775–1776, twelve of twenty-three townships had JPs. By 1778, JPs lived in all twenty-three townships.[96]

Not only did the leaders of the new state find it imperative to break up the counties into smaller districts for the better administration of justice, hey also created 10 new counties. They created counties in the most western regions of the state and divided the large southeastern counties, such as Philadelphia and Chester, into several smaller, more manageable areas. Rationalizing space with more counties resulted in an explosion in the number of governing institutions and officers throughout the state. The number of courts, jails, magistrates, sheriffs, undersheriffs, and coroners nearly doubled.

Pennsylvania's politicians also reformed key aspects of the judiciary, broadened the powers of law enforcement officials, and connected those officers to the state. During the war, JPs gained the "shocking power" to fine, jail, or deny bail anyone they deemed inimical to the "State of Pennsylvania" at their discretion.[97] Further linking JPs with a rising central authority, those officers obtained jurisdiction over capital crimes while under the supervision of a state supreme court judge. At the end of 1778, Pennsylvania had its first regular oyer and terminer courts staffed by twenty-two county JPs and three supreme court judges. Just as significant, those supreme court judges rode a circuit broken up into western and eastern districts, where they could provide uniformity of law in capital cases and oversee civil litigation through appeals. Such changes were profound. By 1778, Bedford County, which had had sporadic oyer and terminer courts commissioned by executive fiat during the colonial period, had quarterly oyer and terminer courts that sat for at least eleven days.[98] Through these changes, state leaders could ensure a uniformity of decisions while demonstrating the preeminence of state institutions over local spaces.

Throughout the 1780s and into the 1790s, the government repeatedly used the reform of the judiciary to consolidate and centralize power in the state. In many ways, the state had to institute such reforms. During the late 1770s and early 1780s, Pennsylvania suffered from both internal and external threats to state authority and legitimacy. Not only did the revolution divide the people into two opposing camps, but the state constitution separated those people loyal to the American cause. Add to this dark reality the state's initial failure to rectify the crumbling status of civil government, and one gets the impression of a state on the brink of collapse. Every instance of the state's inability to uphold the law posed as a testament to state failure. For instance, when the government failed to capture two highway robbers, citizens suspected that the state was, as one writer put it, "weak" in "the execution of government." Surely," the author wrote, "the power of the State of Pennsylvania is superior" to two criminals. Pennsylvanians, he ended, "are entitled" to a "vigorous exertion" by the state for their "security and protection."[99] That was the point; the revolution was supposed to fix the problems of governance, not make them worse.

State leaders responded to such criticisms by reforming the judiciary and tightening state control of law enforcement. In 1780, for instance, the legislature added another supreme court judge and three years later fixed their circuit further by establishing four circuit districts that ran all year around. In 1791, they increased the number of circuit districts to five and added district presidents answerable to the state executive. Each district, moreover, was separated into subdivisions for courts of oyer and terminer, courts of quarter sessions, courts of common pleas, and orphans' courts. The district presidents directed and supervised the law enforcement and judicial affairs of each district. They controlled the direction of judges, justices, sheriffs, and coroners. They could issue writs of habeas corpus and certiorari, and they could mobilize the force of the district to put down internal unrest. Such changes, many thought, would "secure an efficient, safe and *uniform* administration of the laws" and provide for "the good Order of Government."[100]

Not only did such changes offer a uniformity of decisions, but they forcibly demonstrated the power of the state over the lives of citizens. In opening the sessions of the supreme court in the counties and districts of Pennsylvania, for example, the judges mimicked royal displays of authority and paraded through the counties with a retinue of state officials, both civil and military. When the day came to open the supreme court, sheriffs, coroners, county lieutenants, presidents of the court of common pleas, and a detachment of cavalry met the judges of the supreme court at the county line and escorted them through an elaborate parade to the courts. Reflecting on the courts of his youth and of his parent's generation, David Paul Brown argued that "with all their professed republican principles," the state judges "followed and imitated, at no great distance, the example of the judges of the English Court of King's Bench." Public processions, Brown concluded, had the same purpose as those in England, to "enjoin reverence to the sovereign."[101]

State panoplies of power, then, served a purpose. As one writer noted, the opening of the courts strikes "great terror" into the hearts of the state's internal enemies and provides "comfort and security" for "the good people thereof."[102] Through the revolution, the state supreme court had been raised to such a power over the social, moral, and economic life of citizens that one onlooker noted that the president of the state served as the mere "Footman" of the "Chief Justice [who] rides in the Body of the Carriage, and the *People* run whooping and hollowing along side, choak'd with Dust and bespatter'd with Mire."[103] Such an augmentation of state power through the supreme court was a product of the transformation of the legal institutions and officers during the American Revolution.

In Virginia, a similar trajectory of the standardization of law and the centralization of power took place. Also, as New Hampshire and Pennsylvania, these changes were the product of a long-drawn-out dispute rooted in the problems of the colonial past. In Virginia, the structure of the courts, the power of the state over local spaces, and the uniformity of state law all came to a head in the divisive days of the 1780s. The colonial system had perpetuated the dominance of local oligarchs that left the imperial state weakened and confined to the geographically confined space and popularly assumed corruption of Williamsburg. It seemed, to all and sundry during the colonial period, that the system did not meet the needs of inhabitants as their daily lives were altered by societal forces that they could not control, much less come to grips with. Independence, however, released constraints on reform. Despite the determination of some to maintain the structure of the colonial government, Virginians overhauled the institutions and officers that directed and regulated the daily activities of citizens. It was only through these changes that the state could claim to be anything other than a glorified continuation of the colony that preceded it.

The 1776 state constitution began the process of change in Virginia. In that instrument, not only did Virginians claim sovereign power by wresting away control from royally appointed officials, but they also reformed those most important of officers, the judges. Unlike New Hampshire, Virginians had little difficulty outlining a strict separation of power between the branches of government and to give real meaning to that separation. The constitution reserved the selection of judges to a joint ballot of the General Assembly and stipulated that judges held their office "during good behaviour" with "fixed and adequate Salaries"[104]—change they could never have achieved as a colony under the constraints of royal instructions.[105] Just as significant, the constitution abolished plural officeholding, pushing Virginia one step closer to eradicating the personal nature of colonial governance. Such stipulations, necessary as they were considering the grievances of the colonial past, gave teeth to the idea of separate powers. No longer could a governor manipulate legal proceedings—nor, as many pointed out, could the legislature. With these reforms, as historian Kevin R. C. Gutzman argues, Virginia created the "first distinct judicial branch, in the modern sense of the term, in the world."[106]

In the first few years after independence, state legislators put the ideas inspired by the constitution into working form. The obliteration of royal and executive powers had real and practical ramifications for legal proceedings in the state. Not only had the crown been the court of last resort, but the governor and his council functioned as the only high court in the colony, with both law and equity powers. Instead of replicating this judicial framework, legislators, between 1776 and 1779, fashioned three new high courts in the state. They created a general court detached from the executive, separated its law and equity functions with the creation of the high court of chancery, and relinquished its appellate jurisdiction with the formation of the supreme court of appeals. Instead of a two-tiered judiciary, as existed in the colonial past, there were three levels of superior courts with distinct powers in law and equity.

On the surface, these transformations augured a significant delineation between the colonial past and the new future under the state. Nevertheless, much of the old system of local governance remained intact. The highest courts in the state still confined their meetings to Williamsburg, and county magistrates, a singular cause of colonial contempt, maintained their control of local governance. According to the constitution, the executive branch could not even remove a local magistrate without the "recommendation of the respective County Courts," thus preserving that institution's autonomy and dominance.[107] It was, as petitioners from Fairfax County pointed out, "a very faulty Part of our Constitution."[108]

While such a stipulation belies the idea of a transformation from colony to state, the entire thrust of the revolutionary period proved the undoing of those institutions and the local elite's absolute control over them. The rise of a central authority to oversee, and in some ways control, local institutions was a goal of revolutionary reformers from the beginning. In 1776, state legislators established a committee to republicanize and standardize law in the state. They wanted to remove vestiges of a monarchical past and make the disparate parts of the state legally holistic. This popularly known committee for the "Revision of the Laws" included such legal luminaries as Thomas Jefferson, George Wythe, Edmund Pendleton, and, for a time, George Mason. Together, those men fashioned a new trajectory for the state of Virginia. They created a long-range program to alter the penal code, restructure the courts, codify religious freedom, and establish a publicly funded educational system. The committee crafted 126 bills, half of which became laws within five years, with another half following in the late 1780s into the 1790s. Crucially, many of these laws highlight the lawmakers' efforts to break the power of local oligarchies using newly fashioned state institutions.

Of the acts restructuring the courts, one of the most significant for the future of Virginia's legal system was a bill creating a circuit for the general court. Although the legislature initially refused to implement the act, the goals of the reformers and the debate over the bill in the 1780s paved the way for judicial reform. Realizing the difficulty of eradicating the autonomy of local judges, "a self-contained Body, with the Power of filling their own Vacancys," the reformers put together a bill creating a powerful general court that could control those officers by providing "superior wisdom and uniformity of decisions" throughout the state by going on circuit.[109] Yet, it was a hard-fought battle. In the initial hearing in 1776, the legislature removed all sections pertaining to a circuit court and thus perpetuated problems Virginians railed against for years.[110] When the bill received a new hearing in 1784, it again met defeat. According to John Marshall, "the circuit Court system meets with too much opposition from selfish individuals to be adopted." The principal members of the opposition, Marshall argued, were "those [local] Magistrates who are tenacious of authority." They would "not assent to any thing which may diminish their ideal dignity."[111] In the end, "the fate" of the bill, which represented "the work of an Age," was "destroyed by a set of D—Asses."[112]

The sheer level of animosity and vitriol leveled against opponents of the bill speaks to the doggedness with which reformers adhered to reorganizing the courts and extending state authority. Within less than two years after the second refusal, legislators finally passed a circuit bill that, as James Madison noted, "is nearly a transcript from the bill originally penned in 1776."[113] By reflecting on the origins of the bill, particularly its place within the "Revision of the Laws," which even contemporaries viewed as a revolutionary initiative, Madison connected ongoing court reform and the expansion of the state to the revolution.

Less than two years after the circuit bill, Madison and other legislators pushed court reform even further. They created a geographically diffuse system of state courts that represented a significant departure from the past and a radical reorientation of the place and authority of the state over local spaces. Instead of a circuit system, Virginians expanded the reach of the general court—and thus the state—through the erection of state district courts. From James Monroe's perspective, "Of the general court after this term, nothing is left but the name." Each "district court," he went on, "bears the same relation to the County Courts within it that the general court did to all the counties."[114] Now, instead of a general court that only had the power on paper to direct legal proceedings in the province and therefore curb the power of the county courts, there were eighteen district courts with state judges established throughout the commonwealth "cloathed with all the powers of the General Court."[115] In result, there would be, as Judge Pendleton mused, "regular Subordination and uniformity of Judgments" to correct the "confused Ideas" that all the courts in the state were not "but branches of the same Court." Connecting all the courts together as "branches of the same Court" was a significant step toward the centralization of state authority over the whole.[116]

By 1788, then, the state of Virginia, in both form and function, looked nothing like its colonial predecessor. The two-tiered judiciary had been replaced with three high courts and eighteen district courts staffed by state judges that took away from the power and authority that local magistrates and county courts had wielded for over a century.[117] It was through such reforms that state judges, now powerfully backed by a formidable judicial structure, could claim such ideas as judicial independence, and, importantly, judicial review. It is no coincidence that judges like St. George Tucker, George Wythe, Edmund Pendleton, and Spencer Roane asserted such powers on the heels of judicial reform.[118] The state judges had become, as Judge Tucker pointed out, the "censors of the republic."[119]

These three histories provide a picture of the transformations wrought by the revolution to the emergence of new states. One may reasonably question what three distinct colonies-cum-states with expansive frontiers can offer our understanding of the revolution in general. After all, each colony/state had its own unique experiences and trajectories. Yet, the crisis of governance that characterized the revolutionary period in those places, spanning the mid-eighteenth century through the 1780s and 1790s, occurred throughout revolutionary America. Though the timing of the crises, or what John Brooke has defined as the "revolutionary beginnings" and "revolutionary settlements" may have differed, we can see shared experiences in the history of the Carolinas, the regulator movements there, and the ongoing debates that shaped the very character of those states after independence. The same is true in New York, as the state government moved to solidify its ever-extending jurisdiction and thus project its authority over the peoples within it, or in Maryland, as the initial constitutional moment failed to reflect the needs, hopes, and aspirations of its citizens and forced a reckoning with the purpose of government and whom that government served as the "price of revolution." Or, again, we can see the story unfold in Connecticut, which did not alter its constitution in the immediate aftermath of independence but still augmented the authority of state institutions such as the executive and the judiciary to govern the state during the revolutionary war. We can also see this prolonged struggle in Massachusetts, as regulators in the 1780s pushed for a "satisfactory and legitimate restructuring" of their "civil institutions."[120]

Massachusetts is a case in point. There, as in New Hampshire, Pennsylvania, and Virginia, colonists (and then new citizens) complained of unequal access to the institutions of justice, eastern elite monopolization of important judicial offices, and the failure of the state to incorporate "the people" into the body politic. There, too, we see not only a democratic deficit spanning the 1760s into the 1780s, but through that, a legitimation crisis. As Brooke points out in his work on western Massachusetts, the "revolutionary beginnings" that shaped popular responses to the colonial government were characterized by "widespread concern with the continuing inaccessibility of justice." On the eve of the revolution, Brooke found that "roughly 65 percent of the people in Hampshire County and 45 percent of Berkshire County lived in towns without a resident Justice of the Peace." This inequality continued well after independence, thus significantly shaping western resistance to the state government and the continuance of their struggle for a satisfactory "revolutionary settlement" for an inclusive system of government that was accessible, equitable, and took into consideration expansive problems and experiences in the ways it governed. Government, from that perspective, was not and should not be dedicated to the special interest and emolument of the few, but should be directed to solve the problems and cater to the needs of the many.[121]

The decade of the 1780s, what Fiske viewed as the Critical Period of American history, was, in a sense, "critical" because it was a divisive moment in the history of the United States in which Americans were in the midst of working out long-term problems in an effort to achieve a revolutionary settlement that, at the very least, had a broad base of popular support. Such a transition and transformation could and did not happen overnight or easily. That push for ongoing change informed elite perceptions of a spreading insurgency lit by the "combustibles in every state," an argument about people and their rights that has had significant purchase throughout American history.[122]

Importantly, however, that hard-won *first* settlement was not achieved by the United States Constitution—the miracle that saved America, according to Fiske—but rather by an ongoing struggle to form governments that citizens viewed as legitimate repositories of the people's sovereign power. How that sovereign power translated into a national identity with national programs and national rights was still far in the future in the late eighteenth century. For some people in the revolutionary era, settlement began and ended in their states.

The dedication to an idea of government that can change and adapt to new problems, acting equitably and efficiently, is central to an ideal of American governance. It continues to inspire Americans to fight for the realization of the basic promises of revolutionary settlements that have been too often denied to large segments of the population. The revolutionary era was one moment in a series of moments in the fight for inclusion, equity, and, importantly, equal access to and treatment before the law. That struggle was not solved by that first settlement or by the ratification of the U.S. Constitution—in fact, they only reaffirmed the necessity of popular mobilization to resist policies and visions that do not adequately reflect the needs and interests of "the people."

The definition of "*the* people" has fundamentally changed since the revolutionary era. Who could and should be included in that vision and have access to the levers of power has been an enduring struggle. A dedication to that realization inspired popular mobilizations deemed dangerous "riots and rebellions" by those in power at the time, such as Gabriel's Rebellion, the Whiskey Rebellion, or Fries's Rebellion. However, those movements, like today, were not against government, but rather *for* government—a government that has the ability, wherewithal, and political will to protect and enhance the lives, fortunes, and sacred honor of "*the* people." This essay has focused on one foundational moment—a moment revolutionaries understood as dedicated to an idea that government should be "the choicest blessing Heaven ever has bestowed on the human race," rather than a "necessary evil."[123] Revolutionaries may have worked out the basic ideals and institutional framework of governments dedicated to that principle, but achieving the *actual* equity of *every* American that those governments represent, serve, and govern is still ongoing.

## Notes

1. John Winthrop to John Adams, June 1, 1776, in *Papers of John Adams,* ed. Robert J. Taylor, Mary-Jo Kline, Gregg L. Lint (Cambridge, MA: Belknap Press of Harvard University Press, 1979), 4:224.
2. John Fiske, *The Critical Period of American History, 1783–1789* (Boston, 1888), 64–69.
3. Jack P. Greene, *Understanding the American Revolution: Issues and Actors* (Charlottesville: University of Virginia Press, 1995), 51, 364, 369.

4. Gordon S. Wood, *Creation of the American Republic, 1776–1787* (Chapel Hill: University of North Carolina Press, 1969); Wood, *Radicalism of the American Revolution* (New York: Knopf, 1992).

5. Peter Onuf, *Statehood and Union: A History of the Northwest Ordinance* (Bloomington: Indiana University Press, 1987); Peter Onuf and Nicholas Onuf, *Federal Union, Modern World: The Law of Nations in the Age of Revolutions* (Madison, WI: Madison House, 1993); Daniel Hulsebosch, *Constituting Empire: New York and the Transformation of Constitutionalism in the Atlantic World, 1664–1830* (Chapel Hill: University of North Carolina Press, 2005); David Hendrickson, *Peace Pact: The Lost World of the American Founding* (Lawrence: University of Kansas Press, 2003); Douglas Bradburn, *The Citizenship Revolution: Politics and the Creation of the American Union, 1774–1804* (Charlottesville: University of Virginia Press, 2009); Brian Philips Murphy, *Building the Empire State: Political Economy in the Early Republic* (Philadelphia: University of Pennsylvania Press, 2015); Gary Gerstle, *Liberty and Coercion: The Paradox of American Government from the Founding to the Present* (Princeton, NJ: Princeton University Press, 2015); Steve Pincus, *The Heart of the Declaration: The Founders' Case for an Activist Government* (New Haven, CT: Yale University Press, 2016); William J. Novak and Steven Pincus, "Revolutionary State Formation: The Origins of the Strong American State," in *State Formations: Global Histories and Cultures of Statehood,* ed. John L. Brooke, Julia C. Straus, and Greg Anderson (Cambridge, UK: Cambridge University Press, 2018), 138–55.

6. Oscar Handlin and Mary Handlin, *Commonwealth: A Study of the Role of Government in the American Economy; Massachusetts, 1774–1861* (Cambridge, MA: Belknap Press, 1947); Louis Hartz, *The Liberal Tradition in America* (New York: Harcourt Brace, 1955).

7. Max Edling, *A Revolution in Favor of Government: Origins of the U.S. Constitution and the Making of the American State* (Oxford, UK: Oxford University Press, 2003); Patrick Griffin, *American Leviathan: Empire, Nation, and Revolutionary Frontier* (New York: Hill and Wang, 2007).

8. Christopher Marshall, *Extracts from the Diary of Christopher Marshall,* ed. William Duane (Albany, 1877), 223; *Pennsylvania Gazette (Philadelphia),* November 15, 1780.

9. Ibid.

10. Douglas Bradburn, "The Rise of the States: The Problem of Order and the Causes of American Independence" (paper presented at the American Historical Association, Washington, DC, January 3–6, 2008; Christopher R. Pearl, "Franklin's Turn: Imperial Politics and the Coming of the American Revolution," *Pennsylvania Magazine of History and Biography* 136, no. 2 (2012), 117–39; Pearl, *Conceived in Crisis: The Revolutionary Creation of an American State* (Charlottesville: University of Virginia Press, 2020); Gerstle, *Liberty and Coercion,* 17–88.

11. Jeremy Belknap, *The History of New-Hampshire* (Dover, 1812), 2:262–263; Daniell, *Experiment in Republicanism: New Hampshire Politics and the American Revolution, 1741–1794* (Cambridge, MA: Harvard University Press, 1970), 17; Daniell, "Politics in New Hampshire under Governor Benning Wentworth, 1741–1767," *William and Mary Quarterly* 23, no. 1 (1966): 76–105; James Kirby Martin, "A Model for the Coming American Revolution: The Birth and Death of the Wentworth Oligarchy in New Hampshire, 1741–1776," *Journal of Social History* 4, no. 1 (1970): 41–52.

12. Daniell, *Experiment in Republicanism,* 66n69.

13. Clifford K. Shipton, *New England in the 18th Century* (Cambridge, MA: Harvard University Press, 1963), 390.

14. Carl Bridenbaugh, *Mitre and Sceptre: Transatlantic Faiths, Ideas, Personalities, and Politics, 1689–1775* (Oxford, UK: Oxford University Press, 1962), 178, 183, 208, 263; Daniell, *Experiment in Republicanism,* 4–5, 18, 63; Martin, "A Model for the Coming American Revolution," 47.

15. Belknap, *The History of New-Hampshire.* 3:193; Peter Livius, *The Memorial of Peter Livius, Esq. One of his Majesty's Council for the Province of New Hampshire, in New England, to the Lords Commissioners for Trade and Plantations* (London, 1773), 1–30; Paul W. Wilderson, *Governor John Wentworth and the American Revolution* (Hanover, NH: University Press of New England, 1994), 204–5; James Kirby Martin, "A Model for the Coming American Revolution," 47–50; George Adrian Washburne, *Imperial Control of the Administration of Justice in the Thirteen American Colonies, 1684–1776* (New York: Columbia University Press, 1923), 147–49; Daniell, *Experiment in Republicanism,* 19; Joseph Henry Smith, "Appendix A: Statistics on the Appellate Jurisdiction of the Privy Council, 1696–1783," in *Appeals to the Privy Council from the American Plantations* (New York: Columbia University Press, 1950), 667, 670.

16. Daniell, *Experiment in Republicanism,* 49; John J. McCusker, "Colonial Statistics," Tables Eg 97–109, in *Historical Statistics of the United States, Earliest Times to Present: Millennial Edition,* ed. Susan B. Carter et al. (New York: Cambridge University Press, 2006), 5:658.

17. *New Hampshire Gazette,* February 25, 1774.

18. Livius, *The Memorial,* 39.

19. Daniell, *Experiment in Republicanism,* 49–50.

20. *New Hampshire Gazette,* October 11, 1771.

21. *New Hampshire Gazette,* March 18, 1774.

22. In Grafton County, for instance, five of the six appointed magistrates were either recent settlers of that county or absentee landlords, and all were connected to the governor. Two of the magistrates, John Fenton and John Hurd, held official positions in multiple counties. Fenton, for example, a native of Ireland, moved to New Hampshire after Governor Wentworth gave him 3,000 acres of land in the province. By 1774, he had become a close associate of the governor and was rewarded with the positions of militia colonel, magistrate for Portsmouth, magistrate for Hillsborough County, magistrate for Grafton County, clerk of the inferior court of common pleas in Grafton, and judge of the probate court for Grafton.

23. Daniell, *Experiment in Republicanism,* 50.

24. *Documents and Records Relating to the Province of New Hampshire, From 1764 to 1776,* ed. Nathaniel Bouton (Nashua, 1873), 7:348–49.

25. William Henry Fry, "New Hampshire as a Royal Province" (PhD diss., Columbia University, 1908), 465.

26. *Documents and Records,* 7:313–14; *New Hampshire Gazette,* March 18, 1774; *New Hampshire Gazette,* June 19, 1767, and May 6, May 13, June 10, and October 7, 1768.

27. *New Hampshire Gazette,* April 1, 1774

28. *Pennsylvania Archives,* ed. William Henry Egle (Harrisburg, PA, 1896), ser. 3, vol. 8:703–4.

29. Dr. William Shippen to his brother, Judge Edward Shippen of Lancaster, July 17, 1776, in "Notes and Queries," *Pennsylvania Magazine of History and Biography* 44, no. 3 (1920): 286.

30. *Pennsylvania Archives*, ed. Charles F. Hoban (Harrisburg, PA: State Printer, 1935), ser. 8, vol. 8:6819.

31. Pearl, *Conceived in Crisis*, 59–60.

32. *Pennsylvania Archives*, ser. 8, vol. 6:4543

33. *Continuance Docket #11*, Northampton County Courthouse, Easton, PA.

34. *Pennsylvania Archives*, ser. 8, vol. 7:5408.

35. William Allen to Thomas Penn, March 8, 1767, Thomas Penn Papers, 1729–1832 (hereafter TPP), reel X, 94–98, Historical Society of Pennsylvania (hereafter HSP); *Supreme Court Dockets (Pennsylvania), 1753–1799*, vol. 1, HSP; G. S. Rowe, *Embattled Bench: The Pennsylvania Supreme Court and the Forging of a Democratic Society, 1684–1809* (Newark: University of Delaware Press, 1994), 97–118.

36. *Pennsylvania Archives*, ser. 8, vol. 7:5580–81.

37. Allen to Penn, March 8, 1767, reel X, 94–98, TPP.

38. Jack D. Marietta and G. S. Rowe, "Violent Crime, Victims, and Society in Pennsylvania, 1682–1800," *Pennsylvania History* 66 (1999): 45.

39. "Proceedings of Council from 1762–1771," *Colonial Records* (Harrisburg, PA, 1852), 9:682–83.

40. *Pennsylvania Archives*, ser. 8, vol. 9:6749.

41. Lewis Ourry to James Hamilton, August 26, 1763, Burd-Shippen Papers, Series 1: Correspondence, box 3, American Philosophical Society (hereafter APS), Philadelphia; "A Petition," January 18, 1769, *Pennsylvania Archives*, ser. 8, vol. 7:6319–20, ser. 8, vol. 9:6819, 7042.

42. *Pennsylvania Chronicle*, February 8 and 15, 1768; Joseph Galloway to Benjamin Franklin, March 10, 1768, *Papers of Benjamin Franklin*, ed. William B. Wilcox (New Haven, CT: Yale University Press, 1972), 15:71.

43. A. G. Roeber, *Faithful Magistrates and Republican Lawyers: Creators of Virginia Legal Culture* (Chapel Hill: University of North Carolina Press, 1981), 115–16.

44. Richard R. Beeman, *The Evolution of the Southern Backcountry: A Case Study of Lunenburg County, Virginia, 1746–1832* (Philadelphia: University of Pennsylvania Press, 1984), 44.

45. Landon Carter, *The Diary of Colonel Landon Carter of Sabine Hall, 1752–1778*, ed. Jack P. Greene (Charlottesville: University of Virginia Press, 1965), 2:668–69.

46. *Executive Journals of the Council of Virginia*, ed. Wilmer L. Hall (Richmond: Virginia State Library, 1945), 5:378–79.

47. *Journals of the House of Burgesses of Virginia*, ed. H. R. McIlwaine (Richmond: Virginia State Library, 1909), 7:190.

48. *Virginia Gazette*, October 24, 1771.

49. See, for instance, the petitions of inhabitants in Princess Ann and Fairfax Counties, March 23, 1752, in *Executive Journals*, 5:379–80. See also Roeber, *Faithful Magistrates*, 153–59.

50. Carter, May 9, 1770, in Greene, *Diary*, 1:405.

51. Quote of William Rind in Roeber, *Faithful Magistrates*, 153.

52. Michael A. McDonnell, *The Politics of War: Race, Class, and Conflict in Revolutionary Virginia* (Chapel Hill: University of North Carolina Press, 2007), 29.

53. Carl Lounsbury, *The Courthouses of Early Virginia: An Architectural History* (Charlottesville: University of Virginia Press, 2005), 164–65.

54. Hugh F. Rankin, "The General Court of Colonial Virginia: Its Jurisdiction and Personnel," *Virginia Magazine of History and Biography* 70, no. 2 (1962): 142–53; Roeber, *Faithful Magistrates*, 132.

55. Quote of William Allason, 1765, in Roeber, *Faithful Magistrates*, 131.

56. *Virginia Gazette*, May 30, 1766.

57. John Wentworth to Lord Dartmouth, December 20, 1774, in *Documents of the American Revolution*, ed. K. G. Davies (Dublin: Irish University Press, 1975), 8:248–51; John Wentworth to Thomas Gage, January 21, 1775, quoted in Richard Francis Upton, *Revolutionary New Hampshire: An Account of the Social and Political Forces Underlying the Transition from Royal Province to American Commonwealth* (Hanover, NH: Dartmouth College Publications, 1936), 24.

58. Paul W. Wilderson, *Governor John Wentworth and the America Revolution* (Hanover, NH: University Press of New England, 1994), 221–65.

59. *New Hampshire Gazette*, March 18, 1774.

60. *New Hampshire Gazette*, April 1, 1774.

61. Ibid.

62. *New Hampshire Gazette*, April 22, 1774.

63. *New Hampshire Gazette*, October 7, 1768.

64. John Wentworth to Lord Dartmouth, December 20, 1774, in *Documents of the American Revolution*, 8:250.

65. *New Hampshire Gazette*, March 17, 1775, February 10, 1775, and June 2, 1775.

66. *New Hampshire Gazette*, December 30, 1774; Charles James Smith, *Annals of the Town of Hillsborough, Hillsborough County, N.H.* (Sandborton, NH, 1841), 16–17; Daniell, *Experiment in Republicanism*, 88.

67. *New Hampshire Gazette*, December 30, 1774.

68. *New Hampshire Gazette*, May 5, 1775.

69. Samuel Livermore to Wentworth, January 11, 1775, in *Documents of the American Revolution*, 9:28.

70. *New Hampshire Gazette*, February 3, 1775.

71. *New Hampshire Gazette*, February 17, 1775, February 25, 1775, May 5, 1775, January 20, 1775.

72. *Pennsylvania Journal*, September 27, 1775; *Pennsylvania Packet*, November 20, 1775.

73. Wentworth to Dartmouth, May 17, 1775, in *Documents of the American Revolution*, 9:135–36.

74. Wentworth to Dartmouth, July 13, 1774, in *Documents of the American Revolution*, 8:150.

75. Wentworth to Dartmouth, August 18, 1775, in *Documents of the American Revolution*, 9:76–78.

76. *Pennsylvania Packet*, June 10, 1776.

77. *Pennsylvania Packet*, February 12, 1776; Demophilus, *The Genuine Principles of the Ancient Saxon, or English Constitution* (Philadelphia, 1776), 2, 10, 16, 18, 22, 39–50.

78. Ibid.

79. The ideas presented by revolutionaries on statecraft represent a crucial transition from colony to state. They show, when combined with the reforms they instituted, the importance of both the ideas and actions of people during the revolution to the formation of modern states. One of the central attributes of a modern state, argued by Max Weber and still considered such by modern scholars, is the impersonal nature of a modern state's bureaucracy. Officials, in this sense, are not, as Weber noted, appointed using "ascriptive criteria"; rather, "specialized qualifications" underlie the decision. Significantly, Weber used the example of a judge to highlight this point. In words strikingly similar to those of Jefferson, Weber noted that a judge in a modern state is "an automaton into which legal documents and fees are stuffed at the top in order that it may spill forth the verdict at the bottom along with the reasons, read mechanically from codified paragraphs." While Weber made room for the individual decisions of judges, he highlighted that even those were guided by "the Code." Such an understanding of the state has led leading political scientists, sociologists, and philosophers to argue, as Christopher W. Morris did in 2002, that "modern governance is impersonal." Jefferson to Pendleton, August 26, 1776, *Thomas Jefferson Papers Digital Edition,* ed. Barbara B. Oberg and J. Jefferson Looney (Charlottesville: Rotunda, an imprint of University of Virginia Press, 2008), accessed July 6, 2021, https://rotunda.upress.virginia.edu/founders/TSJN-01-01-02-0210; Max Weber, *Economy and Society: An Outline of Interpretive Sociology,* ed. Guenther Roth and Claus Wittich (Berkeley: University of California Press, 1978), 2:979; Christopher W. Morris, *An Essay on the Modern State* (Cambridge, UK: Cambridge University Press, 2002), 255; Christopher Pierson, *The Modern State* (London: Routledge, 1996), 15–17; Harvey C. Mansfield, "On the Impersonality of the Modern State: A Comment on Machiavelli's Use of *Stato,*" *American Political Science Review* 77, no. 4 (1983): 849–57.

80. Upton, *Revolutionary New Hampshire,* 177.

81. Belknap, "Appendix," *History of New Hampshire,* 419–24; *Documents and Records,* 8:10–13, 61–64; Daniell, *Experiment in Republicanism,* 115.

82. *New Hampshire Mercury,* September 6, 1786.

83. *Laws of New Hampshire,* ed. Henry Harrison Metcalf (Bristol, NH: Musgrove Printing House, 1916), 4:10–11.

84. *Fowle's New-Hampshire Gazette,* May 27, 1785.

85. William Plummer to William Coleman, May 31, 1785, in *Publications of the Colonial Society of Massachusetts* (Boston: Colonial Society of Massachusetts, 1910), 11:384.

86. Jeremiah Mason, *Memoir, Autobiography and Correspondence of Jeremiah Mason* (Kansas City, MO: Lawyers' International, 1917), 25–26.

87. Timothy A. Lawrie, "Interpretation and Authority: Separation of Powers and the Judiciary's Battle for Independence in New Hampshire, 1786–1818," *American Journal of Legal History* 39, no. 1 (1995): 323.

88. Lawrie, "Interpretation and Authority," 319.

89. Mason, *Memoirs,* 25; *An Address of the Convention for Framing a New Constitution of Government for the State of New-Hampshire* (Portsmouth, 1783), 8.

90. Mason, *Memoirs,* 26.

91. Lawrie, "Interpretation and Authority," 332–33.

92. Josiah Bartlett to General Court, January 5, 1791, in *Early State Papers of New Hampshire,* ed. Albert Stillman Batchellor (Concord, NH: Ira C. Evans, 1893), 22:142.

93. Stephen Peabody, *A Sermon Delivered at Concord Before the General Court of the State of New Hampshire at the Annual Election* (Concord, NH, 1797), 13.

94. Thomas Smith to Arthur St. Clair, August 22, 1776, in *The St. Clair Papers: The Life and Public Services of Arthur St. Clair,* ed. William Henry Smith (Cincinnati, 1882), 1:374.

95. PA State Const. § 30, in Francis N. Thorpe, *Federal and State Constitutions* (Washington: Government Printing Office, 1909), 5:3089; *Statutes at Large of Pennsylvania from 1682 to 1809,* ed. Robert L. Cable (Harrisburg, PA: Legislative Reference Bureau, 2001), 9:41–45.

96. The information for the geographic distribution of JPs was determined by cross-referencing Wayne Bockleman, "Continuity and Change in Revolutionary Pennsylvania" (PhD diss., Northwestern University, 1969), 97–104 with an incomplete list of local officers commissioned under the 1776 Constitution located in the *Pennsylvania Archives,* ser. 2, vol. 3:667–794 and the appointments listed in the "Minutes of the Supreme Executive Council" in the *Colonial Records.* I used county histories and extent tax records to find the residence for those JPs that did not have places of residence attached to their commission or were not included in Bockleman.

97. James Burd to Edward Shippen, November 13, 1776, Peale-Sellers Family Collection, series 1: Correspondence, box 1, APS. *Statutes at Large,* 9:240–41.

98. *Statutes at Large,* 9:733; G. S. Rowe, *Embattled Bench,* 129; *Colonial Records,* 15:34, 160; "Expenses for a Court of Oyer and Terminer in Bedford County after 1778–1780," in Bedford County Collection, Pennsylvania Counties, Miscellaneous Records, 1701–1901, box 1, folder 4, HSP.

99. *Pennsylvania Packet,* August 22, 1778

100. Jasper Yeates to Edward Burd, October 3, 1784, Burd-Shippen Family Papers, reel 1, folder 12, Pennsylvania Historical and Museum Commission (hereafter PHMC); PA State Const., 1790, in Thorpe, *Federal and State Constitutions,* 5:3092–103; *Statutes at Large,* 14:110–20.

101. *Pennsylvania Mercury,* October 20, 1786; David Paul Brown, *The Forum: Or, Forty Years of Full Practice at the Philadelphia Bar* (Philadelphia: R. H. Small, 1856), 326, 328.

102. *Pennsylvania Packet,* April 8, 1778.

103. Francis Hopkinson to Thomas Jefferson, September 28, 1785, in Oberg and Looney, *The Papers of Thomas Jefferson Digital Edition.*

104. VA State Const., 1776, in Thorpe, *Federal and State Constitutions,* 7:3817.

105. Pearl, *Conceived in Crisis,* 97.

106. Kevin R. C. Gutzman, *Virginia's American Revolution: From Dominion to Republic, 1776–1840* (Lanham, MD: Lexington Books, 2007), 32.

107. VA State Const., 1776, in Thorpe, 7:3818.

108. "Fairfax County Petition," June 8, 1782, in *The Papers of George Mason, 1725–1792,* ed. Robert A. Rutland (Chapel Hill: University of North Carolina Press, 1970), 2:73337.

109. Ibid.; James Madison to Thomas Jefferson, January 9, 1785, in Oberg and Looney, *The Papers of Thomas Jefferson Digital Edition.*

110. "Bill for Establishing a General Court," November 25, 1776, in Oberg and Looney, *The Papers of Thomas Jefferson Digital Edition.*

111. John Marshall to Charles Simms, June 16, 1784, in *The Papers of John Marshall Digital Edition,* ed. Charles Hobson (Charlottesville: Rotunda, an imprint of University of Virginia Press, 2014), accessed July 6, 2021, https://rotunda.upress.virginia.edu /founders/JNML-01-01-02-0086.

112. Archibald Stuart to John Breckinridge, January 26, 1786, quoted in *The Papers of James Madison Digital Edition,* ed. J. C. A. Stagg (Charlottesville: Rotunda, an imprint of University of Virginia Press, 2010), n 3, accessed July 6, 2021, https://rotunda.upress .virginia.edu/founders/JSMN-01-08-02-023.

113. James Madison to Thomas Jefferson, January 9, 1785, Oberg and Looney, *The Papers of Thomas Jefferson Digital Edition.*

114. James Monroe to Thomas Jefferson, April 10, 1788, in ibid.

115. James Madison to Thomas Jefferson, December 4, 1786, in ibid.

116. Edmund Pendleton to James Madison, December 9, 1786, in *The Papers of James Madison Digital Edition.*

117. Roeber, *Faithful Magistrates,* 203–30.

118. David John Mays, *Edmund Pendleton, 1721–1803* (Cambridge, MA: Harvard University Press, 1952), 2:290–302; Timothy S. Huebner, "The Consolidation of State Judicial Power: Spencer Roane, Virginia Legal Culture, and the Southern Judicial Tradition," *Virginia Magazine of History and Biography* 102, no. 1 (1994): 47–72.

119. Quote of Tucker in Roeber, *Faithful Magistrates,* 216.

120. John L. Brook, "To the Quiet of the People: Revolutionary Settlements and Civil Unrest in Western Massachusetts, 1774–1789," *William and Mary Quarterly* 46, no. 3 (1989), 432; Richard Maxwell Brown, *The South Carolina Regulators: The Story of the First American Vigilante Movement* (Cambridge, MA: Harvard University Press, 1963); Marjoline Kars, *Breaking Loose Together: The Regulator Rebellion in Pre-Revolutionary North Carolina* (Chapel Hill: University of North Carolina Press, 2002); Alan Taylor, *The Divided Ground: Indians, Settlers, and the Northern Borderland of the American Revolution* (New York: Knopf, 2006); Ronald Hoffman, *A Spirit of Dissension: Economics, Politics, and the Revolution in Maryland* (Baltimore: John Hopkins University Press, 1975), 271; David H. Villers, "'King Mob' and the Rule of Law: Revolutionary Justice and the Suppression of Loyalism in Connecticut, 1774–1783," in *Loyalists and Community in North America,* ed. Robert M. Calhoon, Timothy M. Barnes, and George A. Rawlyk (Westport, CT: Greenwood Press, 1994), 17–30.

121. Brooke, "To the Quiet of the People," 436, 437 (table 3), and 441.

122. George Washington to Henry Knox, December 26, 1786, in *The Papers of George Washington Digital Edition* (Charlottesville: Rotunda, an imprint of University of Virginia Press, 2008), accessed July 6, 2021, https://rotunda.upress.virginia.edu/founders /GEWN-04-04-02-0409. See also, Robert A. Gross, "A Yankee Rebellion? The Regulators, New England, and the New Nation," *New England Quarterly* 82, no. 1 (2009), 112–35.

123. *Pennsylvania Mercury,* March 11, 1790.

# Something from Nothing?

## CURRENCY AND FINANCE IN
## THE CRITICAL PERIOD

*Hannah Farber*

> The task of creating wealth out of nothing had become too arduous
> and too thankless to be endured.
>
> —John Fiske

> A craze for fictitious wealth in the shape of paper money ran like an
> epidemic through the country.
>
> —John Fiske, one paragraph later

JOHN FISKE'S DISCUSSION OF American finance in the "Critical Period" features two successive passages that offer, if not outright contradiction of one another, then certainly a dilemma for the reader to consider.[1] In the first passage, Fiske unreservedly celebrates the "brilliant" and "heroic" efforts of Robert Morris in financing the American war effort and establishing the Bank of North America. Morris's financial ingenuity, in Fiske's retelling, enabled Americans to win their war for independence. By 1784, however, frustrated by the "weak and disorderly Confederation," Morris apparently decided that "the task of creating wealth out of nothing had become too arduous and too thankless to be endured" and resigned from his position as superintendent of finance of the United States. In short, in this passage, Fiske characterizes the process of creating wealth out of nothing as a praiseworthy and unique accomplishment.

{193}

In the very next paragraph, however, Fiske condemns a different "something out of nothing" project with language as strong as that with which he praised the efforts of Morris. The target of his condemnation in this passage is the movement among a number of American state legislatures in the mid-1780s to create paper money. Fiske describes this movement as a "craze for fictitious wealth," comparing it to both a delusion and a contagious disease. Thus while Morris's efforts to create "wealth out of nothing" were apparently praiseworthy, patriotic, and successful, those of state legislatures were lunacy.

It is not terribly difficult to understand why Fiske, a northerner writing in the aftermath of the Civil War and the restoration of the U.S. gold standard, would be predisposed to consider paper emissions by the American states as folly, if not sedition. However, Fiske's ambivalence toward making wealth out of nothing also places him within a long tradition in both scholarship and popular culture that observes financial invention with a jaundiced eye.[2] Morris, an individual who apparently created "something from nothing," remains a controversial figure in American history. His critics—then as now—believed he was primarily out to line his pockets.[3] His financially minded biographers, by contrast (like those of his protégé Hamilton), tend to celebrate him as an entrepreneurial figure who both presaged and made possible the wealth and might of the United States.[4] For these latter writers, what Morris made out of nothing was justified because it was for the benefit of the nation, which was no delusion, but a very real polity recently emerged from nothing and bound for a prosperous future of its own.

Scholars who defend paper money emissions of the 1780s tend to have very different politics from Fiske. However, they, like Fiske, tend to find ways to explain why paper money was not in fact something made, capriciously, from nothing. Terry Bouton, for example, places the currency issues of the 1780s in the context of the relatively successful track record of currency issues in colonial America before the revolution. Paper currency, understood in this light, does not come "from nothing" at all, for colonial precedent—history itself—is part of the "something" from which the 1780s currency emerged.

Instead of weighing in on the question of whether Morris or the state legislatures were justified in creating something out of nothing, this essay offers a different premise: that we do not have to see either Morris (whom Fiske praised) or the state legislatures (which he criticized) as creating "something from nothing" at all. We can, rather, view the involved parties as engaging in complex maintenance projects. The success of these projects depended on the protection of existing assets (broadly defined) through the cultivation and maintenance of financial, political, and personal relationships, and even through the cultivation and maintenance of cultural narratives. Morris's success in funding the Revolutionary War depended on his ability to maintain the value of the financial assets and instruments at his disposal. The success of the state legislatures' paper money issues in the 1780s similarly depended on the legislatures' ability to maintain ties between the value of paper money, the value of other extant assets like land, and even the unquantifiable "value" of the reputation of individuals involved in the currency-issuing process.[5]

By focusing on the ways in which the activities of Morris and the states were acts of maintenance, recategorization, and reorganization rather than invention, and by thinking about how these activities were possible because of existing financial networks, communities, histories, and obligations, we can better understand the continuities and dependencies upon which national independence was built. We can also make visible the connections—not one-time but ongoing—between economic value and other, nonmonetary forms of worth.

Appraisals of Morris's activities during the War of Independence and under the Articles of Confederation tend to be filtered through the appraisers' broader opinions on a slew of weighty political concerns: commercial banks, the project of national finance and its effects on the states and the people, the justice of the exertion of power by a financially educated elite, and the rights of lenders vis-à-vis borrowers. Morris himself has been placed by his biographers within a variety of social and political settings. As we have seen, John Fiske considered Morris primarily a protonationalist and applauded him for his efforts on behalf of the new American nation. By contrast, Morris's recent biographer Charles Rappleye, though similarly admiring his subject, characterizes Morris's actions as those of a sophisticated "global capitalist."[6] The warmth of these two portrayals of Morris, and their shared emphasis on Morris as a heroic individual actor, conceal their very divergent perspectives on the actual work that Morris did on behalf of the nation. Both writers portray him as an individual who rescued the nation by creating something out of nothing.

From the other side of the aisle, progressives excoriate Morris for building an American financial infrastructure that benefited an already wealthy American elite at the expense of the broader public.[7] Here, too, Morris can be viewed as either a globalizer or a nationalist, but either way, he is an individual, who opted to enhance his personal wealth at Americans' expense.

The twentieth-century financial historian E. James Ferguson, though more interested in the mechanics of national finance than in Morris's personal character, nonetheless finds Morris an individual by reference to his understanding of the modern firm. Ferguson envisioned a dichotomy between modern business enterprise, conducted by institutions like the chartered corporation, and eighteenth-century commercial enterprise, which seemed to him, by inevitable contrast, to be performed by the "solitary adventurer who performed the whole range of functions involved in the movement and marketing of goods, acting as banker, shipper, wholesaler, retailer, and sometimes as insurer."[8] For Ferguson, then, Morris would appear (like any other merchant of his day) to be an individual.

Recent scholarship on merchant finance and transnational merchant networks can offer a richer context for Morris's career of apparent invention and guide us toward a deeper understanding of what it means to say that Morris accomplished any particular financial goal.[9] Setting aside the questions of whether Morris's financial stratagems were good or bad, and of whether Morris himself was a good or bad man, we can ask: What was the "nothing" out of which Morris created American wealth and orchestrated the funding of the Revolutionary War? If we put the question this way, it becomes immediately obvious that the "nothing" was not actually nothing—it was a lot of different things, put together. While even Morris himself claimed that he built the finances of the independent United States out of his own financial self, this was far from the whole story.[10] What that "self" entailed was a set of relationships, represented by the credits and debits recorded in his account books and by his membership in a specific socially and financially interconnected mercantile community. Morris's financial self also entailed a significant degree of expertise: an understanding of mercantile practices and technologies that could only have grown out of Morris's long experience as a trader and insurer. Much of the actual work Morris did to create "new" American wealth actually involved maintaining the value of existing financial assets of various kinds, applying existing knowledge, and engaging existing personal and commercial relationships. My aim in bringing these characteristics of Morris's "self" to the fore is not to provide grounds for a new moral judgment of Morris himself or the American political economy that Morris helped to create. Rather, I hope to illustrate how Morris's efforts on behalf of American finance—which are often read as one individual's on behalf of either (a) his nation, (b) a nascent American elite, or (c) a global system of capitalism—were actually possible only because Morris was not, in fact, a lone individual making something from nothing.

The most obvious "nothing" Morris used to bring the United States to financial life was his own personal wealth, which he spent on behalf of the revolutionary movement in a variety of ways. Yet the term "personal wealth" does not suffice to characterize Morris's assets. Like other merchants of this period, Morris would have assessed his capital by reviewing the set of obligations recorded on his balance sheets.[11] Many of his most significant assets consisted of the debts that his overseas trading partners owed him. In preparation for the political rupture with Great Britain, Morris actually deepened these debt relationships. In the fall of 1775, as the formal end of trade between Britain and America approached, Morris sent large quantities of grain to England, to the Continent, and to his Mediterranean markets.[12] Another way of putting this, equally logical according to the bookkeeping of the time, was that Morris made a major effort to acquire debt from these British and continental firms, thus deepening his relationships with overseas commercial contacts at a time when political separation appeared to be on the horizon.[13] These debts acquired from foreign private parties were very much part of the "nothing" from which Morris constructed his own and the United States' accounts.

While the American colonies declared their independence at a particular moment in time, the United States came to independent financial life only gradually. Morris's ongoing financial relationships were critical to resolving the gulf between the political and the financial chronologies of independence. Because so much of Morris's early financial work overseas was surreptitious, he often characterized his purchases on behalf of the United States as the purchases of his own firm, Willing and Morris.[14] For the most part, the internal accounts of Willing and Morris were kept separately from those of the United States, but Morris also purchased government supplies on his personal account when the situation required.[15] It is in this light that we should understand Morris's stipulation that he would serve as superintendent of finance only if he could continue to retain his private business connections. Preserving Morris's personal credit connections (and those of his merchant house) was a project that could not, according to prevailing custom as well as wartime necessity, be disentangled from his financing of the war.[16] Public political rupture required ongoing private obligation.

Thinking more broadly yet, the assets out of which Morris created a "something" should be understood to include his membership in a transatlantic mercantile community, a group of lenders and debtors bound together by obligations that often rolled over for decades at a time. As many scholars have demonstrated, in this community, one's reputation was one's credit, and reputation could only be acquired through repeated exchanges and interactions.[17] Morris did not come from a wealthy family, but he did not build his reputation as a solitary individual either. After his father's death, Morris developed commercial skills and business connections through his apprenticeship to the merchant house of Charles Willing. When he reached adulthood, he became the formal business partner of Willing's son Thomas.[18] While the merchant house "Willing and Morris" was named after its two individual principals, the house was a formal legal partnership—a specific institution, defined by law, that possessed its own set of connections to suppliers overseas.[19] These suppliers trusted

Morris and his partner to pay according to his formal agreements and to keep his accounts properly and to adhere to customary procedures and timelines more generally. Under the Articles of Confederation, as states proved inconsistent in committing their funds to the United States, Morris's own reputation in the mercantile community enabled him to continue accessing supplies for the war effort.[20]

Morris's personal assets should also be understood to extend to his knowledge of standard mercantile practices, which we can describe as technologies, institutions, or forms of governance. For example, Willing and Morris was heavily involved in the business of marine insurance. Marine insurance was a type of financial practice that required not only comprehensive knowledge of effective mercantile procedure, but rigorous enforcement of that procedure.[21] For as merchant customers well understood, if shipmasters could not prove that they had followed proper mercantile practice before, during, or after a shipping loss, or if their paperwork did not meet broadly agreed-upon standards, the insurers would not be liable for the loss. Comprehensive knowledge of proper mercantile procedure, as well as related experience with the legality of various kinds of trade (a key concern of insurers throughout the long eighteenth century), would have enabled Morris to perform his work on the Pennsylvania Committee of Safety, smuggling contraband on behalf of the rebelling colonies. Thorough knowledge of proper and legal mercantile procedure would have provided Morris and his collaborators with knowledge of how to circumvent it effectively.[22]

As the Revolutionary War progressed, Morris spent more and more time managing the relationships between the newly independent American states and their public and private foreign creditors. In this capacity, Morris concentrated his efforts as much on preserving the value of existing assets as he did on creating "new" assets. The mechanics of some of the wartime loans from France, for example, required American merchants to accept bills on France from Morris as payments for goods. These bills were redeemable only in Paris, and their value fluctuated according to Americans' perceptions of their worth. Morris's ability to purchase on behalf of the war effort, then, depended on his ability to *maintain* the French bills' value in the American market.[23] Even his domestic financial

projects were intertwined with international ones: after failing to prevent Pennsylvania from printing paper money in the summer of 1781,
Morris was handed £400,000 of the £500,000 currency issue to manage.
Here again, his main challenge was to sustain the value of something
that existed already. To protect this new currency, he shifted around the
other financial assets at his disposal, including the depreciated Continental currency and his remaining credit with France.[24] To sustain the
new, he engaged the old.

Upon resigning his position as superintendent of finance of the United
States, Morris published *A Statement of the Accounts of the United States
of America*. This mammoth accounting document, 216 pages in length,
featured thirteen separate types of accounts of American expenditures,
including, for example, "Expenditures of the Marine" and "Expenditures
of the Paymaster General."[25] The *Statement* would become a source of controversy as Morris's political opposition consolidated, but its sheer existence is remarkable, for it represented the United States, at the war's end,
as a fully fledged financial entity, a real "something" in the world that had
indeed had no prior existence. If one were to open Morris's *Statement,*
however, it would become visible that even the new United States itself
was a "something" composed of its credits and expenditures—that is to
say, it was composed of financial relationships with all kinds of preexisting
people and institutions: sovereign governments, monarchs, administrative bodies, captains, bureaucrats, and merchants (see fig 3).

By tracing the assets, relationships, and techniques that composed the
so-called "nothing" with which Morris funded the war and began to build
the financial infrastructure of the federal republic, we can get a better
sense of what it really means to characterize Morris as a "founder" of the
United States. Morris was not the only important financial figure of the
revolutionary era, and had he not been born, others could have done
the kinds of things that he did; other individuals might, indeed, have
funded the war through a different set of relationships, informed by a
different set of values. However, the crucial point is that when Morris
went to work on behalf of the United States, he did so as an "individual"
who was in fact composed of account credits, a formal trading partnership, his other personal relationships and contacts, and his particular

| | | | | | | | |
|---|---|---|---|---|---|---|---|
| | | *Amount brought over,* | | 1,602 | 28 | 21,961 | 45 |
| October | 15. | To James M'Call, Sec. to the Superintendant of Finance, | 96 19 | | | | |
| December | 4. | Ditto, | 300 | | | | |
| | | | | 396 | 19 | | |
| November | 6. | Patrick Ferrall, for contingent Expences, | 200 | | | | |
| | 8. | Jacob Barge, for one Quarter's Rent of the Office of Finance, | 366 60 | | | | |
| | 20. | John Swanwick, for Paper for his Office, | 8 | | | | |
| December | 2. | Ditto, | 8 60 | | | | |
| | 14. | Ditto, for printing French Bills, &c. | 87 | | | | |
| | | | | 103 | 60 | | |
| | 19. | Catherine Kepple, for Rent of the Comptroller and Regifter's Offices, | 325 43 | | | | |
| | 26. | Mark Wilcox, for Subfiftence Paper, | 133 30 | | | | |
| October | 7. | Jeffe Brown, employed in the Tranfmiffion of Notes, &c. to and from the Eaftern States, | 150 | | | | |
| November | 7. | Ditto, | 100 | | | | |
| December | 10. | Ditto, | 100 | | | | |
| | | | | 350 | | 2,877 | 60 |
| | | OFFICE of FOREIGN AFFAIRS. | | | | | |
| October | 9. | To Robert R. Livingfton, Secretary, for his Salary, and the Gentlemen employed in his Department, | 2,135 65 | | | | |
| | 11. | Ditto, for Salaries of the feveral Foreign Minifters and Agents from 1ft of July to 30th of September, 1782, | 13,563 30 | | | | |
| | | | | | | 15,699 | 5 |
| | | EXPENCES. | | | | | |
| December | 27. | To Robert R. Livingfton, for the Ufe of his Department, | | | | 100 | |
| | | WAR OFFICE. | | | | | |
| October | 9. | To Major General Lincoln, Secretary, for his and the Salaries of the feveral Perfons in his Office, | 2,514 10 | | | | |
| | 19. | Elijah Weed, Keeper of the Prifon, | 544 57 | | | | |
| | | | | | | 3,058 | 67 |
| | | EXPENCES. | | | | | |
| October | 8. | To Jofeph Carleton, Secretary to the Minifter at War, for Firewood, | 160 | | | | |
| November | 21. | Ditto, | 100 | | | | |
| December | 14. | Major General Lincoln, for the Ufe of his Department, | 530 | | | | |
| | | | | | | 790 | |
| | | | | | | 44,486 | 87 |

*Expenditures of the Marine, from 1ft of October to 31ft of December, 1782. (No. 5.)*

| | | | | | | *Dol. 90ths.* | | *Dol. 90ths.* | |
|---|---|---|---|---|---|---|---|---|---|
| October | 5. | To Jofeph Pennell, Paymafter, | | | | 602 | 33 | | |
| | 7. | Ditto, | | | | 100 | | | |
| | 18. | Ditto, | | | | 93 | 5 | | |
| | 21. | Ditto, | | | | 210 | 60 | | |
| | 22. | Ditto, | | | | 22 | 21 | | |
| | 23. | Ditto, | | | | 100 | | | |
| November | 29. | Ditto, | | | | 2,610 | | | |
| December | 9. | Ditto, | | | | 596 | 30 | | |
| | 31. | Ditto, | | | | 4,534 | 69 | | |
| | | | | | | | | 8,869 | 38 |
| November | 19. | Allibone, Patton and Gurney, Commiffioners for defending the River Delaware, | | | | 3,942 | 34 | | |
| | 27. | Ditto, | | | | 23,593 | 4 | | |
| | | | | | | | | 27,535 | 38 |
| December | 31. | Jofeph Diant, Merchant at St. Pierres, Martinique, for fundry Difburfements on the Frigate Hague, | | | | | | 8,591 | 79 |
| | | | | | | | | 44,996 | 65 |

The United States was its own financial entity by the end of the war; its vast numbers of specific credits and debits demonstrate the wide variety of financial relationships it had developed. A single page from *A Statement of the Accounts of the United States of America* makes this immediately apparent. (United States Office of Finance, Philadelphia, 1785) varieties of technical experience. These characteristics were indispensable to the function of American finance during the Revolutionary War and the years thereafter. Viewing Morris as the product of his relationships may perhaps make his accomplishments seem less individually heroic, but it also, to some degree, works against neo-Progressive declension narratives of the republic, in which a brief moment of possibility for freedom and true democracy was foreclosed by the forces of the wealthy elite. Morris's "nothing," out of which the political economy of the United States was created, was already an interconnected group of individuals, a set of rules, an established system in its own right. The extent of the radicalism that would have been required truly to begin from nothing is unimaginable.

In 1786, George Washington wrote a sentence to James Madison that generations of American historians have used to frame the postrevolutionary period as a whole. "No Morn ever dawned more favorable than ours did," Washington wrote, "—and no day was ever more clouded than the present!" For Washington, the clouds that covered the favorable morning were made of paper money. Madison had just relayed news to Washington about the "question of a paper emission" that had recently been put to a vote in the Virginia House of Representatives; both men were relieved that the proposal had failed.[26] Their concerns that such emissions of paper money might trouble the Confederation with unchecked inflation, the breakdown of debt relationships, and the financial fragmentation of the Confederation more generally have been interrogated by countless scholars.[27]

It is easy to follow Washington and Madison's lead in reading movements for paper money, which were successful in seven of the thirteen state legislatures in the mid-1780s, as Fiske did: as attempts to make something out of nothing—to create something that had no connection to "real" wealth.[28] After all, each paper money issue would be created in a pen stroke by a state legislature, and it would not be backed by gold or silver, precious metals that everyone in the late eighteenth century agreed had value.

However, if one looks beyond the moment of the proverbial pen stroke, it becomes evident that the state paper money projects of the mid-1780s were far more complex than simple acts of pen-and-paper creation. Paper money was never made out of nothing. It was brought into existence in relationship to existing assets, communities, and institutions, and, critically, it was created in the expectation that those relationships would endure. Recent scholarship has demonstrated that paper money was always the project of political will. This essay suggests that, in addition, paper money projects, intended to preserve the economic function (and thus the political power) of states over time, ought to be understood as maintenance projects, most legible when traced across extended time periods. The maintenance of the value of the paper currency, broadly defined, was to some degree a legal matter, having to do with the legislative acts themselves; it was partly an economic matter, reflecting the degree to which the state was already perceived to be wealthy or impoverished; it was partly a communal matter, having to do with which groups in the state accepted the paper money and whether and how they came to believe it was fair; and it was partly a cultural matter, as early American narratives engaged in protracted conversations about its legitimacy.[29]

Some of the paper currencies' relationships can be articulated in terms of economic activities. For example, paper money was generated in anticipated relationship to the individuals, institutions, and governments who would be expected to accept it as payment.[30] First and foremost of these were the state governments, which were legally obligated to accept their own bills as tax payments. However, paper money was also issued in implicit relationship to the state residents who were expected to accept the bills as payment for private debts. To a certain extent, this was a formal legal matter—the bills could be made "legal tender" for debts within the states—but the matter was more nuanced than formal phrases like "legal tender" or "public and private debts" might seem to imply. Private citizens were not isolated, autonomous individuals, but members of broader communities, which could not be prevented from having their own ongoing conversations about how much the currency was worth and

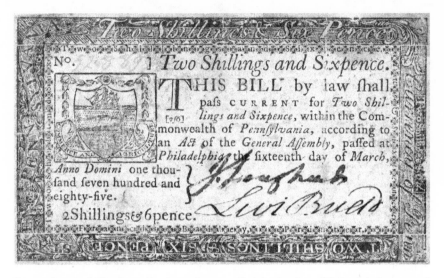

Pennsylvania bill of credit, issued 1785. (Louis Jordan, "Colonial Currency," University of Notre Dame Special Collections, http://www.coins.nd.edu/Col Currency/CurrencyText/PA-03-16-85.html)

whether to accept it, regardless of what the law dictated. Regardless of what the state claimed about its paper money in the moment of issue, it would have no choice but to attend to these communal opinions in its *future* decisions about paper currency.

Paper money was also frequently issued in relationship to land, for land's value was generally believed to be real and enduring.[31] Pennsylvania, for example, issued £50,000 in land-backed "bills of credit" through its state loan offices in 1785. At the loan offices, Pennsylvania residents received these bills, quite literally, as loans; in exchange for the bills, they mortgaged their land to the state, creating an ongoing financial relationship.[32] The state of New York, for its part, emitted £200,000 in bills of credit in the mid-1780s, similarly linking its bills of credit to land. Even the famously contentious $500,000 of paper money issued in Rhode Island was formally anchored to land in a similar fashion.[33] The legislative acts establishing these bills of credit established a legal relationship between each bill and a parcel of land in the state, which, it was supposed, could hardly be worth nothing.

Paper money also came into existence in relationship to existing state debt—a less concrete form of property than land, perhaps, but one that presented just as urgent and enduring a concern for state legislatures. The states that emitted paper money in the 1780s did so partly in response to the problem of their own massive war debts.[34] North Carolina, for one, printed £100,000 in paper money in 1783, then another £100,000 in 1785. This paper was anchored to tobacco, but it soon depreciated, as "the state government paid . . . double specie value" for the tobacco.[35] More broadly, the federal-state relationship was itself a context for the life of North Carolina's paper money. In 1791, federalist North Carolinian William R. Davie explained to Alexander Hamilton that his state was likely to attempt to pay its federal revenue obligations in its own paper currency. This choice was "a matter of Justi[ce]," Davie explained, for it was the state's pro-tofederal obligations that had given rise to the debts in the first place. As Davie put it, "The first emission of this money was [made] for the express purpose of paying the Continental line; the second to purchase Tobacco to pay the interest of the Federal debt, and to answer these purposes more effectually both emissions were made a tender in discharge of private contracts, and have been so received." In other words, federal debt and federal demands from North Carolina had been responsible for the creation of the paper money in the first place; in that paper money, the federal entity would be paid. Attempting to prove North Carolina's fiscal responsibility in spite of such an assertion, Davie reported to Hamilton that the amount of the state's paper money in existence was already in decline: "there are not more than £140,000, now in circulation, the balance having been taken up by the sinking fund and destroyed."[36] By this account, between 1783 and 1791, North Carolina had managed to absorb, through its own taxation, 30 percent of the paper money. Over the course of those years, the "nothing" had retained enough of its reality (its value) that the state was able to accept it in an orderly fashion. If the federal government were, like North Carolina, willing to accept this paper money, Davie wrote, its value would be confirmed still further: "The money would certainly rise to par." Paper money was created in response to existing debt, and the more debt it could legally answer, the more valuable it would remain.[37]

Most concretely, paper money depended on specific, individual people, who had been just as real before the paper money's creation as they continued to be afterward. Legally speaking, paper money came into existence in relationship with particular officials in each state, and its legitimacy, in the perilous moments after its emergence, depended on their virtuous behavior. According to the act establishing New York's 1786 paper currency, for example, the authorizations for bills of credit needed to be signed by specific, named government functionaries and then delivered to the printer. The printer, after printing the bills, was required to swear that he, personally, had overseen their birth and infancy. As the printer's oath put it: "From the time the letters were set and fit to be put in the press for printing the bills of credit now delivered by me to you, until the bills were printed, and the letters afterwards distributed into the boxes I went at no time out of the room."

After thus binding his own reputation to that of the new paper money, the printer was required to transfer the bills to the state treasurer, who subsequently delivered them to the loan officers of each county. The loan officers then gave their *own* oaths and bonds to the county clerk's office, to guarantee legally and financially that they would oversee the distribution of the paper currency honorably. Finally, after so many officials had been personally engaged, the paper money would acquire its intended relationship with American-owned land and American landowners, who had already given that land a value by purchasing it. The bills of credit, as legislation dictated, would be "let out to such as shall apply . . . and can and will give security . . . by mortgage on lands lots or houses lying in the same county."[38] Those who failed to pay interest and principal, as appropriate, on the bills of credit they borrowed would risk having their lands seized.

In sum, while the state government had issued money that did not *represent* any specific existing asset, the currency was only permitted to feature in economic exchange after it had acquired an elaborate set of relationships. In addition, it is worth noting that in the process of emitting its bills of credit, the state engaged an entire administrative structure of oath-swearing, bond-giving individuals, who in the process of creating the currency became implicated in the project of affirming its authenticity and value.

The paper currencies of the 1780s were also brought into existence in relationship to the groups of people who were expected to use them. States, as we have seen, accepted them for the payment of taxes; the very existence of paper money thus signified the enduring relationship of citizen to state. In addition, the opinions of citizens, no matter how humble, continually shaped these relationships. The paper money issue in Rhode Island became contentious not because of any inherent value or lack of value in the bills themselves, but because the state had legally required its inhabitants to accept the bills, and they resisted this forced relationship. By contrast, Pennsylvania paper money circulated relatively successfully because its citizens were generally willing to accept the paper as legal tender for their private debts.[39] Citizens of Georgia, for their part, were required to pledge that they would accept paper money as legal tender at face value—this ritual action aimed to bind the new emissions into existing economic relationships among citizens.[40] The states' decisions yielded varied responses from their inhabitants, but the question of how the paper currencies would be anchored to the states' peoples was in all cases a significant one, and it had a great deal to do with whether the emissions were successful or not.[41]

Paper money emissions of the Critical Period must also be understood to exist in relationship to earlier colonial emissions, in that historical narratives characterizing these emissions as successful effectively "backed" emissions proposed or accomplished during the Critical Period. As observers of the period frequently noted, the British colonies in North America had on a number of occasions issued paper money (both of the land-backed and accepted-as-taxation varieties) in the eighteenth century. The middle colonies, in particular, had done so quite successfully.[42] Contemplating this history, opponents of paper money grounded their own arguments in the more recent history of the Revolutionary War, when paper emissions, in their estimation, had ended in disaster. Thomas Paine emerged in 1786 as a paper money opponent and an ardent supporter of the Bank of North America at a time when the bank was facing public condemnation for resisting the emission of paper money in Pennsylvania. Paine's arguments for the bank (and against state-issued paper money) were grounded in history and in notions of legitimacy in state-citizen relationships. He identified Morris's Bank of North America as the product of a deal made

in specific, dire wartime circumstances, between a group of private "patriotic individuals" and the state.[43] The "individuals furnished and risked the
money, and the aid which the Government contributed was that of incor-
porating them."[44] It was the course of historical events (the "distress of
the times," in Paine's telling) that had legitimized this contract between
private citizens and government, and that had, interestingly, authorized a
new kind of citizen-state relationship—one that was routed through the
relatively novel institution of the joint-stock corporation.[45]

Paine's arguments against paper currency referenced genealogy as well
as history. His visceral understanding of the importance of legitimacy
in the government-citizen contract that produced the bank is most fully
revealed in his discussion of the paper money emissions, which he characterized, by contrast to the actions of the bank, as acts of bastardy. Paper
money, he wrote, was "the illegitimate offspring of Assemblies, and when
their year expire [sic], they leave it a vagrant on the hands of the Public."[46] Paine's logic was as clear as his vulgar (though implicit) wordplay
on "emission." The bank had been the offspring of a relationship between
citizen and state, properly legitimized by law, while the paper currencies
were precipitate and sinful emissions, with a legal relationship to nothing. Subsequent to their birth, these currencies became disruptive, illegitimate progeny without any lineage sanctioned by law.

With all of these relationships in mind, it is clear that state paper money
issues can only be considered "something from nothing" if we understand
the process of creating this money as a literal and instantaneous event,
defined around the moment of its legal instantiation. In the bigger picture, however, contemporaries knew that state paper money issues were
built out of various kinds of things that already existed, including assets
like land and legal enforcement mechanisms. The phrase "something from
nothing" implies an occult act, but state legislatures that emitted paper
currency were not doing magic tricks. It is more productive to envision
the paper money issued in the mid-1780s as a "something" that emerged
out of a powerful and evolving set of existing financial, personal, and
institutional relationships, in and around the American states. Such an
approach makes it easier, if we believe that paper money is a political
project, to understand the *specific* kinds of political power involved in the

creation of paper money. It also makes it easier to identify the similarities between the paper money movements and other financial projects of the day, including Morris's own.

Historical debates over the feasibility and justice of paper money, as well as those over the legacy of Morris, are far from over. Within these debates, "something from nothing" narratives remain appealing for all kinds of political purposes. They resonate with claims for the political novelty of the United States itself, as well as with claims for the uniqueness (whether for good or for evil) of American postrevolutionary capitalism. The stakes are high: Christine Desan has argued, for example, that money is a constitutional project, "colored from the start" by a society's values and aims.[47] Seen in this light, the state paper money movements were unique and novel American projects based on the collective colonial revelation that "value was a functional concept that could be created by collective action." Desan frames Morris's vision, by contrast, as one centered on a faith in private enterprise, with the state serving as "a frame for the creation of value by individuals."[48] Here, too, are serious consequences for the development of American nineteenth-century political economy.

While arguments for the novelty of state paper money issues and those for Morris's inventions have allowed us to look from the Critical Period toward the future of the American state, it is equally important to consider the ways in which the something-from-nothing financial projects of the 1780s were tied to the assets and debts of Americans' present, to the social and commercial networks within which the republic took shape, and to the historical lessons and financial obligations that were the legacy of Americans' past. Morris built American financial independence out of his balance sheets, his network of commercial contacts, and his financial expertise—a "self" inextricable from a transnational mercantile community. Much of his subsequent work was devoted to preserving the value of existing financial assets as well as the personal and political relationships they represented. State paper money issues, similarly, took place in relationship to existing financial assets and debts, existing communities, and even to Americans' prevailing understandings of their own colonial history. "Something from nothing" is in many respects a useful phrase for American histories of the revolution and its aftermath, and to some degree, it is an inevitable one. However, in the realm of finance (as, indeed, in the realm of state making), "something from nothing" is a kind of story that we should employ with particular caution.

# Notes

1. John Fiske, *The Critical Period of American History, 1783–1789* (Boston, 1888), 168.
2. Bubble-and-bust narratives bring this message home to the public with particular clarity. The classic work in this genre is Charles Mackay, *Extraordinary Popular Delusions and the Madness of Crowds* (London, 1841). In American history, the tradition of examining bubbles continues through works such as Jane Kamensky, *The Exchange Artist: A Tale of High-Flying Financial Speculation and the Nation's First Banking Collapse* (New York: Penguin Books, 2009); Jessica Lepler, *The Many Panics of 1837: People, Politics, and the Creation of a Transatlantic Financial Crisis* (New York: Cambridge University Press, 2013); and, taking an even longer view, Scott Reynolds Nelson, *A Nation of Deadbeats: An Uncommon History of America's Financial Disasters* (New York: Knopf, 2012). On the history of defining (and judging) speculation, see Stuart Banner, *Speculation: A History of the Fine Line Between Gambling and Investing* (New York: Oxford University Press, 2017).
3. For eighteenth-century criticisms, see E. James Ferguson et al., eds., *The Papers of Robert Morris, 1781–1784* (Pittsburgh: University of Pittsburgh Press, 1973), 1:21. For contemporary criticisms, see, e.g., Terry Bouton, *Taming Democracy: "The People," the Founders, and the Troubled Ending of the American Revolution* (New York: Oxford University Press, 2007).
4. This tradition runs from Fiske himself through Robert E. Wright and David J. Cowen, *Financial Founding Fathers: The Men Who Made America Rich* (Chicago: University of Chicago, 2006); Thomas K. McGraw, *The Founders and Finance: How Hamilton, Gallatin, and Other Immigrants Forged a New Economy* (Cambridge, MA: Harvard University Press, 2012); and Charles Rappleye, *Robert Morris: Financier of the American Revolution* (New York: Simon & Schuster, 2010).
5. As many scholars now observe, money itself is socially constructed. For a sociologically grounded perspective, see, for example, Nigel Dodd, who in *The Social Life of Money* (Princeton, NJ: Princeton University Press, 2014) defends an understanding of money as an idea and a "claim on society," which is grounded in "social relations among its users" (3–9). The legal historian Christine Desan has argued that money is "a governance project . . . a mode of mobilizing resources, one that communities design for that end and individuals appropriate for their own purposes." Christine Desan, *Making Money: Coin, Currency, and the Coming of Capitalism* (Oxford, UK: Oxford University Press, 2014), 1.
6. Rappleye, 3. For a fairly sympathetic assessment of Morris, which nonetheless portrays him as an "aspiring aristocrat . . . in an egalitarian society," see Gordon S. Wood,

"Interests and Disinterestedness in the Making of the Constitution," in *Beyond Confederation: Origins of the Constitution and American National Identity,* ed. Richard Beeman, Stephen Botein, and Edward C. Carter II (Chapel Hill: University of North Carolina Press, 1987), 100.

7.  Holton, in fact, intentionally reaches for the terminology of contemporary political economic battles, characterizing Morris as a proponent of trickle-down economics. See Holton, *Unruly Americans and the Origins of the Constitution* (New York: Hill and Wang, 2007), 99. See also Terry Bouton, *Taming Democracy.*

8.  E. James Ferguson, *The Power of the Purse: A History of American Public Finance, 1776–1790* (Chapel Hill: University of North Carolina Press, 1961), 71.

9.  This scholarship tends to focus on networks of merchants or on the interconnected activities of merchants and states, although these approaches by necessity overlap. For the former—how networks of merchants worked—see, e.g., Tom Cutterham, "'A Very Promising Appearance': Credit, Honor, and Deception in the Emerging Market for American Debt, 1784–92," *William and Mary Quarterly* 75, no. 4 (October 2018): 623–50; Sheryllynne Haggerty, *"Merely for Money"? Business Culture in the British Atlantic, 1750–1815* (Liverpool, UK: Liverpool University Press, 2012); Pierre Gervais, "A Merchant or a French Atlantic? Eighteenth-Century Account Books as Narratives of a Transnational Merchant Political Economy," *French History* 25, no. 1 (March 2011): 28–47; David Hancock, *Citizens of the World: London Merchants and the Integration of the British Atlantic Community, 1735–1785* (New York: Cambridge University Press, 1995). For merchants, empires, and state making, see, for example, Tyson Reeder, *Smugglers, Pirates, and Patriots: Free Trade in the Age of Revolution* (Philadelphia: University of Pennsylvania Press, 2019); Nuala Zahedieh, *The Capital and the Colonies: London and the Atlantic Economy 1660–1700* (Cambridge, UK: Cambridge University Press, 2010); Cathy Matson, *Merchants and Empire: Trading in Colonial New York* (Baltimore: Johns Hopkins University Press, 1997). This essay aligns even more directly with the claims of Edwin J. Perkins, who characterizes Morris as "among the most important and powerful financial leaders in American history" but, applying his immense knowledge of early American finance, finds descriptions of Morris "in older historical accounts" as the "financier of the revolution" to be "an example of nationalist exaggeration." Perkins, *American Public Finance and Financial Services, 1700–1815* (Columbus: Ohio State University Press, 1994), 106.

10.  "My personal Credit . . . has been substituted for that which the Country has lost." Robert Morris to Benjamin Harrison, January 15, 1782, *The Papers of Robert Morris 1781–1784,* 4:46.

11.  Note, however, that the idea of a "profit" itself was hardly a straightforward one. Pierre Gervais, Yannick Lemarchand, and Dominique Margairaz, "Introduction: The Many Scales of Merchant Profit: Accounting for Norms, Practices and Results in the Age of Commerce," in *Merchants and Profit in the Age of Commerce, 1680–1830,* ed. Gervais, Lemarchand, and Margairaz (New York: Routledge, 2016), 1–12.

12.  Rappleye, 32–33.

13.  For more on the political significance of double-entry bookkeeping, see Caitlin Rosenthal, *Accounting for Slavery: Masters and Management* (Cambridge, MA: Harvard University Press, 2018), and Jacob Soll, *The Reckoning: Financial Accountability and the Rise*

*and Fall of Nations* (New York: Basic Books, 2014). One of the fundamental principles that double-entry accounting makes visible is that a debt is an asset.

14. Ferguson, *Power of the Purse*, 77.

15. Morris wrote on October 3, 1781, "To give you an Idea of my Situation as to money, I think I need only inform you that since I have been in Office I have received the Sum of seven hundred and fifty Pounds Pennsylvania Money from the Treasury of this State and that is in Part Payment of Advances made for them. This is all I have received from the Funds of America. It is true that Colo. Laurens has lately arrived and brought with him a Sum of money from France; And it is also true that I have made use of a very limited Credit given me on France . . . but both these . . . taken together are vastly short of what is necessary." Morris to Nathanael Greene, October 3, 1781, *Papers of Robert Morris, 1781–1784*, 3:14.

16. Morris was far from the only figure associated with the revolution who had to reconcile his private with his public accounts—this was a commonplace challenge for those who handled purchasing for the government. Even George Washington, for example, wrote to Robert Morris in 1777 to balance his own "private Acct with the Public": "I find a credit to it of a blank number of Silver Dollars sent me by you . . . for want of the Sum, I cannot Ball[anc]e the Acc[oun]t." Washington to Morris, August 14, 1777, *The Papers of George Washington Digital Edition*, ed. Theodore J. Crackel (Charlottesville: Rotunda, an imprint of University of Virginia Press, 2008), http://rotunda .upress.virginia.edu.ezp-prod1.hul.harvard.edu/founders/GEWN-03-10-02-0602.

17. Cutterham, "A Very Promising Appearance."

18. Clarence Lester ver Steeg, *Robert Morris, Revolutionary Financier, With an Analysis of His Earlier Career* (New York: Octagon Books, 1976), 3.

19. On the merchant partnership as an institution, see Pierre Gervais, "In Union There was Strength: The Legal Protection of Eighteenth-Century Merchant Partnerships in England and France," in *Market Ethics and Practices, c. 1300–1850*, ed. Simon Middleton and James E. Shaw (Abington, NY: Routledge, 2018): 166–83.

20. Morris's case was not the only one in which the American government's obligations to private parties making outlays on behalf of the independence movement became contentious. Offering his support for the pleas for compensation of one of his partners, a New Orleans merchant who similarly spent his personal funds on behalf of the United States, Morris wrote to the governor of Virginia, "I have had dealings with Mr. Pollock as a Merchant many Years, some of them before this War commenced . . . and have every reason that can arise from long and extensive dealings to believe [sic] him an honest man." The government had accepted the money provided by merchants in their private capacity; it should, therefore, also accept testimony drawn from these merchants' credit records with one another. Robert Morris to the governor of Virginia, January 15, 1782, *Robert Morris Papers*, 4:45. The compensation of another Morris partner, Silas Deane, entangled with that of the fictitious merchant house created by Pierre-Augustin Caron de Beaumarchais, famously became a political fiasco. See Arthur H. Reede, *The Financing of the American Revolution* (Fairport, NY: Rochester Press, 1996), 69–96.

21. Hannah Farber, *Underwriters of the United States* (Chapel Hill: Omohundro/University of North Carolina Press, 2021).

22. For an overview of gunpowder smuggling, see Neil L. York, "Clandestine Aid and the American Revolutionary War Effort: A Re-Examination, *Military Affairs* 43, no. 1 (February 1979): 26–30.

23. Rappleye, 241–45; Ferguson, 126–27.

24. Rappleye, 245; Ferguson, 130.

25. U.S. Office of Finance, *A statement of the accounts of the United States of America, during the administration of the Superintendant of Finance, [. . .]* (Philadelphia: R. Aitken, 1785).

26. George Washington to James Madison, November 5, 1786. The comments were prompted by Madison's report that "in general appearances are favorable. On the question for a paper emission the measure was this day rejected in emphatical terms by a majority of 84 vs 17." Madison to Washington, November 1, 1786, *The Papers of George Washington: Confederation Series*, ed. W. W. Abbot and D. Twohig (Charlottesville: University Press of Virginia, 1995), 4:326–27.

27. See George William Van Cleve, "The Anti-Federalists' Toughest Challenge: Paper Money, Debt Relief, and the Ratification of the Constitution," *Journal of the Early Republic* 34, no. 4 (Winter 2014): 529–60. For a broader introduction to American economic challenges postindependence, see Jonathan M. Chu, *Stumbling Toward the Constitution: The Economic Consequences of Freedom in the Atlantic World* (New York: Palgrave Macmillan, 2012).

28. Ferguson, 142, 165. For a recent argument for the reconsideration of paper money as a political project, see Katie A. Moore, "The Blood That Nourishes the Body Politic: The Origins of Paper Money in Early America," *Early American Studies* 17, no. 1 (winter 2019): 1–36.

29. A great deal of recent historical scholarship has been devoted to deconstructing the idea of the free market and the economic individual. However, in rejecting the individual, scholars cannot retreat to the state as the only other alternate framework. Understanding and articulating other communities within which debts were contracted, within which currency circulated, is critical for a deeper understanding of the relationship between merchants and states. On the ways in which public opinion shaped public credit and on how the question of public credit helped give rise to the notion of public opinion, see Mark Schmeller, "The Political Economy of Opinion: Public Credit and Concepts of Public Opinion in the Age of Federalism," *Journal of the Early Republic* 29, no. 1 (spring 2009): 35–61. On literature, paper money, and counterfeiters, see Todd Barosky, "Legal and Illegal Moneymaking: Colonial American Counterfeiters and the Novelization of Eighteenth-Century Crime Literature," *Early American Literature,* 47, no. 3 (2012): 531–60.

30. For an overview of currency in the colonies, see Leslie V. Brock, *The Currency of the American Colonies, 1700–1764: A Study in Colonial Finance and Imperial Relations* (New York: Arno Press, 1975). In formal economic terms, colonial paper money was backed in one of two ways: by land, when it was issued through land banks, or by promises made by governments that the money could be used for the payment of taxes. The question of whether the promise of redemption through taxation counts as backing has been contentious among economic historians. See Charles W. Calomiris, "Institutional Failure, Monetary Scarcity, and the Depreciation of the Continental," *Journal*

*of Economic History* 48, no. 1 (March 1988): 1. For a response to Calomiris, in which formal economic theories of "backing" and its relationship to money's purchasing power are discussed, see Ron Michener, "Backing Theories and the Currencies of Eighteenth-Century America: A Comment," *Journal of Economic History* 48, no. 3 (September 1988): 682–92. For further differentiation (between "metallic backing," "prospective metallic backing," and "prospective tax backing"), see Scott Sumner, "Colonial Currency and the Quantity Theory of Money: A Critique of Smith's Interpretation," *Journal of Economic History* 53, no. 1 (March 1993): 139n4.

31. Moore, 9, 14. In the colonial period, the receiver of the bill of credit from the land bank promised to make regular repayments to the government: first just the interest on the loan, then gradually, over time, the principal. If the money was not paid, the colonist forfeited the land he had mortgaged. Ferguson, 5.

32. The state authorized an additional £100,000 for the payment of interest on federal and state debt. Perkins, 146–48.

33. "The funds were available for fourteen years at 4 percent interest secured by property valued at twice the loan amount. Borrowers paid interest only during the first seven years and then paid off the principal in seven equal installments beginning in 1793." Perkins, 155.

34. See Holton, especially 82.

35. See Fiske, 201, Perkins, 157–60, and Mary Schweitzer, "State-Issued Currency and the Ratification of the U.S. Constitution," *Journal of Economic History* 49, no. 2 (June 1989): 319. North Carolina printed paper money specifically to ease the payment of taxes.

36. William R. Davie to Alexander Hamilton, November 17, 1791, in *The Papers of Alexander Hamilton*, ed. Harold C. Syrett (New York: Columbia University Press, 1965), 9:503–4.

37. The question of *how* the debt would be redeemed (that is to say, the legal method through which the bills would be removed from circulation) was also an important one; Farley Grubb argues that unclear instructions regarding redemption contributed significantly to the debacle of Continental paper money. "State Redemption of the Continental Dollar, 1779–90," *William and Mary Quarterly* 69, no. 1 (January 2012): 147–80.

38. Jack Richon Pole, *The Revolution in America, 1754–1788: Documents and Commentaries* (Stanford, CA: Stanford University Press, 1970), 307–28.

39. Perkins, 149.

40. Fiske is quite taken with this oath. See Fiske, 202.

41. On legal tender laws, see especially Schweitzer, "State-Issued Currency and the Ratification of the U.S. Constitution," 317.

42. Stephen Mihm, "Funding the Revolution: Monetary and Fiscal Policy in Eighteenth-Century America," *Oxford Handbook of the American Revolution*, eds. Jane Kamensky and Edward Gray (New York: Oxford University Press, 2012), 329–30.

43. [Thomas Paine], *Dissertations on Government, The Affairs of the Bank, and Paper-Money: By the Author of Common Sense* (Philadelphia: Charles Cist, 1786), 21.

44. Ibid.

45. Ibid.

46. Ibid., 48.

47. Christine Desan, "The Constitutional Approach to Money: Monetary Design and the Production of the Modern World," ed. Nina Bandelj, Frederick F. Wherry, and Viviana A. Zelizer, *Money Talks: Explaining How Money Really Works* (Princeton, NJ: Princeton University Press, 2017), 110.

48. Christine Desan, "Money Talks: Listening to the History of Value," *Commonplace* 6, no. 3 (April 2006), http://nrs.harvard.edu/urn-3:HUL.InstRepos:10642452.

# An Excess of Aristocracy

## DEMOCRACY AND THE FEAR OF ARISTOCRATIC
## POWER IN THE 1780S

*Kevin Butterfield*

ARE THEY FEARFUL," WROTE Samuel Bryan in Pennsylvania about the authors of the proposed federal Constitution in 1787, "that if you exercise your good sense and discernment, you will discover the masqued aristocracy, that they are attempting to smuggle upon you, under the suspicious garb of republicanism?" To many of its critics in the ratification debates, the Constitution looked to be a plan for removing power and influence farther from the people. It would create a governing elite, answering to the people only in carefully crafted, often twice-removed ways. It was, perhaps, a "masqued aristocracy." It was, perhaps, a "conspiracy," a "continental exertion of the *well born* in America to obtain that darling domination, which they have not been able to accomplish in their respective states," wrote Bryan. "The hideous daemon of Aristocracy," in the words of one *Boston Gazette* writer opposed to the work of the Philadelphia Convention, was now at work in America.[1]

Aristocracy was "among the accusations most often repeated in the Anti-Federalist press" in 1787 and 1788, according to historian Saul Cornell. Mix together the words "well-born, nine times—*Aristocracy,* eighteen times," and so on, and you had a recipe for a perfectly typical antifederalist essay, wrote someone in the *Pennsylvania Gazette,* and newspapers up and down the coast reprinted the witty and, as it happened, spot-on formulation. That the Constitution was an aristocratic document was a common critique, and it was layered upon a kernel of truth, in that the Constitution clearly placed power at no small distance from the democratic voice of the people. Such accusations did not persuade Americans to reject the new Constitution, however. In the immediate wake of a republican revolution, it can be a bit difficult to understand why the charges that the Philadelphia proposals would create an aristocratic form of government did not more effectively rally opponents to oppose ratification.[2]

The answer is not that elites in 1787 effectively duped the people into embracing a patently less democratic framework of government, though for just over a century many people have argued precisely that. Rather, if one looks back just a few years before 1787, to fears of homegrown aristocracy that took hold in the years immediately following the end of the Revolutionary War, another possible explanation reveals itself: by the time the Constitution was proposed, a youthful American people had grown increasingly confident that any apparent threats of a rising aristocratic power could be and would be quashed. Many of them had come to believe that they had already faced the prospect directly, when a veterans' organization for Revolutionary War officers, a club of national reach that made the ill-received decision to allow membership to pass down to the eldest son of each eligible man, took shape in the closing days of the war. It was called the Society of the Cincinnati, and it had all the makings of a new, indigenous, and dangerous order of nobility.

Exploring the history of what has become known as the "Critical Period" of the 1780s—that period between the end of the fighting and the formation of a new and more stable framework of national government a few years later—is essential to understanding how and why the U.S. Constitution took the forms that it did and why, in fact, it was ratified at all. Efforts to explain how 1787 should be understood in relation to the spirit and the principles of 1776 are among the most contested in American historical writing, I would think, precisely because they are so important. Many and diverse explanations have been offered for why the proffered criticisms of the proposed Constitution—including the accusations that the Constitution was an end run around the republicanism of the states to install in the seat of the federal government a distant but powerful government of elites—were not successful in persuading the state ratification conventions to reject it. It is a live question, and it is one that needs to be explored in the context of the contemporary debates about the threat of aristocracy, for by 1787 many Americans had already given serious thought to whether such fears were real or fanciful. They had already spilled gallons of ink on the subject of where an aristocracy, if indeed one could ever grow in American soil, might take root.[3]

The study of how Americans thought about and reacted to the so-called "excess of democracy" of the 1780s has figured prominently in our inquiries about the origins of the Constitution. In the 1780s, men such as James Madison, Alexander Hamilton, and Elbridge Gerry expressed fears of democratic chaos, that there might be no way to contain popular unrest and the emergence of either mob rule—or, ultimately, anarchy. Anxieties that the new United States were racked and endangered by excesses of democracy were powerful and widespread in the years following the Treaty of Paris. The Regulation of Daniel Shays in Massachusetts in 1786 was only one notable instance of what appeared to be a turn toward lawlessness, helping to produce a reaction in the form of the Philadelphia Convention.[4]

Democracy was not the only monster facing the young American nation in the 1780s. There was also the demon of aristocracy. In the wake of the revolution, many Americans were anxious that some among them might find a way of introducing aristocratic forms of government to the newly independent republics, of planting a hereditary peerage in the free soil of Columbia. Samuel Osgood of Massachusetts was not alone when he worried to John Adams in 1784 that "the aristocratical influence" already "predominates in more than a major part of the United States," and vigilance in defense of republicanism was more crucial than ever. Their current moment, they believed, may be particularly opportune, for if excesses of democracy helped many Americans living through the 1780s to the belief that mob rule was looming, then a reactionary response by elites in one form or another might find support in ways unthinkable in 1776. With the ongoing revisions of the state constitutions that had been drafted early in the revolutionary moment, there were certainly some signs pointing in that direction.[5]

More alarming still, there was also the possibility that, perhaps, no crisis was necessary for an American aristocracy to form. Perhaps cool and deliberate schemes of the most influential citizens of the new republic—namely, those officers of the Continental Army who had formed and joined the Society of the Cincinnati—would hasten the nation toward aristocratic rule. In short, Americans in the 1780s were afraid of excessive democracy. They were afraid, too, of aristocracy. Fears of hereditary, artificial orders of aristocracy during the 1780s shaped American responses to other, less directly counterdemocratic reforms. Ultimately, debates, invectives, and warnings about the possible introduction of a hereditary nobility in the 1780s ultimately helped to diminish the potency of the alarums being sounded in the ratification debates about the looming danger of elite rule.

## The Critical Period for American Aristocracy

What, exactly, is a critical period? I think of it this way: it is a relatively brief period of time in which the potential for social and political change is great, the outcome is entirely uncertain, and—this is key—something more or less describable as the status quo is one possible outcome. In other words, it is a time neither of war nor of revolution, which are unsustainable states. It is also not a time, of course, in which political and civil society go on their course effortlessly. Critical periods are marked, it seems, by serious and concerted efforts just to keep things from flying apart. By that definition, the 1780s fits the bill, as does the decade of the 1850s. At some moments in both periods, it must have appeared that the status quo could be and would be meticulously preserved through compromise and a deeply felt commitment to union; in other moments, disunion and disaster were not just possible but, in sparks and flickers, very real.

The 1850s and the 1780s also share something quite specific that was both a backdrop and an essential ingredient to the sense of crisis: a widely held fear that many of the nation's wealthiest and most honored men were conspiring against the good of the whole, against the welfare of the people. Where a slaveocracy threatened the nation in the 1850s, the prime suspects in the 1780s were, for many watchful Americans, the same men who had just waged war on behalf of liberty. Interestingly, in the early days of the American Civil War, a small pamphlet was published in New York that attempted to outline *A History of Every Attempt at Resistance to the Federal Government.* Its subtitle went on to describe the high points, including—second and third in a list of nine moments that the author believed were genuine threats to the nation—*The Society of the Cincinnati* and *Shays' Rebellion in Massachusetts.* As his nation fell apart at the close of one critical period, the anonymous author looked back at another, and the Cincinnati caught his eye, no less than the infamous uprising of Daniel Shays or South Carolina's later nullification efforts, as a moment when history might have turned out differently.[6]

The beginnings of the organization appeared to be harmless, even laudable. Officers of the Continental Army formed the Society of the Cincinnati on the banks of the Hudson River on May 13, 1783. General Henry Knox, a Boston bookseller-turned-revolutionary, conceived of the Cincinnati as a "Society of Friends, to endure so long as they shall endure, or any of their eldest male posterity." Within a few months, more than a thousand Revolutionary War officers would rush to join this association, which was named for the Roman general Lucius Quintus Cincinnatus (who, rather than seeking power and glory, had returned to his farm after military triumph). They did so by signing a copy of the parchment "Institution," or constitution, of the Cincinnati. Ultimately, just over two thousand American officers would join as original members of the society.[7]

When the public first learned about its institution, however, critics of the idea of forming any kind of ongoing organization of the officers' corps, let alone one with hereditary membership, made their voices heard. From Massachusetts to South Carolina, and even among American diplomats posted in Europe, there were many American citizens who saw the Cincinnati as a genuine threat to the infant American republic. What they saw was a group of the most acclaimed men of the new nation—American officers of the revolution serving at the close of the war or who had honorably resigned with at least three years' service (French officers, too, were invited)—who, it appeared, were forming something like a knighthood, if not a permanent aristocracy. Members of the Cincinnati would gather together on regular, appointed occasions; they would wear an elaborate medal; membership would descend from them to their eldest sons, into perpetuity. From a certain vantage, it looked like a group of men aspiring to become peers of the realm.[8]

The immediate origins of the Society of the Cincinnati, though, were rooted less in aspiration than in desperation. During the closing days of war, the debate about how to provide some sort of pension or retirement pay for the officers of the Continental Army remained unresolved, leading to the famous Newburgh crisis of March 1783. After George Washington was able to defuse the potential for conspiracy and rebellion in the Newburgh encampment, the problem remained of securing pay and respect for the Continental officers who had served their country. Knox drafted his Institution for the Society of the Cincinnati by April 15, 1783, as a way to preserve the collective strength of the Continental officers in voicing their interests to Congress. If they should fail in receiving sufficient support, the members of his proposed society would, at the very least, be able to offer some kind of mutual aid to those among them who fell on especially hard times. A day later, news of the peace reached Newburgh. In less than a month, the institution was being signed, and men began to join while the Continental Army was disappearing into history.[9]

There were, apparently, some officers who from the moment of its creation saw in the Society of the Cincinnati the seed of something dangerous. There are bits of evidence that Timothy Pickering and William Heath of Massachusetts were prescient about the kinds of anger and anxiety that the society would provoke. However, most joined eagerly and for reasons that had nothing to do with a spoken or unspoken desire to wear their eagle badges while lording it over their fellow citizens. Nor did they join in order to launch a conservative, hierarchical reaction to the leveling tendencies of the revolution. Instead, they joined out of heartfelt desires to preserve the friendships forged in the war. According to one Maryland member, their friendships had been "strengthened by adversity, and finally cemented (as our establishment expresses it) by the blood of the parties." These were generally "of too endearing a nature to be for ever dissolved by the separation which necessarily followed the discharge of the army," and, because "no mode so unexceptionable as this could be devised to render them lasting," the Society of the Cincinnati was formed. In 1787, New York's Morgan Lewis described "a gallant band of patriots, who, for eight years, had lived together in the habits of the strictest friendship,—together borne the numerous hardships incident to the soldiers' life—together braved the various dangers of the field—together fought, bled, and conquered, saw themselves on the eve of separation, and could not bear the thought that it should be forever." Their motives were pure and sentimental, not scheming. For the first few months, as hundreds of officers signed the institution and became members of the Cincinnati, there were few who suspected their organization of being anything more than its founding document declared them to be: a society of friends.[10]

That began to change in September 1783, when the public first learned of its existence. The first grumblings, it seemed, had more to do with public anxieties about commutation pay for the officers than with anything else. In October, South Carolina's Aedanus Burke, a justice on the state supreme court, changed everything. Within weeks of his having heard of about the Cincinnati, he penned a tract he entitled *Considerations on the Society or Order of Cincinnati.* Writing under the pseudonym Cassius, one of the conspirators who ended the life of Julius Caesar after Caesar's actions had begun to subvert the republic, Burke offered the short version of his argument in the subtitle: *Proving That It Creates a Race of Hereditary Patricians, or Nobility.* The Society of the Cincinnati might just be the greatest threat to American liberties yet discovered, he would write, and to permit its continued existence "would give a fatal wound to civil liberty thro' the world."[11]

From this point on, most Americans learned of the existence of the Cincinnati in 1783 and 1784 through the diatribes published against it. None came close to having the impact of Burke's *Considerations.* The content of his critiques essentially shaped the intellectual and emotional responses of a great many people to the officers' fraternal society. Burke, an Irish immigrant born in 1743 who came to the American colonies some time before 1769, was already an active critic of what he saw as elitist developments in his home state of South Carolina. In fact, he had already used the pen name "Cassius" once before, earlier in 1783, in his *Address to the Freemen of the State of South-Carolina.* In that pamphlet, he viciously attacked what he saw as unconstitutional and unjust policies of confiscation and political exclusion at the state level. Published in January, the text revealed Burke's hair-trigger fear, by no means uncommon in the closing months of the Revolutionary War, that the American people might soon find themselves deprived of their hard-won republican forms of government. He was worried that "a *few* could set up pretensions to superior political merit, over the whole aggregate body of the people, and setting up an arbitrary government of the *few*." Seven months later, while at a meeting of the Corner Club in Charleston in August 1783, he learned of the existence of a group with just such pretensions and just such goals: the Society of the Cincinnati. By October, his *Considerations* described a crisis that faced the American people.[12]

He did not temper his language. He did not presume good intentions. "I do boldly assert it to be, an *hereditary peerage*," and it must be struck down now, for "in one generation the order of Cincinnati will be established immoveably." The officers had created a society in which members were "invested with the exclusive privilege of wearing a badge of their order," in which they were "elevated above others, and in parity among themselves"—they were "peers of the realm, *pares regni*, and nothing more or less." The Cincinnati had fought on behalf of a revolutionary and noble cause, but now they proposed an aristocratic and hereditary order that, like a "poisonous *exotic* plant," would take root in America and prove to all the world that the people "are too degenerate to govern themselves in a state of liberty." In the coming months, his pamphlet was reprinted in full in Pennsylvania, Connecticut, New York, Massachusetts, and Rhode Island (either in pamphlet form or in newspapers), and excerpts were printed even more widely. As Washington told Thomas Jefferson in April 1784, after many reprintings and much public discussion, "The Pamphlet ascribed to Mr. Burke had its effect. People are alarmed, especially in the Eastern [i.e., New England] States." Coming as it did immediately after the official end of the war, the debate over the Cincinnati—and the aristocracy it seemed likely to produce—can justifiably be called America's first national controversy.[13]

The hereditary aspect of membership led some to believe that the club might result in the creation of an American peerage, even if the officers themselves had had no such intention (and Burke was not quite willing to grant that). Regardless of whether the framers of the current institution had benign motivations, perhaps the next generations would not have the virtue and the fortitude to resist the temptation to lord themselves over "the whole country besides themselves, a mere mob of plebeians." In just a few generations, Burke wrote, we would have "two distinct orders amongst us," a "race of hereditary Nobles" and "the rabble." He was, of course, not alone in his fear of what later generations might do with the achievements of his own, precisely because those accomplishments were so precarious. Jefferson was among those who held the commonplace opinion that "the moderation & virtue of a single character," George Washington, "has probably prevented this revolution from being closed as most others have been by a subversion of that liberty it was intended to establish"—and, Jefferson told Washington himself when asked for advice about the Cincinnati, "He is not immortal, & his successor or some one of his successors at the head of this institution [i.e., the Cincinnati] may adopt a more mistaken road to glory." Those who received membership by lineal descent, said Governor Benjamin Guerard of South Carolina, "might turn out to be the most untrustworthy characters." Samuel Adams, too, worried that "their Sons, if they should not themselves, when they perceive the Multitude grown giddy with gazing, may assume more than the mere Pageantry of Nobility." Even if Americans could trust Washington's officer corps in the years ahead—and there was an "if" there, at least for Burke—how on earth could they know whether they could trust their sons?[14]

We know with the benefit of hindsight that these fears were overblown. They nonetheless need to be understood in light of the uncertainties of the 1780s, and there were a few reasons that American citizens in the mid-1780s had good reason to take the concerns seriously. First, many Americans genuinely believed that, if ever there were a chance to establish a hereditary aristocracy, this would be it. Fame had consequences. The "officers of the American army" that now made up the Cincinnati, wrote Burke, were "the most renowned band of men, that this day walk on the face of the globe." Few would have disagreed. If anyone could create a peerage in America, it would be these men. Second, the whole design of the institution, allowing as it did for the induction of "honorary members," appeared to have the pernicious effect of allowing the Cincinnati to blunt criticism by inviting into its ranks those few Americans, particularly members of the legislatures, with sufficient merit and reputation to resist the aspirations of the society. That point was made by Burke and many others. When William Moultrie, a member of the Cincinnati whose notes of their first national meeting are an invaluable source, compiled the objections that seemed to be mounting nationally, he emphasized four: "Honorary members[,] funds[,] hereditary succession[, and] medling in politicks."[15]

A third reason that many people thought the alarms of the critics of the Cincinnati were worth taking seriously is that they accorded so well with how Americans made sense of human history in the latter half of the eighteenth century. Both of Burke's 1783 pamphlets, notes his biographer, "feature the conspiratorial mode of explanation in which men were assumed to intend the actual or prospective consequences of their actions." Indeed, as Gordon Wood has famously argued, historical explanations in the age of revolutions tended to look to human design and personal intention to explain how and why things happened, including the rise and fall of nations. As opposed to the emphases on divine causes that marked ages past or the accent on impersonal forces that would rise to prominence in the nineteenth century, many sober and serious Americans believed that, for many of the myriad dangers facing the young nation, deliberate conspiracy lay at the heart. When John Adams wrote about the Cincinnati, he saw "the new order of Chivalry" as nothing less than "a deep design to overturn the whole Edifice of our Republican Liberty."[16]

Fourth, and perhaps most important of all, what the Cincinnati were doing looked so remarkably like what had happened in ancient Rome and across the intervening centuries in Europe that to ignore it was to act as if history offered no lessons for America at all. Burke pointed directly at the Roman experience: no one in Rome, he noted, had planned to create a hereditary nobility, but it came about nonetheless. "The Romans had learned from sad experience," Burke (as Cassius) wrote, "that military commanders acquiring fame, and accustomed to receive the obedience of armies, are generally in their hearts aristocracies, and enemies to the popular equality of a republic." The namesake of the American organization, Cincinnatus, had resisted such arrogations, but Burke and many others were worried that the men in his own day were headed down a treacherous path. A convention in Rhode Island specially called to address the apparent threat came to the conclusion that the "Order or Society

Called the Cincinnati . . . Distinguishing themselves from Citizens at Large by a Badge to be by them Worn" appeared to be "endeavouring to create themselves and their Male Heirs patricians or Noblemen." Across European history, Burke would describe, one could find instances of self-created peerages that transformed into permanent hierarchies in society. John Adams had the same worry of transmutation from chivalric order into something even more socially divisive and politically destructive: he hoped the Cincinnati would take their plan and "lay it voluntarily aside. if they do not Knights will make Barons, Earls, Viscounts, Marquises and Dukes and these Princes and Kings, in a very Short time."[17]

Layered on top of these fears of the establishment of a hereditary aristocracy was the fact that the Cincinnati appeared, at least from the outside, to have political goals. In a period when hardly any organization but Congress was truly national in scope, people could see the Cincinnati—with its federal structure; with national, state, and in some places district-level meetings—as something more than a club of former soldiers. It looked all too much like a self-created and parallel government. It reeked of political pretensions: as a legislative committee in Massachusetts reported, this "select Society" planned to "convene expressly for the purpose of deliberating upon, judging of, and adopting measures concerning matters, proper only for the cognizance of the legislative and their determination thereon, or of such other bodies as are known in the constitution." This was, in 1784, a dangerous imperium in imperio, an organization that, united by friendship, might seek its own interests in what was an ideally unified commonwealth, as Johann Neem has explored. Its very existence constituted an internal threat to republican government, one made all the more frightening by the trappings of nobility.[18]

## The Response of the Cincinnati

Washington, who had been named as the obvious choice as president of the Cincinnati, was mortified when the controversy exploded. As he so often did, Washington sought the advice of others about how he ought to respond to the accusations, including Jefferson, who was then serving in the Congress of the Confederation in Annapolis. Washington knew that the first general meeting of the Cincinnati would be the best chance to do something about the problem, and he contacted Jefferson in advance. In a letter sent in reply on April 16, 1784, knowing that the two men would soon have a chance to discuss the matter in person, Jefferson took the opportunity to make a case for why Washington should do everything he could to destroy the Cincinnati.[19]

Jefferson saw the Cincinnati as a dangerous development in a republic of laws. The association, in granting the progeny of its members "pre-eminence by birth," was "against the letter of some of our constitutions; against the spirit of them all." If people like Washington did not halt its progress, the Cincinnati, Jefferson argued, might well be a first step toward a subversion of all of the revolution's accomplishments. Washington was deeply concerned, too. When they met in Annapolis not long after, as Jefferson recalled, "we had much convers[atio]n on the institution," until Washington "declared his determination to use his utmost endeavor to have it entirely abolished." After leaving Jefferson, Washington traveled to Philadelphia and presided over the first meeting of the Cincinnati in May 1784.[20]

Washington, we know, was genuinely upset. He gave two long speeches, delivered, according to an observer, "with much warmth and agitation." The debate over hereditary membership was terribly important, but Washington also leveraged a different point, emphasizing the notion of friendship. As the Cincinnati's organizers had put it in a letter to French officers, the whole point of the society was "riveting more strongly those indissoluble ties" of friendship. Following Jefferson's advice, Washington made the case that it might destroy the friendships forged in war. Creating some kind of formal organization was a faulty substitute for the purer forms of friendly intercourse that the retired officers really sought.[21]

It looked for a while as if Washington would carry the day, for his "warmth and agitation" at the first triennial meeting was accompanied by a list of specific recommendations for the society. Washington sought to abolish hereditary and honorary memberships, to "strike out every word, sentence, and clause which has a political tendency," and to place the funds of each state society in the hands of the state legislature (a proposal amended by committee to a call for state-by-state charters of incorporation). Surely, it would seem, the Cincinnati would have to do something to respond to the accusations being leveled against them. The national meeting of the Society of the Cincinnati, like the Congress under the Articles of Confederation, could do very little, however. Like the articles, any change to the fundamental principles of organization required the unanimous consent of all thirteen state societies.[22]

Many of the Cincinnati stood firmly opposed to Washington's attempts to change the society. New Hampshire's John Sullivan publicly told Washington via a circular letter sent to all thirteen branches that he and his fellow New Hampshire members would have none of it. "We became Members of the Cincinnati upon the original plan & cannot conceive ourselves bound by Articles to which we never subscribed." If a new system was contrived "we shall Individually claim a right to determine for ourselves whether we will become members or we will not." They had consented to join the Cincinnati in its original form, they argued, and no one could transform it without their renewed consent.[23]

People had already begun to defend the Cincinnati in print against the many attacks being made throughout the nation. One anonymous writer made the point, powerfully, that there was little reason to fear a self-created organization such as the Cincinnati when the power of the law so clearly surrounded them and could so easily obliterate them. "The institution of the Order of the Cincinnati is back'd by no power, and consequently attended with no danger," wrote "An Obscure Individual." Because "*The arm of civil authority surrounds it*—only to *will* its destruction would be instant annihilation. If this institution has any tendency to create distinctions, it is," he wrote, "a distinction *without power,* and without any other luster than what it borrows from virtue." Indeed, "suppose the Cincinnati really aspired at nobility," wrote someone in the *Connecticut Courant.* Yet "we have no right to believe, Congress will aid them in their views." Lacking governmental approbation, the Society of the Cincinnati offered nothing but pretense.[24]

The same author in Connecticut was ready to defend the Cincinnati against any and all charges of aristocracy: "It is ridiculous to suppose that every subaltern in the Society of the Cincinnati, by giving up part of his wages for the benefit of the poor of the society, is become in fact a peer of the realm; but it is easy to give names to persons and things, to hold them up in an odious light." This was a club, a mutual benefit society not terribly unlike many others that already existed as early as 1784, and there was no reason to fear that they would aspire to rule the continent. In fact, the Society of the Cincinnati soon made clear that they had no intention of wearing their badge in public on regular occasions, unlike the peerages and chivalric orders of Europe. Only on special celebrations and in regularly called meetings would the ornate eagle badge even be taken out of the house. In the end, perhaps the Delaware Society of the Cincinnati took the best tack in response to public assaults such as Burke's: "The attack, or rather the compliment paid us by the learned *Cassius,* we hope will have no other effect than to excite us to laudable ambition, to engage our attention to maxims of prudence, and to contribute in establishing in us those republican principles of virtue, honor, and honesty, which we hope will ever be the distinguishing badges of the Cincinnati." We will use this moment, they declared, to become even better men and, above all, to be good citizens of the republic. All of the debates surrounding the Cincinnati gave a great many Americans an opportunity to address directly and without mediation one of their worst fears: the possible rise of an aristocracy out of the ashes of a republic. The stakes remained high, but it was beginning to look as if there may in fact be nothing to fear at all.[25]

## The Diminishing Fear of Aristocracy in America

There was no climax to the turmoil over the Cincinnati. It simply faded away while never quite fully disappearing from view. The proposed reforms offered by Washington would have cut to the core of the criticisms being levied against the society by ending the lineal descent of membership, abolishing the power to make honorary members of those lacking the military credentials, and placing control of society funds in the hands of the legislature of each state. As word spread of these reforms, reported Nathanael Greene to Washington, it "seemed to silence all jealousies on the subject." Because the Cincinnati's institution could be amended only by unanimous consent, however, those reforms ultimately failed ratification. Many states took their time making a decision at all: North Carolina's Cincinnati reported in November 1786 that "Our State Society . . . still remain undecided on the Question of the new Institution." In the end, only three state societies both formally adopted Washington's plan for a revised institution and stood by that decision. Three states rejected the proposals outright. Other state societies, in fact, were determinedly indecisive.[26]

Extensive newspaper coverage of the reform efforts led many to await results rather than continue their assaults. Dragged out over three years, between 1784 and 1787, most simply lost interest or were distracted by other, newer threats to the republic, such as Shays's Rebellion in 1786. In sum, many of the state societies and individual members of the Cincinnati stuck to their original plans just long enough for their critics to find other things to worry about. Many of those critics came to see just how innocuous the Society of the Cincinnati had, almost certainly, always been.

A few worried that the worst of all possible things had happened: the vigilance of the people had faltered, and the Cincinnati were "daily acquiring strength," as John Quincy Adams wrote to his father in June 1787. Because no one now "dares attack this institution openly," he wrote, it "will infallibly become a body dangerous, if not fatal to the Constitution" of the Commonwealth of Massachusetts. Others, such as Gerry and Rufus King, also worried that the snake remained in the grass. In a letter that the Massachusetts delegates to Congress sent to Governor James Bowdoin in 1785, they recommended that he not support any efforts to revise the framework of the national government because "the Friends of Aristocracy" were ready to act if given a chance. Among them, "the Institution of the Cincinnati, honourable and beneficent as the Views may have been of the Officers who compose it, We fear, if not totally abolished, will have the same fatal Tendency" of changing "our republican Governments, into baleful Aristocracies." We should give them no opportunity, they wrote. Criticisms continued to appear for a few more years, according to historian Charles Royster, but the public outrage had subsided. By middecade, more and more nonmembers, such as Noah Webster and Joel Barlow, were increasingly willing to speak publicly about the laudable or, at least, relatively harmless Society of the Cincinnati.[27]

Yet the controversy over the possible formation of a hereditary aristocracy in 1780s America had lasting consequences. William Doyle, a historian of France in the age of revolutions, has observed that the American
exchange of ideas about the merits and dangers of the Cincinnati was, in
fact, "an essential step in discrediting noble claims and ideals" in the new
United States. "Americans were forced to confront ambiguous and half-
conscious assumptions about the nature of their society," he writes, and
it helped them better to understand their own republic. Michael Jan Rozbicki has cast the response to the Cincinnati as an expression of a "Revolutionary anti-aristocratism, originally directed against England" that then
"discredited claims of privilege made by the existing elites—such as those
asserted by the Society of the Cincinnati." The assault on aristocracy in
the form chosen by the Cincinnati did not arise solely from a democratic
instinct. Indeed, much of the alarm was sounded by people who in fact did
believe that there were natural distinctions among men and that certain
men ought to lead: people such as John Adams had no doubts on that point,
and yet he utterly despised the Society of the Cincinnati. It was artificial,
and with its hereditary membership it rewarded and enshrined the merito-
rious of this generation, to the detriment of the next—a point that, as Marc
Harris has noted, was also important to Aedanus Burke. One could oppose
the artificiality and exclusivity of the Cincinnati without denying that any
well-ordered society required something akin to rank and hierarchy.[28]

In the Cincinnati controversy of the 1780s, then, there is a lot to be
learned about the presumptions and priorities of Americans in the years
just following their hard-won revolution. Yet it appears that by 1787
Americans were looking elsewhere for threats to the union. Gerry, to be
sure, referred to the Cincinnati in the Philadelphia Convention as a group
that, owing to its national influence, could (by "acting in Concert") select
the president of the United States. George Mason agreed, saying it was
"a Society for the members of which he had great respect," according to
Madison's notes, "but which he never wished to have a preponderating
influence in the Govt." However, theirs were observations about communication and coordination—particular concerns of the framers of the
Constitution, as Madison's *Federalist*, no. 10, shows—and did not reveal
any especially troubling thoughts about a looming hierarchy. There was

little fear here of aristocratic dominion. The debate about the Cincinnati had helped to produce this newfound confidence. All of the public discussions and popular furor over the existence of this newly created hereditary body of former military men had begun to transform American attitudes toward aristocracy, artificial distinctions, and hereditary privilege, making all such things appear increasingly to be little more than distant, fantastical threats in the thirteen United States.[29]

When in 1787 John Stevens published his *Observations on Government* in order to critique John Adams's *Defence of the Constitutions* and its argument for a "natural aristocracy" of "virtues and abilities," he argued that, in America, "perfect equality . . . exists amongst us. We have no such thing as orders, ranks, or nobility." In his *Creation of the American Republic,* Wood depicted Stevens as being far better in touch with how Americans were thinking by 1787 than was John Adams, and Stevens's take on aristocracy seems to confirm that reading. One thing Stevens took for granted was that "foreigners, who are accustomed to view titles and orders, as matters of importance, cannot easily conceive in what contempt the pretensions of these are held by the people of this country." He made no mention of the Cincinnati; he did not have to. Still, the controversy over its existence no doubt shaped his belief—one shared more and more by Americans throughout the young nation—that "it would be impossible to succeed in the scheme of forming a nobility."[30]

The fact that the debate over the Cincinnati as a hereditary peerage fizzled out and that nothing seemed to come of the dire predictions of their critics may ultimately have narrowed the field of vision of politically attuned Americans in 1787 and 1788. To many, it appeared that the thirteen republics had faced the test of potential elite rule and survived. Americans north and south had contemplated the possibilities of an aristocracy arising domestically and had determined it to be far-fetched. The greater extreme to be feared was of democratic excess, not aristocratic power. Antagonism toward the chivalric order of the Society of the Cincinnati offered lessons for many Americans in how to evaluate and to confront elitist threats to the welfare of the people. One of those lessons seemed to be that aristocracy could never find a foothold in the United States. When the ratification debates took place, those discoveries shaped how people responded to proposals to create explicitly governmental institutions that were removed from the direct will of the people through indirect election: most obviously, the national executive and the national Senate proposed in 1787.

There was still concern, to be sure, that the Philadelphia Convention's plan for a new federal government would give authority to the "wealthy and ambitious, who in every community think they have a right to lord it over their fellow creatures," as Samuel Bryan wrote in 1787. In his Centinel essays in the ratification debates in Pennsylvania, he was worried about nothing so much as the fact that ordinary people not long removed from a republican revolution would, understandably, continue to defer to the more learned and more eloquent, the "lawyers, doctors and divines," whose political opinions were both better educated and better funded. Those arguments, however, did not carry the weight that they might have if the nation had not just weathered what had initially appeared to be a genuine threat of noble privilege. Having done so, other forms of potentially aristocratic power lacked quite the power to instill fear that they might have once had. Writing as "An American Citizen" in September 1787, for instance, Tench Coxe was able to assure people that the Senate, "not being hereditary," was no threat. "They will have none of the *peculiar follies and vices of those men who possess power merely because their fathers held it before them.*" With the rise and fall of an apparent threat of hereditary nobility, many Americans felt better prepared to consider—and more willing to accept—other forms of political organization that placed authority at a greater remove from the voice of the people. Having stared down one form of aristocracy, Americans became more willing to experiment in mechanisms of government that had some of the substance, but not the trappings and the suits, of aristocratic power.[31]

## Notes

1. Centinel [Samuel Bryan?], no. 3, *Independent Gazetteer* (Philadelphia, PA), November 8, 1787, in *The Complete Anti-Federalist*, ed. Herbert J. Storing (Chicago: University of Chicago Press, 1981), 2:156; A Federalist, *Boston Gazette*, November 8, 1787.
2. Saul Cornell, "Aristocracy Assailed: Backcountry Opposition to the Constitution and the Problem of Anti-Federalist Ideology," *Journal of American History* 76 (1990):

1156; "A Receipt for an Antifederalist Essay," *Pennsylvania Gazette* (Philadelphia, PA), November 14, 1787, in *Documentary History of the Ratification of the Constitution*, ed. John P. Kaminski and Gaspare J. Saladino (Madison: State Historical Society of Wisconsin, 1983), 14:103.

3. See George William Van Cleve, *We Have Not a Government: The Articles of Confederation and the Road to the Constitution* (Chicago: University of Chicago Press, 2017); Woody Holton, *Unruly Americans and the Origins of the Constitution* (New York: Hill and Wang, 2007); Michael J. Klarman, *The Framers' Coup: The Making of the United States Constitution* (New York: Oxford University Press, 2016). The forum in the *William and Mary Quarterly* in 2012 on Pauline Maier's *Ratification: The People Debate the Constitution, 1787–1788* (New York: Simon and Schuster, 2010) is a good recent guide to the range of interpretations: *William and Mary Quarterly*, 3rd ser., 69 (April 2012): 361–403.

4. Elbridge Gerry, May 31, 1787, in *The Records of the Federal Convention of 1787*, ed. Max Farrand (New Haven, CT: Yale University Press, 1911), 1:48.

5. Samuel Osgood to John Adams, January 14, 1784, in *Letters to Delegates of Congress, 1774–1789*, ed. Paul H. Smith (Washington, DC: Library of Congress, 1994), 21:277; Willi Paul Adams, *The First American Constitutions: Republican Ideology and the Making of the State Constitutions in the Revolutionary Era* (Chapel Hill: University of North Carolina Press, 1980); Donald S. Lutz, *The Origins of American Constitutionalism* (Baton Rouge: Louisiana State University Press, 1988).

6. *A History of Every Attempt at Resistance to the Federal Government [. . .]* (New York: William E. Chapin, 1861). The nineteenth-century work that launched the term "Critical Period" as a descriptor for the 1780s, John Fiske's *The Critical Period of American History 1783–1789* (1888; repr., Boston: Houghton Mifflin Company, 1916), includes a section on the Cincinnati controversy, beginning with his observation that "men of the present generation who in childhood rummaged in their grandmothers' cosy garrets cannot fail to have come across scores of musty and worm-eaten pamphlets, their yellow pages crowded with italics and exclamation points, inveighing in passionate language against the wicked and dangerous society of the Cincinnati" (114).

7. Edgar Erskine Hume, ed., *Society of the Cincinnati: Rules of the State Societies for Admission to Membership* (Washington, DC: Society of the Cincinnati, 1934), 3; Bryce Metcalf, *Original Members and Other Officers Eligible to the Society of the Cincinnati, 1783–1938: With the Institutions, Rules of Admission, and Lists of the Officers of the General and State Societies* (1938; repr., Beverly Hills, CA: Historic Trust Eastwood Publishing, 1995); Minor Myers Jr., *Liberty without Anarchy: A History of the Society of the Cincinnati* (Charlottesville: University Press of Virginia, 1983), chap. 2 and appendix; diary of Thomas Jefferson, March 6, 1788, in *The Writings of Thomas Jefferson*, ed. Andrew A. Lipscomb and Albert Ellery Bergh, (Washington, DC: Thomas Jefferson Memorial Association, 1903), 17:249–50; North Callahan, *Henry Knox: General Washington's General* (New York: Rinehart, 1958), 216.

8. On the Cincinnati as a knighthood, see Richard Beale Davis, ed., *Jeffersonian America: Notes on the United States of America Collected in the Years 1805-6-7 and 11–12 by Sir Augustus John Foster, Bart.* (San Marino, CA: Huntington Library, 1954), 69, where Foster refers to Charles C. Pinckney as "a Knight of Cincinnati." Abigail Adams made a similar judgment, referring to "knights of the order" in a letter to another critic of

the Cincinnati, Mercy Otis Warren, May 10, 1785. Richard Alan Ryerson, ed., *Adams Family Correspondence, December 1784–December 1785* (Cambridge, MA: Belknap Press of Harvard University Press, 1993), 6:139.

9. Markus Hünemörder, *The Society of the Cincinnati: Conspiracy and Distrust in Early America* (New York: Berghahn Books, 2006), 15–17; Charles Royster, *A Revolutionary People at War: The Continental Army and American Character, 1775–1783* (Chapel Hill: University of North Carolina Press, 1979), 355–56; Myers, *Liberty without Anarchy*, chap. 1; David Head, *A Crisis of Peace: George Washington, the Newburgh Conspiracy, and the Fate of the American Revolution* (New York: Pegasus Books, 2019).

10. Wallace Evan Davies, "The Society of the Cincinnati in New England, 1783–1800," *William and Mary Quarterly*, 3rd ser., 5 (1948): 9; Hünemörder, *Society of the Cincinnati*, 25–26; Curtis Carroll Davis, *Revolution's Godchild: The Birth, Death, and Regeneration of the Society of the Cincinnati in North Carolina* (Chapel Hill: University of North Carolina Press, 1976), 3–59; *A Member of the Society of the Cincinnati, A Reply to a Pamphlet, Entitled, Considerations on the Society or Order of Cincinnati &c.* (Annapolis, MD: Frederick Green, [1783]), 28; Morgan Lewis, address appended to Robert R. Livingston, *An Oration Delivered before the Society of the Cincinnati in the State of New-York: In Commemoration of the Fourth Day of July* (New York: Francis Childs, 1787), 19–21; John Sullivan to George Washington, February 5, 1785, in *Letters and Papers of Major-General John Sullivan, Continental Army*, ed. Otis G. Hammond, in *Collections of the New Hampshire Historical Society*, vol. 15 (Concord: New Hampshire Historical Society, 1939), 394–97.

11. Cassius [Aedanus Burke], *Considerations on the Society or Order of the Cincinnati; Lately Instituted by the Major-Generals, Brigadier-Generals, and Other Officers of the American Army [. . .]* (Philadelphia: Robert Bell, 1783), 7.

12. Cassius [Aedanus Burke], *An Address to the Freemen of the State of South-Carolina [. . .]* (Philadelphia: Robert Bell, 1783); Kerby A. Miller et al., eds., *Irish Immigrants in the Land of Canaan* (New York: Oxford University Press, 2003), 576–85; John C. Meleney, *The Public Life of Aedanus Burke: Revolutionary Republican in Post-Revolutionary South Carolina* (Columbia: University of South Carolina Press, 1989), chap. 4.

13. Burke, *Considerations*, 7–8; Marc L. Harris, "'Cement to the Union': The Society of the Cincinnati and the Limits of Fraternal Sociability," *Proceedings of the Massachusetts Historical Society* 107 (1995): 135; George Washington to Thomas Jefferson, April 8, 1784, in *The Papers of George Washington: Confederation Series*, ed. W. W. Abbot and Dorothy Twohig (Charlottesville: University of Virginia Press, 1992), 1:275–76.

14. Burke, *Considerations*, 6, 14, 4; Thomas Jefferson to George Washington, April 16, 1784, in Abbot and and Twohig, *The Papers of George Washington*, 1:287–92; *Charleston South Carolina Gazette and General Advertiser*, February 10, 1784, quoted in Hünemörder, *Society of the Cincinnati*, 39; Samuel Adams to Elbridge Gerry, April 19, 1784, in *The Writings of Samuel Adams*, ed. Harry Alonzo Cushing (New York: Putnam, 1908; repr., New York: Octagon Books, 1968), 4:298–99.

15. William Moultrie, "Proceedings of the General Societe of the Cincinaty," May 5, 1784, bound volume, Manuscript Department, New-York Historical Society.

16. Meleney, *Public Life of Aedanus Burke*, 96; Gordon S. Wood, "Conspiracy and the Paranoid Style: Causality and Deceit in the Eighteenth Century," *William and Mary Quarterly*, 3rd. ser., 39 (1982): 401–41; John Adams to Arthur Lee, April 6, 1784, in C. James

Taylor et al., eds., *The Papers of John Adams: February 1784–March 1785* (Cambridge, MA: Belknap Press of Harvard University Press, 2012), 16:108–9.

17. Burke, *Considerations*, 7, 10–11; Myers, *Liberty without Anarchy*, 50; "Convention of Members Chosen by the Towns of Westerly, North Kingston, South Kingston, Charleston, Exeter, Richmond, and Hopkinton," April 1, 1784, Rhode Island Historical Society Manuscripts, box 14, folder 369, Rhode Island Historical Society; Adams to Lee, April 6, 1784, in Taylor, *The Papers of John Adams*, 16: 108–9.

18. Quotation from "The Committee of both Houses of the General Court, appointed to enquire into the Existence, Nature, Object, and probably Tendency or Effect of an Order or Society called the Cincinnati [. . .]," *Independent Chronicle* (Boston), March 25, 1784, quoted in Johann N. Neem, *Creating a Nation of Joiners: Democracy and Civil Society in Early National Massachusetts* (Cambridge, MA: Harvard University Press, 2008), 42, see also 40–42, 47; Edgar Erskine Hume, "Early Opposition to the Cincinnati," *Americana* 30 (1936): 597–638.

19. George Washington to Thomas Jefferson, April 8, 1784, in Abbot and Twohig, *The Papers of George Washington*, 1:275–76.

20. Thomas Jefferson to George Washington, April 16, 1784, in ibid., 1:287–92. See ibid., 1:351–52n16, where Jefferson describes his conversations with Washington in a comment he drafted in response to John Marshall's *The Life of George Washington, Commander in Chief of the American Forces, During the War Which Established the Independence of His Country, and the First President of the United States*, vol. 5 (Philadelphia: C. P. Wayne, 1804–1807). See Thomas Jefferson to Martin Van Buren, June 29, 1824, in Lipscomb and Bergh, *Writings of Thomas Jefferson*, 16:62–64; Hünemörder, *Society of the Cincinnati*, 89–90; Dumas Malone, *Jefferson the Virginian* (Boston: Little, Brown, 1948), 414–15. Though he hated the idea of the Society of the Cincinnati, Jefferson perceived, better than most critics, that the organization had genuinely admirable origins. He never swayed from that view, even years later. He would repeat that version of the story two years later when he corrected the French encyclopedist Jean Nicolas Démeunier, who had painted a much more nefarious picture of the Cincinnati. The criticisms of the Cincinnati came about, Jefferson informed him, when men around the country read the plans for the Society "in their closets, unwarmed by those sentiments of friendship which had produced them, inattentive to those pains which an approaching separation had excited in the minds of the institutors." If they had shared those feelings, they would have at the very least understood the impulse that had produced the order. "Jefferson's Observations on Démeunier's Manuscript," in *The Papers of Thomas Jefferson*, ed. Julian P. Boyd (Princeton, NJ: Princeton University Press, 1954), 10:49–50; Jefferson to Washington, November 14, 1786, in Abbot and Twohig, *The Papers of George Washington*, 4:363–66.

21. Ibid., 1:330–32; see ibid., 332–54, for Winthrop Sargent's journal of the first general meeting, May 4–18, 1784, quotation on 335. For the letter from the Society of the Cincinnati to "Senior Land and Naval Officers and Others, Members of the Society of the Cincinnati in France," May 1784, see Sargent, "Journal of the General Meeting of the Cincinnati in 1784," *Memoirs of the Historical Society of Pennsylvania* 6 (1858): 111–12; Kevin Butterfield, "Friendships and Bylaws: Formal Association versus Friendship

in the Early Republic" (paper presented at the Society for Historians of the Early American Republic annual meeting, Baltimore, MD, July 2012).

22. See Washington, "Observations on the Society of the Cincinnati," [May 4, 1784] in Abbot and Twohig, *The Papers of George Washington*, 1:330–32; Hünemörder, *Society of the Cincinnati*, 94–101; Myers, *Liberty without Anarchy*, 58–60, 76–79; Henry Hobart Bellas, *A History of the Delaware State Society of the Cincinnati: From Its Organization to the Present Time [. . .]* (Wilmington: Historical Society of Delaware, 1895), 12–16; Winslow Warren, *The Society of the Cincinnati: A History of the General Society of Cincinnati with the Institution of the Order* (n.p.: Massachusetts Society of the Cincinnati, 1929), 3–9.

23. John Sullivan to George Washington, February 3, 1785, in Abbot and Twohig, *The Papers of George Washington*, 2:320–23; circular letter by Sullivan of Exeter, NH, February 3, 1785, in *Papers of the Connecticut State Society of the Cincinnati, 1783–1807* (Hartford: Connecticut Historical Society, 1916), n.p. Thomas C. Amory, *The Military Services and Public Life of Major-General John Sullivan, of the American Revolutionary Army* (Boston: Wiggin and Lunt, 1868), 197–98, 254–55; E. Wayne Carp, *To Starve the Army at Pleasure: Continental Army Administration and American Political Culture, 1775–1783* (Chapel Hill: University of North Carolina Press, 1984), 203–4; Charles P. Whittemore, *A General of the Revolution: John Sullivan of New Hampshire* (New York: Columbia University Press, 1961), 190; Sullivan to George Washington, February 5, 1785, in Hammond, *Letters and Papers of Major-General John Sullivan in Collections of the New Hampshire Historical Society*, vol. 15 (Concord: New Hampshire Historical Society, 1939), 394–97; Gerald D. Foss, *Three Centuries of Freemasonry in New Hampshire* (Concord, NH: Grand Lodge of New Hampshire, 1972), 180–83.

24. An Obscure Individual, *Observations on a Late Pamphlet Entituled "Considerations on the Society or Order of Cincinnati," Clearly Evincing the Innocence and Propriety of That Honourable and Respectable Institution* (Hartford, CT: Hudson and Goodwin, 1784), 13; *Connecticut Courant, and Weekly Intelligencer* (Hartford, CT), April 13, 1784.

25. Ibid.; Myers, *Liberty without Anarchy*, 63–64; Roger N. Parks, ed., *The Papers of Nathanael Greene*, (Chapel Hill: University of North Carolina Press, 2005), 13:291–92; Delaware State Society of the Cincinnati, November 6, 1783, in *Papers of the Connecticut State Society of the Cincinnati*, n.p.

26. Nathanael Greene to George Washington, August 29, 1784, Roger N. Parks, ed., *The Papers of Nathanael Greene*, vol. 13 (Chapel Hill: University of North Carolina Press, 2005); report of the North Carolina Society of the Cincinnati, *Papers of the Connecticut State Society of the Cincinnati*, n.p.; William Doyle, *Aristocracy and Its Enemies in the Age of Revolution* (Oxford, UK: Oxford University Press, 2009), 136.

27. John Quincy Adams to John Adams, June 30, 1787, in *Writings of John Quincy Adams*, ed. Worthington Chauncey Ford (New York: Macmillan Company, 1913), 1:33; Massachusetts delegates to the governor of Massachusetts [James Bowdoin], September 3, 1785 (in the hand of Elbridge Gerry), in *Letters of Members of the Continental Congress*, ed. Edmund C. Burnett (Washington, DC: Carnegie Institution of Washington, 1936), 8:206–10; Royster, *Revolutionary People at War*, 357–58; Noah Webster Jr., *Sketches of American Policy . . .* (Hartford, CT: Hudson and Goodwin, 1785), 26; Richard Buel

Jr., *Joel Barlow: American Citizen in a Revolutionary World* (Baltimore: Johns Hopkins University Press, 2011), 94–95.

28. Doyle, *Aristocracy and Its Enemies*, 136; Michael Jan Rozbicki, *Culture and Liberty in the Age of the American Revolution* (Charlottesville: University of Virginia Press, 2011), 103–4; Harris, "'Cement to the Union,'" 136.

29. Notes of James Madison for July 25–26, 1787, in Farrand, *The Records of the Federal Convention*, 2:114, 119; Holton, *Unruly Americans*, 207–8; Hünemörder, *Society of the Cincinnati*, 67.

30. A Farmer, of New-Jersey [John Stevens], *Observations on Government, including Some Animadversions on Mr. Adams's Defence of the Constitutions of Government of the United States of America [. . .]* (New York: W. Ross, 1787); Gordon S. Wood, *The Creation of the American Republic, 1776–1787* (Chapel Hill: University of North Carolina Press, 1969), 583–84.

31. Centinel [Samuel Bryan?], *Independent Gazetteer* (Philadelphia, PA), October 5, 1787, in Storing, *Complete Anti-Federalist*, 2:137; Saul Cornell, *The Other Founders: Anti-Federalism and the Dissenting Tradition in America, 1788–1828* (Chapel Hill: University of North Carolina Press, 1999), 105; An American Citizen [Tench Coxe], in *The Documentary History of the Ratification of the Constitution: Pennsylvania*, ed. Merrill Jensen (Madison: State Historical Society of Wisconsin, 1976), 2:142.

# Epilogue

## TURN DOWN THE VOLUME!

*Johann N. Neem*

I N 1987, IN RECOGNITION of the 200th anniversary of the Constitutional Convention, some of America's leading historians of the founding offered their insights in the volume *Beyond Confederation*, published by the Institute of Early American History and Culture in Williamsburg, Virginia. The essays in that volume reflected a century of debate about the founding's meaning and legacy, provided a framework for what to teach in early American history courses, and shaped the agenda of countless scholars. Reading *Beyond Confederation* today, after reading the essays in this volume, leaves me with a sense of wonder and uncertainty. It is hard to believe that the scholars in 1987 were writing about the same period, the same people, and the same Constitution as the scholars who gathered at the Fred W. Smith Library at George Washington's Mount Vernon in 2014.

In 1987, the historiographical conversation was dominated by how to reconcile ideas and interests. The work of Bernard Bailyn, J. G. A. Pocock, and Gordon S. Wood influenced the agenda. The framers appear in *Beyond Confederation* as shaped by classical republican ideals, but these ideals did not produce stoic disinterestedness. Instead, the contributors to *Beyond Confederation* suggested a sense of urgency and even panic as the framers confronted the gap between their intellectual ideals and the realities playing out during what we call the Critical Period. Although not all the contributors were preoccupied with these issues, the overall worldview of the volume was James Madison's. Nothing could save the republic but a republican solution for republican problems. However, those problems were themselves defined by republican lenses—thus it was difficult to see beyond them.[1]

The essays in this volume ask us to see beyond them. Indeed, there is very little mention of republicanism, and even of the great debate—dating at least as far back as 1913, when Charles Beard published *An Economic Interpretation of the Constitution*—of how to connect "big ideas" and intellectual frameworks to base economic interests. The language of panic is missing. The volume dial is turned down. Unlike in 1987, when the framers appeared to be eighteenth-century thinkers, far removed from us, the framers presented here are practical men. They are less foreign to us than were the people offered up by the likes of Bailyn and Wood. Indeed, if there is a moral to this book, it is that the framers of the Constitution, responding to the problems of their time, relied less on their inherited ideas than on a kind of experimental pragmatic spirit—which Caroline Winterer has identified as central to the Enlightenment itself.[2]

Much is gained from this perspective, but something is lost too. I remember as a graduate student reading Wood's path-breaking *The Creation of the American Republic*.[3] That book is bulky, but it left me breathless. At its heart is a discussion about the democratizing impulse in the states and the fears that democratization spurred among elites. The period between the revolution and the Constitutional Convention, Wood showed with words that painted pictures in my mind, was a time when classical politics ended as deference came crashing down. It was a world turned upside down, in which elite federalists sought to put the top back on but never quite could. Wood masterfully wove together the competing accounts of consensus and conflict, Whiggish and Progressive narratives, and ideas and interests to produce one of the classics of American historiography. It was a book that suggested that behind action were deep intellectual frameworks, and it was those frameworks that led Americans to interpret events and policies as they did. Ideas were central to the American founding and the conflicts it spurred. Understanding them reconciled dichotomous accounts of the era and also explained the framers' sense of crisis.[4]

I recall how weird it was later to read Merrill Jensen's *The New Nation: A History of the United States During the Confederation*. Although published before *Creation of the American Republic*, I read them in reverse order. To Jensen, the Critical Period was a time of real progress. State governments were stabilizing, economies were rebounding, and things were improving slowly but steadily. It was not Sturm und Drang, as I had imagined it when I first made my way through *Creation*. Yes, the Confederation period faced challenges, but ordinary people had faith in the future. Jensen concluded, "contemporary opinion in America plainly does not support the picture of unmitigated gloom so often set forth by the writers of history who follow in one another's footsteps with more faith than research."[5] However, if it was not a time of crisis, if things were not falling apart, if Madison's panic-laden words were not definitive, how to explain the Constitution?

We have come to see the era between Yorktown and the ratification of the Constitution as the most significant in American history. At some point, this is just a truism. Because the American Revolution gave birth to the United States, and because the federal Constitution provided the framework to govern the new republic, by definition, for Americans, this era matters significantly. But we have overlaid a sense of awe that encourages inflationary rhetoric. To John Fiske, who coined the term "critical period" in 1888, "it is not too much to say that the period of five years following the peace of 1783 was the most critical moment in all the history of the American people." Indeed, Fiske said to his readers, "We are about to traverse a period of uncertainty and confusion, in which it required all the political sagacity and all the good temper of the people to save the half-built ship of state from going to pieces on the rocks of civil contention."[6] Such rhetoric remained central to those who celebrated—as well as those who condemned—the Constitutional settlement. For example, in his 1979 work *E Pluribus Unum*, Forrest McDonald concluded that in the midst of the great crisis of the 1780s, "there were giants on the earth in those days, and they spoke in the name of the nation."[7] Compared to the "men of little faith" who opposed the Constitution, the framers emerge as America's saviors.[8]

Fiske's perspective remains alive. One need only learn about the Constitution in popular outlets to be reminded of our continued celebration of the framers as saviors. For good reasons, too. The framers of the Constitution designed a system of government that, for all its flaws, enabled the new United States to take its place among the powers of the earth.[9] There is much to be thankful for, as George Van Cleve makes clear in his recent *We Have Not a Government.* In response to the kind of abstract intellectual frameworks that spurred Wood and others, Van Cleve usefully returns to narrative and to the specific causes behind the Articles of Confederation's failure. Even as he brings us down to daily political realities, however, Van Cleve echoes Fiske when he reasserts the critical nature of the period leading up to the Constitutional Convention. Van Cleve argues that the compounding impact of specific challenges—economic, fiscal, social, political—led to political stalemate that could only be resolved by the dramatic transfer of sovereignty to a more powerful federal government. But Van Cleve, thanks to his own work as well as those of others, knows the Constitution required compromises, most notably in regard to slavery. Thus, the Constitution, Van Cleve writes, was both a "brilliant solution to the Confederation's stalemate," and a "pragmatic political compromise" with "flaws."[10] But the brilliance remains.

If much of the writing about the era is inflationary, the contributors to this volume are decidedly deflationary. They want to tone down the rhetoric. These essays rarely raise the volume to 11. There are no stressful, anxious, deep-seated ideologies. There is precious little moralizing. There is no effort to judge who was right and who was wrong. Whether one is a consensus historian or a Progressive historian, a conservative or a radical—or, like Wood, someone trying to bring the pieces together—one would wonder what to do with this book. Like the framers, it depends on the issue. And that's what's so great about it. As Hannah Farber writes in this volume of efforts to glorify or to condemn merchant Robert Morris, "The pressure to draw useful moral lessons from the republic's formative period continues to flatten Morris's role into one in which either heroic and intelligent individuals came to the aid of the republic or the people stood unsuccessfully against the desires of individual merchant-capitalists."[11]

The only time the dial gets close to 11 is in Kevin Butterfield's contribution about the debate over the Society of the Cincinnati, but Butterfield's goal is to turn the volume back down. Yes, he admits, there were concerns when Continental Army officers sought to form a fraternal society in which membership would be inherited. Was this a new nobility emerging in the wake of a democratic revolution? However just as the volume rises, Butterfield responds that, actually, the debate proved that there was little to fear. While pages, and books and books, have been written about the aristocratic aspirations of some American leaders and the democratic efforts to check them, Butterfield says the debate was over before it began. As Americans realized that the Cincinnati was hardly a threat, and as its leaders sought to reconfigure their association to be less offensive, it became clear that the actual threat of a new aristocracy was minimal. Thus, during the ratification debates, when antifederalists once again raised the specter of aristocracy, Butterfield concludes, "Such accusations did not persuade Americans to reject the new Constitution."[12]

Indeed, the Constitution was ratified by what may have been the most expansive franchise in world history. In the majority of states, voting qualifications or the qualifications for delegates to ratifying conventions were, in Akhil Amar's words, "more populist and less property-focused than normal." Americans seemed to understand that a convention of the people required a broader representation of the people than other elections. Moreover, whether or not fears of aristocracy were legitimate, the Constitution itself prohibited the establishment of a titled nobility.[13]

The Constitution, however, was just the beginning. It established a framework. The question remains whether that framework resolved the challenges that faced the new United States. To answer this question, it is useful to look backward from the early republic. In doing so, we find that in many ways it did, but that it also spurred new tensions and issues that the federal government was not always equipped to resolve. When we approach the Constitution and the framers intellectually and we mine their ideas and words for deep concepts, we in turn tend to read the subsequent history as a continued struggle over meanings and political philosophies. However, if we accept the invitation from this volume to turn down the dial and to see the framers not as philosophers but as tinkerers, we are allowed also to see how the contraption they cobbled together responded to the specific problems of their era.

Douglas Bradburn argues that the long-term conflict pitting Whigs against Tories was transmuted in the Critical Period into federalists against antifederalists and transmuted once again in the early republic into the conflict between the Federalist and Jeffersonian Republican parties. Building on the insights of John Murrin and Pocock, both of whom claimed that the revolutionary moment drew much from what came before in English history, Bradburn suggests that path-dependent intellectual forces ensured that, despite a revolution and the ratification of the Constitution, deeper ideological-political presumptions continued to determine how now-Americans thought about and divided over political questions, including the expectation that Americans would divide into two parties.[14] From this perspective, the Constitution is less a fundamental turning point than one more point on a line. Where does this line lead? What are some of the next points?

When Fiske wrote his volume, he observed that the federal union ensured that "the continent of North America should be dominated by a single powerful and pacific federal nation instead of being parcelled out among forty or fifty small communities, wasting their strength and lowering their moral tone by perpetual warfare, like the states of ancient Greece, or by perpetual preparation for warfare, like the nations of modern Europe."[15] Today, we too see the Constitution as a "peace pact" between the newly independent states, who formed a stronger union to avoid interstate conflict as well as to be able to protect each other from external and internal threats.[16]

However, we are, perhaps, less convinced of the pacific nature of that union. Indeed, although this particular volume is silent on the issue of violence, one of the important outcomes of the federal union was a state capable of exercising force against foreign threats. Henry Adams, in his *History of the United States during the Jefferson and Madison Administrations,* had admired Jefferson's commitment to a foreign policy that sought, as much as possible, to avoid war. Even under Jefferson, however, the new state relied on its still-limited military capacity to engage with the Barbary pirates. Moreover, whatever Jefferson's vision of a peaceful, expanding republic of republics, we know that westward settlement depended on the capacity of the state to organize settlement and to clear the land of Native American rivals.[17] In Kathleen DuVal's words, "By ceding some sovereignty to the new government created by the Constitution, the states established a framework for dominating the nineteenth-century west."[18]

Yet domination did not come easy. The stronger federal union may have ensured the new United States' capacity to preserve itself and make claims on foreign powers, but in the mid-nineteenth century, the most powerful polities in the region between the Mississippi River and the Rocky Mountains remained Native American, especially the Commanche and Lakota empires.[19] This does not mean that the U.S. state was impotent. Using the tools of diplomacy and military force, the American government made Native, European imperial, and Mexican land available for American settlers. It also determined how that land would be distributed and pursued trade agreements to make the produce of that land profitable. "By 1867," concludes Max Edling, the United States was able to extend its territorial sovereignty to the Pacific Ocean because of "state-organized and state-directed violence." Edling estimates that four-fifths of federal expenditures between the revolution and Civil War were devoted to military and foreign affairs, including western expansion.[20]

Facilitating the settlement of western land was an essential goal of a stronger federal union, as Susan Gaunt Stearns shows in her important contribution reframing westerners' relations with the Confederation during the 1780s. The West was almost lost to the United States not because of a lack of nationalism, as some have previously argued, but because the Congress of the Confederation lacked clear jurisdiction over western land; institutional capacity and will to protect western settlers from Native American violence; and the ability to secure, and fight for, the West's economic interests. In other words, despite westerners' appeals to Congress, Congress failed the West, which led western settlers to question their relationship to the new United States. It was only when the federal government was able to impose order and security that the West was secured for the American nation.[21]

A stronger federal union also strengthened slavery. As we know, the Revolutionary War almost destroyed slavery as an institution, as enslaved people, inspired by the hope of securing their freedom by reaching British lines, abandoned plantations by the thousands.[22] It took a lot of work to put slavery back together—and southerners demanded a federal commitment to protecting white lives and livelihoods from potential slave rebellions as part of the deal to form a stronger union.[23] Yet, as Nicholas Wood demonstrates in this volume, the Constitution's relationship with slavery is complicated. The Articles of Confederation did not empower Congress to prohibit the slave trade. Petitions from antislavery Quakers ensured, however, that the issue would remain part of the national agenda, ultimately working its way, Wood argues, into the Constitution. Were antislavery activists right that the formation of a national government would limit slavery over time, even if it meant accepting a proslavery compromise in the short term? This is a hard question to ask, since any compromises over slavery affected real human beings. Wood, however, convincingly argues that the Constitution did, in fact, create opportunities to limit slavery, especially the slave trade. It was not the provisions concerning servitude in the Constitution that led to slavery's expansion but, in Wood's words, "the more general development of stable government that could regulate commerce and command fiscal-military resources in an international context."[24]

That is why slavery benefited from the Constitution. The new federal government not only protected slavery through such policies as fugitive slave laws, but its capacity to raise an army helped secure the southwest for the plantation economy.[25] Yes, as Van Cleve also argues, by granting taxation and military authority to the federal government, President Abraham Lincoln was provided the tools necessary to fight the Civil War and end American slavery. "The deeply flawed Confederation could never have won that great a victory for human freedom," Van Cleve writes.[26] However, the burden of evidence falls on the other side. The Civil War was caused because the Constitution did not resolve the issue of slavery while also creating a federal government that facilitated westward expansion. In addition, slavery did not just benefit from the Constitution, but itself contributed to the expansion of state power and capacity. The U.S. government devoted significant resources to preventing the illegal slave trade; using military resources to prevent enslaved people from running away, culminating in the Seminole Wars; and capturing fugitive slaves, culminating in the Fugitive Slave Law of 1850. Enslaved labor was also employed to perform public work.[27] No wonder Donald E. Fehrenbacher concluded,

"Because it substantially increased the power of the national government, the Constitution had greater proslavery potential and greater antislavery potential than the Articles of Confederation. Its meaning with respect to slavery would depend upon how it was implemented."[28]

One of the most important arguments for a stronger federal union, Dael Norwood makes clear in his contribution to this volume, was the United States' inability to secure commercial treaties with European powers. The Constitution did encourage more foreign investment. Ironically, by the 1830s, it was this success that caused the United States to be subject to powerful global forces beyond its reach. As both Jessica Lepler and Alaisdair Roberts argue, American politicians in the 1830s would find themselves powerless to respond to the jitters and ultimately panic of European, and especially British, investors in American land, stocks, and state government bonds. In a globalized economic context, the relative weakness of the American state and the relative smallness of the American economy meant that the United States depended on foreign investment which, in turn, meant that the United States economy, and thus its politics, depended on foreigners.[29] The Constitution's very success in encouraging foreign investment thus produced new forms of dependence.

As obvious as it might seem, one of the most important outcomes of the ratification of the Constitution was a new government. Scholars of American political development and the history of the state have demonstrated the various ways in which the new federal government slowly developed its institutional and fiscal capacity.[30] Political parties formed around the need to distribute resources, including patronage, and federal institutions such as the Post Office reached into every community, spurring social conflict, as exemplified by debates over Sunday mail delivery.[31] The government's capacity to raise revenue independent of the states also created distributive problems, including whether and how to support internal improvements in the states.[32] It mobilized Americans to fight in the Barbary Wars, the War of 1812, and the Mexican-American war, as well as in wars against Native Americans. Its legal capacity to prohibit or permit slavery in the western territories spurred the most intense sectional conflicts, an ironic outcome of the framers' success in creating a national domain overseen by the federal government rather than the states. Indeed, the levers of national power were sufficient that for some Jeffersonian Republicans, liberty itself was at risk, while for others, the federal government's potential to encourage westward expansion and the relatively equal distribution of land would sustain American liberty over time.[33]

Because it created a new government with important powers, the Constitution established a national venue for politics and identity, and the two built on each other. Bruce Ackerman has argued that the founders' inability (or perhaps unwillingness) to imagine national politics and national parties is one of their greatest failures.[34] That may be, because at the time of ratification, the Constitution offered what John Murrin called, in his epilogue to *Beyond Confederation,* "a roof without walls." In Murrin's words, Americans "had shown that they would fight and even confederate to protect the rights of the parts. They had yet to discover whether they could create enough sense of common identity to provide for the needs of the whole."[35]

One imagines George Washington a bit like Hamid Karzai in Afghanistan, endowed with power on paper, but lacking the institutional capacity to act and popular support for his new government. Most experiments such as this fail, and Washington and his treasury secretary Alexander Hamilton were well aware of this fact. Earning Americans' loyalty, and thus their willingness to respect the Constitution and obey the federal government's authority, would depend on what Carol Berkin calls "the hard work of governance."[36] That is one reason why they chose a strong response to the Whiskey Rebellion. They worried that the federal government would crumble if citizens could ignore its laws without penalty, as states had done during the Confederation era.

Ultimately, however, the new government did not sustain itself primarily by using force against its free citizens. Instead, citizens came to see themselves as part of a new nation. They formed bonds of union based on affection, not just coercion. The nation itself was thus one of the most important outgrowths of the Constitution. Most free settlers prior to 1776 considered themselves to be provincial Britons. Like other postcolonial societies, after the revolution, Americans continued to look to Britain as a cultural example.[37] It would take time for Americans to come to see themselves as a distinct nationality and to develop their own cultural traditions and feelings of national belonging.[38] As Bradburn writes in his contribution to this volume, the new United States "lacked traditions and a distinctive national character." It was this need that George Washington's Mount Vernon plantation filled for many Americans. In the days immediately after independence, Bradburn argues, Mount Vernon allowed identity-seeking pilgrims to "begin the process of imagining a shared country after independence."[39]

The United States could never have survived without national sentiments. National identity were the walls that would keep the roof above Americans' heads. But those sentiments required not just rituals, but institutions. Far from a failing, therefore, the reemergence of political parties was an essential element in the new government's success. Parties built one of the walls holding up the American roof by connecting Americans to the national government. The very existence of the new national regime made necessary the formation of national political coalitions to elect like-minded leaders with shared policy goals. This, in turn, required mobilizing citizens. As parties formed to gain national office, and as party leaders and partisan editors reached out to voters, they transformed a federal union into an American nation.[40]

If political parties provided one source of connection, so did other institutions. Americans formed federated voluntary associations to promote such causes as peace, temperance, the distribution of Bibles, and charity. They also developed new national denominations. These new associations and denominations connected local chapters and churches with fellow Americans across the nation, allowing citizens in communities across the United States to be part of a new imagined community.[41] However, for such imaginings to take place, people across the nation had to see themselves as connected to each other, and this depended on the existence of a national public sphere. By encouraging the cheap flow of newspapers, magazines, and other media by post, the new federal government subsidized the formation of the nation.[42] Federal immigration and naturalization laws and court decisions also played a role in determining who could be a citizen— who belonged in the nation.[43]

Paradoxically, the very successes of the new federal government and the emergence of a national imagined community contributed to the revival of sectionalism. By encouraging westward settlement, the new federal regime ensured that the 1787 compromise over slavery would not be sustained. Instead, slavery became America's most divisive national issue as the country expanded. For many southerners, the federal union was desirable so long as it promoted security from foreign threats and encouraged foreign commerce. It did. If one goal of the Constitution was to create what Eliga Gould calls a "treaty-worthy nation," it worked.[44] Following the negotiation of the Adams-Onís treaty removing Spanish threats to the south, many southerners felt freer to promote their sectional and state interests in Washington. Indeed, southerners could proclaim the virtues of small government and states' rights precisely because the federal government had used its power to provide southerners the security they sought.[45]

Familiarity bred contempt. The political parties, voluntary associations, and churches that brought Americans together—in person or in print—also taught them of their differences. Especially as debates over slavery's expansion in the West intensified, it became harder for Americans to maintain the national institutions that allowed them to be part of a common national imaginary. By the 1840s, the walls holding up the American roof were starting to give way. Northern antislavery associations were decidedly sectional institutions, lacking connections with the South. However, even national associations struggled and snapped under the pressures generated by disagreements over slavery. On the eve of the Civil War, America's major Protestant denominations had divided into northern and southern wings, a new northern Republican party had emerged, and the Democrats were unable to maintain national unity.[46] Ultimately, the walls could not bear the weight.

In sum, perhaps it makes sense to see the Constitution as one point on a line, rather than as the day the world began anew. Perhaps it did not create a new order for the ages, but instead many of the fundamental questions that Americans faced in the Critical Period—about states' rights, slavery, security, commerce, identity, and politics—continued to shape the actions of, and Americans' perceptions of and relations with, the new union. Jack Rakove, after all, considered the Critical Period's debates to be where one could find "the beginnings of national politics," and the issues and questions faced by Americans during that period carried over into the Constitutional era and beyond.[47]

This is not, of course, to say that the Constitution did not matter. It's unclear whether the new republic would have survived without a stronger federal government. The Constitution secured, in a world of monarchs and empires, a government premised on the consent of the governed. It allowed the state governments to flourish and to develop into more popular democracies, as Christopher Pearl writes in this volume.[48] It fostered a national culture that was more egalitarian and individualistic than what came before. However, it did not end the questions that animated the Critical Period, and it did not, if one accepts the perspectives offered in this volume, resolve some of the most important issues that led to its passage in the first place.

Moreover, the new powers of the state were part and parcel of the limits of state power. The Constitution gave, but it also structured how it gave. Famously, in his dismissal of the need for the amendments that became the Bill of Rights, James Madison argued that the Constitution granted only discrete powers to the federal government and thus the government could not violate Americans' rights. Jefferson, astutely, noted that the Constitution's transformation of a league of states into a true government would almost necessarily mean that the new government had the potential to expand its sphere of influence, and Hamilton, of course, aspired for it to do so.[49]

On the one hand, the Constitution was a limited grant of authority because many Americans were suspicious of centralized power. On the other hand, as Brian Balogh argues, Americans wanted more from their national government than it seemed empowered, on paper, to accomplish. However, by the early republic, the Constitution had become, in Jonathan Gienapp's phrase, "fixed," and thus any federal action would have to be justified within the terms of the original grant of power from the 1780s.[50] Even Madison struggled with this fact in his decision to support the constitutionality of the Bank of the United States after the War of 1812 (something he had earlier opposed) but yet to veto federal support for internal improvements. In the bank's case, Madison had come to recognize its necessity and propriety to deal with the basic issues that the federal government existed to address—borrowing money for defense. In his veto, Madison encouraged Americans to amend the Constitution to grant the government the authority to use its public money to support building canals, turnpikes, and other infrastructure. He urged legislators to embrace the work of "improving it [the Constitution] as experience might suggest." In vetoing the so-called Bonus Bill, then, did Madison embrace a fixed Constitution or did he continue to believe that the Constitution could be and should be amended as necessary when new needs arose? Was he in fact suggesting that the Constitution should not be fixed in time, but updated when doing so serves the public good?[51]

This is exactly the issue that Gary Gerstle struggles with in his history of the American state, *Liberty and Coercion*. Even if the framers had believed that the Constitution was a framework to be updated continuously, in practice, "amending the Constitution has almost always been a notoriously difficult process." Absent amendments, however, as policymakers sought to update the federal government's powers and duties to meet changing domestic and external challenges, they had to do so with a Constitution "burdened by its past." They thus turned to what Gerstle calls "surrogacy," relying, for example, on the commerce clause to regulate activities tangentially related to "buying and selling commodities across state lines." Forced by the fixed Constitution to improvise legal justifications, however, advocates of a stronger, more active federal government invited resistance as the government engaged in activities without amendments "sufficient to bestow on the federal government constitutional authority commensurate with its vastly expanded power."[52]

But what if we stopped thinking of the Constitution as fixed?

The Constitution, when it was first ratified, was not yet a sacred document. It would become so over time. It was instead a framework for government, full of compromises. Nothing more. If that is what we learn from this volume, and I think it is, I will admit I feel a sense of loss. I miss the big debates—Whigs versus Progressives, patricians versus plebians, ideas versus interests, republicans versus liberals, consensus versus conflict, heroes versus villains. I miss the idea that this was a period where the stakes were existential, an era of such intense debate and social conflict that it produced not just a new Constitution but new ideas about politics and new ways of inhabiting the world. I liked it when the volume dial was turned to 11. I want framers who think big, offer profound meditations on politics and the human condition, sound paranoid at times, and ask much of us. I also want Americans who demand a more egalitarian society, who resist the framers for being elitist or power hungry, and give us hope that we might have a more participatory, more inclusive democracy.[53] I want to ask, How much freedom and for whom? I want to be inspired by what Lincoln called a "new nation, conceived in liberty, and dedicated to the proposition that all men are created equal."

In its deflationary moves, however, this volume reveals the stakes of the Constitution and its limits for us today. The big stories, so fun to teach, put too much pressure on the people, elite and ordinary, who lived through the Critical Period. They are placed on stage to usher in a new world order. Their lives must serve narrative purposes that force them to embody principles and morals that transcend the actual capacity of real, flawed human beings. They are good stories, but the authors in this volume oblige us to ask, do those kinds of stories offer the right morals for a democratic people like ourselves?

The framers that emerge from this volume are neither heroes nor villains. They did not seek to undermine popular liberty, nor were they animated by ideals alone. They were human beings placed in positions of influence, shaped by the revolutionary experience, committed to republicanism, and trying to make a go of things. They examined the specific problems that Americans faced and sought specific solutions. They disagreed, they compromised—sometimes in ways that we find, looking back, unconscionable, such as over slavery. On the other hand, there is something refreshing in seeing the framers as problem solvers. They had no Constitution to idolize or to condemn. They were frightened by the prospect of the revolution failing. They wanted republican liberty to survive in a hostile world—hostile not only because of the presence of powerful Native American and European threats, but also because the premise of popular sovereignty was exceptional. When it came to how to do it, they looked to government not in deductive but inductive terms: what policies, what institutions, and what relationships between the states and the federal government will most likely promote the general welfare and secure the blessings of liberty?

Answering those questions in their time meant dealing with the issues that the United States faced in their time. The essays in this collection make clear what those issues were and where and why compromise was called for. The framers here emerge as human beings. They were not ideological, but they were principled, and of course they had interests. They did not deduce what government could or could not do, but devised solutions for the actual problems they faced. These answers were responses not to abstract problems of political theory, but to specific tangible issues of policy and economy.

The framers depicted here believed that the purpose of government is to solve today's problems. As Christopher Pearl writes in this volume, we cannot understand the Critical Period without exploring the "centrality of governance."[54] Doing so requires adapting institutions to the needs of the era. It means that resolving today's problems might generate new problems—or ironies—downstream, as the Constitution did in the early republic. However, those too can be addressed. The essays in this volume point to a profound failure of government authority under the Articles of Confederation. Far from securing Americans' welfare and liberties, too limited a government failed to protect liberty and promote the general welfare. What Americans learned quickly after the revolution, whether the realm be domestic or foreign policy, whether the concerns were economic or cultural, was that the people's liberty, prosperity, and security would be more effectively achieved by the appropriate application of government power. The Constitution was an incomplete work in progress and the framers anticipated, in Gienapp's words, that it would "grow with experience."[55]

It should be noted, however, that this is not just a story of expanding government power for the sake of government power. Instead, it is the very specificity of the essays in this volume that help us understand what we might continue to look for in our framers: not just their idealism, but their lack of dogmatism. Government must solve problems. To solve those problems citizens and leaders must work together, compromise, and adapt institutions to what the situation calls for. This is not at the expense of ideas and principles. Instead, it is because we must find ways to sustain our ideas and principles in a changing world.

For too long, scholars, divided into conservative and Progressive, and neo-Whig and neo-Progressive, camps have struggled over whether the Constitution secured or betrayed the revolution. No doubt, depending on who one was, it did both. That historiographical debate, as important as it remains, can hide some other truths that this volume brings to light. Instead of being the product of giants who roamed the earth or enemies of democracy, the Constitution that emerges in this volume was a response to the specific issues facing the new United States under the Articles of Confederation. There are conflicting ideas and ideals and disagreements over specific policies, but almost no ideologies.

The Constitution, according to the volume's authors, required compromise but successfully met many of the primary issues facing Americans at the time. Again, nothing more, but also nothing less. It produced new problems that needed new answers down the line. In this sense, we have had many critical periods that call for innovation and imagination. Solving today's problems will lead to new ones that will require us to adapt our tools of governance. When power is called for, it should be granted. Where it threatens liberty, it should be curtailed. Humbling and deflationary as this seems, what better lesson for American leaders and citizens today?

## Notes

1. Richard R. Beeman, Stephen Botein, and Edward C. Carter II, eds., *Beyond Confederation: Origins of the Constitution and American National Identity* (Chapel Hill: University of North Carolina Press, 1987). On republicanism, see Robert E. Shalhope, "Toward a Republican Synthesis: The Emergence of an Understanding of Republicanism in American Historiography," *William and Mary Quarterly* 29, no. 1 (January 1972): 49–80; Isaac Kramnick, "Republican Revisionism Revisited," *American Historical Review* 87, no. 3 (June 1982): 629–64; Daniel T. Rodgers, "Republicanism: The Career of a Concept," *Journal of American History* 79, no. 1 (June 1992): 11–38.

2. Caroline Winterer, *American Enlightenments: Pursuing Happiness in the Age of Reason* (New Haven, CT: Yale University Press, 2018).

3. Gordon S. Wood, *The Creation of the American Republic 1776–1787* (Chapel Hill: University of North Carolina Press, 1969).

4. Gordon S. Wood, "Intellectual History and the Social Sciences," in *New Directions in American Intellectual History*, ed. John Higham and Paul Conkin (Baltimore: Johns Hopkins University Press, 1979), 27–41.

5. Merrill Jensen, *The New Nation: A History of the United States During the Confederation 1781–1789* (New York: Knopf, 1950), 255.

6. John Fiske, *The Critical Period of American History, 1783–1789* (Boston, 1888), 55, 89.

7. Forrest McDonald, *E Pluribus Unum: The Formation of the American Republic, 1776–1790* (Boston: Houghton Mifflin, 1965), 371.

8. Cecilia M. Kenyon, "Men of Little Faith: The Anti-Federalists on the Nature of Representative Government," *William and Mary Quarterly* 12, no. 1 (January 1955), 4–43.

9. Eliga Gould, *Among the Powers of the Earth: The American Revolution and the Making of a New World Empire* (Cambridge, MA: Harvard University Press 2012); Leonard J. Sadosky, *Revolutionary Negotiations: Indians, Empires, and Diplomats in the Founding of America* (Charlottesville: University of Virginia Press, 2009).

10. George Van Cleve, *We Have Not a Government: The Articles of Confederation and the Road to the Constitution* (Chicago: University of Chicago Press, 2017), 298. Van Cleve, *A Slaveholder's Union: Slavery, Politics, and the Constitution in the Early American Republic* (Chicago: University of Chicago Press, 2010). On the importance of narrative to understanding the framers' actions, see Peter S. Onuf, "Reflections on the Founding: Constitutional Historiography in Bicentennial Perspective," *William and Mary Quarterly* 46, no. 2 (1989): 341–75.

11. Farber, "Something from Nothing? Currency and Finance in the Critical Period," in this volume.

12. Butterfield, "An Excess of Aristocracy: Democracy and the Fear of Aristocratic Power in the 1780s," in this volume.

13. Akhil Amar, *America's Constitution: A Biography* (New York: Random House, 2005), 7, 124–26; Pauline Maier, *Ratification: The People Debate the Constitution, 1787–1788* (New York: Simon & Schuster, 2010).

14. Douglas L. Bradburn, "'Parties Are Unavoidable': Path Dependence and the Origins of Party Politics in the United States," in *Practicing Democracy: Popular Politics in the United States from the Constitution to the Civil War*, ed. Daniel Peart and Adam I. P. Smith (Charlottesville: University of Virginia Press, 2015), 23–45; John L. Murrin, "The Great Inversion, or Court versus Country: A Comparison of the Revolution Settlements in England (1688–1721) and America (1776–1816)," in *Three British Revolutions: 1641, 1688, 1776*, ed. J. G. A. Pocock (Princeton, NJ: Princeton University Press, 1980), 368–453.

15. Fiske, *Critical Period*, vi–vii.

16. On the Constitution as a "peace pact" between the thirteen states, see David M. Hendrickson, *Peace Pact: The Lost World of the American Founding* (Lawrence: University Press of Kansas, 2003); Peter S. Onuf and Nicholas G. Onuf, *Federal Union, Modern World: The Law of Nations in an Age of Revolutions, 1776–1814* (Madison, WI: Madison House, 1993).

17. Bethel Saler, *The Settlers' Empire: Colonialism and State Formation in America's Old Northwest* (Philadelphia: University of Pennsylvania Press, 2015); Aziz Rana, *The Two Faces of American Freedom* (Cambridge, MA: Harvard University Press 2010); Patrick Griffin, *American Leviathan: Empire, Nation, and Revolutionary Frontier* (New York: Hill & Wang, 2007).

18. Kathleen DuVal, *Independence Lost: Lives on the Edge of the American Revolution* (New York: Random House, 2015), 344.

19. See three works by Pekka Hämäläinen: "The Shapes of Power: Indians, Europeans, and North American Worlds from the 17th to the 19th Century," in *Contested Spaces of Early America*, ed. J. Barr and E. Countryman (Philadelphia: University of Pennsylvania Press, 2014), chap. 1; *The Commanche Empire* (New Haven, CT: Yale University Press, 2008); and *Lakota America: A New History of Indigenous Power* (New Haven, CT: Yale University Press, 2019).

20. Max Edling, *A Hercules in the Cradle: War, Money, and the American State, 1783–1867* (Chicago: University of Chicago Press, 2014), 12–13. See also Brian Balogh, *A Government Out of Sight: The Mystery of National Authority in Nineteenth-Century America* (New York: Cambridge University Press, 2009), 151–218; Jeffrey Pasley, "Midget on Horseback: American Indians and the History of the American State," *Commonplace*, published October 2009, http://commonplace.online/article/midget-on-horseback; Alan Taylor, *The Civil War of 1812: American Citizens, British Subjects, Irish Rebels, and Indian Allies* (New York: Vintage Books, 2011); Rana, *Two Faces*.

21. Stearns, "Federalism and the Frontier: Secession and Loyalty in the Trans-Appalachian West," in this volume. See also Griffin, *American Leviathan*.

22. Douglas Egerton, *Death or Liberty: African Americans and Revolutionary America* (New York: Oxford University Press, 2009); Paul Gilbert, *Black Patriots and Loyalists: Fighting for Emancipation in the War for Independence* (Chicago: University of Chicago Press, 2012); Gary B. Nash, *The Unknown American Revolution: The Unruly Birth of Democracy and the Struggle to Create America* (New York: Viking, 2005); Sylvia R. Frey, *Water from the Rock: Black Resistance in a Revolutionary Age* (Princeton, NJ: Princeton University Press, 1991).

23. Van Cleve, *A Slaveholder's Union*; Donald E. Fehrenbacher, *The Slaveholding Republic: An Account of the United States Government's Relations to Slavery*, ed. Don E. McAfee (New York: Oxford University Press, 2002).

24. Wood, "Abolitionists, Congress, and the Atlantic Slave Trade: Before and After Ratification," in this volume.

25. See, for example, Adam Rothman, *Slave Country: American Expansion and the Origins of the Deep South* (Cambridge, MA: Harvard University Press, 2005).

26. Van Cleve, *We Have Not a Government*, 296.

27. David F. Ericson, *Slavery in the American Republic: Developing the Federal Government, 1791–1861* (Lawrence: University Press of Kansas, 2011); Ryan A. Quintana, "Slavery and the Conceptual History of the U.S. State," *Journal of the Early Republic* 38, no. 1 (Spring 2018): 77–86.

28. Fehrenbacher, *The Slaveholding Republic*, 47. For a good overview, see John Craig Hammond, "Race, Slavery, Sectional Conflict, and National Politics, 1770–1820," in

*The Routledge History of Nineteenth-Century America,* ed. Jonathan Daniel Wells (New York: Routledge, 2018), 11–32.

29. Jessica Lepler, *The Many Panics of 1837: People, Politics, and the Creation of a Transatlantic Financial Crisis* (New York: Cambridge University Press, 2013); Alasdair Roberts, *America's First Great Depression: Economic Crisis and Political Disorder after the Panic of 1837* (Ithaca, NY: Cornell University Press, 2013). See also Sharon Ann Murphy, *Other People's Money: How Banking Worked in the Early American Republic* (Baltimore: Johns Hopkins University Press, 2017), 71–102.

30. Max Edling, *A Revolution in Favor of Government: Origins of the U.S. Constitution and the Making of the American State* (New York: Oxford University Press, 2003), and Edling, *A Hercules in the Cradle.* See also Richard R. John, "American Political Development and Political History," in *The Oxford Handbook of American Political Development,* ed. Richard Valelly, Suzanne Mettler, and Robert Lieberman (New York: Oxford University Press, 2016), 185–206.

31. Richard R. John, "Private Enterprise, Public Good? Communications Deregulation as a National Political Issue, 1839–1851," in *Beyond the Founders: New Approaches to the Political History of the Early American Republic,* ed. Jeffrey Pasley, Andrew Robertston, and David Waldstreicher (Chapel Hill: University of North Carolina Press, 2004), 328–54.

32. John L. Larson, *Internal Improvements: National Public Works and the Promise of Popular Government in the Early United States* (Chapel Hill: University of North Carolina Press, 2001).

33. Drew McCoy, *The Elusive Republic: Political Economy in Jeffersonian America* (Chapel Hill: University of North Carolina Press, 1980).

34. Bruce Ackerman, *The Failure of the Founding Fathers: Jefferson, Marshall, and the Rise of Presidential Democracy* (Cambridge, MA: Harvard University Press, 2005). See also Gerald Leonard and Saul Cornell, *The Partisan Republic: Democracy, Exclusion, and the Fall of the Founders' Constitution, 1780s–1830s* (Cambridge, UK: Cambridge University Press, 2019).

35. John L. Murrin, "A Roof without Walls: The Dilemma of American National Identity," in *Beyond Confederation,* 333–48, quote at 340.

36. Carol Berkin, *A Sovereign People: The Crises of the 1790s and the Birth of American Nationalism* (New York: Basic Books, 2017), 6.

37. Kariann Yokota, *Unbecoming British: How Revolutionary America Became a Postcolonial Nation* (New York: Oxford University Press, 2011); T. H. Breen, "Ideology and Nationalism on the Eve of the American Revolution: Revisions Once More in Need of Revising," *Journal of American History* 84, no. 1 (June 1997): 13–39.

38. Among many sources, see Waldstreicher, *In the Midst of Perpetual Fetes: The Making of American Nationalism* (Chapel Hill: University of North Carolina Press, 1997); Lloyd Kramer, *Nationalism in Europe and America: Politics, Cultures, and Identities since 1775* (Chapel Hill: University of North Carolina Press, 2011); C. Edward Skeen, *1816: America Rising* (Lexington: University Press of Kentucky, 2003).

39. Bradburn, "America's Court: George Washington's Mount Vernon in the Critical Period," in this volume.

40. On this point, see Joel H. Silbey, *The Partisan Imperative: The Dynamics of American Politics before the Civil War* (New York: Oxford University Pess, 1985); Waldstreicher, *In the Midst of Perpetual Fetes.*

41. Johann N. Neem, "Taking Modernity's Wager: Tocqueville, Social Capital, and the American Civil War," *Journal of Interdisciplinary History* 41, no. 4 (spring 2011), 591–618. See also Ben Wright, *Bonds of Salvation: How Christianity Inspired and Limited American Abolitionism* (Baton Rouge: Lousiana State University Press, 2020); Elisabeth S. Clemens, *Civic Gifts: Voluntarism and the Making of the American Nation-State* (Chicago: University of Chicago Press, 2020); Theda Skocpol, *Diminished Democracy: From Membership to Management in American Civic Life* (Norman: University of Oklahoma Press, 2004). The phrase "imagined community" is from Benedict Anderson, *Imagined Communities: Reflections on the Origin and Spread of Nationalism* (London: Verso, 2006).

42. Richard R. John, *Spreading the News: The American Postal System from Franklin to Morse* (Cambridge, MA: Harvard University Press, 1998); David Paul Nord, "Newspapers and American Nationhood," in Nord, *Communities of Journalism: A History of American Newspapers and Their Readers* (Urbana: University of Illinois Press, 2001), 80–91; Balogh, *Government Out of Sight,* 219–33.

43. Douglas L. Bradburn, *The Citizenship Revolution: Politics and the Creation of the American Union, 1774–1804* (Charlottesville: University of Virginia Press 2014); Rogers Smith, *Civic Ideals: Conflicting Visions of Citizenship in U.S. History* (New Haven, CT: Yale University Press, 1999).

44. Gould, *Among the Powers of the Earth,* 12.

45. Brian Schoen, "Lower South Jeffersonians: States and the Federal Imagination," in *Jeffersonians in Power: The Rhetoric of Opposition Meets the Realities of Governing,* ed. Joanne B. Freeman and Johann N. Neem (Charlottesville: University of Virginia Press, 2019), chap. 8.

46. Neem, "Taking Modernity's Wager"; John L. Brooke, "Cultures of Nationalism, Movements of Reform, and the Composite-Federal Polity: From Revolutionary Settlement to Antebellum Crisis," *Journal of the Early Republic* 29, no. 1 (2009): 1–33; John, *Spreading the News.*

47. Jack N. Rakove, *The Beginnings of National Politics: An Interpretive History of the Continental Congress* (Baltimore: Johns Hopkins University Press, 1979).

48. Pearl, "'Such a Spirit of Innovation': The American Revolution and the Creation of States," in this volume.

49. Kenneth R. Bowling, "'A Tub to the Whale': The Founding Fathers and Adoption of the Federal Bill of Rights," *Journal of the Early Republic* 8, no. 3 (October 1988): 223–51; Andrew Shankman, *Original Intents: Hamilton, Jefferson, Madison, and the American Founding* (New York: Oxford University Press, 2018).

50. Jonathan Gienapp, *The Second Creation: Fixing the American Constitution in the Founding Era* (Cambridge, MA: Harvard University Press, 2018).

51. Balogh, *Government Out of Sight,* 132–39. Compare Leonard J. Sadosky, "How the Jeffersonians Learned to Love the State: Consumption, Finance, and Empire in the Madison Administration" and Richard Samuelson, "The Constitutional Statesmanship of

James Madison," in *Jeffersonians in Power,* ed. Joanne B. Freeman and Johann N. Neem, chaps. 7, 12. See also Saul Cornell, "President Madison's Living Constitution: Fixation, Liquidation, and Constitutional Politics in the Jeffersonian Era," *Fordham Law Review* 89, no. 5 (2021): 1761–81.

52. Gary Gerstle, *Liberty and Coercion: The Paradox of American Government from the Founding to the Present* (Princeton, NJ: Princeton University Press, 2015), 7–8.

53. On this point, see, for example, Nash, *Unknown American Revolution;* Terry Bouton, *Taming Democracy: "The People," The Founders, and the Troubled Ending of the American Revolution* (New York: Oxford University Press, 2007); Woody Holton, *Unruly Americans and the Origins of the Constitution* (New York: Hill & Wang, 2007). On recent historiography, see Jack Rakove, "The Real Motives Behind the Constitution: The Endless Quest," *Reviews in American History* 48, no. 2 (June 2020): 216–28.

54. Pearl, in this volume.

55. Gienapp, *The Second Creation,* 77–81, quote at 77.

CONTRIBUTORS

DOUGLAS BRADBURN, president and CEO of George Washington's
Mount Vernon and the former founding director of the Fred W. Smith
National Library for the Study of George Washington at Mount Vernon, is an award-winning author and well-known scholar of early
American history. He is the author and editor of three books and
numerous articles and book chapters with a specialty in the history
of the American founding, leadership, and the history of American
citizenship. Before coming to Mount Vernon, Bradburn served as a
professor of history and director of graduate studies at Binghamton
University, State University of New York (SUNY). He left as chair of
the history faculty. Bradburn earned his PhD in history from the University of Chicago and his BA in history and economics from the University of Virginia.

KEVIN BUTTERFIELD, executive director of the Fred W. Smith National
Library for the Study of George Washington at Mount Vernon, is a
historian of eighteenth- and nineteenth-century America. Before
coming to the Washington Library, Butterfield held a tenured appoint-
ment as associate professor of classics and letters at the University of
Oklahoma. He is the author of *The Making of Tocqueville's America: Law
and Association in the Early United States* (University of Chicago Press,
2015).

HANNAH FARBER is an assistant professor of history at Columbia University. She specializes in the political economy of colonial North

America, the early American republic, and the Atlantic world. Her first book, *Underwriters of the United States* (Omohundro Institute/ University of North Carolina Press, 2021), explains how the transnational business of marine insurance influenced the establishment and early development of the American state. Her additional research interests include the cultural history of interest rates and the visual and material culture of ocean commerce. She holds an MA and a PhD in history from the University of California, Berkeley.

JOHANN N. NEEM is a professor of history at Western Washington University. He is author of *What's the Point of College? Seeking Purpose in an Age of Reform* (Johns Hopkins University Press, 2019), *Democracy's Schools: The Rise of Public Education in America* (Johns Hopkins University Press, 2017), and *Creating a Nation of Joiners: Democracy and Civil Society in Early National Massachusetts* (Harvard University Press, 2008). He coedited the volume *Jeffersonians in Power: The Rhetoric of Opposition Meets the Realities of Governing* (University of Virgina Press, 2019). He is currently coeditor of the *Journal of the Early Republic*.

DAEL A. NORWOOD is a historian of the nineteenth-century United States, specializing in the global dimensions of American politics and economics. He is currently an assistant professor at the University of Delaware. Since earning his doctorate at Princeton University in 2012, Norwood has served as the Schwartz Postdoctoral Fellow at the New-York Historical Society and the New School, the Cassius Marcellus Clay Postdoctoral Associate in the Department of History at Yale University, and an assistant professor of history at Binghamton University. Norwood is now finishing his first book, titled *Trading in Freedom: How Trade with China Defined Early America*. He is also working on a new project that uses print culture conversations about capitalism as a career in order to understand how "the businessman" became a potent political and cultural identity in America.

CHRISTOPHER R. PEARL is an associate professor of history at Lycoming College. His work focuses on governance and state formation in the colonial and revolutionary periods. He is the author of *Conceived in Crisis: The Revolutionary Creation of an American State* (University of Virginia Press, 2020).

SUSAN GAUNT STEARNS is an assistant professor of history at the University of Mississippi. Her work focuses on how trans-Appalachia came to be incorporated into the American union in the 1780s and 1790s and on the role of the West within the political economy of the Early Republic. Stearns received her BA in history from Yale University and her PhD from the University of Chicago.

NICHOLAS P. WOOD is an assistant professor of history at Spring Hill College. He has served as a National Endowment for the Humanities Postdoctoral Fellow at the Library Company of Philadelphia and as a Cassius Marcellus Clay Postdoctoral Associate at Yale University. His articles on slavery, race, and politics have appeared in publications such as the *Journal of the Early Republic* and the *William and Mary Quarterly*. He is completing a book manuscript, tentatively titled *Let the Oppressed Go Free: The Revolutionary Generation of American Abolitionists*. He received his PhD from the University of Virginia.

# INDEX

*Page references in italics indicate illustrations.*

abolitionists, 93–114; drafting of Constitution and, 100–103; after ratification of Constitution, 103–14; Quakers as, 95–100, 246

Ackerman, Bruce, 248

Adams, Abigail, 234n8

Adams, Henry, *History of the United States during the Jefferson and Madison Administrations,* 244

Adams, John: on aristocratic power, 218, 231; on British trade restrictions, 35–36; on commerce as goal of diplomacy, 28; *Defence of the Constitutions,* 232; on Society of the Cincinnati, 225–26; trade regulation and, 24, 39, 55n57, 55n60

Adams, John Quincy, 230

Adams, Samuel, 224

Adams-Onís Treaty (1819), 250

agriculture, 74–76, 79

Allen, Andrew, 161

Allen, William, 161, 162

Amar, Akhil, 243

American Convention of Abolition Societies, 111

Anderson, Benedict, 259n41

Anglican Church, 158

antifederalists, 84–85, 216

aristocratic power, 216–33; diminishing fears of, 229–33; prerogative and, 37, 156–57, 160–61, 163; Society of the Cincinnati and, 220–29

Articles of Confederation: currency and finance under, 195, 199; federalism and, 82; slavery and, 94, 95, 98, 113, 246; trade regulation and, 37, 40–41, 55n54, 99; Western territories and, 127, 129, 134–35, 136, 141

autonomy, 129, 132–33, 135, 144

Bache, Sarah Franklin, 78

Bailyn, Bernard, 239

Balogh, Brian, 147n15, 251

Bank of North America, 193, 207

Bank of the United States, 251–52

Barbary pirates, 32–33, 55n45, 244, 247

Barlow, Joel, 66, 84, 230; "The Vision of Columbus," 78

Battle of Fallen Timbers (1794), 145

Beard, Charles, 15, 53n37; *An Economic Interpretation of the Constitution of the United States*, 6–7, 240

Beard, Mary, 7

Beaumarchais, Pierre-Augustin Caron de, 212n20

Belknap, Jeremy, 157, 158

Benezet, Anthony, 96, 97

Bentley, Arthur F., 6

Bergmann, Michael, 151n70

Berkin, Carol, 146n8, 248

bills of credit, 204, *204*, 206, 214n31

Bockleman, Wayne, 191n96

Bodley, Temple, 150n50

Bond, Phineas, 58n106

Bouton, Terry, 15, 194

Bowler, Metcalf, 76

Bradburn, Douglas, 12, 60, 109, 128, 146n5, 154, 243–44, 249

Brissot de Warville, Jean-Pierre, 72–74, 76, 79

Britain: Navigation Acts, 31; Quaker antislavery movement in, 98, 100, 103; trade relations with, 31, 35–36, 46, 139; Western territories and, 126, 145n3

British East India Company, 33

Brooke, John, 183, 184

Brown, Christopher L., 119n60

Brown, David Paul, 178

Brown, John, 141, 143

Brown, Moses, 98

Brown, Robert E., 7

Bryan, Samuel, 216, 233

Burke, Aedanus, 222–26, 231; *Address to Freemen of the State of South-Carolina*, 222; *Considerations on the Society or Order of Cincinnati*, 222–23

Butterfield, Kevin, 15–16, 216, 242–43

Calomiris, Charles W., 213n30

Carey, Mathew, 80

Carter, Landon, 164

Castiglioni, Luigi, 68

Castor, Peter J., 148n20

Cayton, Andrew, 151n70

Chase, Jeremiah, 36

Chernow, Ron, 118n54

Cherokee, 135, 136

Chickamauga, 136

Chickasaw, 135

China, trade relations with, 23–24, 33, 36, 55n47

Cincinnatus, 64, 79, 88n6, 220, 225

Clark, George Rogers, 138, 150n50

Clymer, Elizabeth Meredith, 78

Comanche, 245

commerce and trade, 23–48; Articles of Confederation and, 37, 40–41, 55n54, 99; Constitution and, 100, 105, 246, 247, 250; Continental Congress and, 34–47; currency and, 195, 196–97, 209, 211n9; economic development and, 30–31, 53–54n38; embargoes, 37; international, 10–11, 42; national identity and, 25; sovereignty and, 28–30; state power and, 30–34; treaties as protection for, 27; in Washington's "Circular to the States," 82

Constitution: abolitionists and, 100–114; aristocratic power and, 217; commerce regulation and, 42, 58n105, 100, 105, 246, 247, 250; ratification debates, 42, 45, 58n104, 216, 219, 232–33, 243; slavery and, 9, 93–94, 100–103, 107–8, 242, 245–47; sovereignty and, 242, 244–45; taxes and, 45–46, 58n105; Washington's support for, 85; Western territories and, 142

Continental Congress: commerce and, 26, 28, 34–47; economic sovereignty prioritized by, 26; Madison on, 60; slavery and, 97–99; state formation and, 169–70, 172; Western territories and, 130

Cooper, David, *A Serious Address to the Rulers of America, on the Inconsistency of Their Conduct Respecting Slavery*, 97

Cornell, Saul, 216

coronavirus pandemic, 1–3

courts: county courts, 162–65, 182; district courts, 173, 182; general courts, 165, 180–82, 191, 236; superior courts, 173–75, 180; supreme courts, 84, 161–62, 178–80, 222. *See also* judges

Coxe, Tench, 43, 233

Creek, 135, 141

currency and finance, 193–210; Articles of Confederation and, 195, 199; Bank of North America, 193, 207; bills of credit, 204, *204*, 206, 214n31; commerce and, 195, 196–97, 209; creditworthiness and, 51n17; debts and, 15, 197–98, 203, 209; land banks and, 15, 213–14nn30–31; as social construct, 210n5; taxes and tariffs facilitated by, 203, 207; trade facilitated by, 196

Daniell, Jere R., 159

Darwin, Charles, 5

Davie, William R., 205

Dawson, Henry B., 6

Deane, Silas, 212n20

debts: currency and, 15, 197–98, 203, 209; *A Statement of the Accounts of the United States of America*, 200, *201;* state vs. federal, 111, 205

Declaration of Independence, 97

Delaware Indians, 135, 136

Démeunier, Jean Nicolas, 236n20

Demophilus (pseudonym), 170–71, 176

Desan, Christine, 209, 210n5

DiGiacomantonio, William Charles, 122n103

distributive justice, 170, 176, 247

district courts (state), 173, 182

*Documentary History of the First Federal Congress* (eds. Bowling, DiGiacomantonio, and Bickford), 121n79, 123n104

Dodd, Nigel, 210n5

Doyle, William, 231

Drinker, John, 96

DuBois, W. E. B., 123n113

DuVal, Kathleen, 244–45

Dwight, Timothy, "The Prospect for America," 66

Edling, Max, 27, 51n17, 154, 245

*Edward* (ship), 24

Egerton, Douglas R., 119n60

Einhorn, Robin, 27, 58n105

Elliot, Jonathan, 57n90

Ellsworth, Oliver, 43–44, 102

emancipation of enslaved people, 79, 95–97, 100, 103, 105–6, 108–10

embargoes, 37

*Empress of China* (ship), 23, 33, 49n3

Enlightenment philosophy, 29, 44

Fairfax, Ferdinando, 80

Fairfax, George William, 75, 80

Farber, Hannah, 15, 193, 242

*Federalist*, 44, 58n102, 143, 231

federalists: aristocratic power and, 233; commerce regulation and, 28, 42–43, 45; in Critical Period, 4, 243–44; fears of dissolution of the United States, 9; Mount Vernon and, 80–86; slavery and, 113; Western territories and, 126–27, 129, 131, 133–35, 137, 139–44

Fehrenbacher, Donald E., 246–47

Fenton, John, 187n22

Ferguson, E. James, 196

finance. *See* currency and finance

Finkelman, Paul, 123n119

Finney, Walter, 138, 150n50

Fiske, John, 8, 15, 25, 57n90, 127–28, 155, 193–94, 241; *The Critical Period of American History, 1783–1789*, 4–5, 153, 234n6; *Outlines of Cosmic Philosophy*, 5

Foreign Slave Trade Act of 1794, 95, 112–13

Foster, Abiel, 106, 108–9

Foster, Augustus John, 234n8

France: Ohio River Valley and, 145n3; trade relations with, 32, 35, 37, 51n18; wartime loans from, 199

Franklin (state), 133–34, 141–42, 147n17, 149n35. *See also* Tennessee River Valley

Franklin, Benjamin, 29, 53n38, 101, 105–6

Franks, David S., 24, 49n6

French and Indian War (1754–63), 96

Freneau, Philip, 23

Fries's Rebellion (1799–1800), 185

Fugitive Slave Law of 1850, 246

Furstenberg, François, 145n3

Gabriel's Rebellion (1800), 185

Gardoqui, Don Diego de, 139, 141

Garmon, Frank W., 54n38

Garrison, William Lloyd, 6, 93, 114n3

Gates, Horatio, 76

general courts (state), 165, 180–82, 191, 236

George III (king), 63

Georgia: currency and finance in, 207; slavery in, 98, 101, 106, 113

Gerry, Elbridge, 36, 137–38, 218, 230, 231

Gerstle, Gary, 154; *Liberty and Coercion*, 252

Gervais, Pierre, 211n11

Gienapp, Jonathan, 251, 254

Gilbert, Felix, 29

*Gilman v. M'Clary* (New Hampshire 1791), 175

gold standard, 194

Golove, David M., 51n17

Gordon, William, 76, 79

Gould, Eliga, 27, 51n17, 52n24, 250

governance: currency and, 199; local vs. national, 2, 11, 180; state formation and, 152–54, 156, 159, 161, 167, 169, 178, 183, 248; in Western territories, 126, 130. *See also* state formation

Graham, Catherine Macaulay, 69

Greene, Jack P., 153

Greene, Nathanael, 229

Griffin, Patrick, 154

Griswold, Rufus, 87n3

Grubb, Farley, 214n37

Guerard, Benjamin, 224

Gutzman, Kevin R. C., 180

Hamilton, Alexander: abolitionist movement and, 101, 118n54; aristocratic power and, 218; state powers and, 251; trade regulation and, 44; as Treasury Secretary, 111

Hamilton, James, 161

Handlin, Oscar and Mary, 154

Harmar, Josiah, 49n6

Harris, Marc, 231

Harrison, Benjamin, 71, 82

Hartz, Louis, 154

Hatter, Lawrence, 51n18

Heath, William, 221

Hendrickson, David, 9, 27, 154

Henry, Patrick, 142

Hogan, Larry, 2

Holroyd, John. *See* Sheffield, John Holroyd, Lord

Holton, Woody, 15, 145n1, 211n7

Hopkins, Lemuel, 66

Houdon, Jean Antoine, 77

Howell, David, 98

Hulsebosch, Daniel, 51n17, 154

Humphreys, David: on antifederalists, 84–85; "Life of General Washington," 89n22; at Mount Vernon, 67–68, 75, 76–77, 81, 92n76; "Ode to Mount Vernon," 67; "On the Happiness of America," 66–67

Hunt, Freeman, 23

Hunter, Robert, Jr., 68

Hurd, John, 187n22

imagined communities, 249, 259n41

indigenous peoples: Ohio River Valley and, 145n3; in Western territories, 70, 126–27, 135–36, 141, 244–45. *See also specific tribal groups*

Innes, Harry, 138, 141, 143

interstate slave trade, 99, 102–3, 119

Irwin, Douglas, 50n10

Jackson, James, 105, 120n74

Jay, John: abolitionist movement and, 101, 118n54; Jay Treaty negotiations, 38–39, 51n18, 139–40; on state powers to regulate trade, 37, 55n67; trade regulation and, 30, 38–39, 44

Jefferson, Thomas: commerce and, 29; foreign policy of, 244; Society of the Cincinnati and, 224, 226–27, 236n20; state formation and, 171, 181; state powers and, 251; trade regulation and, 36, 39

Jensen, Merrill, 7, 15, 53n37; *The New Nation: A History of the United States During the Confederation*, 240–41

Johnson, Thomas, 83

JPs. *See* justices of the peace

judges: in New Hampshire, 158, 160, 172; in Pennsylvania, 160–64, 177, 178–79; state

formation and, 14, 155, 170; in Virginia, 165, 181, 182–83. *See also* courts

justices of the peace (JPs): in New Hampshire, 157, 159, 168, 172–73; in Pennsylvania, 161, 176–77, 191n96

Kaminski, John P., 123n113

Kentucky: Constitution opposed in, 142; European and Indigenous rivals surrounding, 126–27; population growth in, 130, 145n3, 148n18; statehood of, 145; warfare and violence in, 135–37, 149n41. *See also* Western territories

King, Rufus, 100, 143, 230

Knox, Henry, 81, 220, 221

Lafayette, Marquis de, 69–70, 74, 78–79

Lakota, 245

land banks, 15, 213–14nn30–31

Land Grab Act of 1783 (North Carolina), 133

Land Law of 1779 (Virginia), 133

League of Armed Neutrality, 55n50

Lear, Tobias, 75

Lee, Richard Bland, 77

Lee, Richard Henry, 28, 98

legislatures: aristocratic power and, 224, 229; currency and, 194–95, 202, 205, 208; slavery and, 95, 98, 100, 105; state formation and, 155, 159, 163, 166–67, 172–75, 178, 180–81; trade regulation and, 34, 36, 37–38, 43; Western territories and, 131–35

Lemarchand, Yannick, 211n11

Lemisch, Jesse, 8

Lepler, Jessica, 247

Lewis, Morgan, 221–22

Lincoln, Abraham, 246

Logan, Benjamin, 150n50

Lynd, Staughton, 26

MacKay, James, 69

Madison, James: on advantages of large republic, 143; aristocratic power and, 218, 231; Articles of Confederation reforms and, 40; Bank of the United States and, 251–52; on Continental Congress, 60; court reforms in Virginia and, 182; currency and, 202, 213n26; on powers granted by Constitution, 251; slavery and, 105; trade regulation and, 35, 43, 46–47

Main, Jackson Turner, 7, 8

Margairaz, Dominique, 211n11

Marlborough, Duke of, 66

Marquez, Leonard, 123n119

Marshall, John, 181; *The Life of George Washington*, 236n20

Martin, Alexander, 134

Maryland: Potomac River navigation and, 71–72; slavery in, 79, 98–99, 102

Mason, George, 181, 231

Massachusetts: aristocratic power fears in, 226, 230; Shays's Rebellion (1786) in, 43, 218, 220, 230; state formation in, 152, 183–84; trade regulation in, 37

Matson, Cathy D., 59n109

Maurice of Nassau, 66

Mazzei, Philip, 68

McDonald, Forrest, 7; *E Pluribus Unum*, 241

McHenry, James, 84

McLaughlin, Andrew C., 5

merchants: commerce and, 26, 30, 33, 35, 42, 44–45; currency and, 196–97, 200; slavery and, 93. *See also* commerce and trade

Miami Indians, 135

Michener, Ron, 214n30

Mifflin, Warner, 102–3, 104, 111, 119n65

Millet, Anne Flore, 77

Mississippi River, 33, 38, 138–39, 144

Model Treaty (Continental Congress), 28–29

Monroe, James, 137, 182

Morgan, Philip, 79

Morris, Christopher W., 190n79

Morris, Gouverneur, 74

Morris, Robert, 15, 30, 34, 49n3, 83, 193–209, 212n20, 242; *A Statement of the Accounts of the United States of America*, 200, 201. *See also* currency and finance

Morse, Jedidiah, 68, 89n22

Moultrie, William, 225

Mount Vernon, 60–86, *61, 73,* 249; agriculture at, 75–76; federalism and, 80–86; slavery and, 12–13, 78–79, 91n62; visitors to, 68–70, 81; Washington's "court" at, 70–80, 87n3

Murphy, Brian Philips, 154

Murrin, John, 244, 248

Nash, Abner, 99

Nash, Gary, 8

national identity, 25, 87n4, 249

Native Americans. *See* indigenous peoples

natural rights, 94, 97, 131

Navigation Acts (Britain), 31

Neem, Johann, 226, 239

Newburgh Conspiracy (1783), 149n45, 221

New Hampshire: colonial government in, 156, 157–60; mobilization for imperial crisis in, 166–69; population growth in, 158; state formation in, 171–75; trade regulation in, 37

New Jersey: slavery in, 97; trade regulation in, 38

New York: currency and finance in, 204, 206; state formation in, 183; trade regulation in, 38

New York Manumission Society, 101, 118nn53–54

New York Meeting for Sufferings, 99, 105

North Carolina: Act of Cession (1784), 133–34; Constitution opposed in, 142; currency and finance in, 205; Land Grab Act (1783), 133; secession movements in Western territories and, 128, 130, 132–33; slavery in, 97, 106, 121n83; Society of the Cincinnati in, 230; warfare and violence in, 138

Northwest Ordinance of 1787, 117n30, 128, 130–31, 146n8

Norwood, Dael A., 11–12, 23, 247

Novak, William, 154

Ohio River Valley, 128, 135–36, 145n3. *See also* Western territories

Onuf, Peter, 10, 27, 59n109, 154; *The Origins of the Federal Republic,* 147n16

Osgood, Samuel, 218

Page, John, 110

Page, Mann, 63

Paine, Thomas, 127, 207–8

paper money. *See* currency and finance

Parker, Josiah, 104, 105

Parkyns, George Isham, *Mount Vernon, 61*

Parrish, John, 104, 106, 111

PAS. *See* Pennsylvania Abolition Society

patronage, 156, 157, 160–61, 163

Peabody, Stephen, 175

Pearl, Christopher, 14, 152, 251, 254

Pemberton, James, 97, 99, 103, 104–5, 107, 121n79, 123n108

Pendleton, Edmund, 181, 182, 183

Penn, Ann Allen, 78

Pennsylvania: colonial government in, 156, 160–63; currency and finance in, 200, 204, *204;* mobilization for imperial crisis in, 169; state formation in, 170, 175–79; trade regulation in, 36

Pennsylvania Abolition Society (PAS), 100, 103, 104–6, 118n52, 121n83, 122n94, 122n103

Pennsylvania Committee of Safety, 199

Perkins, Edwin J., 211n9

Philadelphia Meeting for Sufferings (PMS), 96, 99, 112, 115n13, 116n15

Pickering, Timothy, 221

Pinckney, Charles, 38–39, 234n8

Pinckney's Treaty (1795), 145

Pincus, Steven, 154

piracy, 32–33, 55n45

Plummer, William, 174

PMS. *See* Philadelphia Meeting for Sufferings

Pocock, J. G. A., 239, 244

political economy, 28–29, 32, 46, 48, 202, 209

Potomac Navigation Company, 71, 80–81, 83

Potomac River, 71

Powell, Elizabeth Willing, 78

Powell, Samuel, 80

Pownall, Thomas, 29, 54n40

prerogative, 37, 156–57, 160–61, 163

Price, Richard, 30, 39

Prior, Edmund, 100

Putnam, Israel, 77

Quakers: abolitionist movement and, 95–100, 104–5, 115n13, 121n83, 246; Philadelphia Meeting for Sufferings (PMS), 96, 99, 112, 115n13, 116n15

Rakove, Jack, 250–51; *Original Meanings and the Origins of the Constitution,* 126

Rappleye, Charles, 196

Read, Jacob, 36

republicanism, 216–18, 240, 253, 255

Rhode Island: currency and finance in, 204, 207; Society of the Cincinnati in, 225–26; trade regulation in, 34

Richards, Leonard, 123n126

Rind, William, 165

Roane, Spencer, 183

Roberts, Alaisdair, 247

Roney, Jessica Choppin, 147n17

Rotch, William, 93

Royster, Charles, 230

Rozbicki, Michael Jan, 231

Rumsey, James, 71

Rush, Benjamin, 102

Ruston, Thomas, 52n22

secession movements in Western territories, 128, 137–45

Sevier, John, 136, 141

Shaw, Samuel, 33, 55n50

Shawnee, 135

Shays's Rebellion (1786), 43, 218, 220, 230

Sheffield, John Holroyd, Lord, 32, 47, 54n41

Shippen, Edward, 161

Simons, A. M., 6

slavery, 93–114; Articles of Confederation and, 94, 95, 98, 113, 246; Constitution and, 9, 93–94, 100–103, 107–8, 242, 245–47; emancipation of enslaved people, 79, 95–97, 100, 103, 105–6, 108–10; foreign slave trade, 105, 112, 118, 123; Fugitive Slave Law of 1850, 246; interstate slave trade, 99, 102–3, 119; Mount Vernon and, 12–13, 78–79, 91n62; westward

expansion of United States and, 250. *See also* abolitionists; *specific states*

Slave Trade Act of 1819, 122n98

Smith, J. Allen, 6

Smith, William L., 105, 108–9

Society of the Cincinnati, 80, 217, 219, 220–29, 232, 242–43

South Carolina: aristocratic power in, 222; slavery in, 98, 101, 103–4, 106, 113, 120n70

sovereignty: commerce and, 25–31, 34, 42–43, 47; Constitution and, 242, 244–45; in Western territories, 127, 134, 136–37, 144

Spain: Mississippi River navigation and, 33, 38, 138–39, 144; Ohio River Valley and, 145n3; trade relations with, 32, 46, 139, 141; treaty negotiations with, 138–39; Western territories and, 126

Spanish Conspiracy (Kentucky 1787–88), 128, 140–41, 144, 150n58

Spencer, Herbert, 5

state authority, 2, 174, 177, 182

state courts: district courts, 173, 182; general courts, 165, 180–82, 191, 236; superior courts, 173–75, 180; supreme courts, 84, 161–62, 178–80, 222

state formation, 152–85; Continental Congress and, 169–70, 172; courts and, 84, 161–65, 173–75, 178–82, 191, 222, 236; criteria for, 190n79; governance and, 152–54, 156, 159, 161, 167, 169, 178, 183, 248; legislatures and, 155, 159, 163, 166–67, 172–75, 178, 180–81; in Massachusetts, 152, 183–84; in New Hampshire, 171–75; in New York, 183; in Pennsylvania, 170, 175–79; in Virginia, 179–83. *See also* governance

state power, 30, 34, 179, 246, 251

Stearns, Susan Gaunt, 13, 126, 245

Stevens, John, *Observations on Government*, 232
Stiles, Ezra, 29–30
Sullivan, John, 228
superior courts (state), 173–75, 180
supreme courts (state), 84, 161–62, 178–80, 222
Sword, Kirsten, 116n16

taxes and tariffs: Constitution and, 45–46, 58n105; currency and, 203, 207, 213n30; on imported slaves, 105–6, 120n74; Quakers refusing to pay, 96; states imposing, 38; on trade, 34–35
Tennessee, statehood of, 145
Tennessee River Valley: European and Indigenous rivals surrounding, 126–27; population growth in, 148n18. *See also* Western territories
Thatcher, George, 120n74
Thomas, Robert E., 7
Thornton, Thomas, 66
Timoleon, 64
trade. *See* commerce and trade
Treaty of Amity and Commerce (France-US 1778), 37
Treaty of Ghent (1814), 51n18
"treaty worthiness," 51n17
Trescot, William Henry, *Diplomatic History of the Administrations of Washington and Adams*, 5
Trumball, John, Jr., 66, 84
Tucker, St. George, 183
Tudor, Thomas, 120n74
Turgot, Anne-Robert-Jacques, 30
Turner, Frederick Jackson, 5

Van Cleve, George, 94, 109, 113, 122n94, 123n113, 246; *We Have Not a Government*, 242

Van der Kemp, Francis Adrian, 72
Varlo, Charles, 68–69, 90n29
Vaughn, Samuel, 74
Virginia: colonial government in, 156, 163–66; Declaration of Rights, 126; Land Law of 1779, 133; mobilization for imperial crisis in, 169; Potomac River navigation and, 71–72; secession movements in Western territories and, 128, 130, 132–33; slavery in, 79, 98–99, 102, 121n83; state formation in, 179–83; trade regulation in, 55n68; warfare and violence in, 138

Wabash, 135
Waldstreicher, David, 26, 94
War of 1812, 247, 251
Washington, Bushrod, 84
Washington, George: "Circular to the States," 82–83, 88n5, 92n69; currency and, 202, 212n16, 213n26; Farewell Address, 51n19; federalism and, 80–86; Newburgh Conspiracy and, 221; resignation of commission (1783), 62–63; slavery and, 78–80; Society of the Cincinnati and, 223–24, 226–27, 236n20
Washington, Martha, 74–75
Watlington, Patricia, 149n41
Wayne, Anthony, 119n66
Weber, Max, 190n79
Webster, Noah, 67–68, 119n64, 230
Wentworth, Benning, 157
Wentworth, John, 157, 159, 169
Western territories, 126–45; opposition to Constitution in, 142; population growth in, 129–30, 148n18; secession movements in, 128, 137–45, 245; warfare and violence in, 135–37, 149n41. *See also* Kentucky; Ohio River Valley; Tennessee River Valley

Whiskey Rebellion (1791–94), 185, 248

White, Alexander, 122n99

White, James, 141

Wilentz, Sean, 94, 101–2, 109

Wilkinson, James, 140–41

Williamsburg, Virginia, 163, 165, 179–80, 239

Williamson, Hugh, 36

Willing, Charles and Thomas, 198

Winterer, Caroline, 240

Winthrop, John, 152

Wood, Gordon, 53n37, 102, 153–54, 225, 239; *Creation of the American Republic, 1776–1787*, 7–9, 232, 240

Wood, Nicholas, 12–13, 93, 246

Wythe, George, 181, 183

Yglesias, Matt, 47

Young, Arthur, 75–76

Recent books in the series
## Early American Histories

*From Independence to the U.S. Constitution: Reconsidering
the Critical Period of American History*
DOUGLAS BRADBURN AND CHRISTOPHER R. PEARL, EDITORS

*Washington's Government: Charting the Origins of the Federal Administration*
MAX M. EDLING AND PETER J. KASTOR, EDITORS

*The Natural, Moral, and Political History of Jamaica, and the Territories
thereon Depending, from the First Discovery of the Island
by Christopher Columbus to the Year 1746*
JAMES KNIGHT, EDITED BY JACK P. GREENE

*Statute Law in Colonial Virginia: Governors, Assemblymen,
and the Revisals That Forged the Old Dominion*
WARREN M. BILLINGS

*Against Popery: Britain, Empire, and Anti-Catholicism*
EVAN HAEFELI, EDITOR

*Conceived in Crisis: The Revolutionary Creation of an American State*
CHRISTOPHER R. PEARL

*Redemption from Tyranny: Herman Husband's American Revolution*
BRUCE E. STEWART

*Experiencing Empire: Power, People, and Revolution in Early America*
PATRICK GRIFFIN, EDITOR

*Citizens of Convenience: The Imperial Origins of American
Nationhood on the U.S.-Canadian Border*
LAWRENCE B. A. HATTER

*"Esteemed Bookes of Lawe" and the Legal Culture of Early Virginia*
WARREN M. BILLINGS AND BRENT TARTER, EDITORS

*Settler Jamaica in the 1750s: A Social Portrait*
JACK P. GREENE

*Loyal Protestants and Dangerous Papists: Maryland and the
Politics of Religion in the English Atlantic, 1630–1690*
ANTOINETTE SUTTO

*The Road to Black Ned's Forge: A Story of Race, Sex, and
Trade on the Colonial American Frontier*
TURK MCCLESKEY

*Dunmore's New World: The Extraordinary Life of a Royal Governor in Revolutionary America—with Jacobites, Counterfeiters, Land Schemes, Shipwrecks, Scalping, Indian Politics, Runaway Slaves, and Two Illegal Royal Weddings*
JAMES CORBETT DAVID

*Creating the British Atlantic: Essays on Transplantation, Adaptation, and Continuity*
JACK P. GREENE

*The Evil Necessity: British Naval Impressment in the Eighteenth-Century Atlantic World*
DENVER BRUNSMAN

*Early Modern Virginia: Reconsidering the Old Dominion*
DOUGLAS BRADBURN AND JOHN C. COOMBS, EDITORS

CPSIA information can be obtained
at www.ICGtesting.com
Printed in the USA
LVHW040921120522
718583LV00004B/373